OXFORD S....
OF RELIGION

EDITORIAL BOARD

Oxford Studies in Philosophy of Religion

Volume 8

Edited by
JONATHAN L. KVANVIG

OXFORD
UNIVERSITY PRESS

OXFORD

UNIVERSITY PRESS

Great Clarendon Street, Oxford, OX2 6DP,
United Kingdom

Oxford University Press is a department of the University of Oxford.
It furthers the University's objective of excellence in research, scholarship,
and education by publishing worldwide. Oxford is a registered trade mark of
Oxford University Press in the UK and in certain other countries

Published in the United States of America by Oxford University Press
198 Madison Avenue, New York, NY 10016, United States of America

British Library Cataloguing in Publication Data
Data available

Library of Congress Cataloging in Publication Data
Data available

ISBN 978–0–19–880696–7 (Hbk.)
ISBN 978–0–19–880697–4 (Pbk.)

Printed and bound by
CPI Group (UK) Ltd, Croydon, CR0 4YY

Contents

Editor's Introduction

This is the eighth volume of the *Oxford Studies in Philosophy of Religion*. As with earlier volumes, the essays follow the tradition of providing a non-sectarian and non-partisan snapshot of the subdiscipline of philosophy of religion. This subdiscipline has become an increasingly important one in philosophy over the last century, and especially over the past half century, having emerged as an identifiable subfield within this timeframe along with other emerging subfields such as the philosophy of science and the philosophy of language. This volume continues the initial intention behind the series of attracting the best work from the premier philosophers of religion, as well as including work by top philosophers outside this area when their work and interests intersect with issues in the philosophy of religion. This inclusive approach to the series provides an opportunity to mitigate some of the costs of greater specialization in our discipline, while at the same time inviting wider interest in the work being done in the philosophy of religion.

This volume includes winning essays by Ross Inman and Kenneth Pearce for Sanders Prizes in the Philosophy of Religion and by Dustin Crummett for an essay prize for graduate students funded by contributions from the Templeton Foundation. Congratulations to each of these authors for the high quality of their essays and their contribution to this volume.

List of Contributors

ROBERT AUDI, John A. O'Brien Professor of Philosophy, University of Notre Dame

T. RYAN BYERLY, Lecturer in Philosophy of Religion, University of Sheffield

JOSEPH CORABI, Professor of Philosophy, Saint Joseph's University

DUSTIN CRUMMETT, Graduate Student, University of Notre Dame

DANIEL M. EATON, Graduate Student, University of Texas at Austin

WILLIAM HASKER, Distinguished Professor Emeritus, Huntington University

DANIEL HOWARD-SNYDER, Professor of Philosophy, Western Washington University

ROSS D. INMAN, Assistant Professor of Philosophy, Southwestern Baptist Theological Seminary

ROBIN LE POIDEVIN, Professor of Metaphysics, University of Leeds

MEGHAN PAGE, Assistant Professor of Philosophy, Loyola University Maryland

KENNETH L. PEARCE, Ussher Assistant Professor in Berkeley Studies, Trinity College Dublin

TIMOTHY H. PICKAVANCE, Associate Professor of Philosophy, Biola University

MICHAEL SCOTT, Reader in Philosophy, University of Manchester

JAMES P. STERBA, Professor of Philosophy, University of Notre Dame

MARK R. WYNN, Professor of Philosophy and Religion, University of Leeds

1

Cumulative Case Arguments
in Religious Epistemology

Robert Audi

It is characteristic of philosophers to give multiple arguments for their important controversial views. The reasons for doing so are not always clear even to philosophers themselves. Most philosophers would perhaps agree to this much: at their best, arguments are paths to understanding, pillars of conviction, providers of confirmation, nourishment for the intellect, and, sometimes, sources of important truths. But how should we unpack these metaphors? And however we explain them, may we conclude that several plausible arguments for the same conclusion create a cumulative case for it? If so, just what does that mean, and is such a case stronger in one or another way than the totality of the arguments taken singly? Still another question, particularly important for religious epistemology, is whether a cumulative case can be mixed—composed of both arguments and non-propositional grounds supporting the same conclusion. These questions are the topic of this paper, and in exploring them I hope to show some major ways in which cumulative cases may be valuable.

I. KNOWLEDGE AND JUSTIFICATION

Philosophers offer arguments to show something, in a sense of 'show' that implies that the premises enable one to know the conclusion or at least be justified in believing it. I say 'at least' because it usually takes better evidential grounds—and in that way better justified and so, in a sense, stronger—premises—to yield knowledge than to yield justified belief; and justified belief is typically produced by whatever produces knowledge. The reason why knowledge-conferring grounds are in a certain way stronger than justification-conferring grounds is not simply that the existence of justification for a belief does not in general entail the truth of what is believed, whereas only truths can be objects of (propositional) knowledge. It is also possible to have grounds ample for justification for believing a proposition and even entailing its truth but insufficient for one's knowing it. A highly plausible attempt to prove a theorem might illustrate the point. The "proof" might have a defect (such as a subtly false premise) extremely difficult to discover and thus justify believing the theorem, yet not be a basis for knowledge of the theorem, whose truth it might nonetheless entail. Still another factor important for distinguishing grounds for knowledge from grounds for justification is the role of reliability in the process linking the basis of a belief to the proposition believed. This will be illustrated shortly.

What is often not noticed—and is easily obscured by asking the natural question, What must be added to justified true belief to render it knowledge?— is that knowledge does not entail justification. As I have argued at length elsewhere (as have others), knowledge is a matter of a certain relation between the fact that p and a belief that p which constitutes knowledge. Take a case that illustrates (but of course does not prove) the point. A person's knees could be sensitive to climatic conditions in such a way that they cause true beliefs about weather in the next few hours. The person might be puzzled by having such a belief and unable to detect any grounds for it. Still, if the process sustaining the belief is sufficiently reliable, the belief might surely constitute knowledge. Knowledge is what we would commonly attribute to the person—at least if we knew the "mechanism" and its reliability.[1]

I am presupposing that there is a fairly determinate concept of justification in question here. I agree with William P. Alston's view that there are many epistemological desiderata one might confuse with justification, but I would argue that we need not conclude, as he does, that there is no basic concept of justification.[2] Here are two of its anchors, one attached to the process of justifying a belief, the other to the property of its being conducive to knowledge.

---

[1] The literature on justification, knowledge, reliability, and their interconnections is very large. Recent discussions are found in Sven Bernecker and Duncan Pritchard, eds., *The Routledge Companion to Epistemology* (New York: Routledge, 2011). My own detailed case for the views just expressed on this topic is summarized in *Epistemology: A Contemporary Introduction to the Theory of Knowledge* (New York: Routledge, 2010).

[2] For the most detailed and most recent statement of this view see William P. Alston, *Beyond "Justification": Dimensions of Epistemic Evaluation* (Ithaca, NY: Cornell University Press, 2005).

First, we know, intuitively and in broad terms, what it is to justify a claim by citing propositional evidence. In this light, a justified belief may be conceived dialectically: as one based on grounds such that properly citing them in *justifying* it suffices to justify it. I presuppose that we have a sense of what justifying a claim is: roughly, offering grounds (such as perceptions and memories) of certain supportive kinds. Legal contexts are a prominent case in point, but the same notion of justification figures in contexts in which scientific evidence is considered. In this light—and in view of the plausible idea that there is an essential connection between the process of justifying and the property of justifiedness—we can understand a justified belief that p as one that is based on grounds the citing of which (normally) *would* justify p.

Secondly, we can arrive at the same or a very similar conception of justified belief by appealing to the idea that such belief is of a kind that rests on accessible knowledge-sufficing grounds: grounds accessible to introspection or reflection and such that, if there is no fourth-condition problem and p is true, then S knows that p. Without this knowledge-sufficing conception in the background, the Gettier problem would have little traction. If it were not natural to think of justified true belief as knowledge, surely the justified true belief account of knowledge would not have been so long in the ascendency.

Why is justification particularly important for religious epistemology? One reason is that knowledge can be a sheer gift, even if difficult or virtually impossible to recognize as such. We may possibly have a *sensus divinitatis* through which we know that God exists even in the absence of grounds that justify believing this. We may know this, moreover, not only without justification but, in some cases, with at least some degree of justification for doubting or perhaps even for disbelieving that we know it. Knowledge without justification is like a jewel that only some possess, few can appreciate, and fewer still will buy.

Moreover, philosophers and probably intellectuals in general tend to feel uncomfortable believing what admits of evidence but (so far as they can tell) cannot in any of the usual ways be *evidenced* or, in the process sense, justified, and for some people this discomfort is not dispelled by the belief that one nonetheless has knowledge. Third, and related to this, from those we care about who disagree (for many of us a huge number when it comes to religious matters), we want—and want to deserve—not just toleration but respect. Justified beliefs merit respect. Indeed, a good justification calls on rational beings interested in the subject either to agree on the conclusion or to find some defeating consideration.

II. THE LOGIC OF CUMULATIVE CASE ARGUMENTS

Think of a set of valid arguments for the same conclusion, say 'a and b, hence c', 'p and q, hence c', and 'x and y, hence c'. Viewed logically, their premises may be conjoined (say into a&b&p&q&x&y) and retain all their entailments, including, of course, c. Why not for explicitness simply conjoin premises whenever we have two or more such arguments, rather than merely cumulate, say in a listing, the arguments in which they individually figure? (I assume that the premises are, singly and conjunctively, consistent.)

A major reason for not conjoining all the premises is that unless all of the premises of the arguments in question are certain, in a sense entailing that they have a probability of 1, then if they are independent of one another, the objective probability of the conjunction will be not only lower than that of the most probable but not certain premises, but also no higher than the least probable.[3] Even if each non-certain premise is highly probable, their number may be such that the probability of their conjunction is below ½. Then one's conjunction would be more likely than not to be false.

Moreover, suppose the premises are non-certain and that we must grant this—the usual case in controversial matters. Then—unless we have an independent argument for their compatibility—we must, logically speaking, grant the possibility of not just reduced probability, but also of inconsistency owing to one of the premises entailing the negation of another premise. We may, to be sure, have an independent argument for their compatibility, but even then we might not have adequate reason for thinking that no one premise reduces the objective probability of another. Two reports of religious experiences, for instance, might on analysis turn out to have probabilistically conflicting content, one representing God's will as favoring forgiveness and amnesty toward someone and another representing it as favoring hard-hearted disapprobation and punishment.

Consider now the inductive case, in which one's premises do not entail one's conclusion. Philosophically interesting inductive arguments often proceed by reasoning from analogy or by abductive reasoning, such as inference to the best (or a suitably good) explanation. In neither case is it common to have, or anyway to have strong reason to think we have, certainty in our premises. Take Aquinas's argument from governance or other commonly used arguments from design. In both cases there is a

---

[3] I do not assume conjunctivity even for epistemically certain propositions since I take epistemic certainty to entail accessibility of a kind that is not in general conjunctive; but one can frame an absolute conception of certainty for which conjunctivity holds.

multitude of natural facts consonant with our ultimate premises. Even if we may claim certainty for at least many of the relevant propositions, it is best not to conjoin them. What we can say is that each argument may raise the probability of the conclusion. But how much is it raised? We cannot always assign a number. We cannot even be precise about when knowledge-sufficing justification arises. But we can speak of reasons for believing. I will return to this.

III. THE PSYCHOLOGY OF CUMULATIVE CASE ARGUMENTS

One might think that conjunctive arguments arise naturally from cumulative case arguments because belief is conjunctive, at least where one considers two propositions assentingly. This is not so.[4] It can be most easily seen with propositions whose complexity puts them at the limit of one's comprehension (I am referring to persons with finite minds not radically unlike ours). If p is at the limit of my comprehension, I cannot believe the conjunction of p with any other proposition.[5] In any case, even if conjoining one's premises for a view is in some cases desirable (as where premises of two or more arguments are "mutually reinforcing"), it need not be desirable. Take the following complementary cosmological arguments: one argument has the premise that God's creation of the universe best explains why there is something and not nothing; the other has the premise that there cannot be an infinite chain of causes extending infinitely into the past. If one conjoins these and believes the conjunction, this could be beneficial to the strength of one's conviction regarding the conclusion but a liability in dialectic, which usually drives the parties toward dealing with one proposition at a time.

Even if neither comprehensibility nor probability dropped with conjunction of premises, dialectical unwieldiness might still be a liability: complex premises and, correspondingly, complex arguments, tend to be dialectically unwieldy. Can one even count on remembering a proposition that is a conjunction of a dozen premises drawn from half a dozen distinct arguments? Could an interlocutor be expected to grasp it without resort to a written

[4] One might think this point is obvious. But there are cases of commitment to conjunctivity of a precisely parallel kind. For example, John R. Searle has held that "intentions, like desires, are closed under conjunction." See *Intentionality: An Essay in the Philosophy of Mind* (Cambridge: Cambridge University Press, 1983), p. 104.

[5] There may be special exceptions to this, but the idea is that I one cannot comprehend any proposition more complex (in some sense) than p, then one cannot at the time comprehend p & q for any q.

formulation? Even then, decomposition into self-contained arguments would likely be necessary for critical discussion among disagreeing parties.[6] Dialectical unwieldiness is related to a major function of belief: to guide thought and action. Our belief systems are our maps of the world. Much as a map that shows many paths to a destination provides one with a choice of which path is best, a multitude of arguments can offer dialectical choices and indeed different routes to understanding or to shoring up conviction in one's own case. By contrast, a single route with multiple lanes—the cartographic counterpart of a conjunction of many premises—reduces choice and may complicate travel.

IV. THE EPISTEMOLOGY OF CUMULATIVE CASE ARGUMENTS

Justification, like probability, comes in degrees, and, like probability, may drop with conjunction of individually justified propositions. The same holds for rationality. These points suggest that a cumulative case should in general not be represented as a conjunctive case.

In thinking about justification, whether in cumulative or in singular cases, we should not lose sight of its application to an important psychological variable: degrees of conviction, understood as something close to belief strength, as well as in relation to belief *simpliciter*. Here one may remember Locke and others: the wise proportion their conviction to the strength of the evidence—or at any rate of the accessible evidence. With some qualifications, this is plausible.[7] But we now face a problem: if a cumulative case should not be represented as a conjunctive one, how do we combine the relevant degrees of conviction? I see no simple solution to this problem, nor is there any way I know of that produces, for the whole set of

---

[6] An anonymous reader for the Press has pointed out that, in *Pensees*, Pascal noted that "The metaphysical proofs for the existence of God are so remote from human reasoning and so involved that they make little impact, and, even if they did help some people, it would only be for the moment during which they watched the demonstration, because an hour later they would be afraid they had made a mistake" (190). I agree but am here emphasizing problems in conjoining even simple sets of premises in arguments that are each simpler than the kind Pascal refers to. In a sense, my stress is more on syntactic than semantic complexity, his on the latter; but the two kinds of complexity may of course combine to make conjunctive cases even further from ordinary comprehensibility.

[7] Degree of conviction is best not considered equivalent to strength of belief, as I have argued in ch. 4 of *Rationality and Religious Commitment* (Oxford: Clarendon Press, 2011). But the point need not be argued here since the principle in question is perhaps equally plausible for both.

premises or the conclusion, some overall convictional value.[8] Conviction, moreover, seems largely involuntary, at least in cases like this, and that raises further complications. We may say that the more good arguments one has (with independent premises), the better. But it may not be possible to assign, for each premise, a number representing either its probability or the believer's convictional level regarding it. It certainly may not be possible to assign a number to the probability of the conclusion given each premise that supports it (but does not entail it, in which case the probability would be 1, though the convictional level might be much lower).

In speaking of degrees of probability, I may seem to be implicitly inviting a picture on which for every belief we have, we may always reasonably posit a degree of probability for the proposition believed or for the strength of the belief itself, or for both. This is at best a misleading picture. If the former is a matter of the believer's actual or hypothetical probability assignments, it does not cover the whole doxastic realm. A person may have no idea how to assign a probability, or even a definite range of probabilities, for some proposition the person believes. As to the psychological strength of belief as a psychological variable (say as a matter of its resistance to being eliminated by respected objections), in most cases, ordinal "measurement" is all we have for this doxastic strength. Moreover, on my view, strength of belief is not equivalent to the degree of probability that one does or would ascribe to the proposition in question.[9] The vagueness we encounter here is not, however, crippling. We may still be able to determine, often enough, that p is better justified for us than not-p and that a case someone makes for p is better than a case someone else makes for not-p. We may also be able in practice to determine, and also rationally maintain, that a case for p is amply strong or even conclusive.

So far, I have said little about evidence, as opposed to premises that simply provide a degree of justification. Is evidence conjunctive? If, as is plausible for evidence in propositional form, it is factive, then yes.[10] May we then

---

   [8] For a defense of attributing epistemic certainty to some important premises relevant to theism, see Nevin Climenhaga, 'Knowledge and Rationality: A Defense of Cartesian Epistemology' (a dissertation in progress).

   [9] This is discussed in some detail in ch. 3 of *Rationality and Religious Commitment* but is perhaps easily seen if one accepts the view that beliefs by their nature have some strength and that having beliefs is possible without having the concept of probability (as with tiny children) or at least without using the concept in the way the position in question requires.

   [10] Arguably, someone can be said to *have* evidence when the person has plausible grounds even if these are false propositions; these would then be said not to be good evidence or perhaps misleading or not genuine. There is a parallel here to reasons: *There is reason* to believe p seems factive; *I have reason* to believe p does not. Detailed discussion of these subtleties is not needed here.

suppose that justification and rationality for believing p go up with quantity of independent evidence for it? Arguably, we may; but one needed qualification would be that there might be maximal justification or rationality for actual beliefs, in which case there could not always be such an increase. If there is maximal justification, then independent evidence could be redundant for a person who already possesses as much justification as is possible for the person. The millionth eyewitness report one receives favoring a well-established proposition simply might not add to one's justification. I have some doubt, however, that the redundancy is more than pragmatic or psychological, at least mainly a matter of how much evidence one can in some sense deal with.[11] In any case, it seems doubtful that there is maximal justification at least for empirical propositions. There is no need to evaluate these matters here. Neither is likely to affect any of the issues that concern genuine philosophical or scientific disagreements: in neither domain is there any plausible candidate for a major thesis for which we might have maximal justification, and the status of unneeded confirmation may be left aside at least for this paper and most philosophical disputes.

What of non-propositional grounds, which may include the "evidence of the senses," say a visual impression of a wild turkey leading her chicks across a nearby field? Such non-propositional grounds surely do constitute a kind of evidence, but we can represent them propositionally, for instance by saying that someone is appeared to *F-ly*, say arboreally, for the case of someone viewing a tree in normal light. The notion of evidence, then, can do much epistemological work and, in being conjunctive (when in the form of true propositions), contrasts with that of justification for belief. This is important, but it would be a mistake to think that because justification for belief may rest on evidence one has, and because evidence is conjunctive, justification is conjunctive too. One can, for example, *have* evidence without realizing one does, and one can believe an evidence proposition unjustifiedly. We can also justifiedly believe each of several evidence propositions but, even though the proposition constituting their conjunction is true, fail to believe that proposition or believe it unjustifiedly. The conjunctivity of evidence, where evidence propositions are truths (as I am here assuming), is that of truth itself; it is not psychological.

---

[11] To see the problem here, note that we can gain justification from receiving increasing evidence even when we do not keep count, or lose count, of the evidential items. There may be a limit to how many pieces of evidence we can in the relevant way respond to; and, if a count is kept for us, the number might ultimately surpass our comprehension. Still, there seems no way to rule out that evidence can become better and better in force, so that evidential increase is a complicated matter of quality in relation to quantity.

Conjunction is not, however, the only direction one might go in responding to a cumulative case. It is indeed more natural to move to a higher-order perspective. Alvin Plantinga has done this in presenting dozens of arguments he has formulated for the existence of God.[12] He has indeed said that the very fact that there are so many good ones itself yields a good argument for their common conclusion. If there is a principle here, it might be called the *Plantingian Plenitude Principle*: Other things equal, the greater the number of good, independent arguments for a proposition, the more likely it is to be true. (Perhaps 'plausible' is preferable to 'good' here, provided it is not understood subjectivistically.) From the point of view of philosophical theology, this may be compared to the (or a) principle of simplicity on which, other things equal, the simpler of two hypotheses is more likely to be true.[13] Since we seem wired to respond positively to both principles—being in some way guided by them in forming and relinquishing beliefs—we might think that, especially on the assumption of God's existence, they are both true.

Let me suggest here an abductive interpretation of the plenitude principle as applied to a number of arguments with independent sets of premises and each rendering its conclusion at least as probable as its negation or, minimally, raising its probability relative to what we may otherwise assume. Suppose further that we can understand the arguments as a group, holding all of them in memory even if the conjunction of their premises is too complicated to consider as a candidate for belief (thus, on plausible assumptions, even to believe). In a case like this, we might be able to argue that the best—and only good—explanation of the probability of the diverse set of premises (taken individually, not conjunctively) and of their shared conclusion entails God's existence. The explanation might be, for instance, that God has so structured the world that the premises and conclusion are true, and this entails God's existence.

It is important to see here that although the key premise of the abductive theistic argument refers to the set of all the premises and asserts something about them, their *conjunction* is not a premise and is not a proposition that

---

[12] For Plantinga's paper see his "Two Dozen (or so) Theistic Arguments," in Deane-Peter Baker, ed., *Alvin Plantinga: God's Philosopher* (Cambridge: Cambridge University Press, 2007), 203–28, and for a recent collection of papers discussing the many arguments it presents, see Jerry Walls and Trent Dougherty, eds., *Two Dozen or So Theistic Arguments: The Plantinga Project*, forthcoming.

[13] The same principle holds even for propositions with low probabilities; the crucial point concerns what explains a combination of propositions that each raise the probability of a hypothesis over the probability it would otherwise have. Similarly, the plenitude principle applies to a set of arguments no one of which has premises making its conclusion more probable than its negation.

must be presupposed. Granted that one needs a higher-order belief about the premises and not merely to believe them individually, this is not a particularly problematic kind of higher-order belief. One's cumulative case, on this approach, is made by wielding accumulated premises in an overall way, not by conjoining them.

V. CUMULATIVE GROUNDS FOR THEISTIC CONCLUSIONS

We have seen that grounds for a proposition need not be premises. Grounds as I construe them include diverse existing phenomena, and, at least when they are non-propositional they are evidences even if not propositionalized, as they may be by formulating propositions asserting their occurrence. My seeing a windblown spruce tree bending toward the earth with shivering branches (or even my just seeming to see this movement) is a ground for believing there is a wind; the true proposition—and, correspondingly, the fact—that the tree is bending in this way is evidence that there is a wind; and that proposition is a potential premise for the conclusion that there is a wind.

Something more should be said here. Consider the justificatory force that a true proposition asserting the existence of a ground for p, such as a sensory experience *as of p*, has for a belief supported by that proposition or ground, say the belief that q. Let the experience be a visual impression of the spruce bending toward the earth with shivering branches; let q be the proposition that there is a wind; and let g be the proposition affirming the existence of the ground, here the proposition that I am having this visual experience. Does the justificatory force of the ground-affirming proposition, g, equal that of the occurrence of the (non-propositional) ground itself? I doubt this, but in any case, in supporting the belief that q, the *psychological* weight of the ground itself and that of believing g may be (and apparently are) very different. From the proposition that someone is seeing a tree—or experiencing God's love—the existence of these things follows, since what we actually see or experience is real; but my knowing these ground-affirming propositions does not give me the same basis of justification I have if I am the person who *has* the experiences (and I know I am)—the effect depends on self-knowledge of a kind, as distinct from knowledge based on a definite description that uniquely designates me). The difference is not just psychological: the supporting experience grounds the truth of the evidential proposition and is in that way more basic than that proposition, even though their entailments—within a certain range—are the same. (Experiences do not literally entail propositions; but propositions asserting their existence under appropriate descriptions do entail them and may justify them.)

Given the importance of religious experience in *mixed cumulative cases*—cases with both propositional and experiential grounds—for theism, we should note two further points about the difference between a mixed cumulative case for a conclusion and the corresponding unmixed "propositional" case for it.

One point is that where a proposition supporting, say, the belief that God has forgiven one is challenged, one can properly cite the experience on which the belief is based, for instance an experience as of God's forgiving one. That experience, if veridical, corresponds to the truth of the proposition. The occurrence of the (veridical) experience is, indeed, equivalent to the truth of the proposition, but the proposition is true in virtue of the occurrence of the experience; the experience does not occur in virtue of the truth of the proposition. The experience, then, is ontologically more basic than the proposition affirming its occurrence, and this seems epistemologically significant.

Secondly, where a proposition—at least any we can understand—simply expresses the fact that the experience occurs, it does so under some identifying description, but not under one indicating *all* the qualities of the experience. Even if there is such a proposition, it would be either too complex for comprehension by the subject or, even if comprehensible, too fine-grained and rich to be formulable by any normal subject of the experience.[14] Some of the qualities of the experience that are confirmatory will figure in its justificatory power; it would be normal for many more experiential qualities to figure in this way than can be captured in the corresponding proposition—the proposition affirming the occurrence of the experience. The point here is not that experiences—or some of them—are ineffable. That may be so, but my point is that the properties whose presence an experience reveals are often too numerous or too difficult to describe, at least without exceptional literary powers, to be expressed in a dialectically accessible argument. Where a case for some view includes testimony affirming an evidential experience, the experience must normally be described in terms of a dialectically manageable and usually small set of properties.

To develop this idea, we need phenomenology. A beginning here is to note that there is something it is like to feel God's forgiveness or even seem to feel it; but even with the power of poetry, one could not well capture all

---

[14] I here ignore "Russellian propositions" since they actually contain individuals with all their myriad properties and are not objects of thought in the way propositions as abstract entities are.

the distinctive elements that support one's belief that God is forgiving one. Here we may have not only complexity but a kind of ineffability. There might be a sense of release, a feeling of being uplifted, a change in attitude toward oneself, an empathy toward the person one has ill-treated, a power over one's consciousness comparable to that of perception as it creates impressions. Such experiences are not conclusive evidence, but they can have more justificatory power than any accessible set of propositions one can formulate in framing a propositional case for God's existence.[15]

Doubt is more difficult to connect with the justificational difference between a ground and its propositionalization. For instance, when one has an experience as of x's being F, this tends to give more support—certainly psychological support but apparently justificatory support as well—to belief than when, for instance in arguing for the proposition that x is F, one later assentingly considers the counterpart true proposition (that one has had an experience as of x's being F). This difference has great dialectical signifi-cance. We should try to get those we hope to convince to share the kinds of experiential grounds we have and not just to accept our affirmations of their reality. The power of narrative lies in part in its ability to elicit certain grounds.

Grounds differ from one another in justificatory force. But at least where they represent a basic source of justification, such as perceptual experience, they yield prima facie justification. I do not take the five senses to be a priori exhaustive of the kinds of perceptual grounds we can have. Nor are all non-propositional grounds perceptual or even sensory. There are, for instance, inner states, such as pain, anxiety, and joy, that justify self-ascriptions. I doubt that, a priori, we can close the list of their possible sources. I am thinking of them as internally accessible, as with experiential seemings. Grounds of knowledge—or at least bases of knowledge—may be even wider, but of course we must construct our case for a view we are defending, whether cumulative or singular, from what is accessible to us.

Religious experience is a special case here. The range and even the nature of such experience is difficult to describe.[16] Can there be experience 1. of a perfect being, as such? 2. of the Holy Spirit, as such? 3. of rebirth, divine love, or divine forgiveness? Let us consider these in turn, simply with a view to how they might figure in a cumulative case argument.

---

[15] For a detailed case supporting the view that religious experience may have justifica-tory power, indeed may even represent a kind of perception of God, see William P. Alston, *Perceiving God* (Ithaca, NY: Cornell University Press, 1991).

[16] A detailed theory of religious experience, with numerous examples of it and much discussion of diverse literature on the subject, is provided by Alston's *Perceiving God.*

For all three cases, the possibility of an experience that is in some sense *of* the divine is clear, but this possibility by itself has limited significance for religious epistemology. It is one thing to experience something, another to experience it *as* something in particular, and still another to experience it as having some property the experience of which or the perception of which provides some justification for a theistic conclusion. One might see an infinite stream without seeing its infinity. Even a good view might provide no hint of infinite extent. Somewhat similarly, experience of an aspect of a perfect being need not provide justification for taking it to be a perfect being—even for perfection in any single one of the three attributes (omniscience, omnipotence, and perfect goodness) that, jointly, are commonly considered minimally sufficient. It may be otherwise with the Holy Spirit, though if our concept of the Holy Spirit contains the idea that it is fully divine, in a sense entailing that it represents or is a perfect being, then a similar problem arises. In the third case, which I take to be closely connected with the second, there are similar entry points for skepticism but also a multitude of possible manifestations: love alone has many facets, and the conception of divine love appropriate here combines with that of forgiveness and that of rebirth and renewal in a way that yields, under some conditions, abductive grounds for theistic belief and certainly for theistic faith or hope. Faith that God is (say) sovereign does not entail certainty of this; hope that the same theistic proposition is true does not even entail believing it (though it is incompatible with disbelieving it). For a given person, the best explanation of a pattern of experiences might be that, for instance, they represent the work of the Holy Spirit. In some this might lead to strong conviction, in others faith that does not imply such conviction, and in still others simply hope.[17]

The background and context of experiences is important in these cases. Consider Christianity as a context. It makes available not only a rich array of conceptions under which the objects of religious experience have a particular meaning; the context also includes the historic witness of the Christian community—some of which is testimony that reports multifarious religious experiences. The relevant testimony can be counted as evidence even if it is conceived as having just some significant probability rather than assumed to be true at the outset. Indeed, though its content may be supernatural, its existence is a natural phenomenon. There is also scriptural

---

[17] Detailed discussion of psychological certainty, belief, faith, and hope in theistic matters is provided in ch. 3 of *Rationality and Religious Conviction*. Pertinent discussion of these and related matters are found in recent work by Lara Buchak, Daniel Howard-Snyder, and Daniel McKaughan.

inspiration—experienced by many as the apparently inspired character of so much in the Bible, especially the New Testament. This experiential element—which also need not be assumed to be veridical—is most forceful in the associated framework of theological interpretation, but does not depend on that. Might religious experience not gain in evidential power for properly sensitive subjects in this kind of context? Testimony in particular is an important element. Its weight, particularly in regard to miracles, is much disputed, but that it has prima facie justificatory weight is highly plausible and rarely questioned.

This brings us to a category I have so far only foreshadowed, that of mixed cumulative case arguments. These arguments have two kinds of premises: at least one premise reporting a non-propositional ground for the conclusion, say an experience as of God's speaking to one, and (other) propositional grounds, such as the arguments of natural theology and also the fact (if this fact is not itself a natural one) that others report the same sense of divine speaking and the same message expressed by it. By extension, a mixed case may be conceived as one or more arguments for a conclusion together with one or more experiential grounds for it. Someone having such a case might also be described as having *mixed grounds*, propositional and non-propositional, though of course a *statement* of the case will be propositional. It will be obvious that narratives supporting the conclusion may, for the person in question, be available or at least constructable when such an argument (or an experiential ground for the same conclusion) is at hand. Experiences are indefinitely rich, and the self-ascription of religious experiences is often a good beginning point for a narrative that can complement or even implicitly contain a cumulative case.

Here, then, we find room for a cooperation between natural theology and an experientialist approach to supporting a theistic outlook. In many lives, both kinds of grounds, the propositional kind, usable as premises, and the non-propositional, experiential kind, occur. Experiential grounds are, I have suggested, not *justificationally commensurable* with propositional grounds. But their propositional expressions can figure in arguments, and these can be joined with other arguments to comprise a cumulative case. With perhaps a few exceptions, the case should not be represented conjunctively. It may be dialectically represented in many ways. It may also be narratively expressed, and there its justificatory power may be undiminished—depending on how much of the propositional content it preserves, while its aesthetic, emotional, and moral power may be enhanced. A cumulative case may or may not lend itself to narrative expression or even to containment in a narrative in which it is not central. But the connection between the two forms of support for a view, especially a worldview, should not be missed. This topic, however, goes beyond the scope of this paper.

* * *

Theism is one thing, perfect being theism still another, and Christianity something more and, on some interpretations, possibly less. For process theologians, it *is* in one respect less, since they do not consider omnipotence a divine attribute. Does theism need perfect being theology? Yes and no. Yes, by tradition and to maximize the basis and incentive for reverence and humility. No, if the basis of inquiry is what a philosopher may be forgiven for calling the "worship-worthiness" of God: a basis for reverence, ultimate faith, appropriate humility, and, arguably, fidelity to at least the central elements of scripture. It would seem that, even without the almighty triad, God can have perfect goodness and all the power and knowledge that matter for a major kind of worship-worthiness. Even if we accept this possibility, we still should not find it easy to construct a powerful cumulative case for God's existence. But the task is not entirely intellectual: for many kinds of lives, a good mixed cumulative case seems within reach. A life itself can be a kind of witness to God's existence in the form of a divine presence in one's experience. The cumulative case possible in such a life will be indefinitely rich. It will provide some confirmation, but it will also fit a narrative, or even yield the outline of an encompassing narrative for human life. Justification for living within that narrative may come both from the cumulative case and from the beauty, power, and moral strength of the narrative as a framework for living.[18]

[18] The chapter has benefited from discussion on the occasion of its presentation at the Society of Christian Philosophers' Pacific Regional Meeting at Azusa Pacific University and from comments by Nevin Climenhaga and two conscientious anonymous referees for the Press.

2

The All-Powerful, Perfectly Good, and Free God

T. Ryan Byerly

This paper develops a simple and attractive account of the traditional divine attribute of omnipotence which makes available equally attractive resolutions of two difficult puzzles in philosophical theology concerning the compatibility of traditional divine attributes. The first puzzle concerns the compatibility of the attributes of omnipotence and perfect goodness, while the second puzzle concerns the compatibility of perfect goodness and freedom. The account of omnipotence here developed is sufficiently plausible and sufficiently different from other competing contemporary accounts of this attribute to merit attention on its own; but, it is even more deserving of attention given the unique resolutions of the aforementioned puzzles it makes available.

In Section I, I briefly engage the recent history of philosophical treatments of omnipotence, arguing that the analysis of this attribute developed here accounts for the insights and demands identified in this literature quite well. Thus, the account of omnipotence proposed here is attractive when this attribute is considered in isolation from other attributes. In Section II, I explicate the puzzle of omnipotence and perfect goodness and the puzzle of perfect goodness and freedom, showing that someone who adopts the proposed account of omnipotence has the resources to dissolve these puzzles in an attractive manner unique in the current literature. Indeed, more than this, they are equipped to present novel positive arguments in favor of the compatibility of these attributes. Thus, the account of omnipotence proposed here is also attractive when this attribute is considered alongside other attributes.

I. OMNIPOTENCE TAKEN IN ISOLATION

This section briefly explores recent philosophical discussions of the nature of omnipotence where this attribute is considered in isolation from other divine attributes. Here we set aside concerns about what an account of omnipotence should say if omnipotence is to be consistent with perfect goodness and other divine attributes and simply ask what an account of omnipotence should be expected to say in its own right. After examining the literature on this topic (I.a), I will introduce my own account of omnipotence and show that it accommodates the key insights and demands of this literature (I.b). As a result, the account proves attractive as an account of omnipotence where this attribute is considered in isolation from other divine attributes.

I.a. Recent Philosophical Treatments of Omnipotence

My approach here will be to survey recent philosophical literature about omnipotence by briefly entertaining a number of proposals about how to understand omnipotence and explaining key difficulties faced by these proposals.

An initially tempting proposal is to define omnipotence as simply the ability to perform any action whatsoever.[1] An omnipotent being is one that can do any action, period. Philosophers have almost universally rejected this account of omnipotence, since it implies that an omnipotent being must be able to do actions which are logically impossible—like make things entirely out of wood without those things being made of wood.

An easy revision to the first proposal suggests itself. What we should say is that an omnipotent being is one that is able to do any logically possible action.[2] But, unfortunately, this view runs into several difficulties as well. One of these is the famous stone paradox.[3] It would seem that the action type *making a stone so big one cannot lift it* is logically possible—nearly any one of us could token an action of this type. But, could an omnipotent being do this—make a stone so big *it* could not lift it? The foregoing account of omnipotence suggests a positive answer. But, if an omnipotent being is able to make a stone so big it cannot lift it, then there is after all something logically possible that it is unable to do—namely *lift the stone it has just made.*

Due to examples of this sort, one might be tempted to say that omnipotence has to do not with being able to do any logically possible action, but with being able to do any action logically possible for *oneself* to perform.

---

[1] This view is traditionally attributed to Descartes 1984–91 (see especially 2:294 and 3:23–6), and is called "voluntarism."

[2] See Geach 1973 and Sobel 2004 for defenses of this view.

[3] For contemporary statements of the paradox, which itself goes back at least to the medieval period, see Mackie 1955 and Cowan 1965.

That is, an omnipotent being is one that is able to do everything it is possible for it to do. Since it is not possible for omnipotent beings to make stones they cannot lift, omnipotent beings needn't be able to do so. Unfortunately, this sort of account of omnipotence runs into the problem of essentially limited beings exemplified by Mr. McEar.[4] McEar is a curious fellow who is such that it is impossible for him to do anything other than scratch his ear. Fortunately, he is able to scratch his ear. So, he is able to do the one and only thing it is possible for him to do. On the proposed account of omnipotence, it follows that Mr. McEar is omnipotent. Since he obviously isn't omnipotent, the proposed account fails.

Some have been tempted to respond to this kind of example by denying that beings like Mr. McEar are possible.[5] But, this sort of response has not found wide favor. First, modified and more believable versions of the McEar scenario have been proposed.[6] Second, philosophers who have discussed omnipotence, especially recently, have tended to accept that there are some non-trivially true counterpossible claims as well as some false counterpossible claims.[7] The counterpossible claim <if a man were a donkey, he'd have four legs> is non-trivially true, while the counterpossible claim <if a man were a donkey, he'd have eight legs> is false.[8] If these philosophers are correct in accepting a semantics for counterpossibles which allows for non-trivially true counterpossibles as well as false counterpossibles, then these counterpossible claims might be employed to test the metal of accounts of omnipotence. Defenders of the McEar example might use it in this way by proposing that the counterpossible <If McEar existed, he would not be omnipotent> is non-trivially true. Since the aforementioned account of omnipotence implies that this counterpossible claim would not be non-trivially true, it faces a significant difficulty even if the original McEar example isn't modified.

So far, we have focused only on accounts of omnipotence which define omnipotence in terms of action types, saying that an omnipotent being can perform any action type or any possible action type. A different approach

---

[4] The example derives from Plantinga 1967, and the name "McEar" from La Croix 1977.

[5] This is the approach of Wierenga 1983.

[6] See Wielenberg 2000 and Pruss and Pearce 2012.

[7] See, e.g., Morriston 2000 and 2002, Pruss and Pearce 2012, Lembke 2012, and Funkhouser 2006. Merricks 2003 offers a defense of such a non-standard semantics for counterpossible claims in the context of metaphysical disputes. Berto 2009 surveys additional motivations for such a non-standard semantics. Vander Laan 2004 discusses proposed semantics for counterpossibles which will allow non-trivial truth and falsity using the apparatus of impossible worlds. For the opposing view that all counterpossibles are trivially true, see Stalnaker 1968.

[8] This example is taken from Pruss and Pearce 2012.

uses states of affairs instead of action types.[9] One view in this vein proposes that an omnipotent being can bring about any possible state of affairs.[10] One difficulty for this view, however, is that it implies that omnipotent beings are able to bring about just any *necessary* states of affairs, since these are possible states of affairs. But, it is doubtful whether any being could bring about just any necessary states of affairs. Such states of affairs are generally not up to anyone.[11]

We might, then, modify the proposal by claiming that an omnipotent being can bring about any contingent state of affairs. Two difficulties with this proposal concern the past and human freedom. First, on the present analysis, an omnipotent being must be able to bring about past states of affairs, since many of these are contingent. But, arguably, no being can bring about past states of affairs. At least, there are *some* past states of affairs that cannot be brought about at times future to those states.[12] So, the present analysis rules out all too easily the possibility of an omnipotent being. Second, the present analysis requires that an omnipotent being be able to bring about states of affairs involving exercises of freedom on the part of agents other than the omnipotent being. For instance, if God is omnipotent, then the present analysis requires that God be able to bring about Joe's freely choosing to mow the lawn, since Joe's freely choosing to mow his lawn is a contingent state of affairs. However, those philosophers who hold to libertarian views of free will—and many of them are the same philosophers interested in giving an account of omnipotence—will not accept this picture of free will. On their view, Joe's freely choosing to mow the lawn is inconsistent with any other agent bringing this contingent state of affairs about. Thus, again, they will reject the present account of omnipotence because it makes omnipotence too hard to come by.

The failure of these initially attractive and fairly simple accounts of omnipotence led to some increasingly complex proposals concerning how to understand omnipotence in the early 1980s.[13] Two of the focal areas of

---

[9] This approach may help with some of the difficulties faced by act-based accounts. For instance, because the state of affairs *An omnipotent being makes a stone it cannot lift* is not a possible state of affairs, the stone paradox may not threaten states-of-affairs-based proposals. See, e.g., Swinburne 1973.

[10] By a possible state of affairs, I simply mean a state of affairs that possibly obtains. The account is similar for contingent states of affairs—states of affairs that contingently obtain.

[11] Hoffman and Rozencrantz 2012 presses this objection.

[12] I say "some" here to allow that there might be some "soft" features of the past which might be brought about, though there are other "hard" features of the past which cannot be. On the hard/soft distinction, see Todd 2013.

[13] Flint and Fredosso 1983, Hoffman and Rosencrantz 1980, and Wierenga 1983 are classic examples.

these accounts were on the most recently discussed questions concerning whether an omnipotent being must be able to bring about the past or to bring about human free actions. These accounts were constructed in such a way as to rule out these very requirements. As a result, they included in their analyses of omnipotence detailed information about world-segments, counterfactuals of freedom, and the like. By including these details, the accounts made non-trivial metaphysical assumptions. In the eyes of recent writers, these non-trivial assumptions are demerits, rather than merits, of those proposals.[14] A return toward simpler, more intuitive, more theoretically-neutral accounts of omnipotence is evident in the recent literature.

Though I haven't the space here to investigate this contemporary literature thoroughly, I will very briefly discuss two recent examples of this return to simplicity in accounts of omnipotence. Both accounts are motivated in part by a concern to explain how it could be that there are some states of affairs that even an omnipotent being is unable to bring about—a concern to which I will return later. Each account suggests that whether a being's inability to bring about some state of affairs threatens that being's omnipotence depends upon *why* that being is unable to bring about the state of affairs in question. On Wielenberg's (2000) view, so long as the reason the being cannot bring about a state of affairs is not because of any absence of power on the part of the being, the being still qualifies as omnipotent. An omnipotent being is one which is such that there is no state of affairs it cannot bring about because of an absence of power. Pruss and Pearce (2012) instead opt to explain the idea that an omnipotent being might not be able to bring about a state of affairs by appealing to the notion of freedom. For them, an omnipotent being is simply one which is perfectly free and has an efficacious will. Perfectly free beings, however, might be such that there are some things they are unable to will, so long as their inability to will arises from their character and choices in the right way.

I have significant concerns about these accounts of omnipotence which I will not explore at length here. Interestingly, when one considers the details of each account, what one finds is that both views share a commitment to the idea that an absence of basic power to will something needn't affect whether a being qualifies as omnipotent. What matters is unlimited conditional power—roughly, that anything the being were to will, it would intentionally bring about. Following Morriston (2002), I remain unpersuaded of this idea, and I will say a bit more about this in section II. I highlight these accounts of omnipotence now, however, because despite significant disagreement with them in their details, I believe that each provides some

---

[14] See, in particular, Oppy 2005 and Morriston 2002. For critical interaction with the details of these accounts, see Oppy 2005 and Wielenberg 2000.

insight about the nature of omnipotence. Indeed, momentarily, after introducing my own proposal and explaining how it accommodates the key insights and demands of the literature surveyed above, I will argue that this account also provides a deeper explanation for the key insights of these two recent proposals. Where they fail to reach rock-bottom in terms of what is explanatorily fundamental in an account of omnipotence, my proposal reaches the bottom.

I.b. Omnipotence as Possession of All the Powers

Let me, then, turn to my own proposal and to explaining how it accommodates the insights and demands identified in the literature above. I propose that we understand omnipotence in the following way:

(AP) x is omnipotent if and only if x has all the powers.

Like other recent accounts of omnipotence, AP is obviously a very simple account of this attribute. In my view, this is a positive feature in its favor. And, as we will now see, AP accounts for the key insights and demands evident in recent philosophical discussions of omnipotence. Exploring how AP accommodates these insights and demands will also offer us an opportunity to better understand the view.

First, AP does not imply the absurdity that an omnipotent being is able to perform logically impossible actions, like making something entirely out of wood without it being made out of wood. For, as long as there is no power to bring about these logical impossibilities, an omnipotent being needn't be able to bring them about. And, plausibly, there is no such power.

Does AP require that an omnipotent being is able to make a stone so big it cannot lift it, though? One might think, at first glance, that it does. For, it would appear that *the power to make a stone one cannot lift* is a power that some human beings have. So, it is a power. And, AP requires that omnipotent beings have all powers. So, omnipotent beings must have this power. So, they must have the power to make stones they cannot lift. And this just shows that AP's account of omnipotence makes omnipotence incoherent.

But, this line of reasoning can also be resisted by an advocate of AP. For, a key component of the above line of reasoning was the claim that, as illustrated in human cases, there is such a thing as a *power to make a stone one cannot lift*. It is this power that is possessed by some human agents but couldn't be possessed by an omnipotent being. Yet, plausibly, such a view multiplies powers beyond necessity. To see this, imagine two humans S and S′ who are equal with respect to their abilities to make big stones, but unequal with respect to their abilities to lift them. Suppose, for instance, that S and S′ are both such that the maximum sized stone they can make is a 60 pound stone. But, imagine that S′ and not S can lift 60 pound stones. It would be absurd to conclude on this basis that S has powers S′ *doesn't*— namely, *the power to make stones so big one cannot lift them*. No; if anything, S′ is the one with additional powers here. Likewise, when we compare any created thing which can make stones of whatever size but cannot lift them to an omnipotent being, it would be a mistake to conclude that this created being, by virtue of its inability to lift these stones, *possesses* a power the omnipotent being lacks. Rather, the reverse is true. The omnipotent being possesses all of the powers the created being possesses *and more*. In particular, the omnipotent being will possess whatever stone-making powers the created being possesses together with greater stone-lifting powers than the created being.[15] The so-called *power to make a stone one cannot lift* is not a power the created being possesses but the omnipotent being lacks; it is not a power at all. Accordingly, AP needn't succumb to the stone paradox.

Moving on, the example of Mr. McEar also clearly poses no difficulty for AP. Mr. McEar is clearly not omnipotent, given AP, because Mr. McEar lacks many, many powers.

What about the question concerning whether an omnipotent being must be able to bring about past states of affairs? The question concerning whether an omnipotent being must be able to bring about the free actions of creatures? Here I think that what we should hope for from an account of omnipotence is theory-neutrality. An attractive account of omnipotence should not, all by itself, settle the important questions involved here having to do with power over the past and the nature of free action. These are important metaphysical disputes that deserve focused attention of their own. What we want is a theory of omnipotence that neither clearly implies that an omnipotent being must have power over the past nor mustn't, a theory which neither clearly implies that an omnipotent being must be able to bring about the free actions of others nor mustn't.

Again, AP delivers. If there is a power over the past, AP implies that an omnipotent being must have it. If there is a power to bring it about that

---

[15] I ascribe to an omnipotent being some very earthly powers in this paragraph—powers to make stones and push buttons and so on. Some authors have resisted the idea that an omnipotent being must possess *these* kinds of powers—usually calling these powers "physical" powers (see Wielenberg 2000 and Hoffman and Rosencrantz 2012). I think there is significant reason to ascribe these powers to an omnipotent being, however. For, imagine a being O that has all the powers except some of these earthly ones. It seems that the possibility (or conceivability) of a being O2 which has all of O's powers plus the earthly ones O lacks rules out the conclusion that O is omnipotent. For an argument along these lines (though not focused on physical powers, specifically), see Funkhouser 2006.

other agents freely perform certain actions, AP implies that an omnipotent being must have it. But, AP does not by itself settle the question of whether there are such powers. Instead, this question is left as a matter for further metaphysical debate, as it properly should be. Those who find troubling the idea that an omnipotent being could bring about past states of affairs or the free actions of other agents are left free by AP to argue that the relevant powers do not exist; indeed, this is plausibly how their views should be understood. AP, then, fares extremely well as an account of omnipotence taken in isolation from other divine attributes in terms of its ability to accommodate the key insights and demands identified in philosophical treatments of omnipotence up until the most recent proposals.

Finally, AP accommodates the insights of these more recent proposals extremely well also. In fact, it is plausible that AP explains what is right about these proposals, providing an account of what it is these proposals get right about omnipotence in terms of something more basic. In other words, where these most recent proposals fail to reach rock-bottom in terms of explaining omnipotence, AP really reaches bottom.

Pruss and Pearce, we saw, defined omnipotence in terms of two properties—having an efficacious will and being perfectly free. I disagree with these authors about how we should understand possessing an efficacious will and being perfectly free;[16] but, I agree that an omnipotent being will *have* an efficacious will and will *be* perfectly free. Indeed, I think there is a deeper, unified explanation for why an omnipotent being will have these two properties. It is because an omnipotent being has all the powers. A being with all the powers has as efficacious a will as possible. It has the powers necessary to overcome whatever obstacles there might be to its will. And, as I will argue in detail in the next section when discussing the puzzle of perfect goodness and freedom, a being that possesses all the powers is thereby perfectly free. AP, then, explains what is correct in Pruss's and Pearce's account of omnipotence.

---

[16] There are two primary disagreements I have with them. The first is with their analysis of what it is to have an efficacious will. They define an efficacious will using a subjunctive conditional as follows: x has perfect efficacy of will if and only if, for all contingent propositions p, if x were to will that p, then x would intentionally bring it about that p. I am worried that, given Pruss's and Pearce's own commitments to non-trivially true counterpossible claims (which I share), this analysis will require that a being with perfect efficacy is such that it is non-trivially true that were it to will that some other agent freely performs some action, then it would intentionally bring it about that this occurred. I don't agree that an account of perfect efficacy should entail this.

My second disagreement is with Pruss's and Pearce's idea that perfect freedom does not require that one have the power to will atrocities. I discuss this disagreement further in the second full section of the text below.

A similar story goes for Wielenberg's account. Though I disagree with Wielenberg that the following claim explains what it is to be omnipotent, I agree with him that it is true that an omnipotent being is one which is such that there is nothing it is unable to do *because* it lacks the power to do so. I agree with this because I think omnipotent beings lack *no* powers and *a fortiori* aren't unable to do things because they lack powers. Again, AP explains what is correct in Wielenberg's account.

As an account of the traditional divine attribute of omnipotence taken in isolation from other traditional divine attributes, AP is extraordinarily attractive. AP is simple. AP accommodates the key insights and demands identified in recent philosophical treatments of omnipotence. And, I should add, AP has a certain intuitive appeal about it. *Of course* being omnipotent just is being all-powerful! And being all-powerful just is having all the powers. One begins to wonder why on earth recent philosophical treatments of omnipotence have overlooked this idea.

II. OMNIPOTENCE, GOODNESS, AND FREEDOM

That omnipotence is possession of all powers is a simple, attractive, and intuitive proposal when omnipotence is taken in isolation from other traditional divine attributes. But, how does it fare when it is considered *alongside* other divine attributes? Alternative proposals about the nature of omnipotence get part of their appeal from the fact that they are supposedly able to make good sense of relationships among traditional divine attributes whose compatibility has been called into question. One might wonder whether AP, the account of omnipotence I have proposed, can achieve comparable results.

The purpose of this section is to show that one who adopts AP as the account of omnipotence is thereby afforded with attractive ways to defend traditional divine attributes in light of challenges to their compatibility. As I will show, AP affords its proponent unique resolutions to two intractable puzzles about these attributes; and, AP moreover affords its proponent novel positive arguments in favor of the compatibility of these attributes. The specific attribute-pairs on which I will focus here are, first, the attributes of omnipotence and perfect goodness and, second, the attributes of perfect goodness and freedom. For each pair of attributes, I will present an argument for their incompatibility resembling those which have been defended in the philosophical literature, explain how AP affords a response to this argument, and then show how AP provides the resources for defending a positive argument in favor of the compatibility of the attributes.

II.a. The Puzzle of Omnipotence and Perfect Goodness

By ascribing omnipotence to God, it is often thought that theists are ascribing to God necessary possession of the maximum possible degree of power; while, in ascribing perfect goodness to God, it is thought that theists are ascribing to God necessary possession of the maximum possible degree of goodness.[17,18] But, reflection upon these attributes quickly leads to questions about their compatibility. Doesn't God's omnipotence require that it is possible for him to do moral wrongs? But, on the other hand, doesn't God's perfect goodness require that he never would—and indeed, never could—do moral wrongs?

We might work these questions up into an argument against the compatibility of omnipotence and perfect goodness as follows. Suppose, for *reductio*, that:

(1) Possibly, God is omnipotent and perfectly good.

Given that God is omnipotent, it has seemed to many to follow that God must be able to bring about atrocities—events whose very serious wrong-making features are not counterbalanced by right-making features.[19] An example of such an atrocity might be torturing innocent disabled persons. This is something human beings are able to do, and it is difficult to see how an omnipotent being wouldn't also be able to do so. Thus, it has seemed to many that:

(2) Necessarily, if God is omnipotent, then God is able to bring about atrocities.[20]

---

[17] Notably, some theists have turned toward denying the essentiality of these attributes in order to respond to puzzles like the ones I will consider in the text. Pike 1969, for instance, is often interpreted as denying God's essential perfect goodness. For a response, see Garcia 1987.

[18] Hoffman and Rosencrantz 2010 says this about omnipotence. One difficulty with thinking of omnipotence in this way is that it makes omnipotence obviously coherent. But, one might think that there ought to be a substantial question to ask about whether omnipotence is coherent. The account of omnipotence I propose is not subject to this difficulty. See Lembke 2012 for a similar criticism of a closely related view in Nagasawa 2008.

[19] I define atrocities deontologically here in order to address a concern brought up by Tooley 2009. Tooley worries that, by using axiological terms in framing the argument from evil, defenders of this argument unnecessarily open themselves up to resistance on anti-consequentialist grounds. The related term, "horror," is typically defined in the literature axiologically as an event whose bad-making features are not counterbalanced by good-making features.

[20] There is a question about the relationship between God and morality that the defender of this argument must take a stand on, and which I must take a stand on here in order for this paper to move forward. The issue has to do with divine will theories of

Yet, given God's goodness, many have thought that God *cannot* bring about such atrocities. God's perfect goodness does not consist simply in the fact that God doesn't ever in fact bring about such things, nor in the fact that he wouldn't bring them about in a wide range of circumstances.[21] Rather, it has been thought that God's perfect goodness consists, at least in part, in his impeccability—his inability to sin. God is necessarily unable to do wrong. Thus, it has seemed to many that:

> (3) Necessarily, if God is perfectly good, then God is unable to bring about atrocities.

From 1, 2, and 3, it follows that:

> (4) Possibly, God is able to bring about atrocities and God is unable to bring about atrocities.

Since 4 is a contradiction, at least one of 1, 2, or 3 must be rejected. But, the one who presses our puzzle will insist, 2 and 3 are well-supported. So, we must reject our original assumption, 1. That is, we must reject the compatibility of omnipotence and perfect goodness. God cannot possess together each of these attributes which he is traditionally thought to possess essentially.

Arguments against the compatibility of omnipotence and perfect goodness like the foregoing have recently been defended with care by philosophers of religion.[22] Others have attempted to provide responses to these arguments. By far, the more common response from philosophers not persuaded by these arguments is to deny premise 2 in the argument above.[23] The general strategy has been to attempt to provide accounts of omnipotence which appear to match commonsense intuitions about what is required

---

moral rightness. If one adopts a strong divine will theory (like Quinn 1978) according to which an action is right if and only if and because God wills it, and if one also thinks that God is omnipotent, then one will deny 2. For, this theory implies that whatever God wills is morally right. Thus, it is impossible for an omnipotent God to bring about an atrocity (since, in doing so, he will be doing something he willed). Such a view must be rejected for purposes of investigating the issues of this chapter. For a survey of criticisms of it and related views, see Quinn 1999.

[21] Manis 2011 suggests that divine goodness be defined along Molinist lines as there being a wide range of circumstances in which God would not bring about atrocities. For criticism of this sort of Molinist view of perfect goodness (here focused more on the goodness of the redeemed in heaven), see Pawl and Timpe 2009.

[22] Three prominent examples are Morriston 2001, Funkhouser 2006, and Sobel 2004.

[23] This fact is well-noted by Funkhouser (2006), who writes: "Theorists who react to this conflict almost invariably attempt to avoid the difficulty by doctoring the intuitive understanding of 'omnipotence' so that God's omnipotence is compatible with his inability to perform certain deeds (410)." It is precisely this invariability that I wish to challenge here.

for omnipotence and which allow one to deny premise 2—to deny that God's omnipotence entails his ability to bring about atrocities. That one's account of omnipotence is able to deliver this result is taken as a positive feature in its favor.

The accounts of omnipotence we saw earlier from Pruss and Pearce and from Wielenberg are two good examples here. The defenders of each account attempt to show how their account can accommodate the idea that an omnipotent being might be unable to bring about atrocities. In each case, this is because such a being might lack the basic power to will to bring about such atrocities, even if it has sufficient power to bring about anything it wills. Wielenberg, for example, compares the God of classical theism with a color-impaired deity that has the power to make any colored objects it wills to make, but that cannot will to make red objects because it cannot imagine them. The God of classical theism is claimed to be omnipotent in much the same way such a color-impaired deity would be omnipotent. God has the power to bring about atrocities if he wills them; he just doesn't have the power to will to bring them about. Pruss's and Pearce's approach is similar. They think having the power to will to bring about an atrocity is not required for being perfectly free, and so they conclude that a being might lack this power and still be omnipotent if it also has an efficacious will. Both views, then, accept claim 3 in the above puzzle and reject claim 2.

It is not my purpose here to argue against these proposals, though I do think they face significant obstacles.[24] Instead, my interest is in articulating a very different approach to the present puzzle which could be advocated by a defender of AP, the account of omnipotence I have proposed. Since AP is so attractive when we consider omnipotence in isolation from other attributes, and since it plausibly explains the key insights of these alternative proposals, if it could be shown that AP can also make good sense of the relationship between traditional divine attributes whose compatibility has been called into question, then AP will gain the upper hand on these alternatives. For these accounts will lose whatever advantage they had over AP in terms of their ability to solve such puzzles, and at this point it appears this is all the advantage they have over AP.

How should an advocate of AP approach the puzzle of omnipotence and perfect goodness? Plausibly, they should not follow the lead of the majority of recent writers who have wished to resolve this puzzle by denying claim 2—the claim that if God is omnipotent, then God is able to bring about atrocities. For, plausibly, given AP, an omnipotent being *must* be able to bring about atrocities. For, as van Inwagen (1983) has argued, the abilities

---

[24] See brief discussion of these obstacles in the previous section of the text and in n.16.

are naturally taken to be a subset of the powers. And, to deny that God is able to bring about atrocities is naturally taken to involve denying that God has some kind of ability. If God, per AP, has all of the powers and so all of the abilities, then denying claim 2 is simply not an option.

A further reason for the advocate of AP not to follow the majority of recent writers in denying claim 2 is that there is a plausible understanding of what it is to be "able" to bring about a state of affairs which, together with AP, implies that an omnipotent being must be able to bring about atrocities. The understanding of the ability to bring about a state of affairs I have in mind is the following:

> (Ab) x is able to bring about y if and only if there is no obstacle to x's bringing about y which x lacks the power to overcome.

I will say much more on behalf of Ab in the next subsection, where I argue that it provides an attractive account of the "ability" to do otherwise involved in the principle of alternative possibilities typically coveted by libertarians.[25] My suggestion here is that we understand the "able to bring about" in premises 2 and 3 of the puzzle of omnipotence and perfect goodness in this same manner. And, if we do, it follows from AP that premise 2 must be true. An omnipotent being will be one that is able to bring about atrocities. For, an omnipotent being has all of the powers, given AP, and so there can be no obstacles to its bringing about atrocities which it hasn't the power to overcome. To see this simply consider the sorts of obstacles there are to a being's bringing about atrocities and the sorts of powers exercised in overcoming such obstacles. An omnipotent being with all the powers will have all of the powers necessary for overcoming these obstacles.[26]

Instead of denying claim 2 and explaining how omnipotence can be understood without it, the approach that advocates of AP should take is to deny claim 3 and explain how perfect goodness can be understood without it—that is, they should explain why a perfectly good being needn't be a being which is unable to bring about atrocities. To do so, they'll need to offer a way of accounting for what it is that leads us to be inclined to accept 3 without thereby committing ourselves to 3.

---

[25] I say *typically* coveted by libertarians, since there are some libertarians—the so-called "Frankfurt libertarians"—who do not advocate this principle. For discussion of this view, see Timpe 2006.

[26] One salient obstacle to consider here is an obstacle arising from the being's own unwillingness to bring about these atrocities. See below in this section for further discussion of this kind of obstacle. My position is that an omnipotent and perfectly good being with such unwillingness to bring about atrocities has the power to overcome this unwillingness, but necessarily refrains from exercising this power.

What is it that leads us to be attracted to 3—the claim that a perfectly good being is unable to bring about atrocities? As explained above, it is the thought that a perfectly good being's not bringing about atrocities is far from accidental. It is not that this being simply never does bring atrocities about or even that it wouldn't do so in a wide range of circumstances. There is some kind of stronger necessity in its never doing so. One attempt to capture this necessity is encapsulated in 3. The explanation for why the being necessarily refrains from bringing about atrocities is to be found in an inability of that being—the being necessarily does not bring about atrocities because it is unable to bring them about.

But there is another approach to explaining the necessity involved in a perfect being's not bringing about atrocities. It is to explain this necessity in the same way we explain the "volitional necessity" involved in so-called "Luther cases," where we offer a diagnosis of this volitional necessity consistent with AP.[27] The prime example of these Luther cases, unsurprisingly, involves Martin Luther. Luther had published the 95 theses highly critical of practices in the Roman Catholic Church. On April 18, 1521, he was called before the Diet of Worms. Johann Eck placed some of Luther's writings before him and asked Luther whether he was the author and whether he stood by what was written in them. The hope was that Luther might recant. He is famously recorded as having said in response: "Here I stand. I can do no other." The approach I am suggesting here is that the defender of AP explains the necessity involved in a perfectly good being's refraining from bringing about atrocities in the same way she explains the necessity exhibited in these Luther cases.

Not every explanation of the necessity involved in these cases is consistent with AP, however. For example, Pruss and Pearce write that "Martin Luther was both free and morally responsible in his decision not to recant, and yet identified some sort of genuine limitation on his will when he uttered the words, 'I can do no other' (411)." In other words, Pruss and Pearce conclude that the correct way to diagnose these Luther cases is to say that the Lutherized subject lacks a certain basic power to will that which he says he cannot do. If this were the correct explanation of the necessity involved in such cases, then it could not be used by the advocate of AP to explain the necessity involved in God's refraining from bringing about atrocities.

Thankfully, there are alternative diagnoses of these cases according to which the necessity is not due to an absence of power on the part of the

---

[27] See Watson 2004 for discussion of such cases, the interpretation of which remains highly controversial.

subject. Frankfurt appears sympathetic with such a diagnosis, for example, when he writes:

> If a person who is constrained by volitional necessity is for that reason unable to pursue a certain course of action, the explanation is not that he is in any straightforward way too weak to overcome the constraint. That sort of explanation can account for the experience of an addict, who dissociates himself from the addiction constraining him but who is unsuccessful in his attempt to oppose his own energies to the impetus of his habit. A person who is constrained by volitional necessity, however, is in a situation that differs significantly from that one. Unlike the addict, he does not accede to the constraining force because he lacks sufficient strength of will to defeat it. He accedes to it because he is *unwilling* to oppose it and because, furthermore, his unwillingness is *itself* something which he is unwilling to alter (1988: 87).

A plausible interpretation of Frankfurt here is that he thinks that in these Luther cases, the agent's necessity of performing a certain course of action is not due to any absence of power on the agent's part, but only due to a certain stable unwillingness to perform alternative courses of action, perhaps coupled with a higher-order unwillingness to alter this first-order unwillingness. Applied to the case of a perfect God, we would say that God has both the basic power to choose to bring about atrocities and the conditional power to bring them about if he so chooses. Whatever necessity there is in God's not bringing these about is to be explained in another way, by citing God's stable unwillingness to bring these atrocities about and perhaps a higher-order unwillingness to alter this first-order unwillingness. If we understand the necessity involved in God's not bringing about atrocities in this way, it is perfectly consistent with AP. God may have all the powers—including the basic power to will atrocities and the power to bring them about if he wills them—but may still be such that he can't bring them about where the fact that he can't is explained along the lines of a Frankfurtian explanation of the volitional necessity exhibited in Luther cases.

Is this Frankfurtian explanation plausible, though? Is it plausible to think that the necessity involved in these cases is to be explained in terms of unwillingnesses rather than in terms of absences of basic powers? I think it is. Indeed, there is reason to *prefer* this Frankfurtian diagnosis of Luther cases, a diagnosis friendly toward AP, over the Pruss/Pearce interpretation above. The discussion in Wes Morriston 2002 of his example of the imaginary being Jill is helpful here. Morriston's Jill is a being with unlimited conditional power who cannot bring herself to exercise that power in any significant way because she lacks basic power to choose. Tellingly, Morriston characterizes her case as follows: "She would succeed at anything she tried. But she suffers from a kind of mental paralysis. She simply cannot bring herself to make the necessary choices…There is a certain power *over herself* that she lacks (361)." I think Morriston is on to something here. To lack basic power of choice is to lack power over oneself. To have basic power is to gain power over oneself. The two go hand-in-hand. But this observation helps us to see why the Frankfurtian explanation of the Luther cases is preferable to the Pruss/Pearce interpretation. For, in Luther cases, it is clear that the subjects' being such that they can't perform some alternative action is not due to their *lacking* power over themselves. Indeed, if anything, they can't perform alternative actions because they *have* such significant power over themselves. Frankfurt simply offers us a way of understanding what this power over oneself involves—that one is unwilling to pursue the alternative course and unwilling to alter this unwillingness.

Understanding perfect goodness in this way also helps to explain a key difference between the God of classical theism and Wielenberg's color-impaired deity discussed above. The latter plausibly is unable to make red objects precisely because it lacks a certain power over itself. It lacks the basic power to will to make red objects. It is genuinely disabled. But, not so for the God of classical theism. If this God can't bring about atrocities, this is not because it lacks control over itself, not because it is disabled in any way, but because it has control over itself, because it is maximally enabled. This God is just as able to bring about atrocities as Luther was able to recant; so premise 2 of the puzzle above is true.[28] It is premise 3 of that puzzle that is false, since the necessity involved in God's performance, like the necessity involved in Luther's performance, is not due to inability or lack of control but to presence and exercise of control.

So, we have seen a way for advocates of AP to respond to the puzzle of omnipotence and perfect goodness in such a way as to retain the compatibility of omnipotence as they define it with perfect goodness. They should deny 3—the claim that if God is perfectly good, God is unable to bring about atrocities. God is able to bring atrocities about, since God, being omnipotent and satisfying AP, has all the powers necessary for overcoming any obstacle to doing so. But, this omnipotent God can still be perfectly good, since we can account for the necessity involved in God's refraining from bringing about atrocities without accepting 3. We can account for this necessity by explaining it in the same way Frankfurt explains the "volitional

---

[28] Though Frankfurt will agree that the Lutherized subject's necessity is not due to any absence of power, the quote from Frankfurt cited in the text suggests that Frankfurt is still happy to talk of these subjects not being "able" to do otherwise. For some reasons why I do not follow Frankfurt in speaking this way about abilities, see the earlier part of this section where I argue that an advocate of AP should not follow the majority of recent authors in denying premise 2 of our puzzle.

necessity" involved in Luther cases. God can't bring about atrocities because God wills not to do so, and wills not to change this willing. Indeed, God's meta-willings here may go on infinitely.[29]

The resources just tapped in order to develop a response to the puzzle of omnipotence and perfect goodness can in fact be used to offer a positive argument in favor of the compatibility of omnipotence and perfect goodness, where omnipotence is defined by AP. The argument is simple. An omnipotent being, given AP, has all the powers. A necessarily omnipotent being has all the powers in every possible world. But, a being that has all the powers, following Morriston, is in complete control of itself. So, a necessarily omnipotent being is in complete control of itself in every possible world. But a being that is in complete control of itself in every possible world can ensure that in no possible world does it bring about an atrocity. So, an omnipotent being can ensure that in no possible world does it bring about an atrocity. And this is just to say that an omnipotent being can be a perfectly good being.[30,31]

Another way of looking at these issues is as follows. Some might argue that having the powers requisite for committing atrocities is a liability, rather than an ability.[32] This is why a perfectly good God would not have these powers. Instead, I would suggest that having these powers is a liability only for a being not in complete control of itself. Yet, as we have seen, an omnipotent being *is* in complete control of itself. If this being is also morally good, then this complete control over itself will enable it to necessarily abstain from doing certain things—like bringing about atrocities—which it is nevertheless perfectly able to do.

Some philosophers will resist the account I am proposing here because they think there cannot be necessarily unexercised powers. In fact, this view has held great sway on contemporary writers addressing the topic of omnipotence.[33] Given that there cannot be necessarily unexercised powers,

---

[29] I owe this last comment to Jonathan Kvanvig.

[30] Though he denies that God is able to bring about atrocities, Swinburne 1979 explains the necessity of God's never bringing about atrocities in this way as well.

[31] This simple and intuitively powerful argument can be precisified if we focus on how to understand the kinds of necessity and possibility involved in the argument. One way to do this is as follows. The conclusion of the argument is that it is *logically* possible that it is *metaphysically* necessary that an omnipotent being refrains from bringing about atrocities. Below, when I talk of necessarily unexercised powers, I should be understood to be talking about *metaphysically* necessarily unexercised powers.

[32] Mawson 2002 defends this view.

[33] Hoffman and Rosencrantz 2012 note this trend. Rowe 2004 and 2007 appeal to this claim frequently in arguments for the conclusion that a perfectly good being cannot be able to bring about atrocities. Hopefully, the discussion in the text will make plain how an advocate of my solution to the puzzle of omnipotence and perfect goodness

it cannot be that a God that satisfies AP could necessarily refrain from bringing about atrocities. For, given AP, God has all the powers required to overcome any obstacle to his bringing these about. Since, in some world, these powers must be exercised, in some world, the obstacles to God's refraining from committing atrocities are overcome. In my own view, however, the key reason for thinking that there cannot be necessarily unexercised powers is unconvincing. And, it is especially open to dispute in the present context, given considerations we have surveyed above.[34]

The central reason for someone to deny that there could be a necessarily unexercised power is that one might be tempted to analyze powers in terms of subjunctive conditionals of some sort. For instance, I have the power to make a three-pointer just in case, were I to shoot some, I'd intentionally make a good many of them. Or something along these lines.[35] But, the objector will continue, if there were necessarily unexercised powers, then this way of analyzing powers would have no hope. It would have no hope because necessarily unexercised powers would yield trivially true subjunctive conditionals. Supposing, for instance, that God's power to will atrocities were necessarily unexercised, whatever subjunctive conditionals are supposed to be used to analyze God's power to will atrocities will be trivially true. In fact, it will follow that everyone has all of the powers which are necessarily unexercised. But this is untenable. So, the subjunctive conditional analysis of powers will fail, if there are necessarily unexercised powers. But, this analysis cannot fail. So, there must not be any necessarily unexercised powers.

There are two significant replies to this objection I think are worth offering here. First, someone attracted to AP is highly unlikely to grant that powers should be analyzed in terms of subjunctive conditionals of some sort. In fact, they are highly unlikely to grant that powers are to be analyzed at all. A key part of the attraction of AP is that it is supposed to be explanatorily fundamental. It is an analysis of omnipotence which is supposed to explain what is correct in the requirements of other analyses. As such, it is supposed to be working with concepts which reach rock bottom in terms of

would reply to Rowe's question about whether an omnipotent, perfectly good being could bring it about that he was not perfectly good. I would argue that, while an omnipotent perfectly good being has the power to make this the case, it does not follow (as Rowe supposes) that there is some possible world in which this perfectly good being is not perfectly good.

[34] For another author who denies that the power to bring about x entails the possibility that one brings about x, see Conee 1991.

[35] For some classic subjunctive conditional analyses of powers, dispositions or abilities, see Hume 1748, Davidson 1980, Peacocke 1999. For criticisms, see Martin 1996 and Johnston 1992. For an approach that analyzes abilities using subjunctive conditionals *and* basic dispositions, see Fara 2008.

explaining what it is to be omnipotent. Someone who advocates AP, then, like myself, is likely to think that powers are exactly this sort of basic, not-further-analyzable sort of thing. Someone who advocates AP has already given up on analyzing powers in terms of subjunctive conditionals, or in terms of anything else at all.[36]

Second, in the present context, this objection to the proposed method for responding to the puzzle of omnipotence and perfect goodness is especially impotent. This is because the majority of the parties in this debate, as we have seen, are ready to accept that counterpossibles needn't all be trivially true. Thus, the fact that some power is necessarily unexercised does not entail that it is had by everyone, since the relevant subjunctive conditionals may well not be true for everyone. They will be true for some and not true for others. Perhaps those for whom they are true possess the power in question while those for whom they are false do not.

AP, then, offers us a unique and attractive analysis of omnipotence which affords an equally unique and attractive resolution of the puzzle of omnipotence and perfect goodness. AP is simple, it accommodates key insights and demands of recent philosophical treatments of omnipotence, and it explains what is accurate in more recent accounts of omnipotence. Finally, AP affords its defender a unique response to the puzzle of omnipotence and perfect goodness which is defensible against key objections. In the next section, we will see how AP affords an equally unique and defensible response to a second difficult problem in philosophical theology—the puzzle of perfect goodness and freedom.

II.b. The Puzzle of Perfect Goodness and Freedom

We now turn to a second puzzle in philosophical theology concerning the compatibility of traditional divine attributes, this one focused on the compatibility of perfect goodness and freedom, where freedom is understood along libertarian lines. The puzzle about perfect goodness and freedom can be put into the form of an argument very similar to the argument we discussed in the previous section concerning perfect goodness and omnipotence. First, we can suppose, for *reductio*, that:

(1) Possibly, God is both perfectly good and free.

---

[36] In embracing powers as basic, I am following the neo-Aristotelians. For several helpful articles from leading defenders of taking Aristotelian powers to be part of the basic ontology of the world, see Greco and Gross 2012.

Because God is perfectly good, we conclude, as with the previous puzzle, that:

> (2) Necessarily, if God is perfectly good, then God is unable to bring about atrocities.

Yet, there is significant reason to think that:

> (3) Necessarily, if God is free, then God is able to bring about atrocities.

The support for 3 has to do with a libertarian conception of freedom, or of "significant freedom" or "moral freedom," which endorses a strong version of the principle of alternate possibilities (or PAP). This strong version of PAP says roughly that one is free, or "significantly free," or "morally free," only if one is able to bring about both all-things-considered-right and all-things-considered-wrong states of affairs. Significant freedom rests in one's freedom to do both good and evil—one's power to choose and execute both genuine moral rights and genuine moral wrongs. Theists have often insisted that this sort of significant freedom is necessary for moral responsibility, at least in human beings. This has been especially important to advocates of the free-will defense against the problem of evil.[37,38] Those who defend 3 are just applying this version of PAP to God as well. God is significantly free only if God is able to bring about all-things-considered wrongs, like atrocities. In this dialectical context, it is probably best to take "free" in 3 (and 1) to mean whatever sort of freedom is required for moral responsibility.[39] The defense of 3 then requires identifying this sort of freedom with moral freedom.

Unfortunately, 1, 2, and 3 together imply:

> (4) Possibly, God is able to bring about atrocities and unable to bring about atrocities.

Since 4 is a contradiction, we must reject at least one of 1, 2, or 3. But, the person who wishes to defend our puzzle of perfect goodness and freedom as a challenge to the compatibility of these attributes will insist that 2 and 3

---

[37] Two classic sources are Plantinga 1974 and Swinburne 1979.

[38] A similar, though weaker formulation of PAP is advocated by Kevin Timpe 2008: "an agent is free with respect to an action A at a time t only if there are morally relevant alternative possibilities related to A at time t." This principle might be employed in an argument very similar to the one presented here in the text. However, it would complicate the presentation significantly.

[39] Alternatively, we might take "free" to indicate some kind of superior freedom which requires alternative possibilities, even if the sort of freedom necessary for moral responsibility does not.

are well-supported. So, they will conclude that the correct response to our puzzle will be to reject our original supposition, 1. That is, they will conclude that we should reject the compatibility of perfect goodness and freedom. Several prominent philosophers have recently advocated arguments very much like this one for the incompatibility of perfect goodness and freedom.[40] And, as with our previous puzzle, others have responded. By far, the more common response is for opponents of this argument to deny premise 3. In doing so, they suggest reasons for thinking that the sort of freedom required for moral responsibility in God does not require the satisfaction of our strong version of PAP, while the sort of freedom required for moral responsibility in creatures does. Authors who defend this strategy, like Edward Wierenga (2002, 2007) and Thomas Senor (2008), typically argue that in the case of God it is only required for significant freedom and moral responsibility that God be the ultimate source of God's actions, not that God be able to have performed morally significant alternative actions. I will not argue against these approaches here, though I do think they face significant obstacles.[41] My primary goal in this section is instead to explore an alternative strategy available to those who advocate AP. As in the case of the previous puzzle concerning the compatibility of omnipotence and perfect goodness, so with the present puzzle I will show, first, that AP affords its defenders a response to the puzzle and, second, that that it offers its advocates a positive argument for the compatibility of perfect goodness and freedom of the sort that requires PAP.

The first part of the response may be presented very quickly. I have already, in the previous subsection of the paper, explained how those who advocate AP might deny premise 2 of the puzzle of perfect goodness and freedom. They will do this by insisting that a perfectly good being may be perfectly able to bring about atrocities, though necessarily resist bringing any about because of unwillingness. This is especially so if the being is omnipotent in the sense required by AP. For, given that the being satisfies the conditions of AP, it is in complete control of itself. It is able to bring about atrocities, but also necessarily able to resist bringing them about.

The second part requires a lengthier defense. My goal here is to show that, given that AP is the correct account of omnipotence, and given the results of the previous section of this paper, it follows that perfect goodness is compatible with libertarian-style significant freedom. The argument for

---

[40] Two conspicuous examples are Morriston 2000 and Rowe 2004.

[41] Ultimately, I think proposals of this sort must end up resting their case on an appeal to the doctrine of divine simplicity, as Morriston (2000, 2006) argues. Yet, it seems to me that resorting to this doctrine will result in dialectical stalemate, rather than a clear victory for advocates of this approach.

this is as follows. Given that AP is the correct account of omnipotence and given that the results of the previous section of this paper are correct, omnipotence is compatible with perfect goodness. But, as I will argue momentarily, omnipotence, understood in terms of AP, entails libertarian freedom of the sort which requires PAP. So, perfect goodness is compatible with libertarian freedom of the sort that requires PAP (hereafter, I will sometimes just say "libertarian freedom" or "freedom").

The key premise in this argument now in need of defense is the claim that omnipotence, understood in terms of AP, entails libertarian freedom. Libertarians typically identify two key conditions for freedom—a sourcehood condition and an alternative possibilities condition.[42] According to the sourcehood condition, if an agent is to be free they must be the ultimate source of their actions. And, according to the alternative possibilities condition, to be free an agent must be able to do otherwise than they in fact do. On a strong version of PAP, like the one we discussed in presenting the puzzle of omnipotence and perfect goodness, an agent is free only if able to bring about both all-things-considered rights and all-things-considered wrongs (i.e. atrocities). If both the sourcehood condition and alternative possibilities condition are met, then, plausibly, the agent is free in the performance of their action. I want to argue here that, given that AP is the correct account of omnipotence, an omnipotent God satisfies both of these conditions and so has significant freedom.

First, an omnipotent God satisfies the sourcehood condition. This should not be very controversial, especially in this context. I am interested primarily in moving those who tend to respond to the puzzle of omnipotence and perfect goodness and the puzzle of perfect goodness and freedom in ways other than the one I am proposing to give a fuller hearing to my approach. But those who respond to these puzzles in ways other than the way I am proposing tend to emphasize already that God satisfies the sourcehood condition of free will, as we saw above in the cases of Wierenga and Senor. God should be accounted free, in their view, because he is the ultimate origin of his acts. Ultimate origination implies alternative possibilities for humans, but nor for God. For God, on their view, ultimate origination is alone sufficient for freedom. And God satisfies this condition of ultimate origination. I am simply agreeing with these authors' point here that God satisfies this criterion of ultimate origination. There is nothing about AP which would imply otherwise.

---

[42] For an excellent introduction to these two conditions and the role they play in libertarian reflection on freedom, see Timpe 2008.

What about the alternative possibilities condition—especially its strong version? In favor of the view that an omnipotent God satisfies this condition, I argue as follows. As we have seen, an omnipotent being satisfies Ab—my account of what it is to be "able" to bring something about—with respect to bringing about atrocities. But, I will argue momentarily, Ab provides the correct analysis of what it is to be "able" to do otherwise in the sense required by the strong alternative possibilities condition on freedom. Thus, an omnipotent being satisfies the strong alternative possibilities condition on freedom, as well as the sourcehood condition.

The key premise I must defend in this argument is the claim that Ab provides the correct analysis of what it is to be able to do otherwise in the sense required by the strong alternative possibilities condition on freedom. In favor of that judgment, I argue that, if the advocate of the alternative possibilities condition on freedom accepts Ab's proposal concerning what it is to be able to do otherwise, then their alternative possibilities principle will do exactly what it is supposed to do—it will rule out freedom in just those cases it is supposed to, and for the right reason: namely, the ability to do otherwise is lacking in these cases. Thus, Ab is a very attractive account of what it is to be able to do otherwise in the sense required by the alternative possibilities condition on freedom. In arguing for Ab in this manner, I follow Senor's approach to understanding the nature of the "ability to do otherwise" required by PAP. Senor, too, argues that we ought to understand the "ability to do otherwise" in PAP through considering the kinds of cases where PAP is supposed to rule out freedom due to the absence of this ability. I simply disagree slightly with Senor about in exactly which categories of cases PAP ought to rule out freedom and responsibility.

Senor recognizes three kinds of cases where PAP is supposed to rule out freedom. They are (a) cases where an action is determined by past causally sufficient conditions which pre-date the existence of the actor, (b) cases where actors are manipulated by other agents, and (c) cases where actors are compelled to act as a result of internal compulsions with which they do not identify.

Cases of type (a) would obtain if causal determinism were true. If events that occur billions of years before one is born, together with the laws of nature governing those events, conspire to ensure that one acts in a certain way, then PAP is supposed to rule out one's behaving freely in such a case. It is supposed to do so because these past causally sufficient conditions for action preclude one's ability to do otherwise than what these conditions determine one to do. I am somewhat skeptical of Senor's use of this case to illuminate PAP, as I will explain further below.

Cases of type (b) would obtain if one were manipulated by another agent to act in a certain way. The classic examples here are ones which appeal to fanciful neurophysiologists who implant devices into one's brain which cause one to behave in a certain way and prevent one from doing otherwise. Again, PAP is supposed to ensure that actors in these circumstances are not regarded as free or morally responsible.

Finally, cases of type (c) occur where agents are subject to what we might think of as a different kind of manipulation—a kind of manipulation internal to their own psyches. The classic examples here involve addictions or pathologies. Agents who, for instance, because of a pathological fear of being anywhere near red things are unable to draw red pictures are not to be regarded as free or responsible for failing to draw red pictures. PAP is supposed to rule out freedom in cases like this because, due to the redness-aversion pathology, the agent is unable to draw red pictures.

While I agree with Senor's cases (b) and (c), I think he overlooks one more important category of cases where PAP is supposed to rule out freedom and moral responsibility. It is the category of cases where a person is unable to do other than they do because they lack the power to do otherwise—not because of a pathology or because someone is manipulating them or even because they are causally determined to act as they do. Rather, they simply do not have the power in question, and so cannot act accordingly.

Examples which illustrate this sort of absence of power abound. It is because I lack power in this sense that I am unable to make a fifty-foot basketball shot. I just don't have the power to do this. There are a very few people in the world who have this power, at best. It isn't because of manipulation or causal determinism or a pathology that I am unable to make this shot; I just don't have the power to make it. In a similar way, it is because I lack power in this sense that I cannot fly a plane. I've never learned how. Some people have. They've acquired this power. But I haven't. And so, I'm unable to fly. Again, it is because I lack power in this sense that I am unable to donate $1 million to charity. I don't have $1 million, and because of this I lack the power to donate $1 million. And we could keep going.[43]

---

[43] Someone may ask: isn't it causal determinism that rules out the power here? After all, isn't it the case that the past and laws of nature rule out your making the shot or successfully flying the plane? Though in many cases the answer to the second question here may be affirmative, I think there are imaginable cases where it is negative. Suppose we have an indeterministic universe in which sometimes flukes happen in one's favor. That I might flukily get the shot to go down does not entail that I have the power to make that shot, just as the golfer's ability to make putts is not negated by a fluky miss (see Austin 1956).

Now, plausibly, PAP should rule out freedom in these kinds of cases just as well as it does in the kinds of cases which fit neatly into categories (b) and (c). I am not free, or morally responsible, for my failing to make a three-quarter-length shot. I am not free, or morally responsible, for failing to fly planes. And, I am not free or morally responsible for failing to give $1 million to charity. The reason I am not free or morally responsible in these cases is that I couldn't have done otherwise than I did. This is just the sort of thing that PAP is designed to handle. PAP is designed to rule out freedom in those cases where an inability to do otherwise intuitively prevents freedom and moral responsibility. And cases like these fit the bill.

With this understanding of the kinds of cases where PAP is supposed to rule out freedom and responsibility, we can now complete our argument in defense of Ab as an analysis of the "ability" to bring about a morally signifi-cant alternative involved in PAP. Accepting Ab's analysis of ability and con-joining this with the alternative possibilities condition on freedom will plausibly rule out freedom in each of these cases in which it should do so. To see this, let's work backwards, beginning with the fourth kind of case involving the simple absence of power.

The reason the person who simply lacks the power to, say, make a half-court shot is unable to make this shot is that there is an obstacle to their making it which they lack the power to overcome. We might locate this obstacle in the difficulty of the shot itself or in their lacking the strength or precision to throw the ball sufficiently far or sufficiently accurately. The agent does not have the powers necessary to overcome these obstacles. Ab implies that such a person lacks the ability to make the shot. Thus, if the defender of the alternative possibilities condition adopts Ab's analysis of the ability to do otherwise, then that condition will rule out freedom in these kinds of cases, as it should.

A similar result obtains in cases involving psychological maladies. The reason the person with the pathological fear of red objects is unable to make red objects is that there is an obstacle to her making them which the person lacks the power to overcome. This obstacle, of course, is their pathological fear. Ab implies that such a person lacks the ability to make red objects. Thus, if the defender of the alternative possibilities condition adopts Ab's analysis of the ability to do otherwise, then that condition will rule out free-dom in these kinds of cases, as it should.

The same result obtains in cases involving manipulation. The reason the manipulated agent is unable to bring about alternative possibilities is that there is an obstacle which they lack the power to overcome. This obstacle, of course, is their being manipulated by someone else. Ab implies that such a person lacks the ability to do otherwise. Thus, if the defender of the alternative possibilities condition adopts Ab's analysis of the ability to do otherwise, then that condition will rule out freedom in these kinds of cases, as it should.

The first kind of case is, perhaps, the trickiest. It is a case where an agent's actions are causally determined by events and laws that obtained long before one's birth. A libertarian might argue that, in such cases, the agent lacks the ability to do otherwise and so is not free. Of course, it has been highly controversial whether this is correct. Compatibilists have, after all, offered understandings of what it is to be able to do otherwise which a causally determined agent can retain the ability to do otherwise.[44] What we should want from an account of the ability to do otherwise, then, is for it to neither obviously rule out freedom in these cases nor obviously rule it in. We would like this account to leave room for substantive metaphysical debate over whether the causally determined agent is able to do otherwise and thus is free in their actions.

Ab again delivers. For, if Ab is adopted as the correct understanding of what it is to be able to do otherwise in the sense required by the alternative possibilities condition of freedom, then there is room for substantive debate concerning whether the causally determined agent is able to do otherwise. Libertarians might argue that there are indeed obstacles to the causally determined agent's acting otherwise which the agent lacks the power to overcome. For, the past and laws determine the behavior of the agent, who lacks the power to overcome this. Compatibilists, on the other hand, might argue that the causally determined agent *does* have the power to overcome these obstacles (as the causally determined agent has the right kind of power over the past and/or laws[45]), or even that causal determinism presents no obstacle to be overcome in the first place. If Ab is adopted as the correct account of what it is to be "able" to bring something about as this notion appears in PAP, then PAP will play precisely the role it should in debates between compatibilists and incompatibilists about the precise requirements the alternative possibilities condition places on free action.

We have seen, then, that if Ab is accepted as the correct account of what it is to be able to do otherwise in the sense required by the alternative possibilities condition on free will, then this condition will perform its job admirably well. This gives us significant reason to accept Ab as the correct account of what it is to be able to do otherwise in the sense required by this condition. Someone who is able to do otherwise, according to Ab, satisfies the alternative possibilities condition on free will.

---

[44] See, e.g., Ayer 1954.   [45] See, e.g., Lewis 1981.

Given this result, we can now complete our argument concerning the freedom of an omnipotent, perfectly good God. I have been arguing that if this omnipotent, perfectly good God satisfies both the sourcehood condition and the alternative possibilities condition, then this God is free. What is more controversial here is whether this God satisfies the alternative possibilities condition. But, we are now in a position to defend the claim that he does. For, given that this God is omnipotent and given that omnipotence is to be understood in terms of AP, this God has all the powers. Thus, for anything which might serve as an obstacle to God's performing some action, if there is a power that could be used to overcome that obstacle, God has that power. Of course, the specific case we want to know about is the case of bringing about atrocities. God will be able to bring about atrocities, according to Ab, so long as he has all the powers necessary to overcome whatever obstacles there might be to his bringing about atrocities. But, plausibly, God does have all of the requisite powers. For, God has, inter alia, the power to will to bring these atrocities about. And, though he necessarily refrains from willing to bring these atrocities about, it is non-trivially true that were he do to so, they would obtain. Thus, plausibly, God satisfies the conditions Ab requires for the ability to bring about atrocities. And so, as Ab is the correct analysis of what it is to be able to do otherwise in the sense required by the alternative possibilities condition on freedom, God satisfies the alternative possibilities condition on freedom.[46]

That God is omnipotent entails that God is free—as free as one can be. For, God's omnipotence is just his possession of all the powers. But, God's possessing all the powers implies that, for any obstacle there might be to his actions, if there is a power to overcome that obstacle, then God has that power. In particular, God has the power to overcome obstacles to his bringing about atrocities. This is important because it gives God significant or moral freedom. Though God is morally perfect and necessarily refrains from performing morally wrong actions, he has the power to perform them. It is non-trivially true that, were God to exercise his power to perform these actions, he would perform them. In so doing, he would overcome any obstacle to their performance. Thus, he has all of the powers necessary to overcome whatever obstacles there might be to his performing these actions. And the power to do so is just what makes his necessarily refraining from ever performing these actions significantly free.

---

[46] As this passage suggests, I am friendly toward the following sort of analysis: S has the powers P necessary for overcoming an obstacle O to S bringing about X if and only if S has P and it is non-trivially true that, were S to exercise P in an attempt to bring about X, S would bring about X by exercising P.

In this section, we have seen that the puzzle of perfect goodness and freedom dissolves, and that there is even a positive argument for the claim that perfect goodness and freedom are consistent. That argument hinges on the account of omnipotence defended in the previous section. Thus, this account of omnipotence is not only independently plausible, but it makes available unique resolutions to both the puzzle of omnipotence and perfect goodness as well as the puzzle of perfect goodness and freedom.

III. CONCLUSION

This paper has defended a novel account of omnipotence and argued that this account of omnipotence makes available unique responses to two intractable puzzles in philosophical theology. The goal of the paper has not been to provide a knock-down argument in favor of the account of omnipotence and the solutions to these puzzles here explored, however; the goal is more modest. The goal has been to convince philosophers of religion who would not otherwise have seriously considered the present views that they are at least viable alternatives deserving of serious attention—at least as serious attention as their leading contemporary rivals. We have seen that the present account of omnipotence is simple; we have seen that this account accommodates the key insights and demands of recent philosophical treatments of omnipotence; we have seen that what competing contemporary accounts of this attribute have going in their favor is arguably explained by the present account; and, finally, we have seen that the present account affords its advocate unique and defensible resolutions to two intractable puzzles in philosophical theology concerning the compatibility of traditional divine attributes. For all of these reasons, I recommend the present account of omnipotence and the solutions it affords to these puzzles in philosophical theology to the community of philosophers of religion.

REFERENCES

Austin, John L. (1956). "Ifs and Cans." *Proceedings of The British Academy* 42.

Ayer, Alfred J. (1954). "Freedom and Necessity." In *Philosophical Essays*. New York: St. Martin's Press.

Berto, Francesco. (2009). "Impossible Worlds." In *Stanford Encyclopedia of Philosophy*, ed. Edward N. Zalta. <http://plato.stanford.edu/entries/impossible-worlds/>.

Conee, Earl. (1991). "The Possibility of Power Beyond Possibility." *Philosophical Perspectives* 5.

Cowan, J. L. (1965). "The Paradox of Omnipotence." *Analysis* 25.

Davidson, Donald. (1980). *Essays on Actions and Events*. Oxford: Oxford University Press.

Descartes, René. (1984–91). *The Philosophical Writings of Descartes*, trans. John Cottingham, Robert Stoothoff, Dugald Murdoch, and Anthony Kenny. 3 vols. Cambridge: Cambridge University Press.

Fara, Michael. (2008). "Masked Abilities and Compatibilism." *Mind* 117.

Flint, Thomas P. and Fredosso, Alfred. (1983). "Maximal Power." In *The Existence and Nature of God*, ed. Alfred J. Fredosso. Notre Dame, IN: University of Notre Dame Press.

Frankfurt, Harry. (1988). "The Importance of What We Care about." In *The Importance of What We Care About: Philosophical Essays*. New York: Cambridge University Press.

Funkhouser, Eric. (2006). "On Privileging God's Moral Goodness." *Faith and Philosophy* 23.

Garcia, Laura L. (1987). "The Essential Moral Perfection of God." *Religious Studies* 23.

Geach, Peter. (1973). "Omnipotence." *Philosophy* 48.

Greco, John and Gross, Ruth, eds. (2012). *Powers and Capacities in Philosophy: The New Aristotelianism*. London: Routledge.

Hoffman, Joshua and Rosencrantz, Gary. (1980). "What an Omnipotent Agent can Do." *International Journal for Philosophy of Religion* 11.

Hoffman, Joshua and Rosencrantz, Gary. (2010). "Omnipotence." In *A Companion to Philosophy of Religion*, 2nd edn, ed. Charles Taliaferro, Paul Draper, and Philip L. Quinn. Oxford: Wiley-Blackwell.

Hoffman, Joshua and Rosencrantz, Gary. (2012). "Omnipotence." In *Stanford Encyclopedia of Philosophy*, ed. Edward N. Zalta. <http://plato.stanford.edu/entries/omnipotence/>.

Hume, David. (1748). *An Enquiry Concerning Human Understanding*.

Johnston, Mark. (1992). "How to Speak of the Colors." *Philosophical Studies* 68.

La Croix, Richard. (1977). "The Impossibility of Defining 'Omnipotence'." *Philosophical Studies* 32.

Lembke, Martin. (2012). "Omnipotence and Other Possibilities." *Religious Studies* 48.

Lewis, David K. (1981). "Are We Free to Break the Laws?" *Theoria* 47.

Mackie, John L. (1955). "Evil and Omnipotence." *Mind* 64.

Manis, R. Zachary. (2011). "Could God Do Something Evil? A Molinist Solution to the Problem of Divine Freedom." *Faith and Philosophy* 28.

Martin, C. B. (1996). "Dispositions and Conditionals." *Philosophical Quarterly* 44.

Mawson, Tim. (2002). "Omnipotence and Necessary Moral Perfection are Compatible: A Reply to Morriston." *Religious Studies* 38.

Merricks, Trenton. (2003). *Objects and Persons*. Oxford: Clarendon Press.

Morriston, Wes. (2000). "What is So Good About Moral Freedom?" *Philosophical Quarterly* 50.

Morriston, Wes. (2001). "Omnipotence and Necessary Moral Perfection: Are They Compatible?" *Religious Studies* 37.

Morriston, Wes. (2002). "Omnipotence and the Power to Choose: A Reply to Wielenberg." *Faith and Philosophy* 19.

Morriston, Wes. (2006). "Is God Free? Reply to Wierenga." *Faith and Philosophy* 23.

Nagasawa, Yugin. (2008). "A New Defense of Anselmian Theism." *Philosophical Quarterly* 58.

Oppy, Graham. (2005). "Omnipotence." *Philosophy and Phenomenological Research* 71.

Pawl, Timothy and Timpe, Kevin. (2009). "Incompatibilism, Sin, and Free Will in Heaven." *Faith and Philosophy* 26.

Peacocke, Christopher. (1999). *Being Known*. Oxford: Oxford University Press.

Pike, Nelson. (1969). "Omnipotence and God's Ability to Sin." *American Philosophical Quarterly* 6.

Plantinga, Alvin. (1967). *God and Other Minds: A Study of the Rational Justification of Belief in God*. Ithaca, NY: Cornell University Press.

Plantinga, Alvin. (1974). *God, Freedom, and Evil*. Grand Rapids, MI: Eerdmans.

Pruss, Alexander and Pearce, Kenney. (2012). "Understanding Omnipotence." *Religious Studies* 48.

Quinn, Philip. (1978). *Divine Commands and Moral Requirements*. Oxford: Oxford University Press.

Quinn, Philip. (1999). "Divine Command Theory." In *Guide to Ethical Theory*, ed. Hugh LaFollette. Oxford: Blackwell.

Rowe, William. (2004). *Can God Be Free?* Oxford: Oxford University Press.

Rowe, William. (2007). "Divine Freedom." In *Stanford Encyclopedia of Philosophy*, ed. Edward N. Zalta. <http://plato.stanford.edu/entries/divine-freedom/>.

Senor, Thomas. (2008). "Defending Divine Freedom." In *Oxford Studies in Philosophy of Religion*, Volume 1, ed. Jonathan Kvanvig. Oxford: Oxford University Press.

Sobel, Jordan Howard. (2004). *Logic and Theism: Arguments for and against Beliefs in God*. Cambridge: Cambridge University Press.

Stalnaker, Robert. (1968). "A Theory of Conditionals." In *Studies in Logical Theory*, American Philosophical Quarterly Monograph Series 2. Oxford: Blackwell.

Swinburne, Richard. (1973). "Omnipotence." *American Philosophical Quarterly* 10.

Swinburne, Richard. (1979). *The Existence of God*. Oxford: Clarendon Press.

Timpe, Kevin. (2006). "A Critique of Frankfurt Libertarianism." *Philosophia* 34.

Timpe, Kevin. (2008). *Free Will: Sourcehood and its Alternatives*. London: Continuum.

Todd, Patrick. (2013). "Soft Facts and Ontological Dependence." *Philosophical Studies* 164.

Tooley, Michael. (2009). "The Problem of Evil." In *Stanford Encyclopedia of Philosophy*, ed. Edward N. Zalta. <http://plato.stanford.edu/entries/evil/>.

van Inwagen, Peter. (1983). *An Essay on Free Will*. Oxford: Oxford University Press.

Vander Laan, David. (2004). "Counterpossibles and Similarity." In *Lewisian Themes: the Philosophy of David K. Lewis*, ed. Frank Jackson and Graham Priest. Oxford: Oxford University Press.

Watson, Gary. (2004). "Volitional Necessities." In *Agency and Answerability: Selected Essays*. Oxford: Oxford University Press.

Wielenberg, Erik J. (2000). "Omnipotence Again." *Faith and Philosophy* 17.

Wierenga, Edward. (1983). "Omnipotence Defined." *Philosophy and Phenomenological Research* 43.

Wierenga, Edward. (2002). "The Freedom of God." *Faith and Philosophy* 19.

Wierenga, Edward. (2007). "Perfect Goodness and Divine Freedom." *Philosophical Books* 48.

3

The Evidential Weight of Social Evil

Joseph Corabi

INTRODUCTION

In his recent prize-winning essay "Social Evil," Ted Poston examines a variety of evil that typically goes undiscussed in treatments of the problem of evil.[1] In addition to the familiar moral and natural evils, Poston introduces the distinct category of social evils. "Social evil," he says:

> is an instance of pain or suffering that results from the game-theoretic interactions of many individuals. When a social evil occurs, responsibility for the outcome lies with no particular person and no impersonal force of nature; rather it lies with a group of people, each of whom may be morally in the clear.[2]

Although Poston's primary aim is to introduce and describe the phenomenon, he does ultimately conclude that social evil is "problematic" and that it provides an "opportunity to further mine the conceptual resources of theism."[3] In this paper, I take up the challenge that Poston raises. I argue that, while *apparent* social evils are disturbingly common, *real* social evils are surprisingly rare—at least when one adopts an ethical framework that is at home within Christianity (and other traditional theistic religions as well). Moreover, the social evil candidates that remain after scrutiny add little evidential weight to the kinds of non-social evil cases already familiar from mainstream discussions of the problem of evil. Hence, although social evils and apparent social evils raise significant practical challenges for Christians and others deeply invested in promoting a flourishing world, their addition to the mix does not provide significant new evidence against the existence of the Christian God. This is because it does not contribute a large quantity

---

[1] Ted Poston, "Social Evil," *Oxford Studies in Philosophy of Religion* 5 (2014), 166–85.
[2] Poston (2014), 168.   [3] Poston (2014), 185.

of new suffering to the world and moreover that suffering is not of a prob-
lematically novel quality. Thus, my efforts are primarily aimed not at criticizing the general atheological argument from social evil, but at a version of
the argument that targets the Christian God and the God of other religions
that share ethical commitments with Christianity of the sort discussed
below. My hunch, though, is that this will cover a wide range of theistic
positions.

My strategy in the paper will be, first, to describe social evil and give
some paradigmatic examples of apparent social evils, as well as present a few
qualifications and set the issues in context. Second, I will go to work discussing the ways that examples of apparent social evils can be "siphoned
off"—i.e. shown not to satisfy the conditions required to count as social evil
for one reason or another. This process will involve clarifying the nature of
both social evil and Christian moral commitments. Next, I will examine the
kinds of social evil candidates that remain after the siphoning process is
completed, exploring and tying together what evidential lessons about theism can be learned. Objections will be considered, and the concluding section will then sum up the overall findings.

SOCIAL EVIL: PURE AND IMPURE

To get a clear understanding of social evil, we first need a detailed account
of what a social evil is. In his discussion, Poston actually describes two distinct types of social evil, though one receives the bulk of his attention and is
clearly his main target. This first variety is pain and suffering that results
from "the game-theoretic interactions of rational moral individuals;"[4] this
I will call "pure" social evil:

A pure social evil $=_{df}$ A scenario where agents $a_1 \ldots a_j$ all make free decisions and are
morally blameless, yet pain or suffering results for agents $b_1 \ldots b_k$. This pain or suffering is brought about at least largely because of the free decisions made by $a_1 \ldots a_j$,
and would not result if only a small proportion of those specific free decisions were
made.[5] (There may or may not be overlap between the $a_1 \ldots a_j$ and the $b_1 \ldots b_k$, and
there must be at least an a_1 and an a_2.)

---

[4] Poston (2014), 166.
[5] When I refer to "those specific free decisions" here, I mean the specific actions, not
the existence of the choices in the abstract. In other words, to offer an example, if a_{10} faces
a choice between R and S and chooses S, I mean to refer to a_{10}'s choice of S, not the fact
that a_{10} faced this free choice.

I readily admit that it is possible to quibble over this definition. For our purposes, though, it will be good enough—none of my conclusions will trade on any objectionable niceties of formulation, and the definition states at least a necessary condition that any pure social evil will meet. One issue we should be mindful of, however, is that the definition does not specify whether the required blamelessness is restricted to the decision itself (considered in complete isolation) or whether it includes various background decisions in the past that have placed the individual in their present epistemic position. I will not attempt to stipulate a resolution to this issue, as there is no clear precedent to fall back on from previous discussions. In the end, whether we require diachronic blamelessness or merely synchronic blamelessness may matter somewhat for the classification of social evil, but it will not matter to an ultimate appraisal of the evidential importance of the cases. I will return to this issue later in the paper.

There are many classic candidates for status as pure social evils. Poston himself gives a fictional example that he takes to be paradigmatic: residents of Southern California aiming to conserve water during a drought. In his scenario, the Los Angeles area is in danger of running out of an adequate water supply, and so area residents must come together and agree to restrict consumption to prevent more severe consequences. But restricting water use involves a significant cost for most individuals, and many of them are involved in beneficial projects where water use is required. (Some of them take care of beautiful public gardens, for instance, while perhaps others run public swimming pools for kids.) These individuals reason that, if they were to defect and continue to use water as normal, their beneficial projects could continue as before. There would be no effect on the overall plight—after all, they are each just one of millions of agents involved. Each then individually decides to defect, knowing that this will bring about the best overall outcome.[6] But then so many individuals wind up defecting that, together, they produce an outcome which is far worse than would have been the case had they all just cooperated in the first place. (Let us suppose, as Poston does, that what each individual does is completely opaque to all other individuals, and there are enough individuals with good reason to defect that together they create a serious shortage.) The powerful insight is that, blameless and well intentioned though the individuals involved are, their choices collectively lead to a disastrous outcome.

---

[6] It is important to note that each individual is correct that their decision to defect will bring about the best overall outcome, given how other individuals are deciding. The problem is just that, when large numbers of individuals think this way, the overall outcome is far worse than it would otherwise be.

This fictional case is meant as an illustrative example, but there are many real life scenarios that are widely thought to involve social evils. Among these are various kinds of pollution, anthropogenic climate change, traffic congestion, abuse of antibiotics, and overfishing in the world's oceans, along with many lower-stakes everyday situations.[7]

Poston's second and less central variety of social evil is what I will call "impure social evil." Impure social evils are scenarios where at least some of the individuals are blameworthy, but where the game-theoretic machinery produces "an amount of pain and suffering that is disproportionate to the individual choices in the game."[8] Poston gives as examples here the violent conflicts in Northern Ireland and the former Yugoslavia, as well as suffering associated with the practice of dueling in early modern England. (In these cases, individuals in difficult positions acted in mildly blameworthy ways, but those mildly blameworthy actions often had devastating consequences.) It turns out to be very difficult to offer a precise definition of impure social evil—more difficult than to offer the corresponding definition of pure social evil. The reason is that it is extraordinarily tough to pin down what it means for an amount of pain and suffering to be "disproportionate" to individual choices, even if we think we have a rough intuitive grasp of the phenomenon. Fortunately, as I mentioned, these impure social evils play only a peripheral role in Poston's own analysis (rightly in my view), and so I will wait until much later in the paper to address them. Like Poston, I will dedicate the bulk of my attention to pure social evils.[9]

Before getting down to business, though, I should offer the qualification that I am not aiming to offer a demonstration that the world contains very few social evils (at least pure ones) or that whatever social evils remain are scant evidence against the existence of God. Even coming close to offering a demonstration of this conclusion would involve thoroughly examining the myriad of complexities associated with the diversity of sociological and economic interactions the world contains, as well as detailed investigation

---

[7] Incidentally, there are also cases of "social goods"—situations where game-theoretic interactions among bad actors produce beneficial results. Various market mechanisms are famous examples—particularly noteworthy are cases where colluders in a cartel are incentivized to defect and ruin the cartel's exploitative advantage. For a non-technical discussion, see John Cassidy, *How Markets Fail: The Logic of Economic Calamities*, New York: Farrar, Straus, and Giroux, 2009.

[8] Poston (2014), 180.

[9] Social evils are not reducible to natural evils because they involve decisions which are free *ex hypothesi*. They are not reducible to moral evils because the individuals are not blameworthy, or at least not in proportion to the evil. In any case, the classification of evil in terms of natural evil and moral evil needs sharpening, independently of the issues posed by social evil.

into strategies for addressing evidential arguments from evil. This is just not possible in anything short of a monumental tome. My effort should instead be seen as an attempt to render my conclusion plausible and offer helpful guidance for future systematic investigation.

SIPHONING: EGOISM

It is no secret to anyone that Christianity, in virtually all its forms and throughout its entire history, has been unremittingly hostile to egoistic moral views. One of the Gospels' most famous exhortations is to "love your neighbor as yourself."[10] The rest of scripture is filled with admonitions to love others and to make sacrifices for their good, and Christian tradition has followed suit univocally.[11] While certainly not news, it is important to keep this in mind in the context of addressing social evil, since many classic examples of game-theoretic conundrums involve purely rational agents, where "rational" action is stipulated to involve only self-interested motivation.[12] The original prisoner's dilemma is a case in point. The parties involved are concerned only with their own individual welfare, and this concern with their own individual welfare causes each of them to betray their co-conspirator, resulting in a worse outcome for both players than if they had cooperated with one another.[13]

This analysis can also plausibly be extended to many real life cases of prima facie social evil. Consider many instances of pollution, for instance, where an individual's particular polluting actions are unnoticeable in the grand scheme of things, but all of the individuals together collectively make the problem far worse. Often, the agents involved are motivated by nothing more than trivial gains in personal convenience or tiny financial benefits, with little by way of noble motives anywhere in the vicinity.

---

[10] Matthew 19:19 and 22:39, Mark 12:31, and Luke 10:27, with precursor in Leviticus 19:18. Exhortations to love others are also common in John—see for instance 13:34. (See also Romans 13:9.) Some of these particular passages do make references to oneself, but of course they only make reference to oneself as a way of instructing the reader not to act in a merely self-interested way.

[11] Both the Islamic and Jewish traditions also have strong prohibitions against egoistic moral reasoning.

[12] Poston is of course careful to avoid these by stipulating in his examples that the agents involved are rational *moral* individuals. But since these kinds of self-interested cases are so common in the literature, it is worth addressing them.

[13] This is made clear by Poston's Jonathan Edwards-inspired suggestion in section 4.2 of Poston (2014).

The devastating recent financial crisis is another case in point. While replete with potential sources of social evil, many of those scenarios manifestly involved actors who were at least largely selfishly motivated, and whose motivations were clearly wrong according to Christian moral principles—they involved disregard for the welfare of others, and thus were not demonstrations of love. Take, for example, the market analysts and decision-makers who appear to have seen disaster on the horizon but adjusted their forecasts in an optimistic direction to bring them into line with conventional wisdom, thus seeking crowd protection (often successfully) and insulating themselves and their jobs from the wrath of their superiors, investors, and boards. Often this strategy allowed them—particularly high-level decision-makers—to reap hefty financial rewards for longer than they would have by telling the truth.[14]

All of these kinds of examples (with perhaps a scant few exceptions) violate the above definition of pure social evil, because all of them involve actors who are not morally blameless, at least if a Christian moral theory is correct. Their selfishness is a clear violation of basic tenets of Christian morality. One might object, however, that although their behavior is clearly *wrong* by Christian lights, it is not necessarily morally blameworthy by those same lights. These individuals may not know that Christianity is true or even believe in it, after all, and their intuitions may tend in an egoistic direction. Even if these individuals are Christians, they might be blamelessly ignorant of what their religion teaches about such ethical matters. Consequently, their actions may be examples of blameless wrongdoing, which would leave the scenarios they are involved in as serious candidates for pure social evil status.

This is an important objection that we will have occasion to consider in other contexts as we go along. In fact, it is important enough that I will give it a name—henceforth, I will refer to it as the "Blameless Wrongdoing Objection." It is not particularly plausible in the egoism case, though. It is hard to believe that a significant number of the individuals involved in the candidate scenarios under discussion really believe that their selfish actions are morally permissible, or at the very least have come to their warped moral views without previous blameworthy actions (either their own or someone else's) that have put them in an unfavorable epistemic position.

---

[14] See the discussion in Cassidy (2009), 177–9. In a famous example, Angelo Mozilo, the CEO of Countrywide, was not dishonest about future prospects (at least privately), but he did make decisions which were clearly designed to serve his own interests, not those of his shareholders or the broader economy (Cassidy (2009), 246–7).

SIPHONING: PARTICULARISM

While many apparent pure social evils can be disqualified due to the inappropriately selfish motives of the individuals involved, not all cases are so easy to handle. This is because, in many real-world instances, the decision-makers do not seem to be motivated by their self-interest, but rather the interest of some particular group that may not even include them. In some cases, the tendency to promote the welfare of the group is ultimately explicable by self-interest—the manager who looks out for her company's interest so she can get a promotion and buy a fancy new car, for instance, or the man who helps his next door neighbor in anticipation that his aid will be reciprocated. But many real world examples seem to resist such facile assimilation to self-interested explanation. What is to be said about them?

While not as vocal in its condemnation of this kind of preferential treatment as in its condemnation of egoistic moral reasoning, the Christian tradition has also tended to strongly oppose giving special moral treatment to particular groups, especially when one is a member of the group or the group enjoys privileged status in some important way.[15]

Scripturally, perhaps the clearest expression of the theme is in the tendency to use familial and neighbor metaphors to describe all of humanity.[16] In addition to specific sayings and the occasional use of metaphors, there is widespread scholarly agreement that a prominent theme in the Gospels, particularly in Luke, is Jesus' desire that his disciples transcend destructive and oppressive social arrangements that rely on the special treatment given to members of exclusive groups. For instance, this desire is thought to underlie much of the Lucan Jesus' opposition to the agendas of the Pharisees.[17] Consider also Jesus' exhortations to love one's enemies—the ultimate outsiders.

As I mentioned above, the Christian tradition has recognized more instances where special treatment to groups is warranted than where special treatment to self is warranted. Christians typically believe that special obligations accrue to family members in virtue of being family members and in virtue of their role in the family, for instance, perhaps the most prominent

---

[15] There are certainly more caveats and qualifications in the particularism case than in the egoism case, however.

[16] Relevant material includes the story of the Good Samaritan (Luke 10:29–37), the warnings against attachment to family (e.g., Luke 14:26), and Jesus' reactions to his own family (Mark 3:31–5, and softer versions in Luke 8:19–21 and 11:27–8).

[17] See, for instance, the discussion of Jesus' table fellowship with outcasts in Joel B. Green, *The Gospel of Luke*, New International Commentary on the New Testament, Grand Rapids, MI: Eerdmans, 1997, 244–50.

being the duty on the part of children to honor father and mother and the corresponding duty of father and mother to care for children and give them spiritual instruction.[18] In the same vein, Christians commonly hold that we need not show total altruistic indifference to friends and family members as compared with complete strangers, though there are certainly strong limits on how much special favor is tolerable.[19]

It is clear, however, that in many real world cases of prima facie pure social evil where the parties avoid selfish motivation, they do not avoid motivations that are objectionable on the above grounds. The particularity of the interests they take into account transcends the strong limits of appropriate favoritism (or appears in contexts where any particularity is inappropriate), and consequently the cases fail to qualify as pure social evils in spite of initial appearances.[20]

There remains the familiar issue of the Blameless Wrongdoing Objection to deal with, however. And this objection is more plausible in many scenarios where particularistic rather than egoistic motivations are in play, precisely because favoritism for things like family, ethnicity, or nation is more widely believed to be morally appropriate in general than favoritism for self (and arguably more often innocently believed to be such). Hence, it would be much easier for a non-Christian or an uninformed Christian to fall into this sort of epistemological trap without being to blame for it. (Though there would of course be limits—presumably many cases of particularistic motivation would involve giving in to temptation in a blameworthy way, rather than being blameless expressions of the agent's genuine moral convictions.) Let us bracket this worry for the moment, though, and consider what is perhaps the starkest challenge to the claim that pure social evils are much rarer than we might initially think: impartial altruistic cases.

---

[18] See, for example, Ephesians 6:1–4, citing Exodus 20:12 and Deuteronomy 5:16. A recent example of a philosopher affirming that parents have special obligations to children can be found in Alexander Pruss, *One Body*, Notre Dame, IN: University of Notre Dame Press, 2013, especially 184–5 and 381–92.

[19] It may well be that the tradition—even most particular segments of the tradition—does not have precise views about exactly how much special favor is tolerable. But the key is that, while there may be uncertainty or quibbling over the details, there is widespread agreement about many kinds of special treatment going too far. This is all I will rely on.

[20] Included are cases where individuals' behavior mimics that of self-interested parties, but where the motive behind the behavior is protection of family, friends, or some other favored group. Parents who work at jobs that contribute to "social evil" but who do so not out of self-interest but out of a desire to give greater opportunities to their children can easily be examples of this phenomenon.

SIPHONING: CONSEQUENTIALISM

As Derek Parfit pointed out in his ground-breaking book *Reasons and Persons*, multi-person prisoner's dilemmas and other sources of what we are calling "social evil" are not restricted to cases where the parties involved are self-interested or acting on particularized motives—social evil can afflict even purely altruistic actors who favor no particular group or individual.[21] Poston's fictional drought example, discussed in the introduction, is such a case: each of the parties has the general welfare of the world in mind (and is well-informed about the consequences of different courses of action), yet each makes decisions that collectively lead to a much worse outcome than some other set of decisions would have led to.

While such cases may not be exceedingly common in the real world, they certainly do not appear on a first take to be an extreme rarity either. One important thing to notice about all paradigmatic mechanisms that lead to social evil is that they require the actors involved to think in a consequentialist fashion—these individuals must make decisions based on the perceived goodness of *outcomes*, allowing expected consequences to trump other factors.[22] Interestingly, though, there are prohibitions in Christianity against consequentialist motivation in many contexts, even when that consequentialist motivation is purely altruistic and based on the maximization of human well-being or the general good of the world. Part of the reason for this is that Christianity is a religion whose ethical framework is at least largely grounded in love for God and our fellow human beings. But loving our fellow human beings is often incompatible with doing things that make sense when one adopts a consequentialist worldview. Alexander Pruss offers such a case: imagine a misguided billionaire offers to make me a deal. If I approach a destitute stranger, spit in his face, and then spend two minutes verbally abusing him and denying his worth (trying hard to genuinely mean what I say), the billionaire will give the stranger one million dollars. Even suppose that after the episode is over, I will get to explain to

---

[21] Derek Parfit, *Reasons and Persons*, Oxford: Oxford University Press, 1984, 66. Parfit addresses the issue primarily for *pure* altruists—people who treat their own well-being as morally irrelevant and count the well-being of everyone else as of equal importance *ceteris paribus*. But the same issues can arise for people who are merely impartial altruists—i.e. those who count everyone's well-being as of equal importance *ceteris paribus*, including their own.

[22] I am grateful to an anonymous reviewer for pointing out that this problem can arise for anyone who allows consequences or expected consequences to trump other factors, whether or not the individual is a pure consequentialist. For ease of exposition, I will focus on pure consequentialist motivation in the subsequent discussion, but the lesson can be extended beyond such cases.

the stranger what is going on. One can easily imagine that the stranger might be psychologically constituted in such a way that my taking the billionaire up on this deal would give the best outcome overall for him—suffering the verbal abuse and getting the million dollars might easily be better for him, in some normal consequentialist sense, than getting nothing at all. It might even be better overall for the world. Yet, by Christian lights, it would clearly be wrong for me to do this, because verbally abusing the stranger and denying his worth would be inconsistent with loving him as I ought.[23] While this example may be fanciful, the core principle is likely to apply in many real life cases.

It is also worth keeping in mind the long and venerable tradition of non-consequentialist ethical reasoning embodied in the Doctrine of Double Effect, a favored casuistic tool in many branches of Christianity.[24] Even those Christians who do not subscribe to the Doctrine of Double Effect are typically unsympathetic to the idea that we should ignore scriptural injunctions against consequentialism, and for our purposes the rejection of consequentialism is the key aspect of the doctrine.[25]

It is also important to note the lessons that come from the celebration of martyrdom—especially early martyrdom—that one finds in Christianity. As is widely known, many early martyrs died because they would not offer sacrifices to the Roman imperial cult or perform other seemingly trivial acts of betrayal, in spite of the fact that they were often given generous opportunities to do so by authorities. Their refusal undoubtedly had powerful consequences in many cases (raising awareness of Christianity and of the level of commitment of its adherents, for instance), but their reasoning did not typically appear to be consequentialist in nature.[26] These martyrs were and continue to be celebrated, moreover, and the reasons for this have had little or nothing to do with any consequences their actions had or were expected to have (at least not consequences of a problematic sort).[27]

In Christian circles, the actions of martyrs have often been taken to justify strong deontic truth-telling requirements, and Christianity in various forms has been sympathetic to a wide variety of other purely deontic principles.

---

[23] Pruss (2013), 27.

[24] In typical formulations, an action is impermissible, regardless of its consequences, if it is intrinsically bad.

[25] See especially Romans 3:8's implication that we should not do evil "that good may come of it."

[26] Many of these consequences were highly negative, of course, and it was probably the negative consequences of suffering and death that were usually most salient in the moment.

[27] As illustration, consider the passage on martyrs from Latin Father Minucius Felix, *The Octavius*, 37.

While there is undoubtedly uncertainty and disagreement over specifics, within mainstream Christianity there is little controversy surrounding the claim that there are many purely deontic principles that should govern human moral decision-making.

What is crucial for our purposes, of course, is the issue of how many candidates for pure social evil status involve violations of these deontic requirements, in one form or another. (This is because, if deontic requirements are violated, then we have wrongs being done. And if wrongs are being done, individuals are likely to blame for those wrongs, thus ruling out the case from status as a pure social evil.) Obviously, it is difficult to offer a definitive analysis without being clear about exactly what the deontic requirements are and exactly what candidate scenarios exist. As I mentioned above, this would be too much for any single paper to address. Still, we can make significant progress by examining particular cases that appear to be representative and assessing whether there is a deontic principle in the vicinity that Christians will plausibly accept as part of the religion's overall ethical view.

Take, for instance, Poston's sanitized hypothetical case of water conservation. Although not explicitly stated, his description implies that there is an understanding among all the residents that the best way to prevent very bad consequences is to come together and conserve water,[28] and a shared commitment to prevent very bad consequences if possible. Hence, there appears to be some tacit set of mutual promises or at least a tacit agreement among the residents not to violate reasonable water use restrictions (perhaps an application of their obligation to obey legal authorities under normal circumstances). (We can suppose that the L.A. area authorities are trusted—this is a fictional case, after all!—and that they have publicized both the need for water restrictions and the nature of those restrictions.)[29] Thus, residents who decide to defect based on consequentialist reasoning—even if it is altruistic consequentialist reasoning—appear to violate commonly held

[28] If not, we may just be looking at a case of widespread ignorance—ignorance of the ways to handle a water shortage. This ignorance is likely to be either a moral evil or a natural evil, depending on the explanation of why it is present. (In itself, this doesn't guarantee that the present scenario will be disqualified from pure social evil status, but it will have a significant effect on its evidential weight if not.)

[29] If the authorities are not trusted—as may often be the case in real life analogs of this situation—we must ask why. If they are not trusted because they have a track record of lying to the public, for instance, then we may have a case of a moral evil, or at least a social evil of little evidential significance (because it is the product of a moral evil). If they are not trusted because of the laziness of residents, the take-home message is probably similar. If they are not trusted because people do not have the energy to pay careful attention to all of the information they are getting but are blameless in this, we may be looking at a natural evil or a social evil produced by a natural evil. More on these various possibilities later.

Christian tenets about either the importance of promise-keeping or the importance of obedience to legitimate authorities.

Particularly insidious, at least potentially, are cases where an agent is faced with a decision to act on an egoistic or particularistic motive that is inappropriate because of its egoism or particularism, but where the motive can easily be transformed into an altruistic one on a modicum of reflection. How can this occur? It often happens in situations where the individual has very limited options, but can achieve a Pareto improvement by defecting, benefiting himself or his favored group significantly while making no one else worse off. (A Pareto improvement is precisely a situation where one group or individual can be made better off without making anyone else worse off.) Consider Frank the Fisherman. Frank is a man of modest means and supports his children through the revenues from his fishing. Legitimate authorities acting legitimately to curb overfishing have placed restrictions on the size of a catch, but they do not have the resources to adequately police the restrictions (and so any threat of punishment can be safely ignored). Initially, Frank is tempted to defect, take more fish, and benefit his family. But he feels it would be wrong to show this kind of favoritism to his family, since after all they aren't starving or in any desperate need. (Imagine that others like him think the same way—let us suppose that there are many.) But then it dawns on him! If he takes a few more fish, this will do absolutely nothing to the catch of any other fisherman in the entire world.[30] Hence, by taking a few more fish, Frank is not merely improving the welfare of his family—he is improving the welfare of the entire world (the entire human world at least)! In this case, his distaste for particularism will not impede him, and—assuming the others reason similarly—the social evil will be well on its way to being done.

But again, Christianity has something to say about this case. Even though Frank's action produces a Pareto improvement and is justifiable on altruistic consequentialist grounds, it is still impermissible by the Christian's lights. Because Frank failed to obey a legitimate authority's regulations (or perhaps because he failed to abide by an agreement that he made), he has done

---

[30] Let us suppose that this assumption is true. If it is not—if Frank is actually affecting the probability that others will catch fish (either now or in the future)—things will get trickier. We (and Frank himself, if he is being careful) will have to assess the expected effects of his decision. If they are sufficiently small, then his decision will be exactly the same de facto as if his action had no effect. If the effects are large, then we are probably not looking at a social evil candidate anymore. Rather, this will just be a straightforward moral decision that can be analyzed as a potential instance of moral evil if a wrong decision is made, assuming that Frank is to blame for the wrong act. (If not, it is probably going to be a case of blameless ignorance, which is standardly classified as a natural evil.)

wrong.[31] As a result, his case will fail to satisfy the requirements for pure social evil, at least so long as the Blameless Wrongdoing Objection can be overcome. Before finally addressing this objection and other issues, we will consider a handful of miscellaneous siphoning strategies. Thus far, our siphoning strategies have concentrated on cases where agents fail to satisfy the requirements for blamelessness that pure social evil requires. Subsequent ones will focus on the failure of some of the problem-causing game-theoretic idealizations to apply to most real world cases.

SIPHONING: OTHER STRATEGIES

In addition to the strategies we have already seen for explaining away candidates for pure social evil status, there are several others. Three of them are especially important. The first involves noting that a major source of social evil in the abstract is the "simultaneous move game"—a variety of game-theoretic interaction where all of the players act in isolation from information about other players' decisions. Poston's drought example is like this—all of the players make a decision to either cooperate or defect without any specific information about how the other players are choosing. But such situations in the real world are rare. Typically, one is both receiving information about the choices of players who have already moved and broadcasting information about one's own choice for players who have not yet moved. This allows for more effective cooperation among players, particularly when this feature of the interaction is combined with the two other features discussed below.[32]

One other such feature—the source of the second important miscellaneous siphoning strategy—is iteration. Comparatively few real life social interactions involve only one "round" in the way that the classical prisoner's dilemma does (although such interactions may be getting increasingly common in a world where anonymous social encounters in big cities and online

---

[31] Although I will not pursue the suggestion here, it may be that Christianity's insistence on deontological principles even provides a bit of evidence in favor of Christianity, assuming that early proponents of the religion could not have foreseen the usefulness of deontological commitments in forestalling social evils.

[32] It will allow for more effective cooperation for two reasons. First, because there will be additional information that will allow individuals to coordinate their actions. And second, the additional information will alert individuals of the impending dangers and allow those individuals to take steps to confront the behavior that is giving rise to the problem. I am grateful to an anonymous reviewer for pointing out the need for this clarification.

are on the rise). But it is well-known that, when prisoner's dilemma-like scenarios repeat, it will often be possible for the players to cooperate and avoid social evil, because they are able to monitor one another's behavior and issue threats and punishments for defection. Of course, if the players know that the series of interactions is coming to an end, they will revert to the behavior that would be appropriate if there were only a single round. But often, under real-world circumstances, agents do not see this end point coming.

The third relevant feature is the tendency of real-world defection decisions to probabilize the bad effect. In Poston's drought example and other classic candidates for social evil status, defection is especially seductive because the cases are set up in such a way that, by defecting, one does not increase the likelihood at all that the bad effect will occur nor does one tangibly worsen the situation, even in a small way. In the drought scenario, for instance, any individual's choice is stipulated to have no effect on whether the negative outcome is realized (and presumably no effect on the probability that it or the alternative will be realized).[33] But in the real world, things are not generally this tidy, particularly when there are multiple iterations of the interaction and one is broadcasting information via one's choices. But even when there is only one round, often real life is not so simple. My story of Frank the Fisherman above may make this clear. Although I stipulated away this complication originally, a more realistic version of the story would have to acknowledge that if Frank takes more fish, there are likely to be consequences down the road, even assuming Frank and his colleagues are about to sail into the sunset of fishing retirement. These fish will no longer be around to reproduce and increase the fish population, which will probably have small but tangible effects in future fishing efforts.[34] (There may be a small but non-zero chance that it will have large effects.) In some cases, these complications may be enough to affect payoff structures and force moral actors into cooperation with one another, even setting aside worries about the appropriateness of consequentialist reasoning. (Hence, in these instances when

---

[33] I assume here that whenever one has an effect on the probability of an overall outcome (at least in this context), one counts as having an effect on the realization of the outcome (if the outcome in fact occurs).

[34] Because many classical game-theoretic puzzles presume that the parties are motivated by pure self-interest, they often do not have reason to consider such complications in their payoff structures. Even assuming he doesn't retire, Frank's chance of affecting his *own* future catch by taking more fish really is zero, for all intents and purposes. Given that there are billions of fish in the sea, what is the chance that he personally is going to run into this one again or one of its offspring? Interestingly, the U.S. Supreme Court backed legislative attempts to solve coordination problems of this sort in Wickard v. Filburn. (Thanks to Dan Tyman for alerting me to this example.)

cooperation fails to result, we know that we are not looking at pure social evil, at least not unless the parties involved are blameless wrongdoers.)

We have now examined numerous reasons why prima facie candidates for status as pure social evils fail to qualify as genuine pure social evils on a Christian framework. Many of these candidates involve motivation that is blameworthy by Christian lights, while others involve factors (such as iteration and information sharing) that make them disanalogous from the kinds of classic game-theoretic scenarios that those worried about the evidential weight of social evil take as paradigms.

Now that we have examined all the various siphoning strategies, there are likely to be a number of objections. I will examine what I consider to be the most pressing of these in the next section.

OBJECTIONS

(A) Your argument treats acting in self-interest (i.e, acting in an egoistic way) as though it were inherently wrong. But acting in self-interest under some circumstances is morally permissible—indeed, even morally obligatory. But then we wind up with a far greater number of serious social evil candidates than you are letting on.

Reply—I acknowledge that sometimes egoistic decisions—most obviously egoistic decisions made in financial contexts—are neither blameworthy nor wrong. This is because sometimes in these situations the pursuit of self-interest is morally justified and appropriate. (Or, at the very least, sometimes the pursuit of personal economic gain in financial and other markets is appropriate, and such action will often mimic the pursuit of self-interest.) In my view, some cases of this sort do survive scrutiny and do appear to be legitimate social evil candidates. I will address these at greater length later in the evidential section below.

(B) The deontic requirements that Christianity embraces are understood to be defeasible. If I am a doctor and I promise to have lunch with you, for instance, but on the way run into a man having a heart attack, I do not do wrong by stopping to help the man, even if this causes me to miss lunch. Now, one might think that defeasible requirements of the nature we are discussing can be defeated in a case where I produce a Pareto improvement by defecting (i.e. I create a situation where someone is made better off without anyone being made worse off). And, as per Poston's stipulations, by using extra water in his drought case I produce just such a Pareto improvement. Thus, the mere existence of deontic requirements within Christianity does not rule out many social evil candidates.

Reply—The trouble is that the defeasibility standards in these cases are generally taken to be at least fairly high. Turning on a hose to fight a fire that is about to consume my house is one thing; turning it on to water my fruit trees (Poston's example) or a community garden is another. Not just any old Pareto improvement is enough. One might object that this is unprincipled—why would a true moral code not allow an agent to produce the best outcome available to them in a situation like this? Note, though, that there is great wisdom in a moral code designed with prohibitions against bringing about certain kinds of Pareto improvements. This prevents morally upright agents from causing the kinds of widespread social evils that would arise easily if these restrictions were not in place.[35]

(C) Some of your examples rely on Christianity's alleged deontic requirement to obey legitimate authorities, under at least some circumstances. Many branches of Christianity do allow for individuals to disobey authorities when their conscience conflicts with the dictates of those authorities, however.

Allowances for conscientious objection to authorities are notoriously tricky within Christianity, and unfortunately it would take me too far afield to treat them in depth here. In any case, they are unlikely to apply to paradigmatic social evil candidates. The sorts of conscientious objection countenanced by Christianity always involve one of three things: (1) the individual has a conviction that the authorities have false or unjustified beliefs about morally relevant empirical phenomena, (2) the individual has a conviction that the authorities have false or unjustified beliefs about fundamental goods, or (3) the individual disagrees with authorities over the existence of a deontic moral principle. None of these rationales applies in the paradigmatic situations I discuss.

WHAT'S LEFT?

Now that we have completed our survey of siphoning strategies and examined a number of pressing objections, there appear to be several kinds of pure social evil candidates that survive. In this section, we will take stock of what remains, and in the process I will argue that pure social evils due to blameless wrongdoing are not evidentially important and can be safely discounted.

---

[35] I am grateful to an anonymous reviewer for spurring me to expand my discussion of this objection.

Let us first consider scenarios where the Blameless Wrongdoing Objection is plausible—cases where the bad outcome is produced by a collection of free decisions that are wrong (according to Christianity), the bad outcome would not be produced (at least not in full) by any small proportion of the free decisions, but where the agents involved all manage to avoid blameworthiness for their wrong choices. While there are likely to be some cases of egoistic motivation that fit into this category, most will be cases of particularistic or altruistic motivation. (Among moral attitudes that conflict with Christianity, these tend to be the ones that non-Christians or poorly informed Christians are most likely to adopt. Many instances of particularistic or altruistic motivation will not be blameless, though, even if particularistic and altruistic cases are more common among blameless wrongdoing cases. There will be plenty of instances, in other words, where the agents involved are clearly giving in to some temptation, not acting on genuine moral convictions.)[36]

While cases that qualify as pure social evils due to blameless wrongdoing do exist, they are not evidentially important. To understand why, we must classify them further. Blameless wrongdoing cases will be situations where either (A) the parties are blameless in the present decision at least partly because they or someone else is to blame for putting them in a deficient epistemic position,[37] (B) the parties are blameless in the present decision because of natural obstacles that put them in a deficient epistemic position, but whose effects are in no way due to the blameworthy choices of agents,[38] or (C) the parties are blameless in the present decision because of previous pure social evils.

Some cases falling under (A) may not even count as satisfying the definition of pure social evil, because my definition (following Poston's more informal characterization) does not specify whether the blamelessness can be restricted to the present choice considered in complete isolation, or whether it requires blamelessness in relevant choices leading up to the present one. In general, even if they exist, cases falling under (A) are evidentially untroubling to theism, or at least add little or no new troubling evidence. This is because they are examples of moral evils, and moral evils (even horrendous ones) are unfortunately already all too common and familiar.[39]

---

[36] If nothing else, the material above should convince readers that social evils among informed Christians are quite a bit rarer than one might think.

[37] Included are cases where agents deceive themselves about probabilities or payoffs in the scenario.

[38] There are subtleties about the definition of "moral evil" and "natural evil" that are important in the grand scheme of things, but can be ignored for our purposes.

[39] We can understand a moral evil roughly as a bad outcome of a blameworthy decision, and hence the consequences of these social evil situations are also moral evils

Similar things can be said about cases falling under (B)—the seriousness of natural evil, including natural evil that results in the moral ignorance of agents, is already recognized.[40] Such moral ignorance already produces devastating effects in a large number of familiar cases where no problematic game-theoretic interactions occur, so it seems doubtful that piling on some additional negative effects of naturally produced moral ignorance will make much difference.

Cases falling under (C) appear to be non-existent, at least where the social evil traces all the way back to an ultimate source in social evil (i.e. when we continue to trace our way back through the causes of this particular scenario, we never wind up with an explanation that ultimately rests on something other than moral evil, natural evil, or some combination thereof). How plausible is it that the blameless ignorance of the agents involved would be due only to social evil? We have seen strong reasons to believe that pure social evils are rare to begin with—even when we require only synchronic blamelessness—so what are the chances that we are going to find complicated diachronic social evils going all the way back in the explanatory sequence?

While this is possible, it is sufficiently obscure that the burden of proof clearly lies with the atheologian to produce real-life cases where it operates. To put the matter another way, the challenge for the atheologian is to describe a possible world where the only evils are pure social evils, and to provide some reason to think that the actual world shares some of the relevant features with this world.[41]

Aside from instances of blameless wrongdoing, what other kinds of scenarios slip through the cracks? There are cases where egoistic, particularistic, or altruistic consequentialist motivation are morally appropriate, and can lead to suboptimal outcomes. Arguably, there are economic scenarios of this sort. Take, for instance, situations where the "Paradox of Thrift" arises. In these cases, the sensible frugality and caution of all the individual actors in an economy leads to very negative consequences for the economy as a

because they are indirect consequences of blameworthy past decisions. If one prefers to restrict moral evils to *immediate* consequences of blameworthy decisions, then these social evils can be described as effects of moral evils rather than moral evils themselves. The substantive point is the same. (The introduction of impure social evil may require a complication of the basic definition of moral evil, but my arguments below are designed to show otherwise. In any case, there are other reasons to make the classification of evils more subtle than typical discussions of the problem of evil do, but as I mentioned previously these are not relevant for present purposes.)

[40] Some of these problems are likely related to the problem of divine hiddenness, another evidential issue that is already prominent in the theism debate.

[41] I am grateful to Jonathan Kvanvig for suggesting a formulation along these lines.

whole.[42] No one would challenge the wisdom or moral appropriateness of individual frugality in situations of economic stress (especially not Christianity, which has always valued responsible stewardship of resources), but it can collectively lead to serious suffering. An altruistic example that may slip through the cracks—though not necessarily one with many close analogues in real life—is Poston's saintly orphanage case, which he presents as his purest social evil example.[43]

Before continuing on to discuss evidential implications of the cases that remain, it is time to return to the issue of impure social evils. Recall that impure social evils are social evils where not all the parties involved are blameless, but where the bad consequences are "disproportionate to the individual choices in the game," in Poston's words.[44] While game-theoretic interactions (or at least scenarios closely analogous to the interactions game theorists discuss in the abstract) are a very real part of human life, it is exceedingly difficult to understand what it would be for bad consequences to be "disproportionate" to individual choices in them. Surely we cannot readily compare a decision made in a game-theoretic scenario with "the same" one made outside a game-theoretic scenario, since after all it is typically of the very essence of the decision that it was made in a game-theoretic scenario. (The dilemma I face in the drought situation, for instance, is not at all same kind of choice that I would face in a similar scenario where I was the only potential consumer of water in the area. The only way the decision in the scenario could be qualitatively the same as one outside it is if I mistakenly believe that the scenario I am involved in does not include any other individuals whose actions could affect outcomes.) It could be that Poston has in mind that each decision has a level of praiseworthiness and blameworthiness associated with it, and that we can compare different levels of praiseworthiness and blameworthiness in different kinds of decisions— specifically, in our case, the praiseworthiness/blameworthiness of decisions in game-theoretic scenarios with ones outside game-theoretic scenarios. But this won't do either. Regardless of the finer points of one's theory of praiseworthiness or blameworthiness, it seems clear that there is no normal

---

[42] A famous real life mini-example of this paradox occurred in the "Capitol Hill Babysitting Co-Op" in the 1970s. See the description in Paul Krugman, *Peddling Prosperity*, New York: W.W. Norton, 1994.

[43] Poston (2014), 184. In this case, an individual running an orphanage is faced with the decision to make extra phone calls to solicit donations to buy a Christmas gift for an unfortunate child, but where individuals running other orphanages are dealing with similar issues. Even here, there are reasons to be suspicious, on some of the same grounds discussed above.

[44] Poston (2014), 180.

general consequence for any given blameworthiness level which we can use to calibrate what is "proportionate." This is because the same level of praiseworthiness or blameworthiness in different contexts often produces dramatically different consequences, and no context can be identified as *the* standard one. (A small child making a decision with a specific level of blameworthiness and the President of the United States making a decision with the same level of blameworthiness will likely have very different outcomes, even when no game-theoretic machinery is involved.)[45]

I am inclined, then, to conclude that there is nothing mysterious or idiosyncratically problematic about the way that game-theoretic machinery causes bad consequences in the context of blameworthy decisions. These simply are the consequences of the kinds of blameworthy decisions that occur in those scenarios. We must learn to identify them as such in the same way that we learn to identify the different kinds of consequences that occur with blameworthy moral decisions in the diversity of non-game-theoretic contexts we are familiar with from history, politics, and daily life. For those unsatisfied with this response by itself, I should also point out that impure social evils are clearly more corrupted by moral evil than are pure social evils, since moral evil is directly associated with the decisions in the scenarios themselves.

For all of these reasons, I am not inclined to see impure social evils as evidentially threatening, especially if it turns out that pure social evils are not (as I will argue in the next section). After all, the main threat associated with pure social evils is that they introduce a novel kind of evil, supposedly unaddressed by standard theodicy strategies. But there is nothing novel about the kind of evil associated with impure social evil, once we have taken account of pure social evil along with moral and natural evil.[46]

---

[45] Perhaps there is some way of averaging the outcomes of all the decisions with this level of blameworthiness in every possible world, but such a process is likely to be enormously difficult. Moreover the result of the analysis is far from clear, so it will be hard to say which decisions will turn out to have disproportionate effects. There are also cases of natural bad luck, where unforeseen natural circumstances magnify a bad effect of a decision, but the magnification in these cases is much easier to quantify.

[46] Quantity clearly does play some role, and I admit that I cannot fully address messy issues surrounding how the overall quantity of relevant evil in the world is affected by impure social evil. It may also often be more difficult to foresee the consequences of one's choices in game-theoretic cases, but of course it is also often difficult to foresee these consequences in non-game-theoretic scenarios as well. As I mentioned above, this paper should not be seen as an attempt to offer a once and for all demonstration of the evidential insignificance of social evil.

EVIDENTIAL IMPLICATIONS

Now that the siphoning process is complete, we have seen that there are a small handful of candidates that do appear to qualify for bona fide pure social evil status. These include some cases of blameless wrongdoing and some cases where morally appropriate consequentialist reasoning is employed (whether of an egoistic, particularistic, or altruistic sort). The crucial issue now is of course their evidential importance for atheism. In this section, I will argue that the remaining social evils do not constitute significant evidence against theism, because they are rare and ultimately trace back to some combination of moral and natural evil.

The evidential weight of the blameless wrongdoing cases was addressed above. Pure social evils of this sort that are ultimately caused only by other pure social evils don't appear to exist. Other kinds of pure social evils based on blameless wrongdoing appear to be much rarer than we might have initially supposed. Consequently, it is hard to see how they could be of significant evidential weight. Ones that are ultimately explicable in terms of moral evil don't appear to add a great deal to the quantity of moral evil in the world (since moral evils, including severe ones, are unfortunately very common and these kinds of social evils are not). Nor does the quality of the new evil appear very significant. After all, moral evils are already known to produce devastating consequences in all sorts of different ways. If we were to discover that there is a previously unnoticed way that moral evils cause devastating consequences—namely, by creating conditions that give rise to pure social evils—we would not learn something of much evidential significance, because there is no reason to think that God would be more likely to act to prevent indirect bad consequences of moral evils than direct ones. The same basic point goes for such social evils that have their ultimate cause in natural processes—again, natural processes are already known to produce devastating consequences, including natural processes leading to ignorance and cognitive failure. Piling on a few new cases of a subtly different kind does not appear to be of great evidential significance.

What about cases where legitimate consequentialist reasoning is used? These are trickier to deal with, but similar considerations point us toward the same conclusion for them. To understand these cases, we must understand what gave rise to the scenarios *themselves*, as opposed to any moral ignorance that is present in them. (These scenarios do not contain moral ignorance *ex hypothesi*—the individuals in them are not mere blameless wrongdoers, but individuals who positively do right.) Again, there are three basic options (ignoring subtle complications): (1) they are ultimately produced by blameworthy moral choices (even though the scenarios themselves involve no blameworthy choices), (2) they are ultimately produced by natural processes, or (3) they are ultimately produced by further social evil unrelated to either blameworthy moral choices or natural processes.

As with the blameless wrongdoing classification above (but with even more plausibility here), I conjecture that cases of (3) do not exist. While I can offer no demonstration of this thesis, the material I have presented thus far in the paper should have convinced the reader that pure social evils are quite a bit harder to produce than one might initially think, whereas moral evils and natural evils are ubiquitous and occur easily. Thus, it would be surprising if the world contained pure social evils that are social evils to their core, depending not at all on previous blameworthy moral decisions, natural scarcity of resources, or other phenomena already familiar from mainstream discussion of the problem of evil (or natural failure to discern effective solutions to coordination problems).[47] It is hard to fathom what such evils would even look like. Consequently, they can be safely ignored until someone comes forward with plausible examples of them.

Cases of (1) likely comprise a substantial portion of pure social evils that involve no blameless wrongdoing in the social evil scenario itself. But again, these kinds of cases are not of great evidential significance. The world already contains substantial amounts of moral evil, and such a small number of genuine cases of pure social evil remain after siphoning that we are likely looking at little more than a drop in the bucket. And although social evils are different in quality from moral or natural evils, their quality difference does not appear to be of great enough significance to justify a drastic solution on God's part. After all, removing from the world the social evils ultimately caused by blameworthy free choice would require God either to eliminate all free choice (or at least the tangible consequences of free choice) or to selectively eliminate free choices that lead to pure social evils. But, given that pure social evils appear to be rare, it is inelegant for a God who so values free choice that he allows it even in (non-game-theoretic) scenarios where it leads to tremendous destruction to eliminate it as soon as an occasional negative game-theoretic interaction threatens. It is hard to fathom what sort of principle such a God could be operating under.

Similar points go for cases under (2). Many pure social evils will fit in this category, produced by the combined natural processes of scarcity of some valuable resource plus naturally produced cognitive limitations. (The natural cognitive failure could manifest itself in failure to see workable solutions for

---

[47] Arguably, all financial examples of social evil ultimately have resource scarcity as at least part of their explanation.

coordination problems.) But again, severe natural evil is already well known and its evidential implications well explored. It may be that the effects of natural evil are magnified because some natural evils give rise to social evils, but given the wide range of catastrophic consequences of many regular natural evils that are unassociated with game-theoretic scenarios, it is unlikely that the evidential significance of natural evil will be greatly enhanced by the fact that some natural processes cause social evils. The plausibility of commonly produced justifications for natural evil (soul-making, the benefits of stable laws of nature for moral learning or aesthetic beauty, etc.) are not likely to be affected by a few additional cases of suffering thrown on top of the already familiar ones, even if those cases are of a novel sort.[48]

Nearing the end of our journey, the reader might raise one final practical objection. If God's ultimate justification for allowing social evils is just that he *really* likes the kinds of things theodicists always talk about (significant free will, soul-making, natural law stability, etc.), why not write a very short paper saying that?! Why spend so much time "siphoning off" social evil candidate scenarios? My response is that God may really like the kinds of things theodicists talk about without *really really* liking them. At some point, the quality and quantity of suffering may reach a threshold that any God worthy of the name would be unwilling to tolerate, and so such a level would provide clear evidence against the existence of such a God. Adding a high quantity of suffering caused by the choices of blameless moral agents (often acting rightly no less!) might very well push the world over that threshold. Hence, it is important to do our best to show that genuine pure social evils are rare.

As we have already discussed, a key unresolved issue in deciding exactly how much pure social evil exists is settling on whether pure social evil requires diachronic blamelessness or only synchronic blamelessness. But this issue is not important for evaluating the evidence social evil provides against theism. This is because the more permissive synchronic definition will allow for some additional social evils, but the further social evils it permits will be among the least interesting from an evidential perspective—the ones that are brought about as a result of previous blameworthy moral decisions.

---

[48] Poston (2014) does discuss soul-making and natural law stability as theodicy strategies for addressing social evil, but he merely points out that they can't play any role in directly explaining the existence of social evil. This is true, but it discounts the possibility that they play an indirect role, by justifying God in allowing processes that have social evils as consequences.

CONCLUSION

We have now seen a host of siphoning strategies that show that many candidates for social evil status don't qualify. In addition, we have examined a host of reasons to think that the candidates that remain (both the ones that involve blameless wrongdoing and the wholesale avoidance of wrongdoing) do not provide significant evidence against the existence of God, because they appear to be produced by processes that are already familiar from mainstream discussions of the problem of evil. These processes are already known to produce significant suffering in other contexts and are already the targets of much attention by theodicists. The central argument of this paper has been non-demonstrative, however, since offering anything close to a systematic case would require surveys of vast swaths of both empirical and conceptual territory. It is my hope that the ball has been put squarely in the court of the atheologian, though. If there are collections of social evils that are problematic for theism, they have not yet been produced or identified.[49]

[49] Thanks to editor Jonathan Kvanvig, Jamie Hebbeler, Paul St. Amour, Dan Tyman, Brandon Gergel, Becky Germino, and several anonymous reviewers from *Oxford Studies in Philosophy of Religion* for their helpful feedback on previous versions of this paper.

4

Sufferer-Centered Requirements on Theodicy and All-Things-Considered Harms

Dustin Crummett

I. INTRODUCTION

Until recently, the analytic philosophical literature on the problem of evil focused overwhelmingly on questions regarding the world as a whole—whether creation might be more valuable for having evils in it, how good a world would need to be for God to create it, and so on. In recent years, this focus has begun to shift; many are now convinced that successful theodicy[1] requires attention to how evils affect the particular people who suffer them.[2] The thought is that God's concern for the significance of each particular individual would make him unwilling to impose certain sorts of sacrifices upon individuals for the greater good, or that his resourcefulness would make it unnecessary for him to do so. Let a "sufferer-centered requirement on theodicy" be a requirement that our theodicy pay special attention to how God's governance of the world affects the particular people who suffer terrible evils.

---

[1] I will use "theodicy" to refer to both theodicies and defenses. (The difference is supposed to be something like that theodicies try to explain God's *actual* reasons for allowing evil, while defenses merely propose possible reasons. I don't see that the distinction is important for our purposes.)

[2] So the story goes, anyway. This way of framing the contrast is popular, but it might be at least a little too quick. One could hold that the distribution of goods and evils within a world *itself* affects the value of the world, so that one couldn't actually judge the value of a world without paying attention to the stories of particular individuals. The focus on the world/focus on the sufferers dichotomy might then break down. But the theodicists that Stump and Adams are responding to generally have not held this view (or haven't let it noticeably affect their theodicies, if they have held it.)

This shifting of focus to the particular individuals who bear the cost of evils can largely be attributed to the influential work of Marilyn Adams and Eleonore Stump.[3] Both Adams and Stump have endorsed very strong sufferer-centered requirements on theodicy, ones which entail (perhaps with a few qualifications)[4] that, as a result of divine providence, either (in Adams's case) no one is overall harmed by anything that happens to them or (in Stump's case) something overall harmful can happen to someone only if they freely fail to appropriate the goods their suffering made possible. I will call their requirements (and any other, relevantly similar requirements) *the strong sufferer-centered requirements on theodicy*, because they are so strong. William Hasker has objected to the strong requirements' implications about harm, arguing both that they would theoretically undermine morality and that it would be practically bad for us to accept them. In the next section, I will discuss Adams's and Stump's requirements on theodicy. In the third and fourth sections, I will discuss Hasker's objections to their requirements. I claim that Hasker's own arguments, as stated, are extremely problematic. However, I will develop some Hasker-inspired objections to the strong requirements which I think are very powerful. In the fifth section, I discuss why God might not meet the requirements endorsed by Stump and Adams. I also attempt to show how Adams and Stump can modify their accounts to avoid the objections I raise while respecting the considerations that motivated the strong requirements in the first place. The relevant modifications will shift the focus of the requirements from *each evil's* never leaving us worse off to *God's actions and omissions* not doing so, even as particular evils really do sometimes constitute (incredibly severe) all-things-considered harms for us.

II. ADAMS'S AND STUMP'S ACCOUNTS

Adams's theodicy focuses squarely on what she calls "horrendous evils," which are "evils the participation in which (that is, the doing or the suffering of

---

[3] Marilyn McCord Adams, *Horrendous Evils and the Goodness of God* (Ithaca, NY: Cornell University Press), 1999; Marilyn McCord Adams, *Christ and Horrors: The Coherence of Christology* (Cambridge: Cambridge University Press), 2006; Eleonore Stump, "The Problem of Evil," *Faith and Philosophy*, 2(4), 1985; Eleonore Stump, *Wandering in Darkness* (Oxford: Oxford University Press), 2010.

[4] "With a few qualifications" because Stump, in her later work, restricts her requirement to suffering involuntarily undergone and because I'm not exactly sure whether Adams wants her requirement to apply to horrors (see fn. 10). But restrictions like these on the scope of the harms covered by the strong requirement shouldn't fundamentally affect the arguments I'll give in sections III and IV or the modifications I'll suggest to the requirements in section V.

which) constitutes prima facie reason to doubt whether the participant's life could (given their inclusion in it) be a great good to him/her on the whole."[5] Such evils certainly seem to afflict us. Yet Adams also emphatically stresses that God should act for the good of every individual person, not merely the aggregate good of groups of people or to abstract, impersonal goods; the governance of a God who acted with only such global concerns in mind would, Adams tells us, be "at best indifferent, at worst cruel."[6] The problem is immediately clear: how can we reconcile the claim that God will ensure each of his children an excellent life with the fact that his children often suffer or commit evils that threaten to leave their lives total ruins?

In answering this, Adams draws on Roderick Chisholm's distinction between *defeating* goods or evils and merely *balancing them off*. When an evil is merely balanced off, it is countered by an equal or greater amount of good. When it is defeated, however, it becomes part of an organic unity—a collection of value bearers whose total value is not equal to the arithmetic sum of the values of its parts—whose value is at least as good as it would be without the evil (so that, for instance, the disvalue of a discordant part of a symphony is defeated when that part, *in virtue of its very discordance*, makes the whole symphony more beautiful.) Adams believes God's love for us would require him to defeat all evils by making them partial constituents of organic unities which are good *for the person who suffered the evil*:

> At a minimum, God's *goodness to* human individuals would require that God guarantee each a life that was a great good to him/her on the whole by balancing off serious evils. To value the individual qua person, God would have to go further to defeat any horrendous evil in which s/he participated by giving it positive meaning through organic unity with a great enough good *within the context of his/her life.*[7]

God can do this by making our horrendous sufferings moments of identification with the suffering of Christ, or by expressing gratitude to us for the suffering we bore while God carried out his purposes, or by making them moments of contact with the divine, and (in each of these cases) by helping us come to appreciate these values during a wonderful afterlife. Horror-strewn lives will not be *better* than lives without horrors, since God can also give unsurpassably great goods to us without our suffering horrors. But the defeat of the horrors within our lives ensures that horror-strewn lives will not be *worse*, either; rather, both sorts of lives will be incommensurably good.[8] Because horrors will thus be "given a dimension of positive meaning," in the afterlife participants in horrors will "be brought to the point of

---

[5] Adams, *Horrendous*, p. 26.   [6] Adams, *Horrendous*, p. 30.
[7] Adams, *Horrendous*, p. 31.   [8] Adams, *Horrendous* , p. 167.

accepting them and so no longer retrospectively wishing to erase them from their life stories."⁹ It is in this way that God's willingness to set us up for horrors is reconciled with his perfect love for each individual. We can thus say that Adams's position apparently implies what I will call *Adams's requirement*: no suffering that God allows can leave its sufferer worse off than they could have been had the evil not occurred.¹⁰

Eleonore Stump likewise believes that the occurrence of evils must, in some sense, be aimed at the good of their sufferers:

> With considerable diffidence, then, I want to suggest that Christian doctrine is committed to the claim that a child's suffering is outweighed by the good for the child which can result from that suffering. This is a brave (or foolhardy) thing to say, and the risk inherent in it is only sharpened when one applies it to cases in which infants suffer, for example, or in which children die in their suffering.... It seems to me nonetheless that a perfectly good entity who was also perfectly omniscient and omnipotent must govern the evil resulting from the misuse of... significant freedom in such a way that the sufferings of any particular person are outweighed by the good the suffering produces *for that person*; otherwise, we might justifiably expect a good God somehow to prevent *that particular suffering*, either by intervening (in one way or another) to protect the victim. while still allowing the perpetrator his freedom, or by curtailing freedom in some select cases.¹¹

For Stump, our ultimate good is freely achieving union with God, and our ultimate evil is rejecting such union. Unfortunately, our sinful wills prevent us from achieving such union, and sometimes horrific suffering is the best way to heal this defect and encourage us to will union with God. Because the point of the suffering is to encourage a particular free response, it may fail to achieve the desired effect; God cannot make the free decision for the person. Nonetheless, all suffering is *aimed at* the good of the sufferer, just as a medical treatment is aimed at the good of the patient even in unfortunate situations where it fails to achieve this aim.¹²

---

⁹ Adams, *Horrendous*, p. 203.

¹⁰ Anyway, I *think* Adams endorses Adams's requirement. She focuses on horrors and, strictly speaking, only explicitly tells us that *horrors* will be defeated, not that all evils will. But if mundane evils can leave us worse off while horrors can't, this would sometimes leave us in the strange position of wishing, insofar as we are concerned about someone's welfare, that a horror had befallen them rather than something merely bad, so that God would have gone ahead and defeated it. That seems like an unacceptable implication. In any event, nothing in the arguments I give in the next two sections will depend on this; if it is objectionable to say that *no* evils leave us worse off, it's surely about as objectionable to say that the *worst* evils don't leave us worse off.

¹¹ Stump, "Problem," pp. 410–11.

¹² Stump, "Problem," pp. 409–11. In her later *Wandering in Darkness*, Stump expands greatly on what she takes to be the nature of of the defect in our will and the way in which

We may thus say that Stump has endorsed what I will call *Stump's requirement*: the occurrence of any suffering[13] God allows must be such that no other event would be a better[14] way of making the sufferer better off than they could have been otherwise, though it may leave them worse off it they freely fail to appropriate the goods it makes possible.[15] This requirement is stronger than Adams's in one way and weaker in another. It is stronger because it requires that the evil be aimed at making the sufferer *better off* than they would have otherwise been, while Adams is happy to admit that God could have given people lives which were no worse and didn't have any horrors in them. It is weaker because some evils may actually leave their sufferers worse off. Achieving the goods in question requires a particular free response on the part of the sufferer, and some people, believe it or not, may ultimately be so perverse as to not love God no matter *how* horrific the torments God allows to befall them.

Both requirements have implications for how and whether evils can harm us. Suppose—awfully plausibly—that if an event is what I'll call an *overall harm* (sometimes called an *all-things-considered harm*) to someone, they are worse off for the event's having occurred than they would have been if the event hadn't occurred.[16] And suppose that an event is a *pro tanto harm*

suffering can help mend this defect; see *Wandering*, Part 2. She also makes clear that her particular story about how her strong requirement is met—the story about our sinful wills needing healing—is, for purposes of that book, only supposed to apply to "mentally fully functional adult human beings," though she leaves open the possibility that it might also be modified to apply to children and non-human animals (*Wandering*, pp. 4–5). The strong requirement itself, however, is supposed to apply to everyone, however it winds up being fulfilled.

[13] In *Wandering in Darkness*, Stump makes clear that her theodicy is intended to address *suffering* in particular, rather than merely evil in general, and gives an extensive account of what suffering is (*Wandering*, ch. 1). When I speak of "evils" in the context of Stump's theodicy, the term can be understood as involving suffering as she understands it.

[14] Where figuring out whether it would be "better" presumably involves taking account of the severity of the evil, the magnitude of the harm to be avoided or good to be gained, and how the occurrence of the evil affects the probability of the harm being avoided or the good being gained.

[15] In *Wandering in Darkness*, Stump modifies this requirement in two ways (see *Wandering*, ch. 13). One is that the principle is restricted to cover only cases of involuntary suffering. The other is that the principle is strengthened so that, for certain kinds of involuntary suffering, the suffering must be allowed for the sake of a harm being avoided rather than a benefit being gained. Neither of these should make any kind of fundamental difference to the arguments I give against the requirement or the modifications I suggest to it, so, for economy of expression, I'll leave them out from here on.

[16] The popular comparative account of harm *analyzes* overall harm in terms of an event's leaving someone worse off than they would have been otherwise (see, for instance, Ben Bradley, "Analyzing Harm," <http://www.colorado.edu/philosophy/center/rome/RoME_2009_full_papers/Ben_Bradley_Analyzing%20Harm.doc>, accessed July 30,

(sometimes called a *prima facie harm*) for someone if and only if it possesses an overall harm-making feature. A *pro tanto* harm is *merely* that when, despite its harmful features, it fails to make its sufferer worse off on the whole. Surgeries are paradigmatic cases of events that are intended to be merely *pro tanto* harms—one experiences discomfort, incapacitation, etc., but one is (one hopes) nonetheless better off for having undergone the surgery and thus not overall harmed by it.[17]

If these suppositions are true, Adams's requirement entails that all harms are merely *pro tanto* harms, and Stump's requirement entails that overall harms occur only when their sufferers fail to appropriate the goods their suffering made possible.[18] These implications about harm are, I think, pretty central to the work the strong requirements are supposed to be doing: it is easy to reconcile God's concern for the welfare of particular individuals with his willingness to allow their suffering if their suffering will not, in the grand

---

2014). I have not offered an analysis of overall harm; the claim I make involves only a material conditional. This allows us to avoid the most worrisome objections to the comparative account. For instance, the comparative account requires that we treat failures to benefit as instances of harm, since, when I fail to benefit you, you are worse off than if I had benefited you. But this is prima facie implausible; intuitively, in order to *harm* you, I have to actually *do something* to you.

[17] Ben Bradley illustrates the ordinary language distinction between *pro tanto* and overall harms using the example of headlines reporting medical news ("Analyzing," p. 3.) A headline reading "New Study Shows Surgery is Harmful" uses "harmful" in the overall sense; figuring out that surgery involved discomfort, financial expense, and so on would merit neither a study nor a headline reporting it. Meanwhile, "Scientists Develop Harmless Surgical Technique" uses "harmless" in the *pro tanto* sense; if people knew the surgery using the old techniques left patients worse off overall, they wouldn't have been getting it!

[18] It is important to note that the requirements also imply a great deal more than just these claims about harm. Suppose God decreed that, for any harm we suffer, he would give us some compensating good which outweighed the harm, and that he would not give us these outweighing goods if we did not suffer that harm. But suppose his unwillingness to give us the goods if we didn't suffer the harm was a mere matter of whim; there was no interesting relation between the harm and the good, so that God could have made us better off still by just giving us the goods without our suffering. Unless failures to benefit are themselves harms, this would ensure that there were no overall harms, since, given that God wouldn't compensate us without the harm befalling us, no *pro tanto* harm would leave us worse off than we would have been had it not occurred. But proponents of the strong requirements would not be happy with such a state of affairs; they think that, in such a situation, a loving God would just give us the benefits and let us skip the harms. (Thus Adams writes that "Mere balancing off [as happens in the story I just told] of horrors...would leave open the question of why a God Who loved human beings would not—since horror participation is *prima facie* ruinous—omit the horrendous segments altogether" (Adams, *Christ*, p. 46).) This is why I formulated the strong requirements as saying that evils will not merely leave us worse off than we *would* have been without their occurrence, but also than we *could* have been without their occurrence.

scheme, negatively impact their welfare. But these implications about harm are also, I claim, ultimately untenable. I will argue as much in the next two sections.

III. THEORETICAL OBJECTIONS TO THE STRONG REQUIREMENTS

William Hasker has argued that the strong requirements' implications about harm present insoluble ethical problems.[19] It seems to me that there are at least two threads to Hasker's argument. One thread is *pragmatic*— apart from whether they are plausible, we have practical reasons not to accept the strong requirements, either because doing so is itself somehow morally or relationally inappropriate or else because doing so is likely to lead to bad consequences. The other thread is *theoretical*—our moral obligations would be *objectively unjustified* if the strong requirement is true, since the grounds for those obligations would not exist. Since it is incredibly plausible to think that we have such obligations, we have very strong epistemic reasons to reject the strong requirements. I will focus on theoretical objections to the strong requirements in this section and pragmatic ones in the next.

One of Hasker's most sustained presentations of his version[20] of the theoretical objection is in response to Eleonore Stump's endorsing her strong

---

[19] In this section and the next, I will assume, along with Adams, Stump, Hasker, and the vast majority of the rest of the problem-of-evil literature, that if one of the strong requirements is satisfied, it's satisfied because the evils we suffer somehow contribute (whether causally or constitutively) to other harms being avoided or benefits being obtained. There's at least one way to think that what I've called Adams's requirement is satisfied without thinking that this is so. If one thinks that everyone experiences infinite well-being in virtue of having an eternal, blissful afterlife, and one thinks that no life with infinite well-being and only finite ill-being is better than any other (on the grounds, I guess, that an infinite sum minus any finite sum is still just the same infinite sum), one might think that no merely finite *pro tanto* harm can leave anybody worse off on the whole, even if it doesn't lead to any benefit or avoid any other harm. Some people do hold this view, but *I* think it's wild. Of *course* I'm better off if I go to heaven now than if I suffer totally gratuitous, horrible torture for a googol years and then go to heaven (St Paul apparently agreed in the case of a vastly less severe harm; see Philippians 1:21–4.) If this leaves us unable to cardinally rank all evaluatively comparable lives using the resources of standard arithmetic, well, so much the worse for doing *that* (of all things) rather than for avoiding the torture. But in any event, the arguments I present against the strong requirements in this section and the next will apply as-is to this view, with the exception of something I say about the second pragmatic argument in section IV (see n. 51).

[20] Hasker has also, very briefly, presented a similar argument which is aimed specifically at Stump's version of the strong requirement (see William Hasker, "Light in the Darkness? Reflections on Eleonore Stump's Theodicy," *Faith and Philosophy*, 28(4), 2011, p. 450).

requirement.[21,22] Hasker claims that Stump's view implies that "*no person can ever ultimately be harmed* by anything that happens to her or is done to her"[23] and thereby undermines "that (crucially important) part of morality which deals with our obligations towards other people."[24] In fact, if Stump's view is right, we have no moral obligations to one another *at all*; "from the standpoint of any form of consequentialism," Hasker claims, "the very idea of treating another person wrongly disappears," while on deontological views, "obligations to persons might co-exist consistently with Stump's theodicy" but would "in an important way be *unmotivated*."[25] Hasker grounds this final claim in his endorsement of what he calls "Frankena's principle," expressed in the following quotation from William Frankena:

> [M]oral reasons consist of facts about what actions, dispositions, and persons do to the lives of sentient beings, including beings other than the agent in question, and the moral point of view is concerned with such facts.[26]

The thought is supposed to be that if the principle is true, Stump's requirement would entail that we could not wrong others, since we could not

---

A similar argument appears in Jeff Jordan, "Divine Love and Human Suffering," *International Journal of Philosophy of Religion*, 56(2), 2004. As these arguments apply only to Stump's version of the strong requirement, I will set them aside for present purposes, focusing instead on the form of the argument which applies to both requirements. (Jordan *claims* his argument applies to Adams's position ("Divine," p. 172,) but this is incorrect. His argument is directed against a position on which evils make us *better off* than we could have been otherwise, which, we saw above, is not Adams's view.)

[21] In this particular context, Hasker is in fact concerned not with arguing directly for the falsity of the strong requirements, but with arguing that their falsity is compatible with theism: one of them being true would undermine the significance of morality, but God is not obligated to meet one of the strong requirements if doing so would undermine morality's significance, so God is not obligated to meet the strong requirements. But this passage and others also make clear that Hasker also views these considerations as providing a direct argument for the falsity of the strong requirement: if one of the strong requirements is true, we don't have obligations to one another, but we know from common sense and from revelation that we do have such obligations, so the strong requirements are false. See, for instance, William Hasker, "Suffering, Soul Making, and Salvation," *International Philosophical Quarterly*, 28(1), 1988, and Hasker, "Light," p. 450.

[22] An argument similar in many ways to the one presented here is given in Jeff Jordan, "Divine Love and Human Suffering," *International Journal for Philosophy of Religion*, 56(2), 2004.

[23] William Hasker, "The Necessity of Gratuitous Evils," *Faith and Philosophy*, 9(1), 1992, p. 27. We saw above that this isn't quite true, since she allows that evils can harm us overall as a result of our own free actions (and Hasker modifies his claim accordingly in future writings). But it's *close enough* to be true for present purposes that we can let it slide.

[24] Hasker, "Necessity," p. 28.   [25] Hasker, "Necessity," p. 28.

[26] Hasker attributes this quote to William K. Frankena, *Ethics*, 2nd edn (Englewood Cliffs, NJ: Prentice-Hall, 1993) p. 113.

negatively affect their lives by inflicting all-things-considered harms on them. Hasker has the following to say in defense of Frankena's principle:

> This claim of Frankena's is not uncontroversial, but it seems to me that it enjoys strong intuitive support. Frankena's principle does not require a utilitarian or consequentialist morality; it does not stipulate that the only reasons which are relevant to the moral justification of an action are the consequences for sentient beings of *that particular action*. But it does say that morally relevant reasons must *in some way* have to do with the tendency of the action in question, or of the class of actions of that kind, to do good or harm to sentient beings.[27] And it seems to me that this is correct—that if we become convinced that certain ostensibly moral requirements or prohibitions have *no connection whatever* with the weal or woe of any rational or sentient being, then we soon cease to regard such commands or prohibitions as morally serious.[28]

I think there's something to Hasker's argument here, but it is very far from clear whether we should accept the use he wants to make of Frankena's principle.[29] Right or wrong, common-sense morality is against Hasker here, as it recognizes many obligations which are grounded in things other than welfarist concerns. Many people, for instance, believe that agents have a fundamental right to live their own lives as they see fit, and thus think we have moral reason not to interfere with the private behavior of others *even if* doing so will promote their well-being. Many people likewise think we have duties of truth-telling and promise-keeping to others that are not grounded in welfarist considerations; accordingly, W. D. Ross, in his landmark *The Right and the Good*, argues that we have a fundamental duty to

---

[27] Hasker's drawing of the consequentialism/deontology divide at least comes pretty close to conflating consequentialism with act consequentialism ("the only reasons which are relevant to the moral justification of an action are the consequences for sentient beings of *that particular action*") and deontology with rule consequentialism ("morally relevant reasons must *in some way* have to do with the tendency of the action in question, or of the class of actions of that kind, to do good or harm to sentient beings"). I think this winds up being important, as it makes his position look less controversial than it really is.

[28] Hasker, "Necessity," pp. 28–9.

[29] There are also some other worries we might reasonably have. A minor one is that Frankena's principle needs to be read in a particular way—where "do to" means "do to *overall*"—in order to even be relevant to the discussion; someone who thinks merely *pro tanto* harms carry moral weight could otherwise endorse it alongside the strong requirements without issue. A more serious worry is that the truth of Frankena's principle, combined with the impossibility of our ever being overall harmed, can render *all* our obligations to one another empty only if we have an unintuitively broad conception of "harm" on which failing to benefit someone counts as harming them; otherwise we might be unable to harm one another overall but still have obligations to provide each other overall benefits. (In her later writings, Stump, at least, implicitly rejects such a conception of harm, since she thinks there is an important moral difference between helping someone and harming them (*Wandering*, pp. 392–5).)

keep promises that is separate from any sort of welfarist considerations and can sometimes override them:

> If I have promised to confer on *A* a particular benefit containing 1,000 units of good, is it self-evident that if by doing some different act I could produce 1,001 units of good for *A* himself (the other consequences of the two acts being supposed equal in value), it would be right for me to do so?...I think not. Apart from my general *prima facie* duty to do *A* what good I can, I have another *prima facie* duty to do him the particular service I have promised to do him, and this is not to be set aside in consequence of a disparity of good of the order of 1,001 to 1,000 though a much greater disparity might justify me in so doing.[30]

Many more examples could be given.

Arguing that the actions in question—promise-keeping, and so on—nonetheless *tend* to promote well-being, despite not doing so in every circumstance, would be beside the point. The people in question believe that, even if obeying the obligation to (say) keep promises does, as a matter of fact, tend to minimize overall harm, this is not the sole ground for the obligation, so that the obligation has force even in possible worlds where inflicting overall harms on others is impossible. (One of those possible worlds is *this* one, if one of the strong requirements holds.) One might, of course, reject the judgments in question, or one might attempt to modify one's account of welfare to subsume these apparent counterexamples (claiming that having a promise broken to one is intrinsically harmful, say, and that this accounts for our everyday intuitions about the relevant cases.) But even if one accepts these controversial moves, it is just not true that one's opponents—whether ethical theorists or the numerous "folk" whose intuitions their theories attempt to do justice to—think all of our obligations to one another are "morally unserious" apart from welfarist considerations. Indeed, they think these non-welfarist moral reasons are serious enough that we should sometimes act on them, even when doing so is not the best way to promote the important value of welfare.

Hasker's theoretical objection to the strong requirement, then, rests on a *highly* controversial claim, one rejected by many ethical theorists and in tension with much of common-sense morality. Whatever its appeal of Frankena's principle, then, it's not clear whether we should even accept it to begin with, and proponents of the strong requirements will presumably just take their arguments for the strong requirements as confirmation that one of the many live alternatives to Frankena's principle must be correct. Fortunately, Hasker did not really need to rest his argument on Frankena's

---

[30] W. D. Ross, *The Right and the Good* (Oxford: Oxford University Press), 2002, p. 35.

principle at all. His claims can be made significantly weaker—and significantly more plausible—and still pose problems for the acceptability of the strong requirements.

All that's needed for an argument from moral theory to the falsity of the strong requirements is that *some* facts about morality are most plausibly explained by facts having to do with overall harms (ones not of our own doing, in the case of Stump's requirement). It's true that some ethical theorists have developed systems that don't invoke welfarist considerations at all. G. E. Moore and some of his successors even thought the concept of well-being was incoherent (though, of course, *that* position doesn't play well with the spirit of the strong requirements).[31] And let's admit that the question is *not* whether ethical theorists can, *in principle*, coherently give the right answers about what to do without invoking overall harms. They can, and the formula is easy: for any action whose deontic status is supposed to be (at least partly) explained by some fact about an overall harm, find the feature of the state of affairs that will result from the act that is supposed to constitute the harm and say instead that this feature grounds some other disvalue, or that avoiding it leads to some value, or that the feature grounds some non-consequentialist duty to avoid it.

But we still have the question of how *plausibly* ethics can be done without *ever* invoking overall harms, and there I think the prospects are bleak. I promised to meet my friend for lunch and thus have an obligation to do so (one grounded, perhaps, in a fundamental non-consequentialist obligation to keep promises). While I'm walking to the bus stop, I pass her house and see that it's on fire. I can run to a pay phone (this, alas, is in the days before cells) and call the fire department, saving her house, but I'll miss the bus and our lunch date along with it. Pretty obviously I now have an obligation to break the promise and try to save her house. Surely at least *part* of the most natural explanation of why that is will have *something* to do with the harm of having her house destroyed being sufficient to justify my not keeping the promise. Isn't it the case, after all, that the more harm I think is likely to result, the more serious the promise I would be allowed to break?[32]

Or suppose we think, as most Christians do, that we have special obligations to protect the poor, disenfranchised, and vulnerable. Why is this?

---

[31] Roger Crisp, "Well-Being," *Stanford Encyclopedia of Philosophy*, 2013, <http://plato.stanford.edu/entries/well-being/>, accessed July 30, 2014. See especially sect. 2.

[32] Note that, even if the explanation doesn't itself *cite* the harm, it will probably presuppose it: maybe (for instance) the reason why I should break the promise is that, if she knew what I know, breaking the promise is what my friend would want me to do, but surely the most natural answer as to why she would want *that* is that having her house destroyed would be a great harm.

Surely some of the first answers to come to mind are things like: they have already unfairly *suffered many harms* that others weren't subject to; they are, as a result of their disadvantage, more vulnerable to *further harm*; due to considerations of diminishing marginal utility, they will be *more greatly benefited* than if we tried to help those who are *better off*. All three of these are welfarist conderations, and the first two are incompatible with the strong requirements if we interpret the harms being cited as overall ones.

One could attempt to respect our intuitions here by claiming that the harms being cited in these cases, and other similar ones, are *not* overall harms at all but instead merely *pro tanto* ones. The plausible harm-citing explanations would then be compatible with the strong requirements. But I'm skeptical about the prospects here. Maybe merely *pro tanto* harms do carry some moral weight; there's *something* intuitively problematic about the idea of my inflicting a harm on someone in hopes of helping them avoid an exactly equally severe harm (though it's *also* true that there are many ways to account for this intuition other than according intrinsic weight to merely *pro tanto* harms and that there are serious difficulties both in drawing the doing/allowing harm distinction in a way that respects our intuitions about its moral importance and in explaining why it should be morally important to begin with).[33] In any event, even if inflicting merely *pro tanto* harms carries *some* moral weight, inflicting overall harms seems to carry *more*. If I have reason not to throw a rock at somebody to prevent another, equally painful rock from falling on them, surely I (*ceteris paribus*) have more reason not to throw the rock at them when the other rock *won't* hit them; the obligation not to do the second action is weightier, and I am more blameworthy if I perform it. At least *part* of the most natural explanation for this has to lie in the fact that my actions in the second case leave the person worse off while my actions in the second case don't; after all, the greater the amount by which we think my throwing the rock will leave them worse off, the worse it is for me to throw it. But this explanation is incompatible with the strong requirements; if they are true, then the absence of the second rock, combined with God's allowing me to make the throw, ensures that there's some *other* benefit that will accrue to the person as a result of my actions.

In light of considerations like the ones I've raised, even paradigmatically non-consequentialist ethical theorists have *generally* made room in their theories for considerations grounded in harms, telling us that certain actions are forbidden because of the (overall, here and hereon) harms they would cause others, that other actions are obligatory because they are necessary to

---

avert great harms befalling others, that other actions are supererogatory because of the great harms performing them would inflict on us, and so on. Thus W. D. Ross, for instance, recognizes a prima facie duty of benevolence and another, stronger prima facie duty of non-maleficence.[34] The categorical imperative commands me to help others avoid harm, and does so on the grounds that universalizing a principle allowing people to ignore the suffering of others would leave me worse off.[35] Virtue ethicists have generally thought that cost-benefit welfarist considerations sometimes explain why acts count as manifestations of a particular virtue or vice (as instances of generosity, say, or of cruelty).[36] And so on. John Rawls, perhaps utilitarianism's most prominent modern critic, goes so far as to say that "All ethical doctrines worth our attention take consequences into account in judging rightness. One which did not would simply be irrational, crazy"[37] (and while he speaks there merely of "consequences," the remark's situation in a discussion of utilitarianism, combined with the importance of individual welfare in his own theory, makes clear he is thinking primarily of *welfarist* consequences—harms among them).

However, suppose all this is wrong and morality can survive the strong requirements basically intact. Other aspects of practical philosophy still pose problems for the strong requirements that are as or more severe.[38] Consider self-regarding prudential reasoning. Maybe we have self-regarding obligations such that prudential reasons are also moral reasons, but prudential reasoning nonetheless remains a practice distinct from moral reasoning: it can give results incompatible with moral reasoning (I might coherently judge that an action would be bad for me, but the best thing to do morally, or vice versa) and I can engage in it without employing any deontic concepts (even if I fulfill a self-regarding obligation when I wear my seatbelt, it would be *weird* to *think* of myself as doing so).

---

[34] Ross, *Right*, ch. 2.

[35] See, for instance, Jens Timmerman, "Kantian Ethics and Utilitarianism," *The Cambridge Companion to Utilitarianism*, ed. Ben Eggleston and Dale E. Miller (Cambridge: Cambridge University Press), 2014.

[36] See, for instance, Daniel C. Russell, "What Virtue Ethics Can Learn from Utilitarianism," *The Cambridge Companion to Utilitarianism*, ed. Ben Eggleston and Dale E. Miller (Cambridge: Cambridge University Press), 2014.

[37] John Rawls, *A Theory of Justice*, rev. edn (Cambridge, MA: Harvard University Press), 1999, p. 26.

[38] Hasker occasionally employs examples from these other practical arenas, so it might be that the next few arguments I'll give are implicitly present in Hasker. But they aren't *explicitly* present, since he doesn't point out that these situations also fall within the purview of non-moral decision procedures. (I am thankful to Klaas Kraay for encouraging me to point this out.)

Consider a paradigm case of prudential reasoning: I don't want to take this medicine because it tastes foul and makes me twitch, but I decide to start taking it when I realize it's the only thing that can help me avoid a debilitating medical condition. How are we to make sense of this except to say that I think taking the medicine is (*pro tanto*) *bad for me*, but I'll do it because it's necessary to avoid the condition, which I think would be *even worse for me*, and which wouldn't, in its own turn, lead to any compensating harm being avoided or benefit being gained? After all, wouldn't how important I think taking the medicine is vary with how much overall harm I think the medical condition will cause me? Don't I think I should suffer through the medical condition if I find out that it's the only way to avoid another, greater harm? If the medical condition is the only thing preventing another condition which, combined with the medicine, will cause me exactly as much harm as the condition, wouldn't I regard it as a toss-up what to do? Yet if the strong requirements are true, this ordinary piece of reasoning (and all the others like it that we engage in every day) is apparently grounded on falsehood.

The only way I see to have pieces of reasoning like this come out sound is if prudential reasoning is supposed to ignore whatever goods are making the strong requirements come out true—*other-worldly goods*, presumably. I might then take the medicine to avoid what would be an overall harm viewed purely from the perspective of temporal goods, even though heavenly rewards mean I would not be worse off, *sub specie aeternitatis*, if I suffer from the untreated medical condition. But arbitrarily circumscribing our considerations in this way wouldn't make any sense: I *certainly* better not take the medicine if I think doing so will damn me to hell (and this is true even if I akratically take it anyway). And indeed, the Christian tradition within which both Stump and Adams are working has explicitly taught us to prudentially balance mundane and eternal goods against one another:

Lay not up for yourselves treasures upon earth, where moth and rust doth corrupt, and where thieves break through and steal: But lay up for yourselves treasures in heaven, where neither moth nor rust doth corrupt, and where thieves do not break through nor steal: For where your treasure is, there will your heart be also.[39]

And, famously, "For what is a man profited, if he shall gain the whole world, and lose his own soul? or what shall a man give in exchange for his soul?"[40] Every hour of every day, then, every one of us, when engaging in self-regarding prudential reasoning, at least *apparently* commits ourselves to the possibility of our suffering overall harms of sorts incompatible with the strong requirements.

---

[39] Matthew 6:19–21.   [40] Matthew 16:26.

We couldn't avoid doing as much even if we wanted to. And this is true whatever *morality* has to say about harm.

Close analogues to this kind of reasoning occur as we navigate our intimate relationships with one another. We surely have obligations to our loved ones, but again there is a kind of practical reasoning we engage in as we deal with our loved ones that is distinct from moral reasoning: your love for a criminal might recommend your not turning them into the police even as morality commands you to do so; if you think of yourself as fulfilling an obligation when you buy your significant other flowers on their birthday, your relationship's probably not long for this world. And again, the reasoning we employ in these contexts often commits us to the possibility that our loved ones might suffer overall harms. Doesn't everything I said about the case where I decide whether to take the medicine apply equally strongly to the reasoning I employ when deciding whether to make my child take the medicine?

So far I have focused on practical reasoning. But I also think that the fittingness of many of our common reactive attitudes is grounded in the possibility of events being overall harmful to us. When I was a little kid, I slipped away from my mom in the store to go hide under a coat rack. (I guess it seemed like a good idea at the time.) My mother and some of the clerks looked for me and, after a minute, found me. What did my mother feel while they looked? Fear, I imagine, and regret for having let me slip away (even though this certainly wasn't *moral* regret, since she hadn't been negligent and, in fact, probably did an excellent job of watching me). Why? It's impossible to imagine any answer other than that she was worried that something *bad* would happen to me, that I would be *harmed*. And I think she must have been worried about overall harms; we react differently if a harm to our loved one is merely *pro tanto*. (If a harm is merely *pro tanto*, then, *qua* someone who is concerned about our loved one's well-being, it would no longer be appropriate to regret in the same way our playing a role in the harm's occurring.) And examples like the one I have given could be multiplied at will (Chris Heathwood plausibly suggests as "conceptually connected" to welfare "love, empathy, care, envy, pity, dread, reward, punishment, compassion, hatred, and malice";[41] you've probably had such reactions to something today).

What I am trying to get across with all of this is how *incredibly* radical the implications of the strong requirements are. Conflicting with Frankena's

---

[41] Chris Heathwood, "Subjective Theories of Well-Being," *The Cambridge Companion to Utilitarianism*, ed. Ben Eggleston and Dale E. Miller (Cambridge: Cambridge University Press), 2014, p. 201.

principle (of all things) is the least of the strong requirements' problems. Insofar as they claim that we can never be harmed overall, or can be thus harmed only by our own free action, they conflict with commonsensical and very ecumenical accounts of morality, with self-regarding prudential reasoning, with the sort of practical reasoning we employ when relating to our loved ones, and with the presuppositions underlying many of our attitudinal reactions. If one of the strong requirements is true, probably most things anybody ever did or felt were largely ill-grounded, and certainly most of the *important* things anybody ever did or felt were so. Our belief in overall harms is integrated into our practices as deeply as our beliefs in other minds or the external world, and giving it up would give cause to wonder whether we shouldn't abandon the search for truth altogether: if we were *so* wrong about *that*, why think we're right about anything? That's a heavy price to pay, if anything is.

IV. PRAGMATIC OBJECTIONS TO THE STRONG REQUIREMENTS

Hasker also presents some pragmatic arguments against the strong requirements; by my count, there are at least two. I take the following discussion of Adams's position to be a statement of the first:

> Now my objection [to Adams's view] is not to the idea that, in God's good providence, evils may sometimes be defeated and not merely balanced off...what is objectionable, however, is the claim that if God is good then *necessarily* all evils will be defeated....If we knew in advance that any evil that might occur would be defeated, then it would be quite inappropriate, as Chisholm correctly saw, to "regret or resent" its presence in the world. But if we really, seriously, took this attitude toward evils (and thank God, we usually don't, even those of us who are persuaded of it theoretically) this would inevitably have the effect of undermining our own motivation to prevent the evils from occurring.[42]

Elsewhere, Hasker argues that the general claim that all evils lead to greater goods (whether those goods accrue to the sufferer or not) is partly responsible for "a strain of passivity and fatalism that manifests itself among Christians."[43] Hasker discusses specifically the apathy of many southern white Christians in the face of injustices perpetrated against blacks during the Civil Rights Movement. Hasker believes this apathy can be partly attributed to the belief

---

[42] William Hasker, *The Triumph of God over Evil: Theodicy for a World of Suffering* (Downers Grove, IL: IVP Academic), 2008, pp. 216–17.

[43] Hasker, *Triumph*, p. 193.

that all evils lead to greater goods, writing that "Such passivity in the face of evil is…a natural consequence of the doctrine that in the providence of God 'all is for the best.' "[44]

It's hard to know exactly what to make of this argument. It's easy to imagine the doctrine that "all is for the best" eroding moral motivation, and it's easy to come up with cases where it apparently does so, or is disingenuously used to justify moral apathy. But then, it's also easy to think of people who have held this attitude while being moral exemplars, and Hasker's suggestion that these people don't "really, seriously" adopt the attitude in question amounts to little more than begging the question.[45] Further, it's easy to come up with cases where *rejecting* the strong requirements seems to lead to immorality. Demagogues frequently invoke the specter of catastrophic harm to gain support for actions no one would dream of countenancing outside of maddening fear, and perhaps this would be harder if people "really, seriously" believed that their welfare and the welfare of their loved ones was secure in God's hands. Hasker's view is intuitively plausible to me, but it involves a complex sociological question, and giving any kind of very confident answer to it would require extensive empirical investigation of a sort he hasn't done. For what it's worth, I *suspect* that the pragmatic considerations here are ultimately dependent on the success of the theoretical argument. If, from the perspective of common sense, the emptiness of morality is the *correct* conclusion to draw from the truth of one of the strong requirements, then we should expect accepting it to erode moral motivation. On the other hand, if common-sense morality rests our obligations to one another on non-harm related grounds, or is silent about what grounds our obligations, there's less reason to think that accepting the strong requirement would undermine our motivation in that way.

Hasker also presents another pragmatic argument—one which, I think, has more promise than the first. Hasker says the following about Stump's version of the strong requirement:

Such views strike me as both incredible and morally outrageous.…As for the moral outrageousness, imagine yourself visiting the scene of some disaster—the Bhopal chemical leak, for instance—and consoling yourself and others with the reflection that, after all, the victims are really better off as a result of the tragedy—unless, by their own fault, they fail to take advantage of the marvelous opportunity for spiritual

---

[44] Hasker, *Triumph*, pp. 194–5.

[45] It may not even amount to that. After all, if the claim is that it is only "really, seriously" accepting the strong requirements that leads to moral indifference, then to the extent that accepting the strong requirements doesn't lead to "really, seriously" accepting them, accepting them won't lead to moral indifference.

improvement which is thereby afforded them. Isn't it clear we have no right at all to such consolation? But then what is it doing in our theodicy? If theodicy leads us to make such claims as this, I think we are better off without it.[46]

The worry with the first pragmatic argument was that accepting the strong requirements might lead to immorality. The worry here is that accepting the strong requirements might *be* immoral (and not just as a result of leading to further immorality)—the attitudes that doing so involves might be intrinsically inappropriate.

This argument might seem to again be parasitic upon the theoretical arguments. Presumably, for any or just about any tragedy, there's some possible world where that tragedy (as a result of whatever bizarre thought-experimental causal connection you wish) prevented another tragedy which would have been even worse for all its victims. If that knowledge kept us from having our hearts rent by the suffering, Hasker is right that we would be monsters. But surely the right thing to do, in light of that knowledge, would be to prefer that the lesser tragedy happened even while cursing the fact that the greater tragedy could only be prevented at such an unspeakable cost. (What *else* could we be expected to do—be indifferent as to whether the greater tragedy happened? *Prefer* that it had?) And something like this response, rather than consoled indifference, is presumably what Stump wants us to experience when confronted with actual evils. So perhaps the response necessitated by the strong requirements is inappropriate only if the strong requirements are not satisfied.[47]

I think this is too quick, though. Many of us experience moral discomfort about the whole project of theodicy in general. But that there is some *special* moral discomfort accompanying the strong requirements is something often acknowledged even by proponents of the strong requirements themselves. Thus Stump introduces the claim that her strong requirement is satisfied with "considerable diffidence,"[48] acknowledges that the claim is "brave (or foolhardy)" and that there is a "risk inherent in it,"[49] worries that it will seem "inhuman,"[50] and so on. Given that proponents of the strong requirements themselves experience this moral discomfort, it's reasonable to think there's something underlying it that doesn't rest on skepticism about whether the requirements obtain.

---

[46] Hasker, "Suffering," p. 11.

[47] Stump herself comes close to suggesting something like this; see *Wandering*, pp. 410–11.

[48] Stump, "Problem," p. 410.   [49] Stump, "Problem," p. 410.

[50] Stump, "Problem," p. 411.

Here's a suggestion. Again, presumably nearly any evil might, as a matter of contingent causal connection, prevent by its occurrence another, greater evil from befalling its sufferer. But the strong requirements necessitate a very particular connection between the benefit obtained and the evil suffered. If the connection between the harm and the benefit is totally arbitrary, God could get the one without the other, and proponents of the strong requirements would want him to do just that. There must instead be some essential connection such that not even God could achieve, or could be likely to achieve, the relevant end without the occurrence of the evil or some other, relevantly similar one.[51]

Judging whether such a connection might exist, and thus whether the strong requirements might be satisfied, requires committing oneself to certain judgments about the *nature* of the evils suffered and the nature of goods they might relate to. If the victim of a horror judges that the evil they suffered does, or might, bear such a relation to such a good, there is nothing especially uncomfortable about endorsing that judgment. (We might, of course, have reason to think the victim is wrong. A victim of oppression might have internalized degrading attitudes about themselves and thus fail to appreciate the real horror of what happened to them. But surely it is fair to give the victim's judgment the benefit of the doubt.) But victims of horrors often judge that their sufferings could not, or at least probably don't, bear such a relation, and indeed (in my experience) react with not only incredulity but anger at the suggestion that they might. Contradicting the victim's judgment here does indeed risk being a foolhardy thing to do. This seems especially true when what the victim has suffered is not only worse than anything we have suffered, but worse than anything we can *imagine* having suffered (and I guess that for almost anyone who is still coherent enough to do academic philosophy, there are people who have suffered things even more crushing than they have, even if they have themselves suffered unspeakably horrific things).

The foolhardiness here might be, in part, purely epistemic. The victim, who understands what the horror was like from the inside, is often in a better position to judge the nature of their suffering than we are. To the

---

[51] Someone who holds the view (discussed in n. 19) that our infinitely valuable afterlives assure that no merely finite harms can make us worse off could deny that there is any such connection. God, they might say, could have easily avoided the relevant evils without losing anything important, but just didn't have any welfare-centric reason to do so since finite evils don't ultimately lower our welfare. I doubt such a person should feel any more morally comfortable, though; just *try* telling the victim of a horrendous evil that they believe they were harmed only because they fail to appreciate the counterintuitive ways in which infinite sets behave. I *dare* you.

extent that the judgment of victims is that the strong requirements are not satisfied, then we have additional theoretical reasons to reject them. But there is also a moral or relational worry: contradicting the victim's judgment (even if we're not impolitic enough to *tell* them we've done so) represents a potentially problematic refusal to trust their interpretation of their sufferings and how those sufferings fit into the narrative of their life. This pragmatic argument, then, has force apart from the purely theoretical arguments; even if one of the strong requirements turns out to be *true*, there might be pragmatic reasons not to believe as much in cases where the victim has judged otherwise.

There's likely no algorithmic way to apply what I've said here. Victims might, for instance, draw conclusions about the *kind* of evils they suffered which are incompatible with conclusions drawn by other people who they acknowledge to have suffered the same kind of evil, so that deferring to the judgments of victims all the time is not coherently possible. There are hard problems here, and I don't pretend to know how to navigate them. But it is, at any rate, true that less moral discomfort is better than more, and that being committed to the impossibility of our being (except by our own doing) harmed overall is not only a source of serious moral discomfort but is acknowledged as such by some proponents of the strong requirements. So if we can avoid the problematic implication about harm while still showing respect for the victims of horrors in the way that proponents of the strong requirements want, we should want to do so.

V. MODIFYING THE STRONG REQUIREMENTS

In the last two sections, I argued that we shouldn't accept the strong requirements; their implications about harm violate many judgments which are extremely plausible by the light of both philosophical theory and common sense, and we may also have pragmatic reasons for rejecting them. This leaves open the question of what those sympathetic to the strong requirements *should* believe. Specifically, we will want answers to two questions. The first is this: given that God's going to allow the evils, why doesn't God satisfy one of the strong requirements—why *wouldn't* he go ahead and defeat all evils, or ensure (insofar as is compatible with human freedom) that they lead to some outweighing good that probably couldn't be obtained otherwise? The second is this: given that God's not going to satisfy one of the strong requirements, why does he allow the evils at all—why, given God's concern for individual welfare, does he not prevent the evils if they do nothing to benefit or prevent other harm for their sufferers?

I will take the first question first. One possibility is that the responses to evils necessitated by the strong requirements are sometimes just not the appropriate ones. Recent ethical thought has made much of the idea that one of the major differences between normative theories lies in the attitudes they think we should take towards value—whether value always demands that we make as much of it as possible, or whether it sometimes demands other responses.[52] Some people, for instance, think the value of human life demands my treating it as inviolable, so that I cannot take an innocent life even if it is the only way to prevent more innocent lives being taken. In a somewhat analogous manner, one might think that some horrors are so horrendous, so repugnant, and such terrible violations of what is precious that the way to respect the dignity of their sufferers, and for their sufferers to respect themselves, is not to bind them up into positively valued organic unities or try to spin from them greater goods that couldn't have been otherwise obtained, or to want others to do likewise. Perhaps the appropriate response is instead to mourn them, to want nothing to do with them, and to help the victim heal and move on to flourish in other ways while leaving the horrors themselves unredeemed and unredeemable, their only positive purpose whatsoever the same as that served by the buildings we leave standing at Auschwitz: that of being monuments to our madness, testaments to its victims, and reminders of how bad things really got.

Suppose that isn't right, though, and that, where we can, we should always respond to evils in the way the strong requirements necessitate. It may not be the case that God can. Some horrors may just, by their nature, not fit into any positively valued organic unities or probabilify the achievement of goods that couldn't have otherwise been easily obtained. There's not much reason to expect that all evils would be able to bear that special kind of relation to sufficiently valuable goods; indeed, back when people took the logical problem of evil more seriously, it was regarded as a very serious question whether *any* evils did. If some evils can't bear such a relation, there's nothing God can do to change that, absent some radical form of axiological theological voluntarism. And it can't be a strike against God's love or goodness or power that he doesn't do the metaphysically impossible.[53]

It still might, though, be a strike against God's love or goodness or power if he allows the evils knowing that he can't or won't respond to them in the way the strong requirements necessitate. If the horrors will be ultimately regrettable for their sufferers, why does the God of love allow them to

---

[52] For a landmark work on this topic, see Philip Petit, "Consequentialism and Respect for Persons," *Ethics*, 100, 1989, pp. 116–26.

[53] Hasker makes a point similar to this one; see *Triumph*, p. 221.

happen—why not, as Adams suggests, "omit the horrendous segments altogether?"[54] My suggestion is that proponents of the strong requirements modify their views to take account of the familiar distinction between whether it would be better for us *if the event hadn't happened* and whether it would be better for us *if God had prevented the event* (or, perhaps less demandingly, *if God generally prevented such events*, or something of that nature). Specifically, I claim that the proponent of Adams's requirement should instead endorse what I'll call *Adams's requirement modified*: no suffering that God allows can leave its sufferer worse off than they could have been had God intervened to prevent the evil (or perhaps: if God generally intervened to prevent such evils). And I claim that the proponent of Stump's requirement should instead endorse what I'll call *Stump's requirement modified*: for any instance of suffering, God's failing to intervene to prevent it (or perhaps: his not generally intervening to prevent such sufferings) must be the best way of making the sufferer better off than they could have been otherwise, though it may leave them worse off it they freely fail to appropriate the goods it makes possible.[55]

Many theodicists have claimed that certain goods are such that obtaining them necessitates the *real possibility* of certain evils, though not the *actualization* of those evils. Perhaps (to pick a few examples) there is something good in our having free will and in the virtues and relationships and responsibilities that it makes possible, or perhaps (to draw on a speculative hypothesis from Adams herself) God has reasons to let material creation "do its thing."[56] (I use these for illustrative purposes; I make no claims about whether they *really are* really valuable enough to do the job, whether they *really couldn't have been* attained without great risk, etc.) Attaining these ends might require that God give up a degree of control and let things play out in ways he doesn't determine and that might go very badly. We might, then, be able to get the goods in question without anything bad actually happening, if everyone used their free will properly and natural processes happened to do their things in ways that didn't harm us. But God might not be able to *ensure* that we got the goods without the evils, since doing so

[54] Adams, *Christ*, p. 46.

[55] A reviewer asks why we should *accept* this view, even if it does avoid the problems I raised earlier. Doesn't it seem, for instance, that we can sometimes harm people for the greater good? And if we can, why can't God? I'm not saying we *should* accept this view; I'm trying to explain how Adams and Stump might preserve as much of the spirit of their views as possible while avoiding my objections, not trying to defend the spirit of their views. For what it's worth, my own view is that the policy-centered requirements I introduce shortly are more plausible than these, and that modifying those requirements to better fit a contractualist mold (see n. 61) would make them more plausible still.

[56] Adams, *Christ*, p. 39.

would require his re-seizing the control the giving up of which was a necessary precondition for obtaining the good in the first place.

Perhaps, *sub specie aeternitatis*, God's pursuing such projects will allow us to obtain benefits—membership in a wonderful community involving freely formed relationships and blessed union with God and all the saints, or divine gratitude for the part we played in the fulfillment of God's cosmic purposes, or something else beyond our imagining—which, incredible as it may be, are sufficient to balance or outweigh the harms we suffered. They *will* have been real, all-things-considered harms, since any benefits relating to them come from their possibility but still could have been had if they hadn't occurred (though perhaps not if *God* had prevented them). There will be nothing to be said in their defense. The arguments of the last two sections, which were generated by the strong requirements' making it impossible for us to (except by our own doing) suffer all-things-considered harms, will thus not arise.[57] But the modified requirements might also be satisfied. If the goods in question are sufficiently valuable, and if God's intervening to prevent the evils related to them would also prevent our obtaining these goods, then God's allowing them might leave us no worse off, or even better off, than if he'd intervened to stop the evils and also lost the related goods. And this might be true *even given* the many unnecessary evils that pursuing the goods lead to. (Note that, on this proposal, all evils will be (at least so far as welfarist goods are concerned) "non-gratuitous" in the sense of the term most commonly used in the problem of evil literature,[58] but will be so in a way that avoids Hasker's concerns with views on which all evils are non-gratuitous, since we can still be harmed.)

Alternatively, perhaps God could *sometimes* intervene to stop the relevant evils when they occur, but could not do so *too much*. Some people, for instance, have thought that God might sometimes intervene to stop us carrying out evil intentions without undermining our responsibility for one another, but couldn't (provided people choose to carry out evil intentions enough) do so all the time without responsibility being undermined.[59] In that case, even though we would have been better off if one of the evils

---

[57] Well, some of the moral uncomfortability discussed in the last section might remain. I was morally uncomfortable just writing this paragraph. But I'm not sure what more can be done about it, short of pretty drastically abandoning the kind of project that proponents of the strong requirements are engaged in.

[58] That is, the one where an evil is gratuitous if it is "such that an omnipotent being could have prevented it without thereby having prevented the occurrence of some greater good" (Hasker, "Necessity," p. 23).

[59] See Hasker, "Necessity," and Peter van Inwagen, *The Problem of Evil* (Oxford: Oxford University Press), 2006, ch. 6.

God intervened to stop *happened* to be the one that happened to *us*, we might also (if the relevant good is sufficiently valuable to us) have sufficient self-regarding reasons to endorse his general policy of not intervening more than a certain amount—the policy he was acting on when he failed to intervene in our case. This would satisfy my parenthetical suggested amendments to the modified requirements, and would be in keeping with their spirit: if *all* of us can, even in light of the evils we suffered, endorse God's general policy of only intervening sometimes, it is not a mark of cruelty towards us that God happened not to intervene in our case.[60] (On this view, unlike in the first proposal, some evils *would* be gratuitous so far as welfarist goods are concerned, but God's permission of them will be justified by his inability to prevent all of them without losing things that are sufficiently valuable to all of us.)

The fulfillment of the modified requirements should, I think, be enough to meet the desiderata that motivated the strong requirements to begin with. What matters to the question whether God demonstrates adequate concern for his children is not how his children are affected by *what happens* but rather how they are affected by *what God does*. On this model, we have an answer to the question why God doesn't "omit the horrendous segments altogether": we (at the very least) couldn't have been better off if he'd done so. We won't be brought to the point of accepting the horrors that befell us. So much the better; they were unacceptable. But we will—the hope is—be brought to the point of, with full information and perfect rationality,

---

[60] There's a resonance between this suggestion and the contractualist moral theories defended by John Rawls and T. M. Scanlon (see *What We Owe to Each Other* (Cambridge, MA: Harvard University Press), 1998), insofar as both involve the thought that you have no complaint if you are treated according to policies which you would accept in some kind of normatively privileged decision situation, even if that policy disadvantages you in a given instance. There are also differences, inspired by my attempts to hew as closely to the views of Adams and Stump as possible. For one thing, I have assumed that which policies we would endorse are determined solely by consideration of our own welfare, whereas this isn't true for Rawls or Scanlon (Rawls assumes we are motivated by securing our ability to live out our rational plan of life, whereas Scanlon assumes we are motivated by "personal reasons," which need not be egoistic—they might instead, for instance, have to do with the well-being of those we care about, or with fulfilling some project we're invested in, regardless of how those things might impact our well-being). I have also assumed that the parties in question are *uncompromising*, in the sense that they will only accept a policy which benefits them on the whole, whereas the parties in contractualist decision situations are taken either to be ignorant of which person they will be (as in Rawls) or else motivated to reach terms which both they and everyone else will not be able to reasonably reject (as in Scanlon). Either device entails that I might accept a policy which harms me in some important way, if someone else has a stronger objection to our not implementing the policy. Whether these differences make the resulting view more or less plausible is not a question I'll address here.

accepting God's treatment of us, even from a self-regarding perspective. And if that's true, it's hard to see how to accuse God of cruelty or indifference. Here's a final worry we might have. On Adams's account, the defeat of horrors plays an essential role in restoring *meaning* to the lives of their participants. If this is the *only* way to restore meaning to horror-strewn lives, it might not be *possible* to have a worthwhile life without the horrors in it being defeated. It might *then* be impossible to satisfy one of the modified requirements without also satisfying its correlate strong requirement, and we would be back where we started. My answer is that there are many things God can do to restore meaning to our lives other than defeat horrors: he can give us wondrous new goods (including ones only available because of the horrors' possibility), heal the psychological wounds we suffered, and bring about reconciliation and justice. As I mentioned above, sometimes we might not even *want* horrors to be defeated. But even if this isn't right, one hopes the other approaches available to God will be able to do the requisite work.

I have argued, then, that the strong requirements face extremely severe objections. I have also argued that we can modify the strong requirements to avoid their untenable implications while still having them fill the role that the strong requirements were supposed to play. I have *not* attempted to evaluate particular theodicies in light of the modified requirements, nor have I attempted to evaluate how plausible it is that God will satisfy one or both of the modified requirements (except to say that it's more plausible than his satisfying the strong requirements). Those tasks are for other times (and, I hope, for people braver than me).[61]

[61] I am grateful to Neal Tognazzini, Laura Ekstrom, and Adam Potkay for service on the committee for my undergraduate senior thesis (a chapter of which was the basis for this paper), to Klaas Kraay, Nevin Climenhaga, reviewers for *Oxford Studies*, and audiences at the Central and Canadian meetings of the SCP for helpful comments on later versions of the paper, to Marilyn Adams, whose positive response to an earlier version of this paper encouraged me to develop and try to publish it, and to many other people whose contributions have benefited this paper in one way or another.

5

Wagering on Pragmatic Encroachment

Daniel M. Eaton and Timothy H. Pickavance

1. INTRODUCTION

Lately, there has been an explosion of literature exploring the relationship between one's practical situation and one's knowledge.[1] Some involved in this discussion have suggested that facts about a person's practical situation might affect whether or not a person knows in that situation, holding fixed all the things standardly associated with knowledge (like evidence, the reliability of one's cognitive faculties, and so on).[2] According to these "pragmatic encroachment" views, then, one's practical situation encroaches on one's knowledge. Though we won't endorse pragmatic encroachment here, we find the view intriguing, and its popularity warrants carefully considering its implications. One potential avenue of exploration concerns religious epistemology: in particular, whether pragmatic encroachment has consequences concerning the epistemic requirements of atheism. We begin the journey down that avenue by connecting Pascal's Wager to pragmatic encroachment in order to defend this conditional: If there is pragmatic encroachment, then it is *ceteris paribus* more difficult to know that atheism is true (if it is) than it is to know that God exists (if God does exist).[3]

Two comments. First, on the claim that God exists. For the earlier stages of the paper, we stipulate that 'God' refers to the Christian God, the Trinitarian God of Abraham, Isaac, and Jacob as revealed in the Incarnate Christ, if such a being exists. 'God exists' is, then, roughly and contingently

---

[1] e.g. Anderson and Hawthorne (forthcoming); Fantl and McGrath (2002, 2009, ms.); Hawthorne (2004); Kvanvig (2011); Stanley (2005); Ross and Schroeder (2014); Schroeder (2012); Weatherson (2005, 2011); Williamson (2005).

[2] Fantl and McGrath (2002, 2009, ms.) and Stanley (2005) are arguably the most committed of the lot.

[3] Benton (forthcoming) argues for a similar thesis, but uses a different version of pragmatic encroachment to make his argument.

equivalent to 'Classical, Creedal Christianity is true'. Ordinarily, the English word 'God' is more flexible than this. It can refer to, for example, the being worshipped by Muslims, or Brahman, if such beings exist, and need not be an empty name if some non-classical version of Christianity is true.[4] For sociological reasons to do with the religious affiliation of anglophone philosophers, we are initially concerned with Christianity. Further, because the names for the Supreme Being in Christianity overlap with those in Judaism and Islam, some sort of stipulation is necessary here. We've chosen this one to ease the prose, and do not mean to insinuate anything about the relationship between Christianity and Judaism, Islam, Hinduism, or any other religion. When it comes time to consider alternatives to Christianity below, we will alter the terminology. At any rate, denying that "God" exists, given our stipulation, is not equivalent to being an atheist, as 'atheism' is commonly understood. Second, on one proposition's being "more difficult" to know than some other proposition. It is plausible that we can compare the strengths of two people's epistemic positions, at least in some cases.[5] This is especially true when the propositions in question are related in important ways. For example, one person may have some evidence for believing that the earth is flat, another person may have some evidence for believing that the earth is spherical. Even if the evidential bases are disjoint, we might be able to judge that the evidence that one person has is better or stronger than the evidence that another person has, and thereby judge that the former is in a stronger epistemic position than the latter (supposing evidentialism is true). When we say that one proposition is "more difficult" to know than another proposition, then, we mean to say that one must be in a stronger epistemic position to know the former proposition than one must be in to know the latter proposition.

The plan for the paper is straightforward. In section 2, we say more about what pragmatic encroachment is. We do this by introducing and unpacking the technical term 'practical adequacy' and then using this technical term to give a more precise definition of pragmatic encroachment. We then sketch some of the reasons pragmatic encroachers have offered in favor of their

---

[4] Because 'Allah' is simply the Arabic word rightly translated into English as 'God', we do not deem it appropriate to use 'Allah' here. This is another part of the terminological problem we are up against.

[5] We use 'strength of epistemic position' as DeRose (2009) does (cf. pp. 7–9). One's strength of epistemic position is determined by those factors traditionally associated with knowledge, factors like evidence or the reliability or proper functioning of one's cognitive faculties. If one is an evidentialist, then the better one's evidence with respect to p, the stronger one's epistemic position with respect to p. If one is a reliabilist, then the more reliable was the faculty that gave rise to a belief that p, the stronger one's epistemic position with respect to p. And so on.

view. In section 3, we connect this form of pragmatic encroachment and Pascal's Wager. The connection reveals that pragmatic encroachment entails that it's more difficult to know that God does not exist than it is to know that God exists. There are some worries about our argument, so in section 4 we consider and reply to these worries.

2. PRAGMATIC ENCROACHMENT

According to pragmatic encroachers, whether one knows p requires more than having a non-gettiered true belief that p that has the right truth-conducive features. Knowledge also depends on the practical features of one's situation. This characterization of pragmatic encroachment is thin. All it says is that one's knowledge depends on one's practical situation *in some way or other*, and it makes no attempt to characterize the nature of this dependence. There is more than one such characterization, and each corresponds with a particular version of pragmatic encroachment. Some of these versions are expressed in the literature. We will focus on a particularly popular version of pragmatic encroachment, characterized in terms of practical adequacy. Before we articulate that version, we want to note two assumptions that will simplify the discussion. First, we'll assume an evidentialist gloss on strength of epistemic position, such that the strength of one's epistemic position with respect to any proposition p is a function of the strength of one's evidence that bears on p. Second, we'll model the strength of one's evidence in terms of a rational credence function. The overall idea, then, is that the higher one's rational credence in a proposition, the stronger one's evidence must be with respect to that proposition, and the stronger one's epistemic position is with respect to that proposition. We believe that nothing turns on these simplifications.

The practical adequacy version of pragmatic encroachment claims that a necessary condition for some subject S to know that p is that s's epistemic position with respect to p is "practically adequate". Clearly, we need to unpack this term of art 'practical adequacy'. The basic idea is this: one's epistemic position with respect to p is practically adequate when no amount of improvement in one's evidence about p would make a difference as to what actions are rational for one. Anderson and Hawthorne (forthcoming) put it this way:

The gap between one's actual epistemic position and perfect epistemic position with regard to p makes a practical difference to a decision in a scenario just in case…one's actual ranking of actions differs from one's ranking of actions conditional on *p....* We will call a subject's strength of epistemic position 'practically inadequate' when the gap makes a practical difference and 'practically adequate' when the gap does not make a practical difference. (p. 4)

We should work a bit more slowly through this terrain. First, for some subject S and some proposition *p*, if the gap between S's actual strength of epistemic position for *p* and the perfect strength of epistemic position for *p* makes no *practical difference*, then this strength of epistemic position is practically adequate. And the gap between one's actual strength of epistemic position and the perfect strength of epistemic position makes a practical difference if and only if the action that is actually rational for S differs from the rational action for S conditional on *p*. But how are actions ranked? Here's one way. Using standard decision theory, calculate the expected utilities of all the available actions and list them from greatest to least. And what of actions conditional on *p*, how are they ranked? Again calculate the expected utilities of all the available actions, except this time use the probabilities of each proposition conditional on *p*, and list these results from greatest to least. If the lists have different actions ranked first then the gap made a practical difference, and S's epistemic position with respect to *p* is practically inadequate; if the lists have the same action ranked first then the gap made no practical difference, and S's epistemic position with respect to *p* is practically adequate.

An example is helpful. A sea captain is just about to take her ship full of 200 passengers for a harbor tour. Now consider the following proposition: the ship is seaworthy. Suppose that the captain's rational credence that the ship is seaworthy is 0.9, and accordingly that her rational credence that the ship is not seaworthy is 0.1—fill in the details however you like to get these numbers. Here and throughout, we use 'C' to represent an agent's rational credence function. In this case, then, C(seaworthy) = 0.9 and C(not seaworthy) = 0.1. Furthermore, the captain has two available ways in which she could act: she could depart immediately or she could delay the harbor tour to do some further checking to raise her confidence that the ship is seaworthy.

This set-up has two options for action and two world states, so there are four outcomes to consider. First suppose that the sea captain chooses to start the harbor tour on time. If the ship is not seaworthy, then everyone drowns. If the ship is seaworthy, then everyone has a pleasant harbor tour and none of the passengers get upset due to a delay. Now suppose that the sea captain delays the cruise to do some further checking. If the ship is not seaworthy, then the sea captain will discover this and cancel the harbor tour. This would make the passengers angry, and it would lose the captain the revenue that would have been generated by the trip. If the ship is seaworthy, then the captain's extra checking would delay the departure a half-hour, and this would make some of the passengers mildly upset.

We can represent the sea captain's practical situation with the following table:[6]

	ship is seaworthy	ship is not seaworthy
start the harbor tour on time	+10	−10,000
do some further checking	−10	−200

Here and throughout, we use 'EU' to represent an agent's expected utility function. In this case, EU(start on time) = $0.9(10) + 0.1(-10,000) = -991$, whereas EU(do further checking) = $0.9(-10) + 0.1(-200) = -29$. Thus the actual rankings of the sea captain's actions are as follows:

1. Do some further checking
2. Start the harbor tour on time

What about the rankings of the sea captain's actions conditional on the ship's being seaworthy? In that case, EU(start on time) = 10, while EU(do further checking) = -10.[7] Thus the rankings of the sea captain's actions conditional on the ship's being seaworthy are as follows:

1. Start the harbor tour on time
2. Do some further checking

The order of the sea captain's actual rankings differs from her rankings conditional on the ship's being seaworthy. Thus, the gap for the sea captain

---

[6] We picked particular utilities for the outcomes in this case to make the math easy and vivid. Of course, there is a range of values for each outcome that will also make our point. So, if you find our particular utility assignments implausible—for example you might think that −10,000 isn't enough to account for the utility lost by everyone drowning—feel free to use utility assignments that seem more plausible to you. So long as the particular assignments you choose are constrained by the features of the case, then all of our subsequent points are unaffected. (Our thanks to an anonymous referee for bringing up this issue.)

[7] $1(10) + 0(-10,000) = 10$; $1(-10) + 0(-200) = -10$. The second column of the decision table becomes irrelevant when conditional on the ship's being seaworthy, since (if one is rational), C(not seaworthy|seaworthy) = 0.

makes a practical difference, and accordingly, the sea captain's strength of epistemic position with respect to the ship's being seaworthy practically *inadequate*.

The sea captain's strength of epistemic position could become practically adequate if it were sufficiently improved. Obviously if she became certain that the ship is seaworthy, if C(ship is seaworthy) = 1, then her actual strength of epistemic position would be practically adequate. But, what is the minimally strong epistemic position for her that would be practically adequate? That is, what is the rational credence below which the sea captain is guaranteed to have practically inadequate belief? The value of the minimally strong epistemic position is given by the minimal value of $C(p)$ such that an agent's rankings of actions given $C(p)$ has the same top-ranking actions as the rankings of actions conditional on p. In the sea captain case, this value given by solving for x in the following inequality: $x(10)+(1-x)(-10000) > x(-10)+(1-x)(-200)$. Thus the sea captain's belief that the ship is seaworthy is practically adequate when C(seaworthy) > 490/491, approximately 0.99796. Thus it turns out that the sea captain needs a rational credence tantamount to certainty in order to be in a position to know that the ship is seaworthy, given the utilities we've assumed for the possible outcomes.

Let's now consider a subject whose strength of epistemic position, with respect to this same p, is *practically adequate*. Consider Kenji and his friend Smith who both happen to walk by our sea captain's ship right as it is scheduled to start its harbor tour. Kenji likes to bet on everything, so he proposes the following set of bets to Smith. If Smith bets that the ship will sink during its next harbor tour and he's right, then he wins \$5, and if he's wrong, then he loses \$5. Also, if Smith bets that the ship will *not* sink during its next harbor tour and he's right, then he wins \$5, and if he's wrong, then he loses \$5.

It turns out that Smith has the exact same evidence that the ship is seaworthy that the sea captain has, and accordingly C(seaworthy) = 0.9 and C(not seaworthy) = 0.1. We can represent Smith's scenario with the following table:

	ship is seaworthy	ship is not seaworthy
bet ship is seaworthy	+5	−5
bet ship is not seaworthy	−5	+5

EU(bet seaworthy) = 4, whereas EU(bet not seaworthy) = −4. Thus the actual rankings of Smith's actions are:

1. Bet seaworthy
2. Bet not seaworthy

What about the rankings of Smith's actions conditional on the ship's being seaworthy? With this constraint, EU(bet seaworthy) =5, while EU(bet not seaworthy) = −5. Thus the rankings of Smith's actions conditional on the ship's being seaworthy are as follows:

1. Bet seaworthy
2. Bet not seaworthy

The order of Smith's actual rankings do not differ from his rankings conditional on the ship's being seaworthy. Thus, the gap for Smith makes no practical difference, and accordingly, Smith's strength of epistemic position with respect to the ship's being seaworthy is *practically adequate*.

With this understanding of practical adequacy we can repeat with greater clarity the version of pragmatic encroachment with which we'll work. If one knows that *p*, then one's epistemic position with respect to *p* is practically adequate. Notice that if this is right, then Smith knows that the ship is seaworthy while the sea captain does not—even though they have the same rational credence in the same proposition and both of their beliefs are true and ungettiered. Thus, if practical adequacy is a necessary condition for knowledge, then pragmatic encroachment is true. Fallibilism is required for this point to go through, and the practical adequacy version of pragmatic encroachment plausibly entails fallibilism, assuming that practical adequacy is supposed to be a non-trivial necessary condition on knowledge. For suppose fallibilism is false. Then, if S knows that *p*, then S's rational credence with respect to *p* must be 1. But then S's epistemic position with respect to *p* is guaranteed to be practically adequate. Accordingly it would be impossible to construct a pair of cases such that in the first case S knows that *p* and in the second case S doesn't know that *p* merely because S's belief is practically inadequate. Thus, if fallibilism is false, the practical adequacy version of pragmatic encroachment would be false, or at best trivial.[8] We, therefore, assume fallibilism for the remainder of the paper.

Others characterize pragmatic encroachment using practical adequacy. Here again are Anderson and Hawthorne (forthcoming): "This [the distinction between practically adequate and practically inadequate epistemic positions] can be turned into a test on knowledge: one knows p only if one's

---

[8] Cf. Anderson and Hawthorne, p. 5.

strength of epistemic position is practically adequate" (p. 4). And here are Fantl and McGrath (2002), in the first systematic defense of pragmatic encroachment in the recent literature: "S is justified in believing that p only if, for all acts A, S is rational to do A, given p, iff S is rational to do A, in fact" (p. 78).[9] We take our development of this view to be the same as these versions, at least with respect to the features that matter for our purposes.

At this point, we hope we have made clear what the practical adequacy version of pragmatic encroachment *is*. But one is left wondering whether it's worth taking seriously. So the time has come to (very briefly!) motivate the view. Some pragmatic encroachers appeal directly to intuitions about cases like those articulated above. They ask one to consider directly whether the sea captain knows that the ship is seaworthy, and whether the passer-by knows that ship is seaworthy. The idea is to get a difference in intuition in these cases, and then point out that the only difference has to do with one's practical setting. This, of course, doesn't get one all the way to the practical adequacy version of pragmatic encroachment, but it would get one to pragmatic encroachment more generally.

However, there are also more theoretical routes. Here is one.[10] Suppose there is a practical adequacy constraint on rational action. That is, suppose that if one can rationally act on one's belief that *p*, then one's epistemic position with respect to *p* is practically adequate. If the appropriate action conditional on *p* is different than the appropriate action given one's actual credence, then one cannot rightly act on one's belief that *p*. If that is right, then the sea captain cannot rightly act on her belief that the ship is seaworthy, for the reasons noted above. The passer-by, however, can go ahead with that bet. Further, though, many epistemologists are attracted to the thought that there is an intimate connection between knowledge and rational action. To ease the discussion, we'll stick with the most straightforward such connection, the idea that if one knows that *p*, then one can rationally act on one's belief that *p*.[11] Coupled with a knowledge–action principle like this, the practical adequacy constraint on rational action (together with fallibilism) entails that if one knows that *p*, then one's epistemic position with respect to *p* is practically adequate. The examples above, then, display that it's possible for one person to know that *p* while another does not, even if the only difference between them is their practical situation. In the sea captain–passer-by case, for example, the passer-by knows that the ship is

[9] See also Fantl and McGrath (ms.) p. 2. Stanley (2005) defends a similar type of pragmatic encroachment.

[10] For another, see chapter 1 of Fantl and McGrath (2009).

[11] For discussion, see e.g. Anderson (2015), Hawthorne and Stanley (2008), and Williamson (2000).

seaworthy while the sea captain does not. Importantly, even if you deny that *these* cases are examples of this phenomenon, it is still true that the *structure* of these cases is enough to display the possibility, under the relevant assumptions. Committing to such possibilities is just committing to the practical adequacy version of pragmatic encroachment.[12]

3. WAGERING ON PRAGMATIC ENCROACHMENT

Suppose the practical adequacy version of pragmatic encroachment is true. We believe that there is an important consequence of this view for religious epistemology, namely, it is more difficult to know that atheism is true (if it is) than it is to know that God exists (if God does exist). To see this, consider the decision table below, which we can use to represent what one's faced with when one considers Pascal's Wager:

	God exists	atheism is true
believe God exists	Infinite Goodies	Minimal Baddies
believe atheism is true	Infinite Baddies	Significant Goodies

Before we start, it's worth noting that there are a number of problems with this set-up of the decision table, and we'll discuss some of those below. We've deployed this set-up only to illustrate the underlying point we're driving toward. We'll make that point more cautiously as we repair the decision table.

Throughout, our decision tables have 'believe God exists' as one of the relevant actions. By 'believe God exists' we mean believe in that way that classical Christianity has supposed is necessary and sufficient for (though not the ground of!) one's salvation. You might think that belief is not an act that can be undertaken, so that the possible actions in our set-up are inappropriate. Peterson (2009), for example, says that appropriate actions should be "alternatives", and,

the set *A* is an *alternative-set* if and only if every member of *A* is a particular act, *A* has at least two different members, and the members of *A* are agent-identical, time-identical, performable, incompatible in pairs and jointly exhaustive (p. 29, emphasis in original).

---

[12] For a very different variety, see Schroeder (2012) and Ross and Schroeder (2014).

Believing that such-and-such is, according to popular epistemological lore, not "performable", in that what we believe is not up to us. Further, it is likely the case that we can have inconsistent beliefs, and so believing that God exists and believing that atheism is true may not be incompatible. Neither are those believings jointly exhaustive, as we've noted above. If all this is right, then using 'believe that God exists' and 'believe that atheism is true' as the alternative actions is an inappropriate way to set up the table.

Suppose all that's right. We still think our argument succeeds, for there are actions characteristic of God-believing that can serve as one of a pair that forms the right sort of alternative-set. For example, consider the act of repenting of one's sin, or of being baptized in the name of the Father, Son, and Holy Spirit, or of worshipping the Triune God. The set {repent, do not repent} is an alternative-set, in Peterson's sense. Consider the decision table so constructed. (Since there are a great many sub-cases of not repenting, not being baptized, etc., how to fill in certain cells, once the bells and whistles are added, will be a complicated matter.) Faced with such a decision, and attaching all the bells and whistles developed in response to the other worries developed below, it still takes stronger evidence to have practically adequate belief that God does not exist than it does to have practically adequate belief that God exists, if there is pragmatic encroachment. Using the alternative set {believe God exists, believe atheism is true}, however, is easier to understand, so we will stick with that set-up in the sequel.

With those preliminaries in mind, consider what it would take to have a practically adequate belief in atheism: it would take certainty that atheism is true. Why? First, because the costs of error, the costs of falsely believing that atheism is true, are grave indeed: Infinite Baddies. In the calculation of the expected utility of believing that atheism is true, therefore, any chance that God exists is multiplied by an infinite positive value, and will therefore swamp the potential for getting the Significant Goodies that come with truly believing that atheism is true. Second, because you'll lose out on Infinite Goodies by not believing that God exists, if God does. Therefore, in the calculation of the expected utility of believing that God exists, any chance that God exists will be multiplied by an infinite value, and will swamp the potential for getting the Minimal Baddies that come with falsely believing that God exists. Which is to say, unless you are certain that atheism is true, the expected utility of believing that God exists is guaranteed to be greater than the expected utility of believing that atheism is true. Therefore, only certainty that atheism is true can be practically adequate. For the same reason, any non-zero credence that God exists is sufficient for a practically adequate epistemic position for God exists. No doubt one would be irrational for believing that God exists if one's evidence warranted a rational credence of only, say, 0.000001. But if one wound up believing with such slender evidential warrant, one's epistemic position would nonetheless be practically adequate.

If all that is right, our conclusion follows: if practical adequacy is a necessary condition for knowledge, then one needs better evidence to know that atheism is true than one needs to know that God exists. On this set-up, for one's epistemic position to be practically adequate with respect to the proposition that atheism is true, one's evidence must make it rational for one to be certain that atheism is true. On the other hand, one's evidence needn't warrant anything near to certainty that God exists in order for one's epistemic position that God exists to be practically adequate.

Two worries: first, you might think that infinite utilities are problematic, especially in decision-theoretic contexts; second, you might think our decision table is missing columns. As will emerge, these worries warrant mild revisions in the conditional we're defending, but none will impact the fundamental point.

Before getting to those worries, we want to comment on the connection between our claim and Pascal's Wager. We're doing this because, given that we're appealing to Pascal's Wager, it's natural to think that all the problems for Pascal's Wager, of which there are legion, will be a problem for our thesis. This connection might be thought to be supported by the fact that the two worries we claim we'll deal with are equally worries for Pascal's Wager. But it's false that any problem for Pascal's Wager is a problem for our claim. In order to see this, it's helpful to consider (roughly) what the conclusion of Pascal's Wager is, and how it purports to secure this conclusion. The conclusion: one ought to believe in God, or at least set about doing things that will bring about such belief. The path to this conclusion: belief in God is practically rational, and if something is practically rational then one ought to believe it. Notice that our thesis says nothing about what one ought to believe about God, so if Pascal's Wager fails on account of its conclusion this spells no trouble for our thesis. Second, the consequent of our thesis doesn't entail that belief in God is practically rational—it only entails that it is *easier* for belief in God to be practically rational than it is for belief in atheism to be practically rational. Our claim is, for these two reasons, weaker than Pascal's Wager. So the problems for Pascal's Wager that have to do with these two points are not problems for our claim. We will, therefore, focus only on problems for Pascal's Wager that have to do with setting up the decision table. This is where the respective problem classes overlap.

First Worry: Infinite Utilities are Problematic. In the literature on Pascal's Wager, one finds arguments to the effect that invoking infinite utilities in the set-up of the Wager is problematic.[13] And in the literature on decision theory, one finds arguments to the effect that invoking infinite utilities are problematic in every decision-theoretic context.[14] We think it's right that infinite utilities are problematic. Thus, we need to rewrite the table. We might do it like this:

	God exists	atheism is true
believe God exists	Super-Great Goodies	Minimal Baddies
believe atheism is true	Super-Terrible Baddies	Significant Goodies

Even set up this way, it is still the case that one needs better evidence to know that atheism is true than one needs to know that God exists. This is the case because one still needs better evidence to have a practically adequate epistemic position with respect to the proposition that atheism is true than one does to have a practically adequate epistemic position with respect to the proposition that God exists. The reason is similar to that given above, only that certainty is no longer required in order to be in a practically adequate epistemic position with respect to the proposition that atheism is true.

To be fair, the move away from infinite utilities exposes a gap in the argument, but one that can be filled with independently plausible premises. Here is the gap. Suppose one thought, independently of pragmatic encroachment, that there was a "floor" rational credence for knowledge: a rational credence such that, no matter what is going on in one's practical situation, one must have evidence sufficient to warrant a credence above the floor for one to be in a position to know. It is possible, if there is such a floor, that the rational credence required for a practically adequate epistemic position to be below the floor for certain propositions. In such cases, it might still be that the strength of evidence required for a practically adequate epistemic position might be asymmetric. And if

---

[13] Cf. Jeffrey (1983) and McClennen (1994).

[14] Infinite utilities are in conflict with the continuity axiom, an axiom that is normally taken as part of basic decision theory, and thus it's common for decision theorists to deny that there are infinite utilities. Furthermore, denying that there are infinite utilities offers an attractive resolution of the St Petersburg paradox. Lastly, even if there are infinite utilities it's implausible that finite humans are the sort of beings that could ever secure them, so infinite utilities should be effectively ignored for human decision problems. Thus, there are some general reasons to doubt that there are infinite utilities, at all, or at least for humans.

that is so, then the fact that one needs better evidence to be in a practically adequate epistemic position with respect to one proposition than one needs to be in a practically adequate epistemic position with respect to another proposition *does not* entail that one needs better evidence to be in a position to know the former than one needs to be in a position to know the latter. Let's run through a toy example. Say the knowledge floor is 0.8, and consider again our friend Smith, considering whether to bet that the ship is seaworthy, but with the following slightly modified decision table:[15]

	ship is seaworthy	ship is not seaworthy
bet on ship is seaworthy	+10	−5
bet on ship is not seaworthy	−5	+5

In this case, for Smith to be in a practically adequate epistemic position with respect to the ship's being seaworthy, C(seaworthy) > 0.4. On the other hand, for Smith to be in a practically adequate epistemic position with respect to the ship's not being seaworthy, C(not seaworthy) > 0.6. In this case, better evidence is required for Smith to be in a practically adequate epistemic position with respect to the ship's being seaworthy than is required for him to be in a practically adequate epistemic position with respect to the ship's not being seaworthy. But, we are assuming, the floor rational credence needed for knowledge is 0.8. Therefore, if Smith is to be in a position to know either of these propositions, he needs a rational credence of 0.8. If he had that, he would be guaranteed to have a practically adequate epistemic position. The practical adequacy constraint, in such a case, adds no further demand. Therefore, it is true that one needs better evidence for practical adequacy in such a case, but not better evidence to be in a position to know.

We can fill this gap in the case with which we're concerned. The filling comes in two stages. First, the decision table involved with the Wager can be filled in with fairly modest values and still exact a heavy price with respect to the demands it places on being in a practically adequate epistemic

---

[15] We invite the reader to fill in the details of the story in order to make the utilities come out this way.

position with respect to the proposition that theism is false. For example, consider this set-up:

	God exists	atheism is true
believe God exists	+500	−5
believe atheism is true	−200	+50

Here, the assumptions are that it's ten times as good to get an eternal heavenly life than it is to live a finite atheistic life in conformity to the atheistic truth, that it's two and half times as good to go to heaven as it is bad to go to hell, and that it's ten times better to live a finite atheistic life in conformity to the atheistic truth than it is to live a finite theistic life and be wrong that theism is true. This seems to stack the deck *against* the practical rationality of believing God exists. Nonetheless, in such a case, C(atheism) > 0.93 in order to have a practically adequate epistemic position with respect to atheism's truth. (One gets this by using an inequality similar to the one we used for the case of the sea captain in section 2.) If one were to fuss with the ratios noted above in order to make them more favorable to believing God exists, then the rational credence needed for practical adequacy goes even higher. For example, suppose one changed the top left box to +5,000, which would be to insist that, for example, an eternal heavenly life is but 100 times better than a finite atheistic life lived in conformity to the atheistic truth, then practical adequacy for atheism's truth requires C(atheism) > 0.99, which is well-nigh certainty. In our view, that is still a conservative set-up. It can only get harder to have a practically adequate epistemic position that atheism is true.

Now for the second stage in the gap-filling process. It is plausible that the floor rational credence required for knowledge will be lower than what it takes to have a practically adequate epistemic position with respect to the proposition that atheism is true. For there seem to be a number of propositions that we know for which there is nowhere near certainty. Consider, for example, Smith's knowledge that the ship is seaworthy. The floor there seems fairly easy to reach, evidentially speaking. Further, pragmatic encroachers, if they want their pragmatic encroachment to actually matter, ought to go in for a fairly low floor. For the higher the floor, the less space there is for practical adequacy to be a serious necessary condition on knowledge. The closer to certainty the floor becomes, the more the practical adequacy condition becomes trivial. Now, we take no stand on what, exactly, a plausible floor is. Again, though, even with the conservative set-ups above, the demands for being in a practically adequate epistemic position with respect to the proposition that atheism is true are *very* high, higher we think than a plausible floor credence for knowledge.

Some still might object that heaven is simply not only not better than this-worldly goodies, but would actually be a bad thing, were one to get in. If heaven turns out to be more baddies than goodies, then it is clear that our conditional is false. But we don't think this is right. It may be that this objection assumes that one couldn't be wrong about what is good for one. On the classical Christian conception, after all, heaven is meant to be the best possible life, lived for eternity. Whatever that best life is, that sounds pretty great. And no matter what one's theory of the good life is, so long as it doesn't beg the question against heaven being good, we can simply stipulate that in heaven one has that sort of life for a really, really long time. So, whatever makes for this-worldly goodies, in heaven, either you'll just have more of those goodies for longer, or you'll get even better goodies for longer. Either way, getting heaven is getting Super-Great Goodies.

Second Worry: The Decision Table is Missing Columns. You might think that it's not so obvious that one is guaranteed minimal baddies by believing falsely that God exists. For example, maybe Islam is true. Or maybe there's a Deviant Deity (hence, DD), a deity that punishes believers to the exact extent that the classical God punishes non-believers and rewards non-believers to the exact extent that a classical God rewards believers. These possibilities force us to add columns to our decision table, and correspondingly alter the expected utility calculations. We'll first dwell on the DD case in detail, then the Islam case, and then we'll say something more general.

Adding the DD possibility, the decision table might look like so:

	God exists	atheism is true	a Deviant Deity exists
believe God exists	+500	−5	−200
believe atheism is true	−200	+50	+500

To see the impact that this added column has on our thesis, let's suppose $C(God) = C(DD) = 0.1$; thus, $C(atheism) = 0.8$. Accordingly, EU(believe God) = 26, while EU(believe atheism) = 34. The rankings of actions on these credences is, therefore:

1. Believe that atheism is true
2. Believe that God exists

Indeed, given that conditional on atheism, EU(believe God) < EU(believe atheism)—that is, given that the value in the first row-second column cell is less than the value in the second row-second column cell—whenever C(God) = C(DD), one's actual rankings of these actions will be the same as one's rankings of these actions conditional on God's not existing, unless C(atheism) = 0. Putting this together, if C(God) = C(DD), then one's strength of epistemic position for the proposition that atheism is true is almost trivially practically adequate. All one needs is C(atheism) > 0.

However, things change quickly if C(God) > C(DD). For example, suppose C(God) = 0.14 and C(DD) = 0.06; C(atheism) = 0.8 in this case as well. Then EU(believe God) = 54, while EU(believe atheism) = 42. When C(God) is greater than C(DD) by this small margin, EU(believe God) > EU(believe atheism). Thus, when the credences are fixed in this way, C(atheism) = 0.8 is *not* practically adequate. Also, when the rational credences are fixed in this way, C(God) = 0.14 *is* practically adequate for God's existence. Thus, if one's credences were the same as those in the above example, then the smallest rational credence that makes the proposition that God doesn't exist practically adequate is much higher than the smallest rational credence that makes the proposition that God exists practically adequate.[16]

It is here we stick our necks out a little: evidence that God exists is stronger, indeed we think it's quite a bit stronger, than the evidence that a DD exists. Why think this? The only reason to think that a DD exists is that it's not metaphysically impossible for a DD to exist. While God's existence is also not metaphysically impossible, there are many other reasons to think that God exists: historical reasons, empirical reasons, a priori reasons, and so on. This is not the place to inventory these reasons in detail, but we find that they make the probability that God exists significantly higher than the probability that a DD exists, and that this difference is significant enough to make the practical adequacy constraint non-trivial for the atheist. We doubt we're alone in this evaluation. Accordingly, a DD poses no threat to our thesis, even if the probability that God exists and the probability that a DD exists are both very low.

You might think the foregoing argument is too fast, that indeed there is as much evidence to think that a DD exists as there is reason to think that God exists. In fact, you might think that every bit of evidence there is for God's existence is equally good evidence for a DD, since a DD is the kind

---

[16] More generally, with the decision table set up this way, if C(God exists) = 2(C(DD exists)), then practically adequate atheistic belief requires C(atheism is true) > 0.81; and if C(God) = 3(C(DD)), then practical adequacy requires C(atheism) > 0.86. Practically adequate belief in God comes at much smaller credences. See below for insights into how we calculated these values.

of God that would set things up to make people think God exists. Insofar as one takes there to be evidence for God, then, one must also think there is evidence for a DD. This is not so. Here is an analogy: suppose one is married. If the foregoing were true, then every bit of evidence that one has a non-temporally gappy spouse is equally good evidence that one has a spouse who ceases to exist whenever asleep, to be replaced by a robot simulacra that behaves just like a non-temporally gappy spouse would behave when sleeping. But that is crazy. The evidence you have does not equally support these two theories. And it is clear which theory the evidence supports. The general idea is this: if you think that any evidence you have for God's existence is equally evidence for the existence of a DD, then you're a skeptic. If skepticism is true, then this paper is unsuccessful. But this, of course, is a problem for everyone who isn't a skeptic.[17]

Matters are different when it comes to more serious alternatives to God's existence than a DD. For example, Islam, universalist versions of Christianity, and so on pose a more serious challenge. Let's consider the Islam case. We'll need another row in our decision table, since unlike with a DD, believing that the God of Christianity (hereafter, 'C-God') does not exist is not enough to guarantee the goodies or the baddies if Islam is true.[18] Assuming the same utilities as before, and assuming that the heavenly goodies and hellish baddies for Islam and Christianity are equivalent in magnitude, the decision table looks like this:

	C-God exists	atheism is true	I-God exists
believe C-God exists	+500	−5	−200
believe atheism is true	−200	+50	−200
believe I-God exists	−200	−5	+500

In such a set-up, things are much worse for the atheist if $C(\text{C-God}) = C(\text{I-God})$, compared to the DD case. In the DD case, we noted that any non-zero credence in the truth of atheism was sufficient for practical adequacy so long as $C(\text{C-God}) = C(\text{DD})$. When $C(\text{C-God}) = C(\text{I-God})$, the minimally strong epistemic position needed for practically adequate atheistic belief is $C(\text{atheism}) > 0.86$. Here's how we get that value. What we need is the smallest value of $C(\text{atheism})$ such that EU(believe atheism) > EU(believe

---

[17] Thanks to David Sosa for conversation here.
[18] We use 'believe I-God exists' rather than 'keep the five pillars' or some such. Compare the discussion at the beginning of section 3.

I-God) and EU(believe atheism) > EU(believe C-God). Let x = C(I-God) + C(C-God) = 2(C(I-God)) = 2(C(C-God)). Then C(atheism) = 1 − x. On the above table, we can now see that EU(believe atheism) = $(x/2)(-200)$ + $(1 - x)(+50)$ + $(x/2)(-200)$ = 50 − 250x. EU(believe I-God) = EU(believe C-God) = $(x/2)(+500)$ + $(1 - x)(-5)$ + $(x/2)(-200)$ = 145x − 5. So, for practically adequate atheistic belief, one must determine the value of x in 50 − 250x > 145x − 5; this yields x < 55/395, or (roughly) x < 0.14. Since C(atheism) = 1 − x, practically adequate atheistic belief requires C(atheism is true) > 0.86.

Another case: if C(C-God) = 2(C(I-God)), then the minimally strong epistemic position needed for practically adequate atheistic belief is C(atheism) > 0.895. The set-up is as in the previous paragraph, except that instead of $x/2$ in the expected utility calculations one must use 2$x/3$ for C(C-God) and $x/3$ for C(I-God). This is because, under the current assumption, x = C(I-God) + C(C-God) = C(I-God) + 2(C(I-God)) = 3(C(I-God)). Since EU(believe C-God) > EU(believe I-God) when C(C-God) > C(I-God), determine the needed value of x by solving for x in EU(believe atheism) > EU(believe C-God). Using the values from the above table, (roughly) one needs x < 0.105. Thus, practically adequate atheistic belief requires C(atheism) > 0.895. The situation when C(I-God) = 2(C(C-God)) is symmetrical to this one. In the limiting case, in which either C(I-God) or C(C-God) goes to zero while the other remains non-zero, the situation reduces to the original two-column table above. So the minimally strong epistemic position needed for practically adequate atheistic belief is C(atheism) > 0.93.[19] The most it can take, on the other hand, to have practically adequate belief that the C-God exists is C(C-God) > 0.5 because that is the most it takes to guarantee that EU(believe C-God) > EU(believe I-God). If C(C-God) > 0.5 then EU(believe C-God) > EU(believe atheism) no matter how much of one's non-C-God possibility space is occupied by atheism. That 0.5 number decreases as C(atheism) increases relative to

---

[19] These points together flag a problematic consequence of the practical adequacy version of pragmatic encroachment: sometimes, one can go from not knowing p to knowing p by getting evidence *against p*. For example, the atheist might come to satisfy the practical adequacy constraint, and thereby come to know that atheism is true, by getting some evidence that I-God exists. To see this, consider a subject S who has the following rational credences: C(atheism) = 0.9, C(C-God) = 0.1, and C(I-God) = 0. Since this is just a two-column case, S's 0.9 credence in atheism is under the 0.93 practical adequacy threshold, and is practically inadequate. Now suppose some evidence that leaves S with the following set of credences: C(atheism) = 0.88, C(C-God) = 0.6, and C(I-God) = 0.6. Now S is in a three-column case such that C(C-God) = C(I-God), and in such a case S's epistemic position with respect to atheism is practically adequate since S's credence in atheism is > 0.86. See Eaton and Pickavance (2015).

C(I-God). Putting all this together, so long as the floor rational credence required for knowledge is set fairly low, our conditional looks promising. Importantly, this is true as well when one formulates the conditional using 'I-God' rather than 'C-God'. The most it can take to have practically adequate belief that the I-God exists is C(I-God) > 0.5, and that number decreases as C(atheism) increases relative to C(C-God). The cases, so long as the heavenly goodies and hellish baddies are symmetrical, are equivalent.

The foregoing, as we hope we've made clear, assumes a particular way of filling out the decision tables associated with Pascal's Wager. And generalizing these points to different ways of filling out the decision table isn't so easy, since there are so many variables. However, we believe we have stacked the deck in favor of the atheist, and that can be revealed by making two observations. First, we've assumed a modest view of the magnitude of the heavenly goodies and hellish baddies relative to the magnitudes of the goodies and baddies of a this-worldly life. Moving to less modest such views makes it even more difficult to be in a position to know that atheism is true (other things being equal). Second, we've assumed a smallish gap between the heavenly goodies and hellish baddies. The smaller that gap, the less difficult it is to be in a position to know that atheism is true (other things being equal). Alternatively, the larger that gap, the more difficult it is to be in a position to know that atheism is true. We think a more realistic decision table will be less favorable to the atheist on both of these dimensions.

How things work out for our conditional will be a function of how, exactly, goodies and baddies are distributed, and how, exactly, the probability space is filled. Given the number of variables, there is little hope to say much that is both helpful and general in the context of a paper like this. At the end of the day, we leave it to individual readers to test our claim for their particular decision tables. However, three observations are in order, each contingent on the plausible assumption that there are no humanly achievable goodies greater than those of heaven and no humanly achievable baddies worse than those of hell. First, the most it can take to have practically adequate belief that C/I-God exists is C(C/I-God) > 0.5. And second, for the atheist to be in a practically adequate position with respect to the truth of atheism, either C(atheism) must be very high, well above 0.5, or one must take possibilities like a DD to be nearby as likely as the classical religions. We suspect such probability spaces are unusual.[20]

---

[20] If you disagree with us about whether there are infinite utilities, the worry about missing columns becomes much more difficult to deal with. We're very confident we can still respond to the problem posed by a DD if there are infinite utilities. We believe, though are less confident, that we can respond to the problem posed by other monotheistic religions. Since we believe infinite utilities are problematic, and since developing our

Thus concludes our defense of the claim that if there is pragmatic encroachment, then it is more difficult to be in a position to know that atheism is true than it is to be in a position to know that God exists. For this conditional to be true, there must be no infinite utilities, there must be a lowish "floor" rational credence for knowledge, and it must be rational to have a higher credence in a monotheistic God than in a Deviant Deity. These constraints are substantive, but they are very plausible, and can be motivated independently of a desire to defend this conditional. Infinite utilities lead to paradox. Fallibilists, especially pragmatic encroachers, should want a lowish floor rational credence. And thinking that one has as much evidence for a Deviant Deity as one does for a monotheistic God is at best tantamount to skepticism.

One final point. That this conditional is true is important. It is often assumed that theism is an extraordinary claim, and that extraordinary claims require extraordinary evidence; thus, one needs extraordinary evidence to know that a monotheistic God exists.[21] One sees this picture embodied in principles like Anthony Flew's (1976) "presumption of atheism". More recently, Stephen Law (2011) argues, on the basis of these kinds of claims about evidence, that one ought not believe that Jesus of Nazareth even existed. In a similar vein, Paul Kurtz (1986) writes that, "Extraordinary claims thus require extra degrees of evidence. Thus, before we can invoke miraculous or occult explanations that overturn well established laws and regularities of experience and nature, we would need very strong evidence" (p. 50).

It's plausible that Hume is expressing a similar thought in Section X, Of Miracles, in his *Enquiry Concerning Human Understanding*. He argues that whenever one is given the choice between two miraculous options, one rationally ought to believe in the lesser miracle. Thus, when someone tells you some mundane fact, you are faced with a choice: you can believe the mundane fact or you can believe that the testifier in question hasn't spoken truly. Mundane facts aren't at all miraculous. Someone ruining their credibility as a testifier by lying about a mundane fact is very unusual or quite miraculous. Thus, according to Hume's view, one should believe the mundane fact, and not that the testifier in question is lying (or that they have been lied to). When it comes to miraculous facts, however, much stronger testimony is required, that is, "no testimony is sufficient to establish a miracle, unless the

responses in decision theoretic contexts with infinite utilities would take a great deal of space, we will not discuss these matters here.

[21] The principle that extraordinary claims require extraordinary evidence is commonly associated with Carl Sagan.

testimony be of such a kind, that its falsehood would be more miraculous, than the fact, which it endeavors to establish" (EHU 10.13). Thus, greater testimonial evidence is required to establish a miraculous fact than is required to establish a mundane fact. Now suppose that the following is true: the monotheisms make loads of miraculous claims that are only supported by testimony, and that atheism makes no miraculous claims.[22] It follows from this and Hume's view that it takes much greater testimonial evidence to establish any of the monotheisms than it does to establish atheism.

What we have shown is that if the practical adequacy version of pragmatic encroachment is true, then the usual set-up has the situation exactly backwards. Atheism requires more extraordinary evidence than the monotheisms.

We take no stand here as to whether one ought affirm the antecedent or deny the consequent of the conditional we defend. Maybe it's the case that there's an asymmetry between what it takes to be in a position to know that atheism is true and what it takes to be in a position to know that God exists. But maybe pragmatic encroachment is false.[23]

REFERENCES

Anderson, Charity (2015). On the Intimate Relationship of Knowledge and Action. *Episteme*, 12.3, 343–53.

Anderson, Charity and John Hawthorne (forthcoming). Knowledge, Practical Adequacy, and Stakes. In Tamar Szabo Gendler and John Hawthorne (eds), *Oxford Studies in Epistemology*.

Benton, Matthew A. (forthcoming). Pragmatic Encroachment and Theistic Knowledge. In Matthew A. Benton, John Hawthorne, and Dani Rabinowitz (eds), *Knowledge, Belief, and God: New Insights in Religious Epistemology*. Oxford University Press.

DeRose, Keith (2009). *The Case for Contextualism: Knowledge, Skepticism, and Context*. New York: Oxford University Press.

---

[22] We don't think this is true, but this supposition makes it easier to draw out the contrast between Hume's view and ours.

[23] We delivered an ancestor of this paper at the EPS Annual Meeting in November 2012 and defended an ancestor of this paper at the New Insights and Directions in Religious Epistemology Workshop on Religious Epistemology, Contextualism, and Pragmatic Encroachment, at Oxford University, in March 2013, funded by the John Templeton Foundation. Thanks to helpful audiences at those events, and especially Jeff Russell (who delivered exceedingly helpful comments on the paper at Oxford), Charity Anderson, Matthew Benton, Jeremy Fantl, Sandy Goldberg, John Hawthorne, Matt McGrath, and Michael Pace. Thanks as well to Josh Dever, Sinan Dogramaci, Miriam Schoenfield, and David Sosa.

Eaton, Daniel and Timothy Pickavance (2015). Evidence against Pragmatic Encroachment. *Philosophical Studies*, 172.12, 3135–43.

Fantl, Jeremy and Matthew McGrath (2002). Evidence, Pragmatics, and Justification. *Philosophical Review*, 111.1, 67–94.

Fantl, Jeremy and Matthew McGrath (2009). *Knowledge in an Uncertain World.* Oxford: Oxford University Press.

Fantl, Jeremy and Matthew McGrath (ms.). On Two Ultimately Unsuccessful Objections to Pragmatic Encroachment.

Flew, Anthony (1976). *The Presumption of Atheism and Other Philosophical Essays on God, Freedom, and Immortality.* New York: Barnes & Noble.

Hawthorne, John (2004). *Knowledge and Lotteries.* New York: Oxford University Press.

Hawthorne, John and Jason Stanley (2008). Knowledge and Action. *Journal of Philosophy*, 105.10, 571–90.

Hume, David (1748). *An Enquiry concerning Human Understanding*, edited by Tom L. Beauchamp. Oxford: Oxford University Press, 1999.

Jeffrey, Richard (1983). *The Logic of Decision*, 2nd edn. Chicago: University of Chicago Press.

Kurtz, Paul (1986). *The Transcendental Temptation: A Critique of Religion and the Paranormal.* Buffalo, NY: Prometheus Books.

Kvanvig, Jonathan (2011). Against Pragmatic Encroachment. *Logos & Episteme*, 2.1, 77–85.

Law, Stephen (2011). Evidence, Miracles and the Existence of Jesus. *Faith and Philosophy*, 28.2, 129–51.

McClennen, Edward (1994). Pascal's Wager and Finite Decision Theory, in Jeff Jordan (ed.), *Gambling on God: Essays on Pascal's Wager.* Lanham, MD: Rowman and Littlefield.

Peterson, Martin (2009). *An Introduction to Decision Theory.* Cambridge: Cambridge University Press.

Ross, Jacob and Mark Schroeder (2014). Belief, Credence, and Pragmatic Encroachment. *Philosophy and Phenomenological Research*, 88.2, 259–88.

Schroeder, Mark (2012). Stakes, Withholding, and Pragmatic Encroachment on Knowledge. *Philosophical Studies*, 160.2, 265–85.

Stanley, Jason (2005). *Knowledge and Practical Interests.* Oxford: Oxford University Press.

Weatherson, Brian (2005). Can We Do Without Pragmatic Encroachment? *Philosophical Perspectives*, 19.1, 417–43.

Weatherson, Brian (2011). Defending Interest-Relative Invariantism. *Logos & Episteme*, 2.4, 591–609.

Williamson, Timothy (2000). *Knowledge and Its Limits.* Oxford: Oxford University Press.

Williamson, Timothy (2005). Contextualism, Subject-Sensitive Invariantism, and Knowledge of Knowledge. *Philosophical Quarterly*, 55.219, 213–35.

6

Incarnation: The Avatar Model

William Hasker

The Christian faith affirms that Jesus of Nazareth was fully God and also fully human. The classical definition of the Incarnation was given at the council of Chalcedon in AD 451, and has remained the standard for Christological orthodoxy ever since. It is widely acknowledged, however, that the Chalcedonian definition does not explain how the Incarnation took place; rather, it established parameters within which an acceptable explanation must fall. According to historian Frances M. Young, "in the West, Chalcedon has proved less a solution than the classic definition of a problem which constantly demands further elucidation."[1] This further elucidation has taken the form of a rather large number of different theories and models, most of them claiming (successfully or not) to be developments along the lines laid down at Chalcedon. The main purpose of this essay is to present another such model, the Avatar Model, which I claim helps us to make sense of some of the claims involved in Chalcedonian Christology. The avatars on which the model is based are not, as one might suppose, the manifestations of the gods and goddesses of Hinduism (as, for example, Krishna in the *Bhagavad Gita* is an avatar of Vishnu). Rather, the avatars in question here are a principal feature of the science-fiction movie *Avatar*. Before we come to that, however, it is necessary to set out briefly the main theological problem on which the Avatar Model may shed some light. After that, we will consider some proposed solutions to that problem, solutions which I will argue are not satisfactory. This is followed by a presentation of the Avatar Model, and a final section will assess the merits of the model.

---

[1] Frances M. Young, *From Nicaea to Chalcedon: A Guide to the Literature and Its Background*, 2nd edn (Grand Rapids, MI: Baker, 2010), p. 241.

PROBLEM: THE MIND OF THE INCARNATE SON

According to the Chalcedonian formula, Jesus Christ was a single person (*hypostasis* or *prosopon*) who possessed both the divine nature (*physis*) and a complete human nature. As is well known, this raises a number of difficult metaphysical questions Most of these questions will not be discussed here; the Avatar Model is not intended as a solution to the metaphysical problems of the Incarnation. The doctrine also, however, raises what may be termed a psychological question—the question about the mind of the incarnate Son. Persons, we believe, have mental states, but what sorts of mental states should be attributed to this person? We know well enough, in general terms, what sorts of mental states occur in the life of a normal human person. Perhaps we do not know securely, yet we have pretty firm convictions, about some of the sorts of mental states that must occur in the life of a divine person. But the thought of combining both of these in the mental life of a single individual may well boggle the mind. To take only an obvious example, a divine person must be omniscient—such a person knows everything there is to know—whereas human persons are notoriously non-omniscient. But how could a single person be both? So we have a problem.

What may be a pointer towards resolution of this problem comes in the decree of the Sixth Ecumenical Council, which met in Constantinople in AD 680–1. The decree of this council reads in part,

We likewise declare that in him are two natural wills (*dyo physikas theleseis*) and two natural operations (*dyo physikas energeias*), according to the teaching of the holy Fathers. And these two natural wills are not contrary one to the other...but his human will follows and that not as resisting and reluctant, but rather as subject to his divine and omnipotent will.[2]

This council has been less widely commented on than Chalcedon, but its conclusion has traditionally been accepted as a correct interpretation of the Chalcedonian doctrine.[3] In Christ, it says, there are "two natural operations," which seems to say that each of the two natures does pretty much the same sorts of things it would be doing in, on the one hand, a non-incarnate

---

[2] See Henry R. Percival, *The Seven Ecumenical Councils of the Undivided Church: Their Canons and Dogmatic Decrees* (New York: Edwin S. Gorham, 1901), p. 341.

[3] Oliver D. Crisp points out that, even though Protestants may not regard the Sixth Ecumenical Council as authoritative, "Almost all orthodox Protestant theologians have affirmed dyothelitism" (*Divinity and Humanity: The Incarnation Reconsidered* (Cambridge: Cambridge University Press, 2007), p. 61 n. 36; see also p. 49 n. 23). He cites a number of examples in support of this claim; the only exception noted is the Baptist theologian A. H. Strong.

divine person, and on the other hand, an ordinary human individual. This includes, strikingly, the presence of two "wills" in Christ, though the statement is quick to add that the two wills do not—and, I am sure its authors would add, *could* not—conflict, in such a way that the divine will is doing one thing whereas the human will is doing, or attempting to do, something contrary to what the divine will is doing. No doubt we should take the statement to be saying that all the natural operations in the human mind that lead to and culminate in an act of will—that is, a decision to do something—are operative in the mind of Christ, as are also the natural operations in the divine mind that lead to and culminate in an act of the divine will.

So there is, on this view, a natural operation of the human mind in Christ, and also a natural operation of his divine mind. For the same sorts of reasons already alluded to, it is difficult to suppose that these two operations are parts of the very same conscious state. (The sorts of considerations that might lead to a divine decision to perform a particular action surely must include matters that are not part of any human thought-process and could not be contained in any human mind.) So it seems that this council is pointing us strongly in the direction of what has been termed a "two minds" Christology, a view in which there is in Christ both a complete, and self-contained, set of human mental states—a human "sphere of consciousness"—and also a complete, and self-contained, set of divine mental states, a divine sphere of consciousness. It must be added that the human mental states are *accessible to* the divine sphere of consciousness, in the sense that the divine mind is fully aware of them, whereas the reverse situation does not, and indeed could not, obtain.[4] (There will be many things in the divine sphere of consciousness that could not possibly be contained in a human mind.) A two-minds Christology has been championed recently by Thomas Morris, among others, but it is plausible to assert that something of this sort has, in fact, been the mainstream interpretation of Chalcedonian Christology and therefore of Christian orthodoxy.

At this point, however, the specter of Nestorianism raises its head. If there are in Christ two complete minds, each equipped with the full complement of faculties, how is this different from saying that there are two *persons*,

---

[4] Note that it is not asserted that the personal identity between the eternal Son/Logos and the man Jesus *consists in* the asymmetric accessibility of the human mental states to the divine mind. Presumably, a similar asymmetric accessibility occurs in the case of each and every created mind. (Thomas Morris agrees: "The accessing relationship itself does not alone constitute ownership" (*The Logic of God Incarnate* (Ithaca, NY: Cornell University Press, 1986), p. 159).) What the personal identity in question does consist in is a metaphysical question which is not pursued in this essay.

which of course amounts to the heresy of Nestorianism? If in fact the fathers at Constantinople committed themselves to a two-minds Christology, must we not say that they simply had not thought the matter through sufficiently? The point is nicely (and carefully) stated by Joseph Jedwab:

Suppose the Son has not only two systems of powers, beliefs, and desires, but also, and associated with such systems, two conscious spheres and so two conscious perspectives on the world. Then the Son, though strictly speaking one person, is otherwise just like two persons.[5]

He then cites a thought experiment of Derek Parfit, in which a person has a divided conscious life as a result of a device which makes it possible to interrupt at will the connections between the two hemispheres of the brain. If this were true of one, Jedwab says,

though I am one person, having two spheres at once is otherwise just like being two persons at once. And so again if the Son has two spheres at once, though he is one person, he is otherwise just like two persons at once. Strictly speaking, there's only one person here and so, strictly speaking, Nestorianism doesn't hold. But, since the Son is just like two persons, it is appropriate to say that the Son is two persons and so it is appropriate to say that Nestorianism holds. And this is a worry for the Two-Spheres view.[6]

Jedwab is being careful here. He doesn't say outright that the Two-Spheres view is Nestorian: "strictly speaking Nestorianism doesn't hold." But this seems to be a difference that makes no difference, and at best the Two-Spheres view is close enough to Nestorianism that it ought to worry us. And that is surely enough motivation to cause us to look long and hard at a One-Sphere view.[7]

SOME ONE-SPHERE VIEWS

Following up on this, Jedwab proceeds to consider some One-Sphere views. He rejects the Divine-Sphere View, on which "the Son has one sphere typical

---

[5] Joseph Jedwab, "The incarnation and unity of consciousness," in Anna Marmodoro and Jonathan Hill, eds, *The Metaphysics of the Incarnation* (Oxford: Oxford University Press, 2011), pp. 168–85; p. 179. My thanks to Joseph Jedwab for clarifying through e-mail correspondence some matters concerning his view that I had failed to grasp in reading his article.

[6] Jedwab, "The incarnation", p. 180.

[7] Interestingly, Jedwab states in correspondence: "my main motivation in developing the One-Sphere view was to provide an account of the incarnation for those that think that any person can only ever have one sphere. By the way, this does not include me."

of a default divine conscious life." If this were the case, the Son would not be taking on our humanity in the right way. Nor can we accept the Human-Sphere View, on which "the Son has only one sphere typical of a human conscious life in our present condition." In this case, the Son "lacks those conscious states that are necessary to be divine." For a promising solution, Jedwab thinks we must look to a Divine-Human-Sphere View, on which "the Son has one sphere of consciousness, one part of which is, in itself, typical of a human conscious life in our present condition, and the other part of which is, in itself, as typical of a default divine conscious life as being a human in our present condition allows."[8] So we need to see what this amounts to.

The overall strategy of Jedwab's Divine-Human-Sphere View is to ascribe to the Son those conscious states that are essential to being divine, but to understand those states in a way that as much as possible avoids disrupting what is otherwise a normal human mental life. It is assumed that divine knowledge as possessed by the Son does not in itself involve phenomenal consciousness—just as, for us, at any given moment most of the things we know are not consciously entertained, and involve no phenomenal consciousness. The same cannot, however, be true of every divine mental state; in particular, divine intentional actions must of necessity involve phenomenal consciousness. "Every divine subject, being divine, sustains the world, which involves a conscious state. Moreover the Son, being the divine person he is, has a role in spirating the Spirit, which again involves a conscious state."[9] These conscious states, then, must be a part of the phenomenal consciousness of a divine-human person. Jedwab argues, however, that such states need not be introspected; he supports this by the example of human intentional acts that are not introspected, such as the activity of a long-distance driver who performs all the normal driving functions without being introspectively aware of what they are doing. He invites us to "suppose that, when the Son becomes incarnate, he doesn't introspect any divine mental state he has. The Son, being human, introspects some human mental states he has. And before the resurrection he only ever introspects human mental states. So from the inside, his mental life looks very much like that of an ordinary human. The introspective light shines on his mental life. But the light reveals only the human parts."[10] The Son's mental life, then, will be *introspectively equivalent* to that of an ordinary human being. It will not,

---

[8] Jedwab, "The incarnation", p. 182.   [9] Jedwab, "The incarnation", p. 182.

[10] Quoted from correspondence. Jedwab also states, "But actually, this is only one option, though the favoured option. I allow that the Son always introspects every mental state he has, but that there are degrees of introspection and the Son introspects divine states to the lowest degree possible" (for this, see Jedwab, "The incarnation", p. 183).

however, be *phenomenally equivalent* to that of an ordinary human, because the Son's phenomenal experience will of necessity include the divine intentional acts: sustaining the world, spirating the Spirit, and any other acts the Son may perform. Nevertheless, Jedwab thinks this does enable the Son's mental life to resemble our own sufficiently that he "takes on our humanity in the right way."

This proposal, it seems to me, suffers from multiple serious difficulties. First of all, why should we suppose that divine knowledge-states are not conscious? It's true, of course, that at any given moment we humans are not conscious of most of the things we know. This is necessary because of our limited capacity for attention, not to mention the limited processing capacity of our brains. But such limitations would not apply to a divine person, and I should think that the more common view has been that a divine person is always consciously aware of all the things that he knows. And doesn't omnipotence imply that one is able to introspect one's own mental states (though perhaps one might choose not to do so)? But even if his "standing beliefs" are not conscious, it seems harder to apply this to the new knowledge a temporal divine person (and Jedwab does assume that God is temporal) is constantly acquiring—knowledge, for example about "what is happening right now," where the referent of 'now' is of course constantly changing. In most ordinary situations in which a person acquires a new belief or a new piece of knowledge through experience, that person is consciously aware of the experience through which the belief is acquired.

But suppose Jedwab is right about all this. Consider next the divine intentional actions which do, according to the model, occur in the Son's awareness, but are never introspected. Why are they not introspected? Is the Son *unable* to introspect this aspect of his consciousness? That would be a pretty remarkable limitation in the Son's ability to introspect, something that would seem to call for further explanation, which is not provided. (Taking this line would seem to push Jedwab in the direction of a full-fledged kenotic view.) Or is it that the Son *deliberately refrains* from introspecting these phenomenal states? So that the Son is saying, in effect, "I know that I have all these divine phenomenal states in addition to my human states, but I will refrain from introspecting those divine states, because doing so would make my mental life too different from that of ordinary human beings." I submit that anyone who would entertain a thought like that would already be in a mental state vastly different from that of a normal (and sane) human being!

But finally, suppose we waive all these objections, and assume that in all of these respects things do occur in the way supposed by the Divine-Human-Sphere View. There still remains the phenomenal consciousness, in the Son's mind, of whatever is involved in the divine actions of sustaining the world, spirating the Holy Spirit, and whatever else the Son is doing in the universe. Since these acts involve phenomenal consciousness (though they are not introspected), there is "something it is like" to do them. I submit, however, that we humans have no resources even to begin to imagine what it is like to sustain the world in existence, or to spirate the Holy Spirit. One implication of the view must surely be that the Son can never under any circumstances entirely lose consciousness. Whether he is in the deepest sleep, or a drug-induced coma, or is the victim of a blow on the head, the actions of sustaining the world and spirating the Spirit must go on, and so therefore must the Son's phenomenal consciousness consequent upon these actions. Readers are invited to fill out the picture for themselves, to the extent that they feel able and willing to do so. It seems to me, however, that a being in a conscious state such as this would be enormously different from all normal human beings.[11] Perhaps we shall be told that his sphere of consciousness is as close to ours as it can be, given that it is also a divine sphere of consciousness. If so, some of us will be disposed to reply, "Maybe so, but that is not nearly close enough."

A view concerning Christ's consciousness that could be seen as addressing some of the difficulties with Jedwab's proposal has been suggested by William Lane Craig and J. P. Moreland.[12] Their view is also a One-Sphere View, and indeed a Divine-Human-Sphere View, though not labeled by them as such. The most obvious difference between their view and Jedwab's is that they do not postulate, as he does, actual phenomenal consciousness of such actions as the Son's sustaining the world,[13] though they would agree that the Son performs this action throughout the time of his Incarnation. The core of their proposal is stated as follows:

We postulate that the divine aspects of Jesus' personality were largely subliminal during his state of humiliation. We suggest that what William James called the "subliminal self" is the primary locus of the superhuman elements in the consciousness of

---

[11] Jedwab states in correspondence, "I agree the Son's total phenomenal sphere is radically different from that of an ordinary human. The human part, however, of the Son's total phenomenal sphere is not radically different from that of an ordinary human." Quite so; we must of course remember that both parts together constitute a *single* experiential state of the Son.

[12] J. P. Moreland and William Lane Craig, *Philosophical Foundations for A Christian Worldview* (Downers Grove, IL: InterVarsity Press, 2003), pp. 597–614. Of course their proposal was not intended as a response to Jedwab, since it was published several years earlier.

[13] The action of spirating the Holy Spirit is not mentioned here, because Craig and Moreland reject the doctrines of the eternal generation of the Son and the procession of the Spirit. See Moreland and Craig, *Philosophical Foundations*, p. 594.

the incarnate Logos. Thus Jesus possessed a normal human conscious experience. But the human consciousness of Jesus was underlain, as it were, by a divine subconsciousness.[14]

By relegating the divine attributes to the subconscious, Jesus' conscious experience is allowed to be genuinely human and limited. We may question, however, whether the concept of the subliminal can do the work that is required of it in their statement. What is subliminal is "beneath the limit" of human perception: a "subliminal message" is one that is either so faint or so fleeting that humans are unable to consciously register what is said, yet it is supposed that the content of the message (for instance, an advertising slogan that flickers momentarily on a motion picture screen) somehow registers on the mind and influences behavior, in spite of its never being consciously seen or understood. But one may ask, where exactly are the "limits of perception" for a divine person? Obviously the question is absurd: nothing can be so faint or so fleeting as to escape the notice of a divine person; for such a person the notion of the subliminal can have no application. In order to serve the purpose of this proposal, the divine elements in Jesus' life must be excluded from consciousness entirely.

But even that may not be enough. As Jedwab noted, at any given moment almost all of our knowledge is absent from consciousness. Much of it, however, can readily be brought to conscious awareness if we make the effort to do so. Is Jesus' divine omniscience like that? It must be that on various occasions during his life there were things he would have liked to know but in fact did not know. (One would scarcely make the effort of studying if this were not the case.) Was he then saying to himself, "I could know the truth about this easily, were I to access the divine knowledge which I possess. But I choose not to do this, because it would make my experience too unlike that of other human beings"? As was remarked in our discussion of Jedwab, a being who could (sanely) entertain such a thought is already vastly different from all other human beings. It seems, then, that in order to preserve the similarity of Jesus' experience to ours, his divine omniscience must be relegated to the "deep unconscious"; it must be such that, during his earthly life, he not only did not but could not access it. But then we may ask, what does it mean to say that a person "has knowledge" but is totally unable to access that knowledge? Certainly this is very different from knowledge as ordinarily understood. So it is beginning to seem that, during his earthly life, Jesus was not omniscient after all.[15] Yet Craig

---

[14] Moreland and Craig, *Philosophical Foundations*, p. 610 (italics in original).

[15] Joseph Jedwab suggests (in correspondence) a parallel with the situation in psychoanalysis, in which a person "knows" something, but is unable to access that knowledge

and Moreland are staunchly opposed to the idea that Christ at any time divested himself of any of the essential divine attributes, and they do count omniscience as such an attribute.

Problems also arise concerning particular divine actions (as opposed to continuing actions such as sustaining the world) that are performed during Christ's earthly life. One would certainly suppose that there were such actions (the Trinity does not become quiescent for a thirty-year period), and it follows from his omniscience that they would be part of his knowledge, though not, if the argument of the preceding paragraph is correct, of his *conscious* knowledge. But he would be unable to *concur* or to *cooperate* with the Father and the Holy Spirit in performing any such actions, for to do so is an act of will, and the Son does not possess any will other than the one which is in evidence in the human life of Jesus. Craig and Moreland explicitly affirm monothelitism, rejecting the doctrine affirmed at Constantinople in 681:

> The will of the Logos has in virtue of the Incarnation become the will of the man Jesus of Nazareth. This implication of our model is, in our view, one of its advantages, since it is extraordinarily difficult to preserve the unity of Christ's person once distinct wills are ascribed to the Logos and to the individual human nature of Christ.[16]

So during the earthly life of Jesus, the Father and the Spirit perform divine actions of which the Son has no conscious knowledge and in which he does not concur or cooperate. Pretty clearly, this requires us to reject the unity of operation of the trinitarian persons which is axiomatic for the traditional, orthodox doctrine of the Trinity.

By this time I trust that the general thrust of this critique has become clear. Both Jedwab and Moreland and Craig offer One-Sphere views, in which the characteristics of divine and human consciousness are united in a single realm of conscious activity and experience. The burden of the critique is that in order to preserve a sufficient similarity between Jesus' human experience and our own, the divine attributes must be obscured from consciousness in a way that calls his possession of those attributes in question, at least so far as his conscious life is concerned. We are pressed in the direction of a Human-Sphere View, which Jedwab rejects, or of a general kenotic view, which Craig and Moreland criticize severely. I cannot claim to have

---

without the help of a therapist. It seems to me that in such a situation, there is an ambiguity about whether the persons knows or does not know the matter in question. In any case, isn't it out of the question to suppose that divine omniscience is in need of such therapeutic assistance?

   [16] Moreland and Craig, *Philosophical Foundations*, p. 611.

demonstrated conclusively that no view of this general sort is possible, but I think enough has been done to show that there are very serious difficulties standing in the way of such an effort, difficulties which neither Jedwab nor Craig and Moreland have adequately addressed. But are the prospects for a Two-Sphere view any brighter? For that, we turn to the Avatar Model.

THE AVATAR MODEL

As has already been noted, the Avatar Model takes its departure from individuals who are characters in a science-fiction movie. It goes without saying that anyone making such a proposal opens themselves up to criticism. Many will insist that the model is inadequate and, moreover, inappropriate in taking its departure from such a source. On the other hand, fans of the movie may object to the considerable distance which will open up between the avatars deployed in the film and the final version of the model. In my opinion both objections have merit. My response is that any model for the Incarnation is going to be inadequate; it will fail to capture fully what is stated in the doctrine, and may well from some standpoint seem inappropriate. And on the other hand, any analogy that is chosen will need to be modified or supplemented in order to come as close as possible to mirroring the situation it is taken to represent. For the present I merely ask that the reader be willing to accompany me in a modest project of theological exploration.

The Na'vi, the dominant species on Pandora, are intelligent but at a neolithic stage of cultural development.[17] They are bipedal and in many respects human-like in appearance, but there are important physiological differences, and the Na'vi are larger and physically stronger than human beings. (They are also strikingly beautiful, an important adaptation for survival in the Hollywood environment.) Pandora is a moon of the gas giant planet Polyphemus, which in turn orbits the star Alpha Centauri A. An atmosphere which is toxic to humans, as well as other environmental problems, hinder human activity on Pandora. In order to overcome these problems, and to facilitate communication with the Na'vi, the avatar program was initiated. Each Na'vi avatar body is created in vitro and then brought to physical maturity in an amnio tank. Once mature, the avatar body is controlled by a human volunteer, using persona projection technology. While the human

---

[17] The general nature of the avatar project is evident to viewers of the movie, but the information given here is taken from *Pandorapedia: The Official Field Guide*, <www.pandorapedia.com>.

controller remains in a sleep-like state in a psionic link unit, his or her personality inhabits and completely controls the Na'vi body, and believes he or she is actually inhabiting the Na'vi body, with all senses, reflexes, and bodily functions fully operational. The avatar body has no personality of its own, and is inert (except for basic autonomous functions) when not under human control.[18]

Not especially promising, one might think, as an analogue for the Incarnation! But of course, some modifications are necessary, especially concerning the state of consciousness of the avatar and its human controller. In the movie version, the controller's consciousness inhabits the Na'vi body, and its present experiences are mediated through that body, but the background knowledge includes what is retained from previous human experience. To match the situation with the Incarnation more closely, we must imagine the relationship with the controller beginning at the instant at which the avatar body is first formed. The avatar will then grow from infancy in the Pandoran environment, no doubt with a pair of Na'vi as foster parents. In this way a suitable "depth knowledge" of the planet, and of Na'vi society, could be achieved. And on the other hand, in order for the avatar to fully experience life in the manner of the Na'vi, it is plausible that not all of the controller's background knowledge should be available to the avatar consciousness. No doubt suitable arrangements could be made to impart such knowledge as was essential: in particular, the consciousness in the Na'vi body must at some point become aware of the Na'vi's personal identity with the human controller, and of the purposes which are intended to be achieved through the avatar experience.

Yet further changes are called for. We will not want to leave the human controller's body in a "sleep-like state"; rather, the controller will have full awareness, residing in the controller's own body, of that body's surroundings and experiences, and will be able to carry on a generally normal human life at the same time as it inhabits the Na'vi body. This will of course require that the psionic link is miniaturized in such a way as to be portable, or even implantable, so as not to interfere with the controller's day-to-day activities. (Among other advantages, this will prevent the physical deterioration of the controller's body due to inactivity, which threatens to occur in the original version.) Finally, the controller's awareness will include within itself also an

---

[18] An interesting question underlying this account is, What assumptions are being made about the brain-mind relationship? Unfortunately, no information is provided on this topic. (It would be fascinating for us to learn what the philosophers of the future have concluded on the subject!) I will attempt to describe the situation in as neutral a way as possible, but the reader is cautioned against drawing conclusions from the model about the metaphysics of the Incarnation.

awareness of the experiences and actions in the Na'vi body; however, the consciousness residing in that body will not have awareness of the controller's surroundings and experiences. This gives us, then, an analogue for a Two-Sphere model of the Incarnation.

At this point, however, the model may be met with the objection that such a situation is impossible. Now, merely empirical impossibility (such as the non-availability of persona projection technology) can be brushed aside in a context such as this. Nor need we concern ourselves with the limitations of the human brain, which might not be up to the task of processing simultaneously both the experiences mediated through the Na'vi brain and body and also its own, properly human experiences. (Possibly some surgical augmentation of the controller's brain would be required.) However, some will find themselves strongly convinced of what Tim Bayne calls the "unity thesis," which is the claim that "a human being can have only a single stream of consciousness at any one point in time."[19] Indeed, some will wish to accord to the unity thesis the status of a necessary truth. Now, the Avatar Model, as modified above, clearly violates the unity thesis, so if that thesis is a necessary truth the model is impossible and is, presumably, of little or no value for illuminating the Incarnation.

The unity thesis does have an initial air of plausibility, and there is something to be said in its favor. I believe, however, that it is unwise to accord it the status of a necessary truth, and thus rule out the Avatar Model as impossible. My reason for saying this is that there is significant empirical evidence which seems to tell against the unity thesis, evidence arising from the well-known phenomena of "split-brain" research and multiple personality. (More will be said about this later.) It is inadvisable to attempt to resolve such empirical controversies by appealing to an alleged (but controversial) necessary truth. Suppose that, in the days when the possibility of "splitting the atom" was first being mooted, someone had insisted that by definition an atom (*atomos* in Greek) is indivisible, so that the idea of splitting an atom is a conceptual absurdity. The upshot of this would have been the realization that the concept of an atom as essentially indivisible simply does not apply to the "atoms" in the actual, physical world. We should avoid making the same sort of mistake in the present instance. Bayne himself, who defends the unity thesis, does not make this mistake: he states,

I do not claim that it is a conceptual or metaphysical truth that our conscious states are always unified; indeed, I do not even claim that the unity of consciousness is grounded in the laws of nature. Perhaps there are surgical innovations or evolutionary

---

[19] Tim Bayne, *The Unity of Consciousness* (Oxford: Oxford University Press, 2010), p. 3.

developments that could bring about a division in the stream of consciousness; perhaps there are other species in which the unity of consciousness can be lost. My only claim is that we have no good reason to think that any such division has actually occurred in the members of our own species.[20]

I am inclined to disagree with the last claim made here, and to assert that unity of consciousness is in fact lost by human beings under certain special circumstances. (A brief statement of the reasons for my disagreement may be found in the appendix to this article.) For the present, I merely observe that in his concessions about what could be true for another species, or even for surgically modified human beings, Bayne grants everything that is needed in order to affirm the conceptual coherence of the Avatar Model.

ASSESSING THE AVATAR MODEL

A model for the Incarnation serves two main purposes. First, it provides a relatively concrete and intuitively accessible way to imagine what is happening in the Incarnation, thus better enabling us to think about what the doctrine asserts. But second, it provides assistance in seeing the logical and metaphysical possibility, in some respect, of the doctrine, thus helping to deflect the charge that what the doctrine asserts cannot possibly be true. I submit that the Avatar Model scores well as an aid to the imagination; now we need to assess its success in supporting a judgment that Incarnation is possible.

It has already been indicated that the Avatar Model is not designed to elucidate the metaphysics of the Incarnation. Nevertheless, in certain limited respects it does seem to match up fairly well. This is a "concretist" model, according to which the divine and human "natures" are concrete property-instances or tropes, rather than abstract universals.[21] The Na'vi body and brain (and soul, if any is present)[22] correspond in the model to

---

[20] Bayne, *Unity of Consciousness*, p. 17.

[21] In *Metaphysics and the Tri-Personal God* (Oxford: Oxford University Press, 2013), pp. 62–7 and 226–37, I have argued that the common divine nature of the Trinitarian persons must be understood as concrete. If that is correct, then the parallel in terminology between Trinity and Incarnation (with respect to such terms as *ousia* and *physis*) should lead us to understand the two natures of the incarnate Son also as concrete. Oliver D. Crisp also argues for a concrete understanding of Christ's human nature as the best option for an orthodox Christology (see his *Divinity and Humanity*, ch. 2).

[22] It seems to me that it is really quite difficult to make sense of the metaphysics of the avatar project as portrayed in the film. In all likelihood it is not assumed that an immaterial soul is present either in the avatar or in the human controller; the "psionic link unit" does not seem to be the sort of thing that could transfer a soul from the human

the human nature of the Son; the human body and brain correspond (however inadequately) to the divine nature. The human person, the controller, may fairly be said to "assume," to take into union with himself or herself, the Na'vi body and brain, even as the Son assumes humanity. So far, the correspondence seems to be good, but taking the parallel any further may present difficulties.

The primary focus of the Avatar Model, however, is not metaphysical but psychological. And here the main problem that needs to be addressed is the charge of Nestorianism, the claim that there are two persons and not one. This should be no surprise. As we have seen, One-Sphere models of the Incarnation are largely motivated by the desire to avoid Nestorianism. We have concluded that Divine-Human Sphere models are unsuccessful: either they include too much of the divine for the resulting life to qualify as truly human, or they exclude too much for it to be genuinely divine. Accordingly, we revert to a Two-Sphere model, a model such as is implied by Constantinople 681 and arguably already by Chalcedon. But any Two-Sphere model must be prepared to confront the charge of Nestorianism.

Viewed in terms of the Avatar Model, Nestorianism would correspond to the charge that there are in the avatar situation two different persons: the person of the Na'vi avatar, and the person of the human controller. In the situation as initially described, such a charge would have little plausibility: "The avatar body has no personality of its own, and is inert (except for basic autonomous functions) when not under human control." Putting the matter in a more positive light, we may ask, "Are the thoughts, words, and actions performed by the avatar the thoughts, words, and actions of the human being who lives his or her life through the avatar?" Viewers of the movie will have no hesitation in answering Yes to that question; nor do we have any reason to disagree with that judgment.

How then do things change, as the original model is modified? It does not seem that the first step in the modification, in which the Na'vi body grows up from infancy in the Pandoran environment and has only limited access to the controller's background knowledge and memories, poses a major problem. It is still the human controller who thinks the thoughts, says the words, and performs the actions in the Na'vi "incarnation," although

---

body to the avatar body, and then instantly retrieve it when the controller regains consciousness in the human body. The technology seems better suited to communicate information from the controller to the avatar. But then, how is the reverse transfer supposed to take place? It would seem that the avatar body needs to have a transmission mechanism of its own, but nothing of the sort is provided. Once again, I must caution the reader against deriving from the model conclusions about the metaphysics of the Incarnation.

this is done without some of the knowledge the controller possesses in his or her own, properly human, existence. To be sure, some special measures might be required to make sure that the purposes and motivations of the avatar continue to be aligned with those for which the incarnation was originally devised. (In the movie, this was not adequately accomplished, despite the retention of background knowledge: Jake Sully "goes native," and becomes the leader of the Na'vi in their struggle against the human occupiers.) Nevertheless, it is still the human person who is the subject of all those thoughts, words, and actions.

But what about the second step in the modification, in which the controller is able to continue with a human life while at the same time living a Na'vi life?[23] Here, as we have already acknowledged, understandable questions arise about the possibility of such an arrangement. I have claimed, following Tim Bayne, that there is nothing logically or metaphysically impossible about the assertion of a double consciousness. I also claim, in opposition to Bayne, that this possibility receives empirical support through actual phenomena of divided consciousness (split-brain and multiple personality) that occur in human beings. The important point here, however, is that *these questions have no tendency to throw doubt on the assertion that it is the human person who lives, acts, and experiences through the Na'vi body and brain.* The reasons already given for the personal identity between controller and Na'vi remain fully in force; there simply is no space here for an independent Na'vi person to emerge. The avatar equivalent of Nestorianism simply does not get off the ground. And this, I submit, should reinforce our confidence that a Two-Sphere theory of the Incarnation need not be Nestorian.

Tim Bayne has raised another interesting question about Two-Sphere models of the Incarnation, concerning the sense in which Christ's human experiences are "included" in his divine sphere of consciousness. The notion that the very same experiences can exist simultaneously in two distinct spheres of consciousness seems extremely problematic:

How could two consciousnesses literally share the same particular experiences? There seems to be something necessarily private about experience. One has direct access to an experience only by having it, and particular experiences can only be had by a single consciousness.[24]

---

[23] It is interesting to note that, without this final step, we would have a plausible analogue to kenotic theories of the Incarnation. To be sure, just as life in a dream-like state is inimical to a healthy human existence, it may be that the divine analogue to that is incompatible with a properly divine existence.

[24] Tim Bayne, "The inclusion model of the Incarnation: problems and prospects," *Religious Studies* 37 (2001), pp. 125–41; p. 131.

However, Bayne also helpfully provides a solution to this problem: what is present in the divine consciousness is a *representation* of the human experience; in the divine mind the human experience is represented in effect as "my-experience-through-my-human-nature."[25] I would add to this that it by no means follows from this that the representation is either less complete or less vivid in its phenomenal content than the original experience.

The picture of the consciousness of the incarnate Son that emerges from the Avatar Model is thoroughly classical. In his divine nature and consciousness, the Son performs all of the "natural operations" that properly belong to a divine person, operations that are cognitive, affective, and volitional. I believe the model could be adapted to accommodate a view of God as timeless, though I shall not pursue that option here. And on the other hand, the Son's consciousness exercised through his human body and brain is as fully human, and correspondingly as limited, as good theology will expect it to be. There is of course some disagreement about the extent of these limitations. Some have supposed that, at certain points in his life and in certain respects, Jesus had access to his properly divine attributes, in particular the attributes of omniscience and omnipotence. Others will urge that there was no direct access of this sort, and that the supranormal power, knowledge, and insight that he sometimes evinces are the result of something akin to prophetic inspiration, raised to a superlative degree. The Avatar Model does not force a decision one way or the other; the question is left to be decided on whatever grounds we find compelling. However that may be, the model enables us to affirm that the fathers at Chalcedon and Constantinople got it right.

APPENDIX: BAYNE ON UNITY AND DISUNITY

Tim Bayne's *The Unity of Consciousness*[26] may be the most comprehensive study of conscious unity so far available. It is detailed, exhaustively researched, and carefully argued. In it he defends his unity thesis in the context of a number of different phenomena that have seemed to provide evidence for disunity, including hypnosis, schizophrenia, anosognosia, multiplicity, and the split-brain syndrome. My purpose in this appendix is to indicate briefly why I believe that with respect to the last two items mentioned his argument is less than convincing. It seems important to do this, even though he

---

[25] This is my application of his remarks on p. 131. Bayne's article contains a number of additional criticisms of the "inclusion model" as presented by Thomas Morris and by Richard Swinburne (see *The Christian God* (Oxford: Oxford University Press, 1994), pp. 193–215). A full discussion of these criticisms lies beyond the scope of the present paper.

[26] Page numbers in this appendix refer to this book.

has conceded that divided consciousness is both logically and metaphysically possible, which is all that is actually needed for the Avatar Model. Judgments about logical and metaphysical possibility are notoriously open to challenge, whereas it is beyond dispute that whatever is actual is also possible. Readers who find no difficulty in giving up the unity thesis should feel free to disregard this appendix.

It will be helpful to say a little about the split-brain syndrome and multiple personality, so as to show why they seem to pose a challenge for the unity thesis. First, the split-brain cases.[27] In certain hard-to-control cases of epilepsy it has proved beneficial to sever the corpus callosum, the thick sheaf of nerve tissue which forms the main connecting link between the right and left cerebral hemispheres. In many instances this has lessened the severity of epileptic seizures. More surprisingly, this major surgical alteration of the brain has turned out to have relatively slight effects on the patient's normal, day-to-day functioning. However, under controlled experimental conditions some striking results have been obtained. In the interest of brevity I will describe here only two cases, both featuring manipulative skills. One of Roger Sperry's commissurotomy subjects, W. J., was asked to perform a task with his right hand that involved arranging blocks in a predetermined pattern. The right hand, of course, is primarily controlled by the left cerebral hemisphere, which is greatly inferior to the right hemisphere in its ability to perform tasks involving spatial orientation. As a result, the right hand was having difficulty with the assignment. And then,

Slowly and steadily... the left hand creeps in, brushes aside the right hand, and starts building rather more efficiently. The experimenter is seen [on Sperry's film] pushing away the intrusive left hand. After a little while, along comes the left hand again. This time we see W. J. grasping the wrist of the left hand with the right, and pushing it away himself. But... after another pause, in creeps the irrepressible left hand once again. This time W. J. takes his left hand in his right, pushes it away—and sits on it, to stop it interfering further.[28]

Here is the other case:

L. B., an intelligent eleven-year-old commissurotomy patient, was given a pipe to hold in his left hand; a screen prevented him seeing what he was holding. The pipe was removed, and he was then asked to write, with his left hand, the name of the object he had just held. The left hand is of course primarily controlled by the right hemisphere, which had received the 'pipe' input from the left hand's tactual sensing

---

[27] Some of the material in the next few pages is taken from my "Persons and the Unity of Consciousness," in Robert C. Koons and George Bealer, eds, *The Waning of Materialism* (Oxford: Oxford University Press, 2010), pp. 176–81.

[28] Kathleen V. Wilkes, *Real People: Personal Identity Without Thought Experiments* (Oxford: Clarendon Press, 1988), p. 139.

of the pipe. Slowly and laboriously L. B., with his left hand, wrote 'P' and 'I'. At this point the left hemisphere took over—using its ipsilateral control over the left hand—and, changing the 'I' into an 'E', swiftly wrote 'PENCIL'. The right hemisphere took over again, crossed out the letters 'ENCIL', and *drew* a pipe.[29]

In each case, there is a conflict between the two cerebral hemispheres, each apparently operating on a different conception of how the assigned task is to be accomplished. Furthermore, a strong impression is created that we have here two *centers of consciousness*, each seeking to pursue its own agenda. The most plausible reading of the situation seems to be that both hemispheres are somehow conscious, and each is attempting to perform the assigned task in its own way. It strains plausibility to attribute agency to the hemispheres to the extent that is done in the description quoted above, yet insist that one hemisphere is conscious and the other is not. But if both are conscious this would constitute a violation of the unity thesis.

In cases of multiple personality the original personality seems to have become fragmented, leaving parts which are "separate mental aggregates, each with its own memories, which form the nucleus for new, independently functioning constellations."[30] Multiple personality may sometimes have its origin in childhood fantasy and role-playing, but the separate personalities gain a degree of autonomy that clearly distinguishes this syndrome from play-acting. The different personalities display different patterns of brain function, as seen by an EEG, and give different, but internally consistent, sets of responses to the Minnesota Multiphasic Personality Inventory.[31] The MMPI is an extremely sophisticated test, with lie-detection scales built in; systematically faking responses without detection is considered virtually impossible. The syndrome may in some cases be exacerbated by unwise actions of the therapist (for instance, by showing excessive favorable attention to alternates that tends to reinforce their distinctness), but it exists outside the therapeutic setting and cannot plausibly be considered to be the result of therapeutic suggestion.

My present concern is not so much with multiple personalities as such, as with the apparent existence of *simultaneously conscious* multiple person-alities in the same individual. Sally, the most prominent alternate of Morton Prince's patient Christine Beauchamp,[32] claimed to have been

---

[29] Wilkes, *Real People*, p. 138f.

[30] William N. Confer and Billie S. Ables, *Multiple Personality: Etiology, Diagnosis and Treatment* (New York: Human Sciences Press, 1983), p. 16.

[31] See Wilkes, *Real People*, p. 111.

[32] This case was originally reported in Morton Prince, *The Dissociation of a Personality* (London: Longmans, Green, 1905); I am relying on the account given by Wilkes.

"intraconscious"[33] with Christine, aware of all of Christine's thoughts as well as actions, since her early childhood. Sally remembered Christine's thoughts and actions, but emphatically as "hers" and not as "mine." (The name "Sally" was originally chosen because Sally disliked Christine and objected to being called by her name.) Sally was able to recall Christine's dreams in more detail than Christine herself could. On the other hand, Sally was uninterested in schoolwork and inattentive during lessons; she was quite unable to speak or understand French, a language in which Christine was fluent. (This came in handy when the therapist wanted to communicate with Christine while excluding Sally.)

Similarly Jeanne, the main alternate of William Confer's patient Rene, claimed to have been with Rene, and watching over her, virtually all of the time since they first "met" when Rene was four years old. Both Jeanne and Stella, another alternate of Rene, considered that they had a need to protect Rene, which sometimes involved "taking over" when a situation arose which Rene was unable to handle. On one occasion Stella phoned the therapist to say that Rene, after a traumatic experience, was determined to commit suicide by overdosing on her husband's Seconal and Valium. Stella was asked by the therapist to bring Rene to the emergency ward of the hospital, where he would meet her. Shortly thereafter, Rene did appear at the hospital, in a confused state with no recollection of how she had got there![34] Here again, as with commissurotomy, we have phenomena which seem to point to the existence of two or more centers of consciousness in the same human individual.

How does Bayne meet these challenges to his unity thesis? We begin with multiple personality, to which he devotes comparatively less attention. The main problem here concerns cases of "intra-consciousness"—Bayne prefers to call it "inter-alter access"—in which one alter claims to be conscious of the thoughts as well as actions of another. Clearly he cannot take such claims at face value; to do so would immediately violate the unity thesis. He proposes two alternative explanations:

One alternative to the telepathic account holds that reports of inter-alter access are confabulations—'mere hallucinations'—of mental states. . . . The introspective state that the multiple is reporting might be real enough, but the mental state that is its target might be a figment of the multiple's imagination. (p. 108)

---

[33] "The technical term for a subordinate consciousness that is aware of the primary personality's actions but not thoughts is 'co-conscious'; one aware of both actions and thoughts is 'intraconscious'" (Wilkes, *Real People*, p. 113n.).
[34] Confer and Ables, *Multiple Personality*, p. 130.

The other explanation is as follows:

Another alternative to the 'telepathic' account holds that in inter-alter access multiples are aware of genuine mental states, but these states are their own rather than those of some other subject of experience. (p. 109)

Here there may seem to be an ambiguity: when Bayne says, "these states are their own," does he mean that they are the states *of the alter who reports them*, or does he mean that they are states *of the person*, the person who in fact "is" each of the alters, though due to the "delusion of separateness" (p. 162f.) she is unaware of that fact? Upon reflection, it seems that the latter of these must be what is intended. If the states reported were those of the alter who reports them, then if we assume unity of consciousness those states could only have occurred *when the reporting alter was "out"*—that is, in motor control of the organism—and so there would actually have been no such states at the earlier time when they supposedly occurred. If so, this second alternative explanation seems to collapse into the first: the states reported are a figment of the reporting alter's imagination. I believe (though I am not certain about this) that Bayne must mean that all of the states reported are actually states of the single person, the person who successively imagines herself to be each of a number of different alters. So understood, it does provide a second explanation that is alternative to the view that the reporting alter really does enjoy "intraconsciousness" as is claimed by the alter herself.

We have seen that Bayne is not without resources in seeking to explain apparent cases of inter-alter access without admitting exceptions to the unity thesis. But when we apply these alternative explanations to actual cases, what we find may give us pause. Consider again the Rene/Stella "suicide prevention" episode. On the first proposed explanation, Rene's suicidal thoughts and intentions reported by Stella never actually existed; they were a figment of Stella's imagination, perhaps prompted by a desire for attention from the therapist. I should think that in an actual situation one would be extremely hesitant about drawing such a conclusion, presumably thereby concluding also that the suicidal inclinations were fictitious and could be disregarded. Certainly the therapist in the case, William Confer, drew no such conclusion. (Even if our hesitation here is partly motivated by pragmatic concerns, the case brings out the insecurity of the assumption that the suicidal inclinations were not genuine. In some instances there might be independent evidence that the person had acted or had entertained thoughts in a way that conformed to what was later reported by another alter. I do not know whether such evidence exists in this case.) Bayne's first alternative, that the thoughts reported are mere confabulations, might be true in some instances, but one would hesitate to accept it as a general explanation.[35]

In view of this, I believe Bayne's primary reliance needs to be on his second explanation, which affirms that all of the (genuine) thoughts reported are those of the single person who manifests in the guise of the different alters. Here also, however, attention to particular cases may lead to perplexity. Why would Christine be better able to recall her own dreams while presenting as Sally, than when she is "being herself"? And on the other hand, why would she, as Sally, be unable to understand French, a language she in fact knew well? But consider again the Rene/Stella suicide case. On this reading, we have a single person, Rene, who first forms the desire and intention to end her own life, then wishes to prevent this from happening and takes the steps needed to prevent it (the telephone call and the drive to the hospital), and finally relapses into a confused state in which she apparently has little recollection of the entire process. Is this really a clearer, more economical, and more credible explanation than the one accepted by the therapist who was actually involved in the case? It is hard to think that it is—*unless,* of course, one places an overriding importance on avoiding violations of the unity principle. Otherwise, the explanations involving divided consciousness are superior in at least two ways. They render Rene/Stella's actions more readily intelligible, by assigning different patterns of motivation (wanting to attempt suicide, and wanting to prevent such an attempt) to the different alters. Also, they conform to the "natural" way of interpreting the episode, the one that is derived from the patient's statements and was readily accepted by the therapist.

Bayne may well view the split-brain cases as posing the strongest challenge to his unity thesis. He devotes an entire chapter to the topic, and he grants that the argument for disunity in these cases appears to be compelling. But it is not, he thinks, as strong as it appears to be, because he has a viable competing explanation for the split-brain evidence:

Rather than suppose that the patient's two hemispheres are conscious in parallel, we should think of consciousness in the split-brain as moving or switching from one hemisphere to another. Although both hemispheres can process information concurrently, they take turns supporting consciousness. (p. 210)[36]

[35] Keep in mind that Bayne needs to provide explanations adequate to account for *all* instances of putative divided consciousness; explanations that account for some, but not all, cases will not serve his purpose.

[36] This is actually Bayne's second attempt to explain the split-brain evidence in a way that is consistent with the unity thesis. Earlier, writing with David Chalmers, he interpreted the evidence as indicative of a "processing bottleneck," but more recently he has concluded that this explanation is implausible. See Tim Bayne and David J. Chalmers,

It is evident that Bayne has hit on a remarkably powerful explanation for any and all phenomena that might suggest a divided consciousness. Rather than a divided consciousness, there is a single consciousness that alternates between various loci in the brain. This could easily, for example, be used to account for the phenomena of multiple personality: the different alters activate different brain-systems, and consciousness switches between them (perhaps quite rapidly) to create the strange results that are observed. (Bayne does not deploy this explanation to account for inter-alter access cases; he does, however, use it to account for "hidden observer" data that occur in some cases of hypnosis (p. 187f.).) And since it can so readily explain any phenomena suggestive of multiple streams of consciousness, the switching model is in effect immune to empirical refutation. (Whether this is really a strength, rather than a weakness, of the model may however be open to question.)

Bayne cites several types of phenomena as evidence for the switching model, but in my estimation they fall short. There clearly is evidence for the selective extinction, in some circumstances, of information presented to only one hemisphere, but there is no compelling inference from selective extinction to a switching consciousness. But here as with multiple personality, it will be helpful to apply the suggested explanation to an actual case. Consider, then, the "block building" case described previously. An initial observation is that, if this case is to be explained by switching consciousness, the switching must take place very rapidly. The impression received by observers was of continuous, rather than intermittent, effort on the part both of the designated right hand (and the left cerebral hemisphere) and of the interfering left hand (and the right hemisphere). In order to generate this impression, one would think that the switching probably must occur a number of times each second.[37] Another thought that occurs is that the expression "stream of consciousness" may really be out of place here. We don't have a *stream* of consciousness—that is a continuous, coherent, internally causally connected succession of conscious events and processes. What we have, rather is two distinct series of momentary conscious events, with (so far as we can tell) no internal causal connections between the successive events of either series. But a series of disconnected events isn't a stream, any

---

"What is the Unity of Consciousness?" in Axel Cleeremans, ed., *The Unity of Consciousness: Binding, Integration, and Dissociation* (Oxford: Oxford University Press, 2003), pp. 23–58; for my critique of the Bayne-Chalmers proposal, see "Persons and the Unity of Consciousness," pp. 186–90.

[37] The same observation could be made in the pipe/pencil case. The left hemisphere must have been conscious all along, in order for it to become dissatisfied with the slow progress of the right hemisphere in fulfilling the assigned task.

more than a series of raindrops splashing down one after another is a stream. If there is any stream in the neighborhood, it is to be found in the series of brain-events in each of the two hemispheres—and those series go along perfectly well during the intervals in which there is no conscious experience whatsoever. This, however, raises a further question: just what role is consciousness playing in this scenario? It doesn't carry with it memories, beliefs, motivations, or intentions, for each of these can be quite different in the two hemispheres. The impression given is that consciousness simply flickers back and forth, providing neutral (but intermittent) illumination on processes that can go on whether or not consciousness is present. In other words, it is beginning to look as though, in this model, consciousness is epiphenomenal. But epiphenomenalism is incompatible with Bayne's view overall; that is shown by the fact that he appeals to the complexity of the tasks performed by the right hemisphere as evidence that it is a mistake to limit consciousness to the left hemisphere. Although Bayne takes considerable trouble defending his model he does not, so far as I can see, address the questions I have raised here.

What conclusion should we draw? No doubt Bayne has identified alternative explanations which show that divided consciousness is not the only possible interpretation of the multiple personality and split-brain phenomena. But in the absence of a strong reason to prefer explanations that preserve unity, it is extremely doubtful that his explanations are better than those that include a divided consciousness. Bayne, however, fails to provide us with such reasons. As we have noted, he concedes that the unity thesis is not a necessary truth. His positive case for the thesis rests on the "unity judgment," a judgment we make to the effect that "all [one's] current experiences are phenomenally unified with each other—that they occur as the components of a single phenomenal field...that [one enjoys] a single phenomenal state that subsumes them all" (p. 75). We are indeed inclined to make such a judgment in ordinary situations. But surely this has little force *when we are confronted with experiences which strongly suggest to the subjects of those experiences as well as to qualified observers that in a particular case such unity does not obtain.* Prima facie, such experiences present themselves as exceptions to the unity judgment, and the fact that we are persuaded of that judgment in non-deviant cases does little to discredit the apparent exceptions.

Bayne acknowledges that divided consciousness explanations are the most widely accepted, both for multiple personality and for split-brain cases. The reason this is so, I believe, is that disunity explanations provide the most natural, and prima facie plausible, ways of understanding such cases; they are what is naturally suggested by the data. It seems to me that

Bayne is too ready to override the judgment of clinicians and experimenters who have first-hand experience with split-brain and multiple personality cases. Unless we have overriding reasons to insist on preserving conscious unity at all costs, I believe Bayne's explanations are less credible than those they are intended to replace.[38]

[38] My thanks to Joseph Jedwab, Katherin Rogers, John Sanders, Dale Tuggy, and two anonymous referees for comments on earlier versions of this material.

7

The Skeptical Christian

Daniel Howard-Snyder

According to William P. Alston, "Christian faith essentially involves both cognitive and affective-attitudinal elements".[1] The cognitive element, he says, is typically taken to be propositional belief, for example, belief that "Jesus of Nazareth...was resurrected after being crucified and buried, and that he is alive today and in personal relationship with the faithful."[2] Many Christians believe firmly these and other propositions constitutive of the basic Christian story, with utmost assurance.

For them these are facts about which they have no more doubts than they do about their physical surroundings and the existence of their family and friends. Even if they can see how one *could* doubt or deny these doctrines, they are not themselves touched by this. Perhaps this has been part of their repertoire of constant belief for as long as they can remember, and nothing has come along to shake it.[3]

"But," Alston continues, "not all sincere, active, committed, devout Christians are like this, especially in these secular, scientistic, intellectually unsettled times":

Many committed Christians do not find themselves with such assurance. A sense of the obvious truth of these articles of faith does not well up within them when they

---

[1] Alston 1996: 15. I should add that, in all honesty, I feel a bit uneasy about the phrase "Christian faith" when it is used to pick out a *distinctive* certain sort of psychological stance toward the Lord, or the basic Christian story. That's because, used in that way, it sounds a bit like using "Christian fear," "Christian pleasure," or "Christian digestion" to pick out a distinctive sort of psychological state—which seems to me completely wrong-headed. I suspect there are some closely related psychological stances that we pick out with our faith-talk, e.g. faith-in and faith-that, and that these stances can have both secular and religious objects and contents. Thus, the faith that I have when I maintain faith in Frances Howard-Snyder, as a wife, friend, mother, and lover, is exactly the same psychological stance that I have when I maintain faith in the Lord, and the faith that I have when I have faith that my sons will flourish as adults is exactly the same sort of psychological stance that I have when I have faith that the basic Christian story is true.

[2] Alston 1996: 16.   [3] Alston 1996: 16.

consider the matter. They *are* troubled by doubts; they ask themselves or others what reasons there are to believe that all this really happened. They take it as a live possibility that all or some of the central Christian doctrines are false.[4]

These "(quasi) skeptical Christians," as Alston calls them, "do not find themselves believing in, for example, a bodily resurrection of Jesus from the dead in the distinctive sense of belief," not to mention other aspects of the basic Christian story.[5]

Here a puzzle begins to emerge. For if these skeptical Christians lack belief of the basic Christian story, one might well wonder how they can have Christian faith, as Alston says they do. After all, you might think, as he himself points out, Christian faith essentially involves a cognitive element; thus, since these skeptical Christians lack belief, they cannot have Christian faith. We might put the puzzle in the form of an inconsistent triad, call it *the problem of the skeptical Christian*:

1. A person's Christian faith essentially involves a cognitive element.
2. The cognitive element of a person's Christian faith is belief of the basic Christian story.
3. Skeptical Christians have Christian faith but they lack belief of the basic Christian story.

The problem of the skeptical Christian is a merely theoretical problem: each claim seems initially plausible but they can't all be true.

There are two further related problems, neither of which is merely theoretical, one of which—call it *the problem of faith and reason*—can be put in the form of an argument, targeting those who would identify as Christians:

1. If your Christian faith is reasonable, then it is reasonable for you to believe the basic Christian story.
2. It is not reasonable for you to believe the basic Christian story.
3. So, your Christian faith is not reasonable.

(Let the notion of reasonableness be epistemic; and substitute whatever other term of epistemic appraisal you wish, e.g. *justified, rational, warranted, up-to-intellectual-snuff*, etc.) Many Christians won't care whether the conclusion is true, but many others will. Among those who will care, there are those who will deny premise (2), at least with respect to themselves—we all know people like that, especially in the community of Christian philosophers! But there is another sort of Christian who cares whether the conclusion is true, namely those who want to reject it, alright, but who concede that premise (2) accurately describes themselves—Alston's skeptical Christians, for example. They are in a bit of a pickle, not least because it may well seem

---

[4] Alston 1996: 16.   [5] Alston 1996: 17, 26.

to them that, in general, someone has reasonable Christian faith only if it is reasonable for them to believe the basic Christian story. Of course, if they accept the conclusion in their own case, they will thereby have strong *prima facie* reason to abandon the Christian life. The problem of faith and reason, therefore, is particularly acute for the skeptical Christian.

As for the third problem—what we might call *the problem of the trajectory*— anecdotal evidence suggests that, at least in the West, Christians these days struggle more with doubt than their predecessors. For example, it's not uncommon for a young Christian to go off to college assured in his Christian beliefs, take his first philosophy or religion or literature or history or biology class, and meet for the first time powerful defenses of scientific naturalism or atheism from real-life naturalists and atheists, as well as powerful critiques of considerations in favor of theism in general and Christianity in particular. Such students are often thrown into doubt and they think to themselves something along these lines: "I've got to be honest: while the things I'm learning in my classes don't make me *dis*believe (yet), they do make me wonder, even to the point of, well,..., it's hard to admit it, but, even to the point of being in doubt, serious doubt. But if I'm in doubt, I lack belief; and if I lack belief, then I don't have faith. And if I don't have faith, how can I keep praying, attending church, worshipping God, taking the sacraments, singing the hymns and songs, and so on? It seems I can't, unless I'm a hypocrite. So, in all honesty, I should just drop the whole thing and get out." Of course, our newly-skeptical university student is not alone. The just-displayed trajectory from doubt to getting out can be found at just about any phase or place of life. What might we say to the trajectory-treading skeptical Christian?

Of course, many of us will say, *Get out!* But what about those of us who don't want to say that? I think the first thing we must do is affirm the way in which they take the life of the mind so seriously, as well as the integrity they display by aiming to live in accordance with their considered judgment. That's non-negotiable. We can also address the basis of their doubt. But even here, I suspect, it wouldn't be surprising if most of them lacked the ability or time to conduct a fair and thorough appraisal of the objections and critiques, and it is unclear how the epistemology of experts would advise them. Moreover, I wonder whether, even if they did conduct a fair and thorough appraisal, *belief* of the basic Christian story would be the most fitting cognitive response on their part. Be that as it may, the main point is that many of these people will retain a significant degree of doubt, significant enough to preclude belief of the basic Christian story. They have a problem, then, a practical problem: the line of thought indicated by our university student's speech.

To his credit, Alston sees all this. He makes two crucial points about it.

First, he insists that the Christian who lacks belief—the skeptical Christian—"is not necessarily inferior to the *believer*" when it comes to "commitment to the Christian life, or in the seriousness, faithfulness, or intensity with which she pursues it."[6] She "may pray just as faithfully, worship God just as regularly, strive just as earnestly to follow the way of life enjoined on us by Christ, [and] look as pervasively on interpersonal relationships, vocation, and social issues through the lens of the Christian faith."[7] As such, she can be "all in" when it comes to Christian practice, although "[s]he will undoubtedly receive less comfort and consolation," be "less assured of the life of the world to come," and when she does have experiences that she might be inclined to take as "interactions with God," "she will not be wholly free of nagging suspicions that it is all in her own mind."[8]

Second, while some people might propose to solve our three problems by denying that Christian faith essentially involves any cognitive element, Alston does no such thing. That's because, by his lights, although Christian faith essentially involves a cognitive element, belief is not the only way in which that element can be realized. One can instead *accept* the basic Christian story, and one can accept it reasonably and act on that acceptance with integrity. This is the thrust of Alston's solution to to our three problems.

Here's the plan for what follows. After I summarize Alston's views on the difference between belief and acceptance and on the significance of acceptance for Christian faith, I will do two things. First, I'll argue that the cases he uses to illustrate the difference between belief and acceptance, and the cases he uses to illustrate the significance of acceptance for Christian faith, fail to illustrate that difference and significance. As a result, what he has to say about belief, acceptance, and Christian faith only superficially solves our three problems and cannot satisfy the skeptical Christian. Second, I'll argue that the cases he uses to illustrate the distinction between belief and acceptance, and the cases he uses to illustrate the significance of acceptance for Christian faith, in fact illustrate another way to realize the cognitive element of Christian faith, a way distinct from belief and acceptance, a way that can play the role Alston intended acceptance to play in his account of Christian faith, a way that substantively solves our three problems, a way that the skeptical Christian can find satisfying. But before I turn to these two tasks, some preliminary remarks are in order.

---

[6] Alston 1996: 17 (his emphasis).   [7] Alston 1996: 17.
[8] Alston 1996: 17–18.

1. PRELIMINARY REMARKS

First, a methodological point. When I aim to criticize someone's views, I try to assess what they have to say from the perspective of their theoretical framework, as far I can. Thus, although Alston's views of belief and acceptance are ripe for criticism—whose views aren't in this area?—I will for the most part leave them unquestioned. I'm theorizing from his point of view.

Nor will I question Alston's treatment of Christian faith as largely a matter of faith *in* and faith *that*,[9] which leads to my second remark. We'll be in a better position to engage Alston if we are alert to how he thinks about faith in, faith that, and their relation.

Toward that end, according to Alston, faith *that*—i.e. *propositional faith*, as many call it—is like belief that, propositional belief, in that both involve "a positive attitude toward a proposition," but the former differs from the latter in at least two ways. Propositional faith, unlike propositional belief, (i) "necessarily involves some pro-attitude toward its object," looking on its truth "with favor," and (ii) "has at least a strong suggestion of a weak epistemic position vis-à-vis the proposition in question."[10] I tend to think that it involves more—in particular, something like resilience in the face of obstacles to living in light of one's positive cognitive attitude and looking on its truth with favor—and that it need not involve a weak epistemic position but rather a suboptimal epistemic position.[11] Otherwise I am largely in agreement with Alston.

As for faith *in*—*relational faith*, as I will call it—Alston says that "the crucial feature would seem to be *trust*, reliance on the person to carry out commitments, obligations, promises, or, more generally, to act in a way favorable to oneself."[12] Trust may be crucial to relational faith, but that can't be the whole story since the con-artist relies on his victims in just the way Alston describes but they do not have faith in them. What more is involved in relational faith I leave for another occasion.

Regarding the relationship between relational faith and propositional faith, Alston writes that

[o]bviously, faith in a person presupposes that one has some positive attitude toward the proposition that the person exists and that he or she has various characteristics

---

[9] Another alternative is what I call *global faith*. See Howard-Snyder 2016, as well as Audi 2011, Kvanvig 2013, and Kvanvig forthcoming 2018, esp. chs 4 and 5.

[10] Alston 1996: 12.   [11] Howard-Snyder 2013b: 367–8 and 369–70.

[12] Alston 1996: 13. Cf. Swinburne 1981: 110ff.; Penelhum 1995: 72ff.; Schellenberg 2005: 109ff.

that provide a basis for one's faith. But it is not obvious that this attitude has to be properly characterizable as a case of "faith that".[13]

But why, exactly, is that not obvious? Perhaps Alston's point is that one can have faith in a person while being in a strong epistemic position vis-à-vis the relevant propositions. The positive attitude toward these propositions *need not be* propositional faith, which, by his lights, involves a weak epistemic position, but—and this is important—it *can be*. That is, one can have faith in a person only if one has some positive attitude toward the relevant propositions, and that positive attitude can be faith that they are so. Thus, according to Alston, although relational faith is compatible with propositional faith, it does not require it.

But, he says, propositional faith does require relational faith:

> It seems plausible that wherever it is clearly appropriate to attribute "faith that," there is "faith in" in the background. If I have faith that Joe will get the job, I thereby have faith in Joe, of some sort. If I have faith that the church will rebound from recent setbacks, I thereby have faith in the church and its mission.[14]

Is it really true that S has faith that x is F only if S has faith in x? Presumably not. I have faith that Kirsten will beat her cancer but I don't thereby have faith in Kirsten; rather, I have faith in her doctors. Alston might reply that faith that x is F requires some relational faith or other, as with my faith in Kirsten's doctors. I'm suspicious; but instead of pursuing the matter further, I turn to a third preliminary.

Alston focuses on the "cognitive element" of Christian faith, leaving the "affective-attitudinal" element aside. I will follow suit. Our focus, however, should not be taken to indicate that either of us thinks the former is more central to Christian faith than the latter. Not by a longshot.

Fourth, doubt will figure in what follows, as it has already in the expression of our three problems. Alston does not say how he is thinking about it. Here's how I will think about it. We must distinguish having doubts about whether p from being in doubt about whether p, and both of them from doubting that p. For one to have doubts about whether p—note the 's'—is for one to have what appear to one to be grounds to believe not-p or a lack of grounds to believe p and, as a result, for one to be at least somewhat more inclined to disbelieve p, or at least somewhat less inclined to believe p. For one to be in doubt about whether p is for one neither to believe p nor disbelieve p as a result of one's grounds for p seeming to be roughly on a par with one's grounds for not-p. One can have doubts without being in doubt, and one can be in doubt without having doubts. Having doubts and being

---

[13] Alston 1996: 13.   [14] *Op. cit.*

in doubt are not to be identified with doubting that. If one doubts that
something is so, one is at least strongly inclined to disbelieve it; having
doubts and being in doubt lack that implication.[15]

2. ALSTON ON BELIEF, ACCEPTANCE,
AND CHRISTIAN FAITH

According to Alston, belief is something mental, specifically a mental state,
as opposed to a mental act or process, and more specifically still, a dispositional state that manifests itself under certain conditions like those in the
partial dispositional profile he provides:

1. If S believes that p, then if someone asks S whether p, S will tend
   to respond affirmatively.
2. If S believes that p, then, if S considers whether it is the case that
   p, S will tend to feel it to be the case that p.
3. If S believes that p, then, if S takes q to follow from p, S will tend
   to believe q.
4. If S believes that p, then, if S engages in practical or theoretical
   reasoning, S will tend to use p as a premise when appropriate.
5. If S believes that p, then, if S learns [suddenly] that not-p, S will
   tend to be surprised.
6. If S believes that p, then, given S's goals, aversions, and other
   beliefs, S will tend to act in ways that would be appropriate if it
   were the case that p.[16]

Note that the consequent in each embedded conditional involves a tendency to a certain manifestation. That's because whether any such manifestation is forthcoming will depend on whether any psychological or other
obstacles are present. Note also the term "feel" in item (2). By it, Alston
does *not* mean a sensation or emotion. Rather, he means to "convey the idea
that [the manifestation in question] possesses a kind of *immediacy* or *spon-
taneity*, that it is something one *experiences* rather than something that one
thinks out, that it is a matter of being *struck by* (a sense of) how things are
rather than *deciding* how things are."[17] Others, he observes, call the experience

---

[15] For a more thorough discussion of the nature of doubt, see Peels unpublished,
Moon 2017, and Lee 2014.
[16] Alston 1996: 4, slightly altered for uniform readability.
[17] Alston 1996: 3–4.

in question "consciously [or occurrently] believing p."[18] Moreover, we cannot at will stop believing something we now believe, nor can we at will begin to believe something we do not now believe. Belief is not under our direct voluntary control.

As for acceptance, Alston says that, unlike belief, acceptance is, in the first instance, a mental act. One finds oneself with a belief, whereas to accept p is "to adopt" or "take on board" a positive attitude toward p.[19] Moreover, one cannot believe something at will, but one can accept something at will.[20] Furthermore, the *act* of acceptance normally "engenders" a dispositional *state* much like belief, a state also labeled "acceptance."[21] Alston's rationale for this is that "if acceptance were just a momentary act that left no residue, it would have no point." The "residue" is the dispositional state of acceptance. Contrasting the dispositional states of belief and acceptance with reference to the dispositional profile of the former, he writes:

> Belief…will involve more confident, unhesitating manifestations of these sorts than acceptance will. But in the main, the story on these components [specifically (1), (3), (4), (5), and (6)] will be the same for acceptance. (In (3), substitute "tend to accept" for "tend to believe".) By far the largest difference is the absence of (2). The complex dispositional state engendered by accepting p will definitely not include a tendency to feel that p if the question of whether p arises.[22]

So, according to Alston, the *state* of acceptance differs from belief in three ways: its manifestations will tend to be less confident and more hesitating, its dispositional profile lacks a tendency to feel that p if the question of whether p arises, and it can be "engendered" at will.

I want to make two initial points about the way in which Alston distinguishes belief from the state of acceptance.

First, it's not at all clear that the state of acceptance differs from belief in that belief "involve[s] more confident, unhesitating manifestations" than acceptance. For, as Alston points out, one can have "beliefs of a weaker strength" and "[t]here the dispositions, including the dispositions to taking p as a basis for inferences and behavior, are themselves weaker," that is, they are less confident and more hesitating than "firm belief." Moreover, when Alston characterizes this particular difference between belief and the state of acceptance, he qualifies it with "at least firm belief" (that's what goes into the ellipsis in the quotation above). This suggests that, by his lights, weak belief is no different from acceptance when it comes to the degree of confidence and hesitation of their manifestations. So, although the manifestations

---

[18] Alston 1996: 241, n4.   [19] Alston 1996: 8.   [20] Alston 1996: 11.
[21] Alston 1996: 9; the dispositional state is "a result of" the act of acceptance (17).
[22] Alston 1996: 9.

of the state of acceptance will tend to be less confident and more hesitant than firm belief, the state of acceptance will *not* tend to be less confident and more hesitant than weak belief. The upshot is that the first difference mentioned above—that the manifestations of the state of acceptance will tend to be less confident and more hesitating than belief—really isn't a difference between belief *per se* and acceptance.

Second, regarding the difference in dispositional profiles, we must add something to the profile of acceptance, something that is implicit in the text. Alston tells us that accepting that p involves "taking a stand on the truth value of p," specifically "regarding it as true," giving it one's "mental assent," mentally "affirming" it, and mentally "judging" that it is so.[23] What we have here, I submit, is another item on the dispositional profile of acceptance:

> 7a. If S accepts that p, then, if S considers whether it is the case that p, S will tend to take a stand on p's truth in this sense: S will tend to mentally assent to p, mentally affirm p, and mentally judge that p is so.

Oddly, there is no analogue to (7a) on the dispositional profile of belief. The only items that come close are (1) and (2), but (1) has to do with affirmative *verbal* response and (2) has to do with *feeling* p to be the case; neither has to do with the *mental acts* of assent, affirmation, or judgment. Even so, I expect that Alston would consider this an oversight and so I will impute the analogue to him, (7b), which replaces "accepts" with "believes".

So then, as I understand Alston, the difference between belief and the state of acceptance is that item (2), the tendency to feel it to be the case that p when one considers whether p, is on the profile for belief but not acceptance, and acceptance can be "engendered" at will but belief cannot.[24]

And now we are in a position to see the difference, according to Alston, between Christian faith that involves acceptance, rather than belief, of the propositions constitutive of the basic Christian story. Alston writes:

To accept them is to perform a voluntary act of committing oneself to them, to *resolve* to use them as a basis for one's thought, attitude, and behavior. (And, of course, it involves being disposed to do so as a result of this voluntary acceptance.) Whereas to believe them, even if not with the fullest confidence, is to *find* oneself with that positive attitude toward them, to *feel* that, for example, Jesus of Nazareth died to reconcile us to God. That conviction, of whatever degree of strength, spontaneously wells up in one when one considers the matter. And so, at bottom, it is a

---

[23] Alston 1996: 11, 15, 20.
[24] Audi 2011, 80–4, challenges the second difference.

difference between what one finds in oneself and what one has deliberately chosen to introduce in oneself.[25]

Alston can't mean the last sentence here. For, on his own view, *what* one finds in oneself when one believes a proposition is something with an importantly different dispositional profile from *what* one introduces in oneself when one accepts it, a difference that looms large in his discussion, as we've already seen.

3. ALSTON'S ILLUSTRATIONS OF ACCEPTANCE AND ITS SIGNIFICANCE FOR CHRISTIAN FAITH

So far I have articulated Alston's views on belief, acceptance, and Christian faith. Those familiar with his work will know that two things have been absent from my discussion so far: Alston's illustrations of the distinction between belief and acceptance, and his illustrations of the significance of acceptance for Christian faith. I now bring them to the fore.

To illustrate acceptance, Alston gives three examples.[26] Each example is a case in which "it is not at all clear what is the case or what one should do, but the relevant considerations seem to favor one alternative over the others."[27]

The defensive captain. As the captain of the defensive team I am trying to figure out what play the opposing quarterback will call next. From my experience of playing against him and his coach, and given the current situation, it seems most likely to me that he will call a plunge into the middle of the line by the fullback. Hence I accept that proposition and reason from it in aligning the defense. Do I *believe* that this is the play he will call, unqualifiedly believe it, as contrasted with thinking it likely? No. I don't find myself feeling sure that this is what he will do. Who can predict exactly what a quarterback will do in a given situation? My experience prevents me from any such assurance. Nevertheless I accept the proposition that he will call a fullback plunge and proceed on that basis.[28]

The humble philosopher. I survey the reasons for and against different positions on the free will issue. Having considered them carefully, I conclude that they indicate most strongly an acceptance of libertarian free will. Do I flat-out believe that we have that kind of free will? There

[25] Alston 1996: 17.   [26] Alston 1996: 10.   [27] Alston 1996: 10.
[28] Alston 1996: 10.

are people who do feel sure of this. But I am too impressed by the arguments against the position to be free of doubts; it doesn't seem clear to me that this is the real situation, as it seems clear to me that I am now sitting in front of a computer, that I live in Central New York, and that I teach at Syracuse University. Nevertheless, I accept the proposition that we have libertarian free will. I announce this as my position. I defend it against objections. I draw various consequences from it, and so on.[29]

The army general. Consider an army general...facing enemy forces... He needs to proceed on some assumption as to the disposition of those forces. His scouts give some information about this but not nearly enough to make any such assumption obviously true...He accepts the hypothesis that seems to him the most likely...He uses this as a basis for disposing his forces in the way that seems most likely to be effective, even though he is far from believing that this is the case.[30]

I want to make three points about these cases.

First, the protagonist in each case accepts one proposition from among *several credible contraries.* For example, in the case of the defensive football captain, there is a variety of options to the plunge (or dive) that call for different defensive alignments. There are sweeps, draws, counters, traps, end arounds, reverses, the bootleg, the option, and a variety of trick plays; and then there are all the passing options. Even if they are in a position to rule out some of these alternatives, they'll sensibly assign each of the multiple remaining ones a significant probability, driving down the likelihood of a plunge.

Second, the protagonist in each case accepts one proposition over its credible competitors because "it seems most likely" or because the reasons for and against the different positions "indicate most strongly" the one over each of the others. It is important to see here that a proposition can be the most likely among each of several contraries and still be no more likely than its negation. In this connection, notice Alston's slide in the football case from the captain thinking a fullback plunge is the "most likely" call to their "thinking it likely." The latter doesn't follow from the former, and it strains credulity to suppose that any defensive captain worth their paycheck would think it likely that a quarterback will call a plunge, even on fourth and goal at the one. Too many alternatives must be assigned a significant probability.

---

[29] Alston 1996: 10–11.   [30] Alston 2007: 133.

Third, in light of the first two points, it seems extremely implausible that the captain, the general, and the philosopher accept the relevant propositions, given Alston's account of acceptance. That's because, on his account, the dispositional profile for acceptance includes (1) and (7a), and—to focus just on the captain—they will have no tendency to *respond affirmatively* if someone asks them whether the quarterback will call a fullback plunge, and no tendency to *mentally assent* to that proposition or to *mentally affirm* or *judge* that it is so if they bring it to mind. Indeed, if you ask any of our protagonists whether the relevant proposition is true, and you gave them enough time to reflect on their situation, I expect you would hear all sorts of hedging and hemming-and-hawing. And the same goes for their purely mental responses; just as a "sense of the obvious truth" of the target proposition "does not well up within them when they consider the matter," so an affirmative mental response will not be forthcoming when they consider it.[31] That's because, given their evidence, and our charitable ascription of intellectual virtue, there are too many alternatives each of which occupies a significant portion of probability space, rendering the target proposition only "most likely" or "most strongly indicated." It is, therefore, difficult to see these as cases of acceptance, given Alston's account of acceptance.

I now turn to the significance for Christian faith that Alston ascribes to acceptance. He says that many of those who find themselves incapable of believing the basic Christian story might still have it within their power to accept it,[32] and he elaborates on the significance of "the acceptance alternative for Christian faith" by illustrating it with three cases:

Just as the philosopher described previously accepted the thesis of libertarian free will, though she did not spontaneously feel it to be the case, so it is with (quasi) skeptical Christians. This can take several different forms. Perhaps such a person, having carefully considered the evidence and arguments pro and con, or as much of them as she is aware of, judges that there is a sufficient basis for accepting the doctrines, even though she does not find herself in a state of belief. Or perhaps she has been involved in the church from her early years, from a preskeptical time when she did fully believe, and she finds the involvement meeting deep needs and giving her life some meaning and structure. And so she is motivated to accept Christian doctrines as a basis for her thought about the world and for the way she leads her life. Or perhaps the person is drawn into the church from a condition of religious non-involvement, and responds actively to the church's message, finding in the Christian life something that is deeply satisfying, but without, as yet, spontaneously feeling the doctrines to be true. Such a person will again be moved to accept the doctrines as something on which she will build her thought and action.[33]

---

[31] Alston 1996: 15.   [32] Alston 1996: 25–6; cf. 243–4, n. 43.
[33] Alston 1996: 17.

I want to make two points about these three cases.

First, Alston calls the person in each case a "(quasi) skeptical Christian," earlier referring to such people as "troubled by doubts";[34] moreover, he likens them to the protagonists in the secular cases. Here we need to keep in mind not only that each of the protagonists in the secular cases fails to "spontaneously feel" the relevant proposition to be the case, but that each of them "accepts" it on the basis of its seeming to be "the most likely" or "most strongly indicated" from among several credible contraries, when "it is not at all clear what is the case." This suggests that, for Alston, what counts as "a sufficient basis for accepting" the basic Christian story (in the first case) can be pretty thin soup, a suggestion that is confirmed when we see him count T. S. Eliot among the Christians he has in mind. Despite displaying considerable "skepticism" about Christianity, Eliot reported that he "accepted" it "because it was the least false of the options open to him."[35] One does not sincerely report such a thing unless, at best, one is in doubt about it. So my first point is that, through his cases, Alston invites us to think of at least some skeptical Christians along the lines I have just been emphasizing: as Christians who are in doubt about the basic Christian story, even if, by their lights, it's "the most likely" or "most strongly indicated" or "least false" of the options they deem credible. In what follows I accept his invitation.

Second, when I transpose the frame of mind of Eliot, the captain, the general, and the humble philosopher back into the frame of mind of Alston's three skeptical Christians, I don't see how they could accept the basic Christian story, given Alston's account of acceptance and a charitable construal of their intellectual virtue. Despite the attraction of the Christian story for each of them, if they really are as troubled by doubts as Alston says they are and if they really do regard the Christian story as simply the least false or most likely among the options they deem credible, will any of them be happy to hear of acceptance as an alternative to the belief that eludes them? I doubt it. That's because when they learn that acceptance involves a tendency to respond affirmatively when asked whether the basic Christian story is true—to answer aloud and without qualification, "yes, it is true"— and a tendency to mentally assent to that proposition or to mentally affirm or judge that it is so when it is brought to mind—to answer inwardly and without qualification, "yes, it is so"—they will rightly think that acceptance will elude them every bit as much as belief. For although they look on the Christian story with favor and they are prepared to act in accordance with it, what they have to go on prepares them, at best, to verbally assert that it is the "most likely" or "least false" and to mentally assent to its being the

---

[34] Alston 1996: 16.   [35] Alston 1996: 19, quoting William Wainwright.

"most strongly indicated"—all a far cry from asserting *it* or mentally assenting to *it*, both of which the profile of acceptance requires. And why would they want to introduce, at will, such tendencies in themselves anyway, even if they could? To do so would promote cognitive dissonance and violate their intellectual integrity.

This is a good place to consider an important question Alston raises about the epistemic status of belief and acceptance, the question of whether "belief and acceptance have different [epistemic] statuses vis-à-vis the need for evidence, reasons, [or] grounds."[36] According to Alston, belief and acceptance differ in their mode of origin and dispositional profile, but neither difference seems relevant to any epistemic status related to evidence, reasons, or grounds. Suppose acceptance can be introduced into oneself at will and belief cannot. What's that got to do with whether Alstonian acceptance requires more or less in the way of evidence, reasons, or grounds than belief in order to satisfy, say, evidentialist or reliabilist standards or principles for epistemic justification? It seems wholly irrelevant. In that case, all the weight for an affirmative answer to our question lands on the difference in dispositional profile: the profile of belief that p includes a tendency to feel that p is the case when p comes to mind—a tendency to an immediate, spontaneous experience of being struck by (a sense of) p being how things are—while the profile of acceptance that p lacks that tendency. But again: what's that got to do with whether acceptance requires more or less in the way of evidence, reasons, or grounds than belief in order to satisfy, say, evidentialist or reliabilist standards or principles for epistemic justification? It seems wholly irrelevant. And therein lies the rub: there is no other difference between acceptance and belief, on Alston's view. Thus, on his view, belief and acceptance do *not* have different epistemic statuses vis-à-vis the need for evidence, reasons, and grounds. It's not surprising, then, that the skeptical Christian will be disappointed by what Alston has to offer. For what she lacks with respect to belief, she also lacks with respect to acceptance: *sufficient* evidence, reasons, or grounds to believe—or accept.[37]

The upshot is that the cases Alston uses to illustrate the difference between belief and acceptance fail to illustrate that difference, and the cases he uses to illustrate the significance of a Christian faith whose cognitive element is acceptance fail to illustrate that significance. As a consequence, what Alston has to say about that difference and significance seems to me to provide only a superficial solution to our three problems, as I will now try to show.

---

[36] Alston 1996: 26.
[37] Other accounts of acceptance might not fall afoul of the worry about Alston's account that I am expressing here.

Alston aims to solve the problem of the skeptical Christian by denying (2) of our inconsistent triad, the claim that the cognitive element of a person's Christian faith is belief of the basic Christian story. While a person's Christian faith requires a cognitive element alright, says Alston, it need not be belief; it can be acceptance. Thus, he continues, skeptical Christians can have Christian faith without belief while still meeting the demand for a cognitive element. However: although strictly speaking, (2) is false on Alston's view, adding acceptance as an alternative does nothing for skeptical Christians. That's because they won't accept the basic Christian story any more than they will believe it. We can put the point this way. Alston's solution is impotent against a slight variation on the problem:

1. A person's Christian faith essentially involves a cognitive element.

2′. The cognitive element of a person's Christian faith is belief or acceptance of the basic Christian story.

3′. Skeptical Christians have Christian faith but they neither believe nor accept the basic Christian story.

Nothing Alston says allows us to deny (2′) and, given an accurate description of the state of mind of skeptical Christians and a charitable assessment of their intellectual virtue, we cannot deny (3′). That leaves (1), which is non-negotiable for Alston. The problem of the skeptical Christian substantially remains.

As for the problem of faith and reason, Alston would sympathetically engage the perspective of skeptical Christians by denying premise (1), the claim that, if your Christian faith is reasonable, then it is reasonable for you to believe the basic Christian story. "Your Christian faith can be reasonable," he would say, "even if it is not reasonable for you to believe the basic Christian story. That's because the cognitive element of your Christian faith can be acceptance, and accepting the basic Christian story might be reasonable for you even if believing it is not." This solution is superficial as well. For, once again, although strictly speaking, (1) is false on Alston's view, adding acceptance as an alternative to belief does nothing for skeptical Christians. That's because they are no more apt to accept it than to believe it; moreover, what they have to go on renders acceptance no more reasonable for them than belief, as a variation on the problem reveals:

1*. If your Christian faith is reasonable, then it is reasonable for you either to believe or to accept the basic Christian story.

2*. It is not reasonable for you to either to believe or to accept the basic Christian story.

3. So, your Christian faith is not reasonable.

Nothing Alston says allows us to deny (1*), and we can't deny (2*) on behalf of skeptical Christians since what they have to go on makes it true. Therefore, (3) follows, for skeptical Christians. The problem of faith and reason substantially remains.

As for the problem of the trajectory, Alston would address the line of thought exhibited by our skeptical university student as follows: "Although you are in doubt about the basic Christian story, and you lack belief, you can still have Christian faith. That's because you can accept the basic Christian story, and you can practice without hypocrisy on the basis of such acceptance." This too lacks substance. For although Alston is right that, on his view, a lack of belief does not imply a lack of faith, that does nothing to help our student. That's because they are in doubt about the basic Christian story, in which case they lack those tendencies that the dispositional profile of acceptance brings with it; moreover, even if they could accept it, they could not accept it in good conscience, given items (1) and (7a) on that profile. Acceptance, therefore, does not stop the trajectory from doubt to getting out. The problem of the trajectory substantially remains.

I conclude that propositional acceptance, as understood by Alston, seems unfit to play the role in Christian faith that he envisioned. As a consequence, his view permits only a superficial solution to our three problems. Fortunately, there is an alternative.

4. AN ALTERNATIVE POSITIVE COGNITIVE ATTITUDE FOR THE SKEPTICAL CHRISTIAN

To get in a better position to discern the alternative I have in mind, let's return to Alston's secular cases, the case of the defensive captain, the army general, and the humble philosopher.[38]

First, we can easily imagine that none of them believes the relevant propositions. The captain has no tendency to feel it to be the case that the quarterback will call a fullback plunge, the general has no tendency to feel it to be the case that the enemy forces are disposed in such-and-such a position, and the humble philosopher has no tendency to feel it to be case that libertarianism is true. No "conviction, of whatever degree of strength, spontaneously wells up in" them when they consider the matter.[39]

Second, as indicated earlier, it is also extremely implausible to suppose that they accept the relevant propositions, given Alston's account of acceptance.

---

[38] Here I expand on material from Howard-Snyder 2013b: 365–7.
[39] Alston 1996: 17.

In any case, we can easily imagine that they do not accept them. For example, we can easily imagine that the captain has no tendency to assert that the quarterback will call a plunge if asked or to mentally assent to that proposition if it is brought to mind (and that they have no tendency to be surprised upon suddenly learning that the quarterback made another call).

Third, we can easily imagine that each of our protagonists is in doubt about whether the target proposition is true. That's because each of them thinks that, given what they have to go on, the target proposition is only more likely or more strongly indicated or the least false among the credible options, which is compatible with it being no more likely than its negation. In that case, we might easily imagine that it appears to each of them that what they have to go on with respect to the truth of the target proposition is roughly on a par with what they have to go on with respect to its falsity and, as a result, neither believes nor disbelieves it and neither accepts nor rejects it.

Fourth, despite their lack of belief and acceptance, and despite their being in doubt, each of them acts on a certain assumption. The captain acts on the assumption that the quarterback called a fullback plunge, the general acts on the assumption that the enemy forces are situated thus-and-so, and the philosopher acts on the assumption that libertarianism is true. Take note: *there really is some cognitive attitude that each of them acts on*. Each of them *assumes that* some proposition is true. Call this cognitive attitude *beliefless assuming*.

Fifth, each protagonist acts on the basis of their beliefless assumption, and they act in ways you would expect given their beliefless assumptions. The captain belieflessly assumes that the quarterback called a fullback plunge, and so they put six men on the line. The general belieflessly assumes that the enemy is situated thus-and-so, and so they disperse their troops for a pincer movement. The philosopher belieflessly assumes that libertarianism is true, and so they hold themselves morally responsible for things they were able to refrain from.

While the foregoing observations locate one way to understand the cognitive attitude involved in Alston's protagonists, we might wish for a more general understanding of their attitude. What is it, exactly? What is it to belieflessly assume that p, *in those cases*? This is a difficult question. Beliefless assuming of the sort on display in Alston's cases has not been the focus of much discussion, unlike propositional belief and propositional acceptance, both of which enjoy the attention, if not the affection, of many philosophers. Still, in what follows, I'll make several remarks that I hope will shed enough light to indicate how I propose to think of the matter.

First, we use "assume" in different ways. We sometimes use it to refer to the attitude that we have when we take something for granted or to be obvious, as when we assume that the world is more than five minutes old or that there are persons other than ourselves. I do not mean to use "assume" in this way because, so used, it refers to a propositional attitude too much like belief or acceptance—indeed, it just *is* belief, coupled with full assurance—and so does not fit Alston's cases. On other occasions, we use it to refer to the attitude that we have when we introduce a proposition into our thought for the purpose of considering what follows from it, as when we assume for *reductio* that some times are earlier than themselves or we assume for conditional proof that God exists. I do not mean to use "assume" in this way either because, so used, it refers to a propositional attitude that is too little like belief or acceptance—indeed, it seems to be no more than a bit of mental what-if-ery—and so likewise does not fit Alston's cases.

Second remark: in the sense of "assume" that does fit Alston's cases, one can assume that p without believing or accepting it, and while being in doubt about it, as indicated previously. Thus, assuming of the sort in question is not sufficient for belief and acceptance, and so it is distinct from each of them. Even so, belieflessly assuming that p might be necessary for each of them. Let's look into the matter briefly.

If belieflessly assuming is distinct from belief and acceptance but necessary for each of them, then, whenever someone believes or accepts something, they beliefessly assume it too. Consider some such occasion. For example, suppose I have a dominant desire for banana bread and I believe that there's some in my fridge. Naturally, since there is no inner or outer obstacle to my acting on my belief and desire, I walk to the fridge. Whatever else might be relevant to explaining my behavior, it seems that my belief that there's some banana bread in the fridge has some work to do. But if belieflessly assuming that p is necessary for belief that p, then I not only believe that there's banana bread in the fridge, I beliefessly assume that there is as well. Here two options present themselves: either my belief and my beliefless assumption simultaneously explain my behavior or only one does. Since explanatory redundancy should be avoided when possible, we should pick only one option; and, since my banana bread belief can explain more that needs explaining (e.g. it explains why I am disposed to assert that there is banana bread in the fridge, but my beliefless banana bread assumption does not), we should pick the belief over the beliefless assumption. And what goes for this case goes for every case of belief (putatively) co-existing with beliefless assumption and, *mutatis mutandis*, for acceptance too. The upshot is that, unless there is some good reason to think that beliefless assumption is necessary for belief or acceptance (I know of none), we should theorize from the point of view that it is not. At any rate, that's how I will proceed in what follows.

Third, if beliefless assumption of the sort displayed in Alston's cases is distinct from belief and acceptance, compatible with being in doubt, and neither necessary nor sufficient for belief or acceptance, we might wonder how its dispositional profile differs from those of belief and acceptance. In this connection, recall that being in doubt about p is incompatible with belief and acceptance of p because of their dispositional profiles. When one is in doubt about whether p, one *lacks* a tendency to feel it to be the case that p upon considering whether p; one *lacks* a tendency to verbally affirm that p when asked whether p, one *lacks* a tendency to mentally assent to p, or to mentally affirm or judge that p is true; and one *lacks* a tendency to be surprised upon suddenly learning not-p. But now recall that being in doubt about p is compatible with belieflessly assuming that p. It follows that the dispositional profile of beliefless assumption lacks these tendencies as well.

Fourth remark: even though beliefless assumption differs from belief and acceptance in these ways, it functions similarly to them in reasoning and other behavior, as evidenced by the protagonists in Alston's cases. Specifically, if one belieflessly assumes that p, then, if one takes q to follow from p, one will tend to assume that q as well. And if one assumes that p, then, if one engages in practical or theoretical reasoning, one will tend to use p as a premise when appropriate. And, in general, if one belieflessly assumes that p, then, given one's goals, aversions, and other cognitive attitudes, one will tend to act in appropriate ways.

Fifth, we must resist the temptation to identify beliefless assumption with acting as if. One can act as if one believes that p while disbelieving or rejecting p, but one cannot belieflessly assume that p while disbelieving or rejecting p. For when one belieflessly assumes that p, one lacks the dispositional profile of disbelief; but when one disbelieves that p, one possesses it, even though one might dissemble and act as if one believes that p.

With these observations and remarks in hand, let's return to Alston's skeptical Christians. In light of what has been said about beliefless assumption, we are now in a better position to see how the required cognitive element of Christian faith need not pose a stumbling block to them. To keep what follows manageable, I will, like Alston, focus on Christian propositional faith and relational faith, and I will focus on his second case, the woman who "has been involved in the church from her early years, from a preskeptical time when she did fully believe."[40] Alston doesn't say how she became "troubled by doubts," so imagine that her story unfolds as follows.

After a decade of study and reflection that began as an undergraduate and continued throughout her twenties, she now finds herself deeply troubled

---

[40] Alston 1996: 17.

by arguments for atheism that challenge the goodness and love of God, arguments posed by sincere, respectful, and admirable atheists. Moreover, she finds herself stunned by the failure of Christian theologians to articulate unproblematic theories of how it is that God was in Christ reconciling Himself to sinners, especially in light of later doctrinal developments on this score. All this has left her in doubt about the basic Christian story, and therefore she is in no position to believe it or accept it. That's not to say that she fails to appreciate what can be said on its behalf. On the contrary. By her lights, it's the least false of the options she deems credible. At any rate, that's what she would say if you caught her on good day. On a bad day, she might be more inclined to say that, so far as she can tell, it's no more false than the best of the credible options. She vacillates between these skeptical poles. But despite her up-and-down cognitive situation, she continues to find her involvement in the church "meeting deep needs and giving her life meaning and structure," and she finds the way of love modeled by Jesus and many of his followers supremely attractive, so much so that she is motivated to align her will with his as his disciple, and to beliefiessly assume and thereby use the basic Christian story "as a basis for her thought about the world and for the way she leads her life".[41] So, despite her doubt, she continues in the practices of devotional reading, meditation, confession, thanksgiving, intercession, charity, the sacraments, congregational participation, observing the holy days and holidays, singing the great hymns and songs, teaching her children how to live the story, etc., finding these and related activities and commitments not only satisfying, but activities and commitments around which the rest of her life is shaped. In short, our skeptical Christian intentionally opens herself to the presence of the Lord and the power of the Spirit—to no avail, so far as she can tell. But she doesn't let that take the wind out of her sails or the sap out of her bones; she doesn't let that dishearten or discourage her from following Christ.

Our protagonist has Christian faith—or so I say. She has faith *that* the basic Christian story is true, although she neither believes it nor accepts it. The cognitive element of her faith is beliefiess assumption; just as the defensive captain beliefiessly assumes that the quarterback will call a fullback plunge, she beliefiessly assumes the basic Christian story. She also has faith *in* the Lord, despite her doubt. The cognitive element of her faith in him is also beliefiess assumption; just as the general beliefiessly assumes that the enemy is positioned thus-and-so and consequently aligns his troops for a pincer movement, she beliefiessly assumes that the Lord will remain true to his commitments to those who, like herself, put their trust in him, and she

---

[41] Alston 1996: 17.

belieflessly assumes that he will act favorably on her behalf with respect to her salvation; consequently, she aligns her will and acts accordingly. Her faith in him—including her faith that despite her struggles with doubt, he will never leave her or forsake her—provides her with enough stability and hope to battle late-stage breast cancer and its damnable effects, and gives her the impetus to tackle the more ordinary demons of a human life.

It should be clear that our skeptical Christian "is not necessarily inferior to the *believer*" when it comes to "commitment to the Christian life, or in the seriousness, faithfulness, or intensity with which she pursues it."[42]

In this connection, one of the more wacky objections I've heard to my thesis that beliefless assumption can be the cognitive element of Christian faith is that, on my view, it's too easy to have Christian faith. Apparently, a suitably difficult way requires belief of the basic Christian story, perhaps held "with certainty, without any hesitation or hanging back".[43] That way, when your total evidence, reasons, grounds, and whatever else you have to go on changes in such a way that you ought no longer to believe, or you ought to reduce your confidence, you have a magnificent opportunity to exhibit Christian virtue by embracing the tension—perhaps even the contradiction!—wholeheartedly, knuckling down, and believing all the same, with just the same confidence as before. That's true standing up for Jesus! I must leave an examination of this doxolatrous approach to Christian faith for another occasion.[44] As for the charge that my view makes it insufficiently difficult to have Christian faith, two points are relevant. First, in general, and all else being equal, it is more difficult to act in accordance with a proposition you take some cognitive attitude toward if you belieflessly assume it than if you believe it. Second, if you have any doubt about whether Christian faith with beliefless assumption rather than belief as its cognitive element is an exception to the rule, I say, try it out some time. Then you'll have a better idea how silly it is to suggest that it's easier to have Christian faith without belief.

Before I address an Alstonian objection to what I've put forward, let me briefly summarize how beliefless assumption allows us to proffer a substantive solution to our three problems. As for the problem of the skeptical

---

[42] Alston 1996: 17 (his emphasis). Indeed, you might consider her an exemplar of Christian faith. In this connection, we would do well to reflect on the life of Mother Teresa in light of her private writings. See Kolodiejchuk 2007.

[43] Stump 2003: 363; cf. Thomas Aquinas, *Summa Theologica*, IIaIIae.1.4 and IIaIIae.4.8.

[44] For a splendid contemporary example of this approach—embracing contradictions and all—see the "Way of Aporia," which is better labeled the "Way of Dogmatism," in Sullivan 2014.

Christian, we can deny the claim that the cognitive element of Christian faith is belief or acceptance of the basic Christian story since one might well assume them, which, unlike Alston's solution, is at home with the cognitive situation of skeptical Christians. As for the problem of faith and reason, we can deny the claim that if your Christian faith is reasonable, then it is reasonable for you either to believe or to accept the basic Christian story. For even if it is not reasonable for you either to believe or to accept the basic Christian story, it might yet be reasonable for you to belieflessly assume it, which, unlike Alston's solution, is consonant with the cognitive situation of skeptical Christians and keeps their faith reasonable, at least in so far as its cognitive element is concerned. As for the problem of the trajectory, we can explain to our newly-skeptical university student how the trajectory from doubt to getting out can be broken since they might belieflessly assume the basic Christian story and act with integrity on the basis of that assumption, which, unlike Alston's solution, allows them to continue practicing their faith with a clear conscience, although it's likely to be difficult, perhaps very difficult. But whoever said following Jesus would always be easy, cognitively or otherwise? Not Jesus.

5. AN ALSTONIAN OBJECTION TO BELIEFLESS ASSUMPTION AS THE COGNITIVE ELEMENT OF CHRISTIAN FAITH

In a revealing passage, Alston contrasts accepting a proposition with acting on the beliefless assumption that it is true. Here it is in its entirety:

When the press of affairs requires us to act on one assumption or another, we cannot wait for more evidence. This is the situation of our defensive captain. He must dispose his [players] in one way rather than another, based on one or another assumption as to what the offense will do. But he still need not accept a particular hypothesis on that point. He can adopt an *assumption*, a *working hypothesis*, for the sake of action guidance without accepting it. Accepting *p* involves a more positive attitude toward that proposition than just making the assumption that *p* or hypothesizing that *p*. The difference could be put this way. To accept that *p* is to regard it as true, though one need not be explicitly deploying the concept of truth in order to do so. But one can *assume* or *hypothesize* that *p* for a particular limited purpose, as our captain might have done, without taking any stand on truth value. Again, one can assume or hypothesize that *p* for the sake of testing it, trying it out in practice, so as to help one decide whether to accept it.[45]

---

[45]   Alston 1996: 11, his emphasis.

Although Alston does not have in mind here the thesis that beliefless assumption can be the cognitive element in Christian faith, his remarks suggest that he might not look kindly on it.

We might put the objection like this. Christian faith essentially involves a cognitive element, some positive cognitive attitude toward the basic Christian story.[46] However, when one merely beliefflessly assumes the basic Christian story, one does so just for the purpose of trying it out, to see what happens, perhaps as a field anthropologist might do with any eye toward immersing herself in the point of view of the people she's studying,[47] or perhaps, as Alston suggests, our defensive captain might have done. That cognitive attitude, however, is not positive enough. The cognitive element of Christian faith requires one to take a stand on its truth, to believe it or accept it.

The central thought here targets the credentials of beliefless assumption as a positive cognitive attitude. The idea is that, unlike belief and accept-ance, beliefless assumption really isn't a positive cognitive attitude at all since it does not involve taking a stand on the truth of its propositional object. Of course, that raises the question of what taking a stand on the truth of a proposition requires. I suspect that those who are tempted by this idea will answer that in order for a cognitive attitude toward p to involve taking a stand on the truth of p, its owner must have at least some tendency to assert p when asked, or at least some tendency to mentally assent to p when it comes to mind.

But it seems to me that, although the dispositional profile of beliefless assumption lacks these tendencies, it includes other tendencies that consti-tute taking a stand on the truth of what is beliefflessly assumed. For just as when one believes or accepts that p, when one beliefflessly assumes that p, one will tend to use p as a premise in practical and theoretical reasoning when appropriate and one will, more generally, tend to act in ways befit-ting one's goals, aversions, and other cognitive attitudes. This is why we expect that, when the defensive captain beliefflessly assumes that the quar-terback will call a plunge, they will stack six men on the line rather than four; this is why we expect that, when the general beliefflessly assumes that the enemy is situated thus-and-so, they will disperse their troops for a pincer movement rather than a frontal assault; this is why we expect that, when the humble philosopher beliefflessly assumes libertarianism, they will, for example, use it in their theodicy rather than neglect it for that

---

[46] Alston 1996: 15.
[47] For what this might look like in the sociology of religion, see Luhrman 1989 and 2012.

purpose. This is why we expect that, when the skeptical Christian I described earlier beliefAessly assumes the basic Christian story and the trustworthiness of the Lord, she confesses her sins, partakes of the sacraments, realigns her will regularly through prayerful self-examination, gives generously, and so on. *By performing these actions rather than certain others*, each of our protagonists manifests tendencies that constitute taking a stand on the truth of what is beliefAessly assumed, even though tendencies to assert verbally and assent mentally are absent.

Perhaps the worry lies elsewhere. Perhaps the worry is that, even if beliefless assuming involves taking *some* sort of stand on the truth of what is beliefAessly assumed, it isn't enough of a stand. It's too much like just putting one's toes in the water, or just taking a sip, or just holding hands, or smoking pot without inhaling. It's too much like assuming just for the purpose of trying it out, just to see what happens, just to give it a whirl. It's too non-committal, too much like mere hypothesizing or conjecturing.

It is difficult to know what to say in reply. Does the skeptical Christian I described before *look* like she's beliefAessly assuming the basic Christian story *just* for the purpose of trying it out, *just* to give it a test drive, *just* to see whether she wants to buy in? Of course not. She's bought in more fully than nearly all of the believing Christians I know. Moreover, she doesn't beliefAessly assume it *just* "for the sake of action guidance" or *just* "for a particular limited purpose," but rather because it seems to her the most likely, the most strongly indicated, or the least false of the options she deems credible. And, having beliefAessly assumed it, she may as well structure her life around it, and thereby shape her life into a meaningful, purposeful whole.[48]

As for the suggestion that beliefless assumption, *on my understanding of it*, is too much like hypothesizing or conjecturing, three points are relevant. First, unlike beliefless assuming, hypothesizing and conjecturing *are* just for the sake of action guidance. Second, unlike beliefless assuming, one does *not* hypothesize or conjecture something because it seems to one the most likely of the credible options but rather because one wonders what follows from it; hypothesis and conjecture have a what-if-ery quality about them that assuming lacks. Third, unlike beliefless assuming, one does *not* hypothesize or conjecture a worldview and then structure one's entire life around it. We might put the point this way: in the passage quoted above, Alston has a sense of "assuming" in mind according to which to assume that p is merely to adopt it as a "working hypothesis," to make a conjecture. That's not the sense of "assume" I have mind, nor is it the sense of "assume" on which is

---

[48] For more on faith unifying a life, see Kvanvig 2013 and forthcoming 2018, esp. chs 4 and 5, and Dewey 1934, ch. 1.

makes sense to say that the captain, the general, the philosopher, Eliot, or the skeptical Christian acts on the beliefless assumption that the target proposition is true. In this second sense of "assumes," to belieflessly assume that p "involves a more positive attitude toward that proposition than just" hypothesizing or conjecturing that p.

Alston aimed to exhibit how the skeptical Christian could have Christian faith. In my judgment, he failed. However, by examining the ways in which he illustrated his views about belief, acceptance, and their relation to Christian faith, I hope to have shown how his goal can be achieved. We simply need to follow his lead a bit further and broaden our horizons with respect to the variety of ways in which "sincere, active, committed, devout Christians" might meet the cognitive demand of Christian faith.[49] In particular, we would do well to countenance beliefless assumption, perhaps among other ways.[50,51]

REFERENCES

Alston, William. 1996. "Belief, Acceptance, and Religious Faith," in Jeff Jordan and Daniel Howard-Snyder, eds, *Faith, Freedom, and Rationality*. Lanham, MD: Rowman & Littlefield.

Alston, William. 2007. "Audi on Nondoxastic Faith," in Mark Timmons, John Greco, and Alfred R. Mele, eds, *Rationality and the Good: Critical Essays on the Ethics and Epistemology of Robert Audi*. Oxford: Oxford University Press.

Audi, Robert. 2011. *Rationality and Religious Commitment*. Oxford: Oxford University Press.

Dewey, John. 1934. *A Common Faith*. New Haven, CT: Yale University Press.

Howard-Snyder, Daniel. 2013a. "Schellenberg on Propositional Faith," *Religious Studies* 49: 181–94.

Howard-Snyder, Daniel. 2013b. "Propositional Faith: What it is and What it is not," *American Philosophical Quarterly* 50: 357–72.

---

[49] Alston 1996: 16.

[50] See, for example, Audi 2011, Kvanvig forthcoming 2018, esp. chs 4 and 5, McKaughan 2013 and 2016, Pojman 1986, Roeber unpublished, Schellenberg 2005, and Swinburne 1981. For discussion of Schellenberg 2005, see Howard-Snyder 2013a.

[51] For their helpful comments on earlier versions of this paper and the ideas contained herein, I would like to thank Andy Cullison, Keith DeRose, Trent Dougherty, Frances Howard-Snyder, Hud Hudson, Jon Jacobs, Jon Kvanvig, Mark Lance, Dan McKaughan, Paddy McShane, Meghan Page, Rik Peels, Ryan Preston-Roedder, Bradley Rettler, Lindsay Rettler, Blake Roeber, Tom Senor, Meghan Sullivan, Peter van Elswyk, Dean Zimmerman, and an anonymous referee for this journal. This publication was generously supported through a grant from the Templeton Religion Trust. The opinions expressed in it are those of the author and do not necessarily reflect the views of TRT.

Howard-Snyder, Daniel. 2016. "Does Faith Entail Belief?," *Faith and Philosophy* 33: 142–62.

Kolodiejchuk, Brian. 2007. *Mother Teresa: Come Be My Light*. New York: Doubleday.

Kvanvig, Jonathan L. 2013. "Affective Theism and People of Faith," *Midwest Studies in Philosophy* 37: 109–28.

Kvanvig, Jonathan L. Forthcoming 2018. *Faith and Humility*. Oxford: Oxford University Press.

Lee, Matthew. 2014. "Belief, Doubt, and Confidence: A Threshold Account." PhD dissertation: University of Notre Dame.

Luhrman, Tanya. 1989. *Persuasions of the Witch's Craft: Ritual magic in modern culture*. Cambridge, MA: Harvard University Press.

Luhrman, Tanya. 2012. *When God talks back: Understanding the American evangelical relationship with God*. New York: Knopf.

McKaughan, Daniel. 2013. "Authentic Faith and Acknowledged Risk: Dissolving the Problem of Faith and Reason," *Religious Studies* 49: 101–24.

McKaughan, Daniel. 2016. "Action-Centered Faith, Doubt, and Rationality," *Journal of Philosophical Research* 41: 71–90.

Moon, Andrew. 2017. "The Nature of Doubt and a New Puzzle about Belief, Doubt, and Confidence." *Synthese*. doi:10.1007/s11229-016-1310-y.

Peels, Rik. Unpublished. "Doubt."

Penelhum, Terence. 1995. *Reason and Religious Faith*. Boulder, CO: Westview Press.

Pojman, Louis. 1986. *Religious Belief and the Will*. New York: Routledge.

Roeber, Blake. Unpublished. "The Aim of Belief and the Rationality of Faith."

Schellenberg, J. L. 2005. *Prolegomena to a Philosophy of Religion*. Ithaca, NY: Cornell University Press.

Stump, Eleonore. 2003. *Aquinas*. New York: Routledge.

Sullivan, Meghan. 2014. "Uneasy Grace," *First Things*. <http://www.firstthings.com/article/2014/04/uneasy-grace> (accessed July 20, 2014).

Swinburne, Richard. 1981. *Faith and Reason*. Oxford: Oxford University Press.

8

Omnipresence and the Location of the Immaterial

Ross D. Inman

At the heart of many a theistic metaphysic is the view that an exhaustive inventory of reality consists of both material and immaterial entities, and that these two domains interact in some way or other. There is, however, surprisingly little discussion at the intersection of contemporary metaphysics and philosophical theology concerning the precise nature of and relationship between the material and the immaterial and its bearing on Christian theology.

This was not always the case. Medieval philosophical reflection was replete with discussion on the nature of the relationship between God, angels, and the human soul and the material domain. In fact, according to Robert Pasnau (2011a), the medieval scholastics were largely in agreement that immaterial entities, though lacking in material content are, strictly speaking, spatially located or present in some sense or other when relating to material reality. The question that preoccupied medieval philosophical theologians, then, was not *whether* such entities were spatially located or present in their dealings with material beings, but rather, *how* they were located as such. This, of course, assumes an understanding of the material–immaterial divide that is largely foreign to the contemporary context. Yet it is one that is both philosophically interesting, theologically fruitful, and by my lights worthy of serious consideration once again.

In this paper I want to explore the prospects of following on the heels of the medievals in thinking of immaterial beings, God and the human soul in particular, as being spatially located or present in some sense to the material domain. I begin by offering a brief taxonomy of various models of omnipresence that have been offered both in the history of Christian philosophical theology and in the contemporary literature. I then turn to examine a recent account of omnipresence in terms of ubiquitous spatial occupation or location as well as the underlying metaphysics it employs. After highlighting a point of tension for such a view with standard analyses of the concept of 'material object', I offer a historical sampling of Latin medieval views regarding the nature of the relationship between God and the human soul to space. I conclude by noting how such views help carve out a range of alternative analyses of 'material object' that leave conceptual room for a contemporary theist to follow suit in thinking that at least some immaterial entities are spatially located or present to the physical domain.

1. OMNIPRESENCE: A TAXONOMY

To say that God is omnipresent is to say that God is present or located at each and every place (where 'place' in what follows will serve as a generic place-holder for either an existing entity—a region of space—or simply a material object together with the spatio-temporal or distance relations it stands in to other material objects). But what exactly does it mean to say that God, an immaterial being, is present or located at a particular place? Here it appears that we are already in very deep waters indeed.

In the most general terms, models of omnipresence can be classified according to whether God is taken to be located or present at a place in either a *fundamental* or a *derivative* sense. Roughly, for an entity to be located at some place fundamentally is for it to be located at that place *in its own right*; or in other words: the locative facts about where the entity is located obtain in virtue of facts about the entity *itself*, together with the places and the primitive 'is located at' relation that ties them to those places. On the other hand, an entity's being located at some place derivatively amounts to the claim that it is located in virtue of standing in some particular relation or relations to a *distinct entity*, where the latter is itself located at the place in the fundamental sense; or, the locative facts concerning where the entity is located obtain in virtue of the locative facts about where some *distinct* entity is located fundamentally, together with the various relations it bears to the entity in question.

Taking "is located at" as our primitive we can state these two varieties of location as follows (where '*p*' stands for some place):

Fundamental Location: *x* is located at *p* *fundamentally* $=_{df}$ *x* is located at *p* *in its own right*, i.e. not in virtue of standing in relation(s), R(s), to some distinct *y* that is located at *p* in its own right.

Derivative Location: *x* is located at *p* *derivatively* $=_{df}$ *x* is located at *p* in virtue of standing in some relation(s), R(s), to some distinct entity, *y*, where *y* is located at *p* fundamentally.

Material objects, for example, are constituents of reality that are located at a place in the fundamental sense; trees, tables, and tigers are spatially located at a place *in their own right* in that they themselves bear the "located at" relation to the place in question.

Before applying the above framework to divine omnipresence, it may be helpful to consider the following non-theological example illustrating the distinction between **Fundamental Location** and **Derivative Location**. Those who defend an ontology of immanent universals maintain that such entities exist 'in' their instances in that they are located where the particulars that instantiate them are located. Consider, for example, the universal *charge -1* that is shared by all electrons. As an immanent universal, the property *charge -1* is (wholly) multiply located where each and every individual electron is located.

Now consider an individual electron that is located at some place p. For the proponent of immanent universals, the location of *charge -1* at p can be construed in one of two ways: either (i) *charge -1* is located at p only in the sense that it is instantiated by an electron that is itself located at p, or (ii) *charge -1* is located at p in the sense that it is located at p *in its own right*, i.e. not in virtue of bearing a relation to something that is located at p in its own right. Many friends of immanent universals are inclined to think that such properties are spatially located in the fundamental rather than the derivative sense.[1]

Note further the reductive nature of **Derivative Location**: an entity's being located at a particular place is *nothing more* than its standing in some relation or relations to a distinct entity that is itself located at that place in the fundamental sense. To endorse **Fundamental Location**, then, amounts to the claim that x's standing in R to some distinct entity that is located at a place in the fundamental sense is neither necessary nor sufficient for its being located at that place. As stated, **Fundamental Location** and **Derivative Location** are mutually exclusive: an object cannot be both fundamentally and derivatively located at the same place at the same time.

With the above notions of **Fundamental Location** and **Derivative Location** in hand, we can broadly divide models of divine omnipresence along the following lines. Let "L_d" stand for **Derivative Location**, "L_f" for **Fundamental Location**, and read "$L(\text{God}, p)$" as "God is located at p":

(FO) **Fundamental Omnipresence**: $(\forall p)(p \text{ is a place} \rightarrow L_f(\text{God}, p))$

(DO) **Derivative Omnipresence**: $(\forall p)(p \text{ is a place} \rightarrow L_d(\text{God}, p))$

---

[1] See O'Leary-Hawthorne and Cover (1998) as well as Gilmore (2003).

As was the case with **Fundamental Location** and **Derivative Location**, FO and DO are mutually exclusive models of divine omnipresence. An informal test for distinguishing DO and FO models would be if the model entails that God, considered apart from his standing in some relation or relations to objects that are themselves located at p fundamentally, could nevertheless be located at p. If so, then you have an FO model; if not, then a DO model.

A list of thinkers who are commonly thought to endorse an account of omnipresence along the lines of DO include Anselm, Aquinas, Descartes, Leibniz, and Jonathan Edwards in his later writings (to name just a few). DO models differ as to how they construe the particular relation or relations (R or Rs) in which God stands to entities that are located at a place in the fundamental sense.[2]

One common interpretation of Anselm, for instance, characterizes R exclusively in epistemic terms, namely, God's immediate knowledge or awareness of the goings on at every place.[3] Along similar lines, a standard reading of Aquinas on omnipresence is that he closely adheres to a common medieval formula originating with Peter Lombard in terms of (i) God's immediate causal activity at every place, (ii) God's immediate knowledge or awareness of every place, and (iii) God's essence or substance existing at every place. Many interpreters read Aquinas as reducing clause (iii) to clause (i), namely God's directly causally sustaining in existence each and every creature in a place.[4]

The overwhelming majority of work on divine omnipresence in contemporary philosophical theology consists of variants of DO.[5] The likes of Swinburne (1993), Hoffman and Rosenkrantz (2002), Taliaferro (1994), Wierenga (2010), and Craig and Moreland (2003) all broadly follow Aquinas in unpacking Rs in terms of God's standing in immediate (basic) causal relations as well as his immediate knowledge of the ongoings at every place. The recent work of Eleonore Stump (2010, 2013) aims to defend a DO model which includes the notion of shared or joint attention as a more

[2] See Anselm (1998, chs 20–22), Aquinas (1974: III, q. 68), Descartes (1985: 372–3), Leibniz (1989: 683, 690) and Jonathan Edwards (1955: 183–4).

[3] See Blount (1997), Wierenga (1988), and Hudson (2009). Although see Conn (2011), Leftow (1989), Pasnau (2011a), and Zagzebski (2013) for an alternative reading of Anselm on omnipresence.

[4] See Cross (2003), Swinburne (1993), and Wierenga (2010), and Wainwright (2010) for this reading of Aquinas.

[5] Contemporary philosophers of religion who endorse a DO model of omnipresence include Richard Swinburne, Peter van Inwagen, Joshua Hoffman and Gary S. Rosenkrantz, William Wainwright, Edward Wierenga, Charles Taliaferro, Eleonore Stump, Norman Kretzmann, William Lane Craig, and J.P. Moreland.

fine-grained epistemic condition on divine omnipresence, in addition to God's immediate causal activity and cognitive awareness of every place and its occupants.[6]

One interesting thing to note in passing here is that it is difficult to see how on a DO model omnipresence is a distinct attribute over and above divine omnipotence, omniscience, omnibenevolence, or a combination of these divine attributes. For this reason, the proponent of a DO model might consider omnipresence to be *reducible* to or "nothing over and above" one of the above attributes or conjunction thereof.[7]

FO models of omnipresence, on the other hand, are often thought to be few and far between in the history of Christian philosophical theology. Yet FO models were particularly common in the later medieval and early modern period, most notably in the thought of Duns Scotus, Nicole Oresme, Isaac Newton, and the Cambridge Platonist Henry More.[8] More (1995),

---

[6] See Stump (2010: 117), "God's having direct and unmediated cognitive and causal contact with everything in creation is still insufficient for divine omnipresence. In order for God to be omnipresent, that is, in order for God to be always and everywhere *present*, it also needs to be the case that God is always and everywhere in a position to share attention with any creature able and willing to share attention with God." However, Stump is clear both that shared attention is an epistemic state between *persons* (which would suggest that God fails to be present in places where there are no (non-divine) persons, and whether or not God is omnipresent in the sense she defines is partly determined by the state or condition of the creature (p. 117).

[7] Along these lines, consider the following remark by Robert Adams (1994:124) concerning Leibniz's DO account of omnipresence in terms of God's exercising immediate causal action at a place: "In his later years, Leibniz understands God's immensity as omnipresence and seems favorably disposed to the Scholastic reduction of God's presence in a place to 'immediate operation' on things that are in that place. This suggests the view that immensity is not a divine perfection distinct from omnipotence."

[8] Richard Cross, in his "Duns Scotus on Divine Immensity" (2016), defends the position that Scotus held to a view of omnipresence that is broadly classified as an FO model. As I hope to show in much more detail elsewhere, I consider FO models to be much more prominent in the Christian tradition than is commonly thought. There is a case to be made that even the likes of early modern philosophers Nicolas Malebranche and John Locke as well as theologians John Wesley and the early Jonathan Edwards endorsed FO models of omnipresence. The first three thinkers rely on the principle that an agent, whether created or uncreated, had to first be present at a place for it to be able to act or perceive at that place. In responding to an account of omnipresence characterized solely in terms of God's causal operation at each place, Malebranche (1997) (speaking through the character Theodore in his *Dialogues on Metaphysics and Religion*), states "What kind of reality is God's operation as distinguished and separated from his substance? . . . Now, if the act by which God produces or conserves this chair is here, surely God is here himself; and if he is here, he must be here completely and thus in all the other respects in which he operates" (133, dialogue 8, sec. 5); Locke (1975): "Spirits, as well as Bodies, cannot operate, but where they are" (*Essays*, bk. 2, ch. 23, sec. 19); Wesley (1991): "And these sufficiently prove his omnipresence; which may be farther proved from this consideration: God acts everywhere, and, therefore, is everywhere; for it is an utter impossibility

for instance, grounded God's attribute of omnipresence in God's being *identical to space*, where he understood space to be uncreated, necessary, and existing *a se*. Without going so far as to identify God with space, Newton (1934: 545) was of the opinion that (absolute) space was inextricably bound up with the existence of God that while "he is not duration or space, but he endures and is present. He endures forever, and is everywhere present; and by existing always and everywhere, he constitutes duration and space. Since every particle of space is always...certainly the Maker and Lord of all things cannot be never and nowhere." Since God's existence alone accounts for both the existence of absolute space as well as God's being present to each point of absolute space, his existing of necessity demands that God be omnipresent with respect to absolute space from all eternity.[9]

Those who defend a model of omnipresence along the lines of FO are a rare breed in contemporary analytic philosophical theology. There is one rather obvious reason why this may be the case. To maintain that God is located at every place in the fundamental sense is to claim that God is located everywhere, but not in virtue of his direct causal or cognitive contact with creatures that are themselves located in the fundamental sense. But what *other* sense of location or presence could possibly characterize an immaterial being other than the derivative variety in terms of basic causal or epistemic relations? It seems that a more robust and immediate form of location or presence along the lines required by FO models threatens to undermine both the immateriality and the transcendence of God. On first pass, then, it appears that the only way for immaterial beings in general to be located is for them to be located in the derivative sense.

Be that as it may, there are several contemporary philosophers and theologians who defend a variant of an FO model of omnipresence including Hud Hudson (2009, 2014), Alexander Pruss (2013), Robert Oakes (2006), and Luco J. Van Den Brom (1993). As we will see in much more detail below,

that any being, created or uncreated, should work where it is not" (*Sermon* 111 "On the Omnipresence of God"). The early Edwards (1955), most likely reflecting the influence of Henry More, claims that "space is necessary, eternal, infinite, and omnipresent. But I had as good speak plain, I have already said as much as that space is God." (*Of Being*, 19)

[9] Strangely enough, Newton thinks that "no being exists or can exist which is not related to space in some way. God is everywhere, created minds are somewhere, and body is in the space it occupies; and whatever is neither everywhere nor anywhere does not exist" (1962: 103). Yet God's being everywhere present in such a way, for Newton, is no mere function of his causal operation at every place: "He is omnipresent not only *virtually* but also *substantially*; for action requires substance....It is agreed that the supreme God necessarily exists, and by the same necessity he is *always* and *everywhere*" (1999: 941–2).

Hudson and Pruss construe God's omnipresence as his being wholly spatially located at each region of spacetime in a particular kind of way (entension). Oakes, on the other hand, adopts the quasi-Newtonian line that God is everywhere present precisely because his existence constitutes the existence of space itself, that God is "*maximally immanent in space*–and, indeed, *necessarily* so: [since] space is an *essential aspect* of God" (175). Van Den Brom, in what looks to be the only book-length treatment on omnipresence in the last fifty years, defends the view that God is present at each place in our three-dimensional space in virtue of being spatially extended in his own higher-dimensional space, a hyperspace in which our own three-dimensional space is embedded.

What unifies the above FO models is that each affirm that God is located at every place *in his own right*, and not in virtue of his standing in some immediate causal or epistemic relation to objects that are located in their own right. In other words, the locative facts about where God is located obtain in virtue of facts about God himself, together with the places and the primitive 'is located at' relation that relates God to those places. On FO models, omnipresence is independent of any further causal or epistemic (or any other) relations God might stand in to the denizens of spacetime, who are themselves located in the fundamental sense. Consequently, for those who defend a variant of FO, omnipresence is a distinct and non-derivative attribute of God and thereby irreducible to omnipotence, omniscience, omnibenevolence or the like.

There are two important things to note in passing regarding the above general models of omnipresence at play in the contemporary literature. First, there is a consensus in contemporary work on divine omnipresence that what I am calling **Derivative Location** corresponds exclusively to *non-spatial* location, and that **Fundamental Location** corresponds exclusively to *spatial* location. For the vast majority of contemporary philosophers and theologians who defend a DO model of omnipresence, while God is genuinely located at each and every place in virtue of either his immediate causal activity or knowledge or a combination of the two, this variety of location or presence is best understood in a *non-literal* sense; God is literally *nowhere* when present to the material occupants of spacetime. Hoffman and Rosenkrantz (2002: 41) state this view nicely: "We conclude that since God is *not spatially located*, there is no *literal* sense in which he could be omnipresent."

There are, however, a handful of medieval and early modern scholars who reject the above claim that **Derivative Location** and **Fundamental Location** neatly map on to the distinction between non-spatial and spatial location (respectively) when it comes to the development of omnipresence in the Christian tradition.[10] It is argued that a plausible historical case can be made that even many of the DO models of omnipresence purportedly advanced by medieval and early modern philosophers are best thought of along the lines of God's being literally spatially located at or present to every place. As Jeffrey Brower (2014: 224–6) has recently noted, even Aquinas denies that "the mere possession of spatial location is sufficient for being a material object, since he thinks even God and the angels can be said to have spatial location" (225). While God is everywhere present in virtue of his direct causal and epistemic contact with each object that is located at a place fundamentally, it may be argued that even this variety of location was widely thought to be a genuine form of spatial location.[11]

Second, while FO and DO models are strictly incompatible models of omnipresence, it is entirely consistent for FO models to incorporate the notion that God stands in both direct causal and epistemic relations to creatures that are themselves fundamentally located at a place, and even that these types of relations (however coarse or fine-grained) factor into an exhaustive account of God's interaction with material reality. Part of what is at stake between FO and DO models of omnipresence is whether or not the attribute of omnipresence in particular is reducible to God's standing in such relations to material beings; proponents of FO models answer in the negative, those of DO models in the affirmative. While the FO proponent may question the reducibility of divine omnipresence to such relations, they are nevertheless free to help themselves to these or any other relations in order to provide a comprehensive and theologically adequate account of divine action and presence in the world (e.g. conservation, concurrence, Eucharistic presence, indwelling of the Holy Spirit, etc.).

2. OMNIPRESENCE AS UBIQUITOUS ENTENSION

With the above taxonomy in hand, I now want to turn to examine an FO model of omnipresence recently advanced by both Hud Hudson (2009,

---

[10] See Pasnau (2011a, 2011b), Reid (2008), Brower (2014: 224–6), Grant (1981), Goris (2009), Adams (2006), Muller (2003). Muller (2003: 343), for example, sums up theological reflection on divine omnipresence in Reformed Orthodoxy from the period *c.*1565–*c.*1725 as follows: "the divine immensity and omnipresence place God *extra mundum* ["outside the world"] in the sense of being beyond all physical limitation, not in the sense of being physically distanced from the world order."

[11] Even more, however, is the fact that some of these same scholars call into question standard characterizations of the Christian tradition as largely favoring a DO as opposed to an FO model of divine omnipresence.

2014) and Alexander Pruss (2013), what Hudson refers to as "ubiquitous entension." I'll begin by unpacking some of the requisite metaphysics undergirding their view and then flag an untoward theological implication of their account stemming from predominant analyses of the concept of 'material object.'

Within the past few years, analytic metaphysics has seen a resurgence of interest in the variety of location or occupation relations that relate material objects to the places where they are located. On its surface, talk of 'places' smacks of a substantivalist view of space, the view that places exist independently of their contents and are in no way reducible to or derivative upon distance relations between material objects, as the relationalist maintains. While some are of the opinion that substantivalism has achieved something of a consensus among philosophers of physics for good reason, others are hopeful that talk of 'places' or 'locations' can be adequately paraphrased into a suitable relationalist framework. Though I myself lean more towards a substantival view of space, I intend to remain as neutral as possible as to how much ontological weight one ought to assign to talk of 'places' or 'locations' in what follows.

Informally, let us say that I am *entirely located* in my office (where I use 'office' here to denote a mereologically complex place for illustrative purposes) when I am in my office and I am nowhere outside of my office; I am exclusively in my office such that I fail to be in any place that doesn't share a proper part in common with my office. Now if I were to reach my arm outside of my office to get the attention of my colleague, I would cease to be entirely located in my office. I would, however, be *partly located* in my office in so far as at least one of my proper parts is entirely located in my office. Lastly, I am *wholly located* in a particular sub-place of my office when all of me is in that place, there is no proper part of me that fails to be in that sub-place of my office.

More precisely, let us follow Hudson (2005: 99) in taking "is located at" as primitive and define the following location relations:

x is *entirely located* at $p =_{df} x$ is located at p and there is no place disjoint from p at which x is located.

x is *partly located* at $p =_{df} x$ has a proper part entirely located at p.

x is *wholly located* at $p =_{df} x$ is located at p and there is no proper part of x not located at p.

Here I need to say a bit about the difference between an object's being *entirely located* and its being *wholly located* at a place, as the two are often conflated.[12]

---

[12] Helm (1980), for instance, makes the following claim: "A second thing that it seems to mean is that God cannot be wholly present at two or more separated places at once.

In so far as it denotes exclusivity of location, my being *entirely located* in my office excludes my being located at any place that is disjoint from my office; if I am entirely in my office, I am nowhere else. On the other hand, my being *wholly located* in my office in no way excludes the possibility of my also being wholly located at a distinct, non-overlapping place in space; that is, it allows for the possibility of *multi-location.*

On the assumption that places can stand in part–whole relations to one another (places can have other places as proper parts, i.e. proper subplaces), we can define the notion of an object's *entending* and *pertending* a place in space:

x pertends $p =_{df} x$ is an object that is entirely located at an extended (non-point sized) place p, and for each proper subplace of p, p^*, x has a proper part entirely located at p^*.

x entends $=_{pdf} x$ is an object that is wholly and entirely located at an extended (non-point sized) place p, and for each proper subplace of p, p^*, x is wholly located at p^*

For an object to pertend in space is for it to be exclusively located at an extended place and for each of its proper parts to be 'spread out' or distributed across each of the proper subplaces of that place. My body, for instance, is entirely located at an extended place (right *here* and not on a beach in Bermuda), yet it is distributed across space in that it is partly located where my right arm is, and partly located where my head is, etc.

Now consider an object's entending a place in space. Roughly, for an object to entend is for all of it (without remainder) to be exclusively located at an extended place, and for all of it (without remainder) to be located at each of the proper subplaces of that place. Entending objects are not 'spread out' or distributed across space such that they are partly located or present at distinct, non-overlapping places; rather, for each of the places where they are located, they are *wholly* located both at both the places themselves and at each of the proper parts of those places.[13]

Both Hud Hudson (2009, 2014) and Alexander Pruss (2013) have found in the relation of entension renewed prospects for shedding light on the

It seems to be a conceptual truth about any individual in space that it cannot be wholly present in two places at once." Here Helm collapses the distinction between an object's being *entirely* located at a region (*there* and nowhere else) and its being wholly located at a region (every proper part of the object is *there*, without remainder). If the denial of multi-location is a conceptual truth as Helm suspects, then entension (which entails but is not entailed by multi-location) is ruled out from the start.

[13] Note that while entension entails multi-location—an item cannot entend in space without being multi-located in space—the converse does not seem to hold in so far as an object that is multi-located at two distinct places, p1 and p2, need not be wholly located at each of the subplaces of p1 and p2.

divine attribute of omnipresence.[14] They both suggest that divine omnipresence is plausibly construed in terms of ubiquitous entension: that God is wholly and entirely located at the maximally inclusive place, presumably the whole of spacetime itself, and is wholly located at each of the proper subplaces of spacetime.

Recall the two-fold definition of entension above. Given that the whole of spacetime itself encompasses every place whatsoever, it is clear that there is *no* place disjoint from it at which God is located. Moreover, the second clause of the definition is automatically satisfied if one takes God to be altogether devoid of proper parts. On this view, in so far as God has no proper parts at all, he fails to have distinct parts spread out over the various subplaces of space. If one takes God to have proper parts, then God would be wholly located at every subplace of space in so far as every one of His proper parts would be located at every subplace of space.

In response to what he calls *the problem of incorporeality*, the question as to how something can occupy a place in space and fail to be material, Hudson argues that an untoward consequence of the ubiquitous entension model is that God turns out to be a material object, embodied in the whole of spacetime.

The untoward implication turns on Hudson's occupation analysis of the concept of 'material object' stated as follows:

Occupation: x is a *material object* $=_{df} x$ occupies a place in space.[15]

Hudson prefers to bite the bullet of God's being a material object rather than part with his preferred analysis of 'material object.' He notes:

My own view of the matter is that anything that occupies a region is a material object, and that the occupier inherits the shape, size, dimensionality, topology, and boundaries of the region in which it is entirely located. Anyone similarly attracted to the simple occupancy analysis of 'material object' and these related theses has a bullet to bite if he wants to endorse an entension-based reading of omnipresence... to

---

[14] Here I ignore the minor variations between the accounts offered by Hudson (2009, 2014) and Pruss (2013). One notable difference hinges on whether or not ubiquitous entension is compatible with divine timelessness. Hudson answers in the negative, Pruss in the affirmative. Pruss employs David Lewis's distinction between *external* and *personal* time, roughly the difference between objective time and inner time, respectively. To illustrate, consider the following remark by the backwards time-traveler: "In five minutes (internal time) I'll be in the Mesozoic era (external time)." Pruss defines omnipresence in terms of God's being wholly located at every place of space at every external time. He takes God's atemporality to be a matter of his being *internally* or *personally* atemporal, that is, God's inner life has no internal time.

[15] As Hudson endorses a substantivalist theory of spacetime, he glosses **Occupation** in terms of regions of spacetime as opposed to the more neutral 'place.'

be fair, however, the simple occupancy analysis of 'material object' is certainly controversial (and negotiable for the theist) (2009: 211).

I'll argue below that orthodox theists who are sympathetic to a non-reductive model of omnipresence in terms of ubiquitous entension have ample historical motivation to be open to negotiate as to whether **Occupation** correctly demarcates the material from the immaterial.

But note here that the threat of divine materiality is in no way limited to one's endorsement of **Occupation**. Rather, an entension-based reading of omnipresence gives rise to the above untoward theological commitment on similar analyses of 'material object,' ones that have received much wider support in both historical and contemporary settings:

> **Extension:** x is a *material object* $=_{df} x$ is spatially extended.
>
> **Location:** x is a *material object* $=_{df} x$ has a spatial location.

An object is spatially extended, according to some, if it occupies or is located at a non-point-sized region of space.[16] According to **Extension**, materiality consists in being 'spread out' or distributed across space, and not merely occupying or being located at a region of space per se. It is standard to trace the roots of **Extension** to Hobbes and Descartes, though some have recently pointed out that Descartes was sympathetic with the notion that even immaterial entities can be extended in space in a particular sense.[17]

Some philosophers have argued that **Extension** ought to be rejected in so far as it rules out, a priori, the existence of point-sized material objects. If to be material is to be extended in space, then seemingly unextended objects—perhaps quarks, photons, or other subatomic particles—are rendered immaterial on this view. And some might find it rather odd that, according to **Extension**, material objects like trees and bicycles are composed of a vast number of immaterial entities. Others are not as perturbed by the implication that subatomic particles turn out immaterial on **Extension**. In so far as one is inclined to think that an object's being extended in space suggests that it is composed of parts and perhaps has a spatial surface or boundary, one might follow van Inwagen (1990: 19) in thinking that, "talk about the surfaces of submicroscopic objects, or about the stuffs they are made of, tends to verge on nonsense."

By my lights, **Location** is the widely assumed yet rarely argued-for analysis of 'material object' underlying debates in contemporary metaphysics and

---

[16] See Carroll and Markosian (2010: 189–90).
[17] Pasnau (2011b: 334). See Descartes (1985), Letters to More V: 269.

philosophy of mind.[18] Ned Markosian (2000) is a notable exception here in that he has explicitly argued in favor of **Location** and has offered a number of reasons to prefer his view over rival accounts.

Not all are fond of **Location**, however. Hudson (2005: 2–3) rejects the view on the grounds that it misclassifies regions of substantival space as material. While Hudson fails to elaborate on this point, his worry appears to turn on the fact that in contemporary philosophy of physics substantival spacetime, in particular the manifold *M* of general relativity, is widely thought to be an *immaterial* or, at the very least, a *dematerialized* substratum that supports fields, geometrical and topological properties, and also the structures that define absolute motion.[19] Presumably, Hudson takes the "is located-at" relation to be reflexive such that every region of space is located at itself, which misconstrues regions of space as material on the view in question.

The point remains that if one follows Hudson and Pruss in explicating God's omnipresence in terms of ubiquitous entension, then God is both wholly located at (or 'occupies') the maximally inclusive non-point-sized place, and is wholly located at (or 'occupies') every proper subregion of that place, both of which render God a material object by the lights of **Location**, **Occupation**, and **Extension**.

Here I strongly recommend that the orthodox theist not bite any bullets regarding the materiality of God in explicating omnipresence in particular as well as God's relationship to spacetime in general. Instead, I want to offer some friendly advice to those who are attracted to the ubiquitous entension model of omnipresence to explore alternative analyses of 'material object' to those currently on offer in the contemporary literature. I hope to show in what follows that the theist has solid historical precedent in the history of Christian philosophical theology for entertaining the view that immaterial beings in general can be spatially located at various non-point-sized places

---

[18] Two quick examples. Hoffman and Rosenkrantz (2002: 40) claim as "unquestionably true" the following premise in what they call the classic argument against dualistic interactionism in the philosophy of mind: "Necessarily, a body, but not a soul, has spatial location" and "we regard *not being spatially located* as a logically necessary condition of being a soul." Moreover, in addressing the rejoinder to his classic pairing problem for (interactionist) substance dualism that takes the soul to be spatially located, Kim (2005: 90) asks "why aren't souls just material objects, albeit of a very special and strange kind?"

[19] See Wayne (2008). Earman (1989: 155) notes: "When relativity theory banished the ether, the spacetime manifold M began to function as a kind of dematerialized ether needed to support the fields.... [I]n post-relativity theory it seems that the electromagnetic field, and indeed all physical fields, must be construed as states of M. In a modern, pure field-theoretic physics, M functions as the basic substance, that is, the basic object of predication."

in space, and thereby reexamine whether **Occupation**, **Extension**, and **Location** suffice to demarcate the material from the immaterial.

3. LATIN MEDIEVALS ON THE LOCATION OF THE IMMATERIAL

In contrast to the contemporary metaphysical landscape that tends to assume an inseparable link between *having a spatial location or extension* and *being material*, some have recently pointed out, quite independent of recent work in contemporary metaphysics, that Latin medieval thinkers were in broad agreement that immaterial entities such as God and human souls were spatially located in some sense or other in their interactions with material beings.[20]

Consider the following remarks by Robert Pasnau (2011a: 19) on medieval conceptions of divine omnipresence in particular:

Although it is now commonly supposed that God exists outside of space, this was not the standard conception among earlier theologians. Medieval Christian authors, despite being generally misread on this point, are in complete agreement that God is literally present, spatially, throughout the universe. One simply does not find anyone wanting to remove God from space, all the way through to the end of the seventeenth century. Of course, no one wanted to say that God has spatial, integral parts. So the universally accepted view was that God exists holenmerically throughout space, wholly existing at each place in the universe... God can be said to exist everywhere, and at every time, and to exist wholly wherever and whenever he exists.

---

[20] In addition, William of Ockham (1991) offers the following concise statement of the location of angels: "As for the second article, I claim that 'to be in a place' is taken in two ways [viz.] circumscriptively and definitively. What is *circumscriptively* in a place is a thing which is such that (i) a part of it is in a part of the place and (ii) the whole of it is in the whole of the place. On the other hand, a thing is *definitively* in a place when (i) the whole of it is in the whole place and not outside the place and (ii) the whole of it is in each part of the place... I claim that an angel is not through his substance in a place in the first way. For an angel does not have parts and, consequently, is not circumscribed by a place... However, through his substance an angel is in a place in the second way, i.e. definitively. For his whole substance is in the whole of that place, and his whole substance is in each part of the place—not just in the sense that the angel's substance is present to the place (for God is present to the place in that sense), but also because the angel is in some way surrounded by and contained by the place, so that he is in that place and is not outside the place in which he is... *And so just as the located body is in a place, so too an angel who is present to that body and to all its parts is in a place—though the body is in the place circumscriptively and the angel definitively.*" (*Quod.* I, q. 4, a. 3, emphasis mine)

In the place of 'entension' Pasnau adopts the more traditional terminology of 'holenmerism' to characterize the unique way the Latin medievals thought of God's presence to material creation.

My aim in this section is to offer a small sampling of the aforementioned Latin consensus regarding the truth of the conjunction of the following three theses:

> **Extended Location:** God and human souls have non-point-sized spatial locations.[21]
>
> **Immateriality:** God and human souls are immaterial.
>
> **Simplicity:** God and human souls are mereologically simple.[22]

To the contemporary analytic philosopher the above three theses appear to be in deep tension with one another. We have already noted the tension between **Extended Location** and **Immateriality**. Common analyses of 'material object' on offer—**Occupation**, **Location**, and **Extension**—preclude an immaterial object's being located at or extended in any place in space whatsoever. To be related to space in such a manner *just is* what it is to be material. Moreover, the conjunction of **Extended Location** and **Simplicity** is in tension with the principle, which arguably underlies much of the resistance to the possibility of extended material simples: that necessarily, if x is entirely located at a non-point-sized region p and p is mereologically complex, then x is mereologically complex. If, as some are inclined to think, the mereological structure of an object must mirror the mereological structure of the place where it is located, then no simple object can be located at a non-simple place.

With the above tension noted, let's begin by turning to **Extended Location**, **Immateriality**, and **Simplicity** in the work of Augustine.

3.1 Augustine of Hippo

Both early and later medieval discussion concerning the nature and location of immaterial entities was in large part shaped by the work of Augustine

---

[21] More specifically, *subsequent to the creation of the physical universe*, God is located at various non point-sized places in space; and at least *throughout its ante-mortem career*, the human soul has a non-point-sized spatial location.

[22] This, of course, is only one part of the doctrine of divine simplicity. Here I restrict my discussion to the mereological content of the doctrine and ignore issues pertaining to the attribution of distinct properties (whether intrinsic or extrinsic) to God.

(354–430), particularly his discussion of the soul and the various relations in which it stands to the body.

Concerning the immateriality of the soul, Augustine remarks that "the soul is immaterial is a fact of which I avow myself to be fully persuaded" (*Letter* 166, 2.4). He does not, however, infer from the immateriality of the soul that it therefore lacks spatial location. As Goetz and Taliaferro (2011: 43) point out, "Given that the soul isn't corporeal in nature, one would expect Augustine to maintain that the soul is not in space. Nevertheless, he affirms that the soul is in space, but not in the same way in which something corporeal is in space."

For Augustine, matter is located in space in such a way that "[e]ach mass that occupies space is not in its entirety in each of its single parts, but only in all taken together. Hence, one part is in one place; another part in another" (*Immortality of the Soul*, 16.25); elsewhere he makes the same point that matter is located in space by "every part of it [being] less than the whole" (*Letter* 166, 4).

The soul, by contrast, is "in any body…whole in the whole and whole also in any part of the body" (*On the Trinity* 6.2.8). More specifically,

For [the soul] pervades the whole body which it animates, not by a local distribution of parts, but by a certain vital influence, being at the same moment present in its entirety in all parts of the body and not less in smaller parts and greater in larger parts, but here with more energy and there with less energy, it is in its entirety present in the whole body and in every part of it. (*Letter* 166, 2.4)

The capacity for a distinct type of spatial location is partly what sets the soul apart as immaterial for Augustine. In fact, he goes so far as to say that it would be *impossible* for the soul to be wholly located in every part of the body were it material. He notes:

Now, this presence of the mind in all parts of the body at the same moment *would be impossible if it were distributed over these parts in the same way as we see matter distributed in space*, occupying less space with a smaller portion of itself and a greater space with a greater portion. For all things composed of matter are larger in larger places or smaller in smaller places, and no one of them is in its entirety present as any part of itself, but the dimensions of material substances are according to the dimensions of the space occupied. (*Letter* 166, 2.4, emphasis mine)

When discussing the way in which the soul is located in the body in particular, Augustine is at pains to first distinguish the various ways in which the material and the immaterial are related to space in general. He states:

If matter be used to designate nothing but that which, whether at rest or in motion, has some length, breadth, and height, so that with a greater part of itself it occupies a greater part of space, and with a smaller part a smaller space, and is in every part of it less than the whole, then the soul is not material. (*Letter* 166, 4)

For Augustine, then, one of the marks of the material is being located in space *in a particular kind of way*, namely by being partly located at distinct places such that "every part of it [is] less than the whole." With respect to the mereological simplicity of the soul and its mode of spatial location with respect to the body, Augustine says,

When we come to a spiritual creature such as the soul, it is certainly found to be simple in comparison with the body... The reason it is simpler than the body is that it has no mass spread out in space, but in any body it is whole in the whole and whole also in any part of the body. (*On the Trinity* 6.2.8)

In sum, Augustine situates the distinct ways in which the soul and body are located in space within a more comprehensive view of the material–immaterial divide, one that is characterized at least in part by the capacity for distinct ways of being located in space. Like all material objects, the body is located at a place by being partly located at every part of that place; in the parlance of contemporary metaphysics, the body *pertends* in space. Being immaterial, the human soul is located at a place by being, "whole in the whole and whole also in any part of the body" (*On the Trinity*, 6.2.8); in contrast to material beings, the soul *entends* in space.

Turning now to Augustine's view of divine omnipresence, he famously records in his *Confessions* his adolescent struggle to conceive of the divine nature as being anything other than extended throughout space "as a great being with dimensions extending everywhere, throughout infinite space, permeating the whole mass of the world" (1961: 134). He writes, "I could not free myself from the thought that you were some kind of bodily substance extended in space, either permeating the world or diffused in infinity beyond it" (1961: 133). He later goes on to acknowledge the error of his adolescent and Manichean ways by saying: "This was the theory to which I held, because I could imagine you in no other way. But it was a false theory."

Once again, one might think that Augustine's more developed and mature view of God's omnipresence was one that removed God from space entirely. As was the case with the soul above, this would be much too quick. In *Letter* 187 titled "On The Presence of God" where Augustine explicitly addresses the question of *how* God is everywhere present, he is, as with his remarks on the soul above, at pains to situate God's unique presence in the world within a larger framework concerning the material–immaterial divide:

And yet, when we say that God is everywhere, we must resist carnal thinking and withdraw the mind from the senses of the body so that we do not suppose that God is spread out through all things as if by spatial magnitude in the same way that the earth, or a liquid, or air, or this light is spread out. For every magnitude of this sort is smaller in a part than in its whole. (*Letter* 187, 4.11)

The divine nature, for Augustine, is not related to space as material objects are related, namely by having distinct parts that are extended or distributed across space. Along the same lines:

Yet he is not spread out in space like a mass such that in half of the body of the world there is half of him and half of him in the other half, being in that way whole in the whole. Rather, he is whole in the heavens alone and whole on the earth alone and whole in the heavens and in the earth, contained in no place, but whole everywhere in himself. (*Letter* 187, 4.11)

Perhaps the clearest statement of Augustine's positive view of divine omnipresence is found in *Letter* 187 as follows:

On this account is He said to be everywhere, because He is absent to no part; on this account is He said to be whole, because He presents not one part of Himself to a part of things, and another part of Himself to another part of things, equal part to equal parts of things, a less to lesser parts, greater to a greater part; but *He is equally present as a whole not only to the whole of the universe, but also to each part of it.* (*Letter* 187, 17, emphasis mine)

In *Sermon* 277 Augustine vividly illustrates this view of omnipresence by comparing the way that human beings are located at a place—namely, by being wholly located at a single place at a particular time—with the way in which God is wholly located at every place at the same time:

You too, I mean, are the whole of you in your house and the whole of you here in church; but when you're in church you are not in your house; when you're in your house, you are not in church. So it's not the same with him...the whole of him is everywhere simultaneously. After all, he isn't poured out like water, or divided and carted around in bulk like earth. When he is all on earth, he doesn't abandon heaven; again, when he fills heaven, he doesn't withdraw from earth. (*Sermon* 277, 13)

As before in the case of the soul and the body, the point of contrast here is between the distinct (*ways*) in which God and material objects are each located in space, not between *lacking a spatial location* and *having a spatial location*.

Augustine routinely characterizes God's ubiquitous presence not in terms of his being removed from space altogether but, rather, as a particular *way* of being located in the totality of space that preserves God's absolute mereological simplicity and thus in direct contrast to the mode of location exhibited by material beings. While the soul is exclusively located where the body is and is wholly located at each of the parts of the body, God alone is "equally present as a whole not only to the whole of the universe, but also to each part of it."

While it is equally true that Augustine adamantly rejects the notion that God is strictly speaking "in a place," it is important to be clear on what exactly he means by this locution. For an object to be "in a place," for Augustine, is for it to be "contained" in a place such that the object could not exist without being located at a place. Material objects are "contained" in a place in that their existence depends on their being *somewhere*.[23] In his own words: "take from bodies their places and they will be nowhere, and because they will be nowhere they will not exist." By contrast, God "is not contained by those things to which he is present, as if he could not exist without them" (*Letter* 187, 6.18).[24]

Augustine seems to think that it is precisely *because* bodies are contained in space in this particular way (i.e. they *must* be in some place or other) that they are material:

Have no doubts at all about this: that God is not a body. It is proper to bodies to be spread out through space, *to be contained in place*, to have parts, halves, thirds, quarters, wholes. Nothing like that with God, because God is whole everywhere, not half of him in one place, with the other half somewhere else; but all of him is in heaven, all of him on earth. (*Sermon* 277, emphasis mine)

Again, for Augustine the contrast here is between (a) material objects that are (i) mereologically complex, (ii) wholly located at a single place (i.e. not strongly multi-located), (iii) cannot exist without being located at some place or other, and (iv) are partly located at distinct places; and (b) God as an immaterial entity that (i) is mereologically simple, (ii) is wholly located at *every* place, (iii) can exist without being located at a place (say, prior to creation), and (iv) is partly located at no place. Consequently, the reason why God is not "in a place" on Augustine's use of the phrase is that God

---

[23] Where the notion of dependence here, I take it, is most charitably read as generic dependence. While the existence of a material object necessitates the existence of some place or other, it need not necessitate the existence of the place it presently occupies (or else it couldn't change location without thereby ceasing to exist).

[24] See further *Letter* 277: "Only don't let us strive to reduce God to a place, don't let us strive to shut God up in a place, don't let us strive to spread God out in any kind of bulk through extended space; let us not have the nerve to do that, let's not even think of it. Let the substance of divinity remain in its own proper dignity. Let us, certainly, as far as we can, change for the better; let us not change God for the worse." Again, the primary issue for Augustine here is not being located in space per se but to safeguard God's ontological independence from space as well as the absolute simplicity of the divine nature.

(unlike material objects) is neither confined to a single place nor metaphysically dependent on space for his existence.

Consequently, Augustine appears to be committed to the conjunction of **Extended Location**, **Immateriality**, and **Simplicity**. Immaterial objects such as God and the human soul can be wholly located at a non-point-sized place (for God: the maximally inclusive place where the universe is entirely located; for the human soul: the place where the body is entirely located), and wholly located at each part of that place (for God: each subplace of the maximally inclusive place where the universe is entirely located; for the human soul: each subplace of the place where the body is entirely located).

3.2 Anselm of Canterbury

Let us turn now to Anselm of Canterbury (1033–1109), the premier philosopher-theologian of the eleventh century. With his usual precision and clarity, Anselm devotes chapters 20–4 of his *Monologion* to a systematic discussion of God's unique relationship to place and time. He constructs a disjunctive syllogism whose major premise consists of the following three disjuncts. God is either:

(i)   "everywhere and always (i.e. in every place and time)."
(ii) "only somewhere and sometime (i.e. limited to some place and some time)", or
(iii) "nowhere and never (i.e. in no place or time)" (1998: 33–4).

Anselm quickly dismisses options (ii) and (iii) based on considerations of God's absolute simplicity as well as God's universally sustaining creatures in existence. Starting with (iii), Anselm rejects the notion that God exists "nowhere and never (i.e. in no place or time)" on the grounds that absolutely nothing exists without God's immediate sustaining causal activity (cf. *Monologion* 13), conjoined with the more general principle that "Absolutely no essence exists where and when he does not exist, since without him nothing exists" (2007: 28). As Brian Leftow (1991: 187) has pointed out, here Anselm relies on the more general tenet that an immediate cause is present to or located where its effect is located, where and when the effect exists/occurs (assuming, of course, that the effect has a location in space and time).[25] Anselm goes so far as to say, "since nothing at all exists without him, if he exists nowhere and never, then every good thing exists

---

[25] See Leftow (1991: 187).

nowhere and never, and absolutely everything exists nowhere and never. Just how false that is, there is no need to say" (2007: 28).

In rejecting (ii), the thesis that God is "only somewhere and sometime (i.e. limited to some place and some time)", Anselm relies once again on God's direct sustaining of material beings, yet in such a way that does not assume the principle that an immediate cause must be where its effect is located. According to Anselm, God is absolutely simple and thereby devoid of distinct parts and properties. Being absolutely simple, God is identical to his causal activity or power. And since God's sustaining power extends to every place, upholding all things in existence, it therefore follows from divine simplicity that God cannot be present only somewhere and some-time but must *himself* be present in his entirety to every place and time.

In fact, Anselm emphatically rejects the notion that God is capable of being located at every place and time solely in virtue of his immediate causal power, while himself being (non-causally) located at a single place and time. In his own words, "And if it is said that through himself he exists determinately at a certain time and place, but through his power he exists wherever and whenever anything exists, that is not true. For since it is evident that his power is nothing other than himself, his power in no way exists apart from him" (2007: 28). Consequently, Anselm highlights two lines of reasoning in favor of the view that God is "everywhere and always (i.e. in every place and time)" as stated in (i), namely God's immediate sustaining activity in creation and God's absolute simplicity.

In chapter 21, Anselm argues that God must be "everywhere and always (in every place and time)" in one of two ways, either:

(a) existing "as a whole only in the sum of all places and times, and existing in its *parts* in each individual place and time," or
(b) existing "as a whole in the sum of all places and times and existing as a *whole* in each individual place and time." (1998: 34–5, my emphasis)

Note first the striking similarity between Anselm's (a) and (b) and the aforementioned relations of pertension and entension, respectively. Anselm rejects (a) outright on the grounds of God's absolute simplicity: what lacks parts entirely cannot be partly located in any sense. This leaves (b). The nub of Anselm's objection to (b) turns on the seeming impossibility of an entity's being wholly located at more than one place at the same time: he says, "One whole, therefore, cannot be simultaneously in several places as a whole" (35). If such a strong form of multi-location is impossible, it follows that contrary to (b), "There is no way for the supreme essence to exist as a whole in every place and time."

Anselm thus faces a paradox: God is both located at *every* place and time (conclusion of chapter 20) and located at *no* place and time (the conclusion of chapter 21). At this point Hudson (2009: 201), following Wierenga (1997), claims that Anselm resolves the paradox in chapter 22 by positing two mutually exclusive location relations which correspond to the way in which material and immaterial objects are located at a place. As Wierenga puts it: "Anselm then attempted to reconcile this 'contradictory language—but ineluctable logic' by distinguishing between two senses of 'being wholly in a place,' namely, being *contained* in a place and being *present* in a place" (258). Since being straightforwardly located at a place in the way that material objects are located amounts to being 'contained in' that place, God is literally *nowhere* on this reading of Anselm. Yet God can be said to be located at each place in a non-literal sense in virtue of being 'present at' every place, where being present to every material creature in this way need not compromise the absolute simplicity nor the transcendence of God. Paradox is avoided in chapter 22, then, precisely because the sense in which God is *present at* every place and time is distinct from the sense in which he is *contained in* no place and time.

I believe this reading of Anselm's resolution to the paradox in chapter 22 is mistaken. I'm inclined to think instead that Anselm's way out of the paradox turns, at bottom, on his general views concerning the material–immaterial divide. At the start of chapter 22 of *Monologion*, Anselm returns to (b) and asks, "perhaps [God] can exist as a whole in individual places and times." His reason for reconsidering (b) as a minimal condition on omnipresence hinges on a wider, overarching view as to what it means for an entity to be *material*, that is, an entity confined to or "bound by the law of place and time" (1998: 39).

Anselm identifies two principles that govern what he calls "temporal and spatial natures," which are "under the rules and regulations of time and place:"

This, then, is what time and space stipulate: that (and only that) which is enclosed in their limits, neither escapes the logic of (spatial and temporal) parts and wholes, nor exists as a whole in more than one place and time simultaneously. (1998: 38)

It seems that for Anselm, then, an object x is *material* just in case (i) x is composite, and (ii) x is incapable of being wholly multiply located at one and the same time. In true Augustinian fashion (cf. *Letter* 166, 2.4 above), Anselm holds that it is strictly impossible for material objects in particular to be wholly multi-located, that is, wholly located at distinct places at the same time. By contrast, for God qua immaterial being, "the long arm of space and time does not encircle: [and] is neither condemned to the multiplicity of having parts, nor prohibited from being present as a whole in more than one place and time simultaneously" (1998: 38).

On this reading of Anselm, the solution to the above paradox resides primarily in the immaterial nature of the supreme substance. Being immaterial, God is not localized or confined to a particular place like material objects, and hence can exhibit the strong form of multi-location required by (b) above. Being absolutely unlimited, God is capable of being wholly located at every place whatsoever without being 'bound to' or 'contained in' a single part of space or the whole of space in its entirety.

In chapter 22 of the *Monologion*, Anselm is unequivocal that while God and material objects are both related to place in some sense, only the latter are 'contained' in the places where they are located (1998: 39); God in no way depends on place for His existence. In a way that bears a striking resemblance to Augustine's own remarks above, Anselm reasons that for an object "which does not commit its existence to a place and time is neither forbidden nor obliged, by the law of space and time, to be, or not to be, in some place and time" (1998: 39). Though God is wholly located or present at every place and time by his own volition, his existence in no way depends on being related to place and time as such.

Anselm concludes the above discussion with the following remarks in support of (b) as a necessary condition on God's omnipresence:

Since, as I say, this is what time and space stipulate, I do not doubt that the supreme substance is exempt. No time or place, after all, contains it. Now, ineluctable necessity demands that the supreme essence be absent from no place or time. And, further, no space and time legality prohibits it from being present at every place and time simultaneously. *I conclude, therefore, that it is necessary that it be present as a whole simultaneously to all places and times, and to each individual place and time.* (1998: 38, my emphasis)

While Anselm's full account of divine presence in the world no doubt includes more than what is captured in (b) above—namely, God's being directly cognitively aware of and sustaining in existence every material creature—there are good interpretive grounds for thinking that it is certainly nothing less than God's being wholly spatially located in the whole of space, and wholly spatially located in each part of space as well. With Brian Leftow (1989: 354) we can affirm that, for Anselm, God "is literally in space, but not as a material thing is."[26]

---

[26] For an interesting discussion concerning Anselm's fully developed account of omnipresence see the dialogue between Wierenga (1988) and Leftow (1989). Also, see Pasnau (2011a) for an interpretation of Anselm's view of divine eternity that coheres with the interpretation of Anselm's view of divine omnipresence offered here.

It is interesting to note that in *Proslogion* 13 Anselm makes a similar appeal to the material–immaterial divide concerning the mode of location of the body and the soul, contrasting the two precisely in terms of their ability or inability to be wholly located at more than one place at the same time. Anselm remarks:

Certainly that is absolutely limited which, when it is wholly in one place, cannot at the same time be somewhere else. This is seen in the case of bodies alone...That, however, is limited and unlimited at the same time which, while wholly in one place, can at the same time be wholly somewhere else but not everywhere; and this is true of created spirits. For if the soul were not wholly in each of the parts of its body it would not sense wholly in each of them. (1998: 95)[27]

Again, there is no suggestion here that material objects (bodies) have a spatial location and immaterial objects (created spirits) lack a spatial location, and that each bear distinct location relations to place in general. Rather Anselm contrasts the two kinds of objects in terms of the possibility or impossibility of being wholly multi-located. As noted above, for Anselm, the inability of a body to be wholly multi-located at distinct places is constitutive of its materiality, while the ability of the human soul to be wholly multi-located at each place in the body is constitutive of its immateriality.

As was the case with Augustine above, Anselm's view of omnipresence and the location of the soul in the body commits him to the conjunction of **Extended Location**, **Immateriality**, and **Simplicity**. In neither of these Latin medieval thinkers do we find an account of the interaction between the immaterial and the material domain that is explicated in non-spatial terms. Rather, in sharp contrast to the way in which material beings are located in space, both God and human souls are located in space in such a way that preserves both their mereological simplicity as well as their ability to be wholly located at distinct places at the same time.

In claiming that Anselm endorses the conjunction of **Extended Location**, **Immateriality**, and **Simplicity** regarding the divine nature in particular, I take issue with the interpretation of his account of omnipresence offered by Hudson (2009, 2014) and Wierenga (1997). Hudson claims that both Anselm and Aquinas "develop accounts of omnipresence and its characteristic

---

[27] Note here the explanatory ordering: the soul's being wholly located at every part of the body *explains* its ability to sense at each part of the body, and not vice versa. This suggests that the notion of "being located at" or "present to" some place is distinct from an object's having immediate knowledge or sensation at that place. This further suggests, contrary to Hudson and Wierenga, that Anselm does not consider the deepest account of God's omnipresence to be captured in terms of God's immediate sensation or knowledge of the goings-on at every point in space.

'being present at' relation that are parasitic on our understanding of the straightforward, non-mysterious occupation relation with which we are all familiar" (202). For Anselm in particular, Hudson and Wierenga claim that God is not located at every place in a straightforward, spatial sense but, rather, is located at every place only in the sense of having direct cognitive awareness of every material object that is itself located in a straightforward, spatial sense. In short, Hudson and Wierenga construe Anselm as a proponent of what I am calling a DO model of omnipresence.

As was noted above, I think the overarching location relation employed by Anselm in his account of God's relationship to space in *Monologion* 20–2 is the straightforward, ordinary variety of spatial location. Where God and material objects differ in their relationship to space pertains to *the distinct ways in which they are spatially located*, namely by either entending or pertending the places where they are entirely located. While Anselm relies heavily on the relations of entension and pertension (or something very similar) as distinct modes of spatial location exhibited by immaterial and material entities respectively, I take him to be working with a *single*, basic location relation—namely 'present at'—in which entension and pertension are characterized in terms of.

In contemporary parlance, my claim here is that Anselm endorsed something along the lines of what we might call *locational monism*, the view that there is a single, basic (i.e. irreducible) location relation that relates objects to places.[28] And for Anselm the basic location relation that relates material and immaterial objects to space is the 'present at' relation. Entities that stand in the 'present at' relation to some place are, quite literally, spatially located at that place, irrespective of whether they are material or immaterial. Of course locational monism is consistent with there being multiple, *non-basic* location relations that are defined in terms of the single basic notion; and on the reading of Anselm I am offering here, the non-basic location relations of entension and pertension are defined terms of the single basic 'present at' relation.

While Hudson and Wierenga also attribute to Anselm a version of what I am calling locational monism, they nevertheless offer the relation of *containment* as the basic relation at work in Anselm's account. On their reading of Anselm, he defines the derivative 'present at' relation in terms of bearing a relation to an object that is itself 'contained in' a place. On this view, only

[28] One can adopt a monistic or pluralistic stance with respect to a number of relations, whether parthood, causation, identity, etc. As far as I am aware, such terminology was first introduced by McDaniel (2004) in the context of compositional monism and compositional pluralism. See also his (2009).

material objects stand in the basic containment relation to places and, as a result, are the only objects that can be properly said to have a spatial location; God and other immaterial beings, by contrast, exclusively stand in the non-basic 'present at' relation to their respective places, and thus fail to be located in space in the above straightforward or strict sense.

I'll conclude this section by offering one final consideration in favor of interpreting Anselm along the lines of a locational monism that takes the 'present at' relation as the single basic relation that relates *both* material and immaterial objects to places.

In *Monologion* 22 Anselm makes the point that material objects are *both* 'present at' times and places as well as 'contained by' times and places. In addressing the sense in which both God and material objects, i.e. "localized or temporal natures," are 'present at' times and places, Anselm remarks:

> For if that supreme essence is said to exist in a place or a time, even though the very same expression is used both of him and of localized or temporal natures because of our customary way of speaking, there is a different meaning because of the dissimilarity of the things themselves. When it comes to localized or temporal natures, this one expression signifies two things: that they are *present at* the times and places in which they are said to exist, and that they are *contained by* those times and places. But in the case of the supreme essence, only one of these meanings applies, namely, that he is present, not that he is contained by them. (2007: 33, emphasis in original)

If Anselm was of the opinion that being 'present at' and being 'contained in' a place denoted two mutually exclusive relations as claimed by Hudson and Wierenga—which they would need to be in order to avoid the contradiction addressed in ch. 22 of *Monologion*—then it is puzzling that Anselm would affirm that material objects stand in *both* relations to places and times. Far from thinking that the 'present at' relation exclusively relates immaterial beings to space, Anselm is unequivocal that both God and material objects are 'present at' the places where they are located; this alone ought to call into question the above reading of Anselm proposed by Hudson and Wierenga.

It seems more likely that God's failing to be 'contained by' place amounts to the claim that God, in contrast to material beings, is neither metaphysically dependent on place nor delimited by the dimensions of the places where God is located. We need not interpret Anselm as taking the notion of containment as a distinct, mutually exclusive location relation in contrast to the 'present at' relation. God is not contained by any place only in the sense that his nature in no way constrains his ability to be wholly multilocated at distinct places at the same time, or to be located at no place at all.

Consequently, what is doing the heavy lifting in Anselm's account of omnipresence is, at bottom, the notion that God is wholly located at the sum of all places in space, and wholly located at each individual place in space, i.e. (b) above. In contemporary parlance, Anselm is of the view that God's omnipresence amounts to God's entending the totality of space, where the location relation at work in ubiquitous divine entension is the same basic relation that relates material objects to places.[29] While it is certainly true that Anselm is of the opinion that God stands in immediate causal and cognitive relations with material beings (see *Monologion* 13 and 14), it is another thing entirely to attribute to Anselm the view that God's standing in these relations is constitutive of divine omnipresence per se.

In his excellent book-length study that tracing the history of late medieval and early modern metaphysics, Robert Pasnau (2011b: 337) makes the following statement:

Holenmerism [what I am calling 'entension'] is the standard view regarding immaterial entities—God, angels, and rational souls—from Plotinus, Augustine, and Anselm all the way through the scholastic era. Nearly all the leading scholastic authors embrace this position, including Bonaventure, Aquinas, Scotus, Ockham, and Buridan.

Likewise, medieval historian and philosopher of science Edward Grant (1981: 355, n. 33) makes the same general point that what I am calling 'entension' was:

[T]he fundamental medieval concept that God is wholly in the whole of a space and wholly in every part of that space, a concept that was also applied to other spiritual substances, such as souls and angels. It was the common medieval manner of explaining how a spiritual substance could occupy a body or place and yet remain indivisible despite the divisibility of the body or place.

My aim in this section has been to substantiate, at least to some degree, the above claims of Pasnau and Grant regarding **Extended Location**, **Immateriality**, and **Simplicity** in Augustine and Anselm in particular.

4. THE MATERIAL–IMMATERIAL DIVIDE REVISITED

On the overarching theistic metaphysic endorsed by Augustine and Anselm, an entity's being located at an extended or non-point-sized place per se is

---

[29] As a result, I'm inclined to think that Anselm's own view of omnipresence is the same as or highly similar to the one defended by Hudson (2009, 2014) and Pruss (2013), namely ubiquitous entension.

not sufficient to mark it out as material. As was noted above, this sets them in contrast to widely endorsed analyses of the nature of the material in the contemporary literature.[30]

But suppose the theist is attracted to the above line of thinking that allows for immaterial objects to *entend* the non-point-sized places where they are spatially located. How might the theist resist the unorthodox view that God is a material object, given that standard analyses of 'material object' preclude God's being situated in space in this manner? What alternative account might the theist offer in the place of **Occupation**, **Location**, and **Extension**? I conclude by exploring several alternative analyses of 'material object' that are broadly inspired by the views of Augustine and Anselm above.

In what follows, I aim to satisfy what I consider to be historically entrenched theological desiderata concerning the material–immaterial divide. At the very least, I consider the theological desiderata for an analysis of 'material object' to rightly classify paradigmatic instances of immaterial beings in the Christian tradition, namely, God, angels, and human souls.[31] In so doing I aim to carve out space for the relation of entension and its application to immaterial beings as a viable, orthodox option in contemporary Christian philosophical theology.[32]

As a first pass, we might consider modally strengthening **Location** above to the following:

> **Modal Location:** x is a *material object* $=_{df}$ it is part of the nature of x to have a spatial location.[33]

---

[30] Though there are dissenters. William Lycan (2009), for instance, suggests that dualists opt for the view that minds are literally located in space (partly to solve the interaction problem); this would, by his lights, in no way undermine the mind's being immaterial. He then asks, "It may be wondered wherein minds are *immaterial*, if they are spatially located?", proceeding to answer, "In at least two ways: they do not have other physical properties such as mass or charge; and unlike brain matter, they are not made of atoms or subatomic particles" (558–9).

[31] The epistemic grounds for thinking that angels and human souls exist and are immaterial are beyond the scope of my concern here.

[32] The application of the relation of entension to Christian doctrine in particular is far-reaching, even if not employed in an analysis of divine omnipresence. Here I'm thinking of the potential application of entension to the Incarnation, Eucharistic presence, and the indwelling of the Holy Spirit.

[33] Here one could modalize **Occupation** in the same sense, although I limit my discussion here to **Location**. Swinburne (1994: 9) offers a modal view of 'material object' that is in the same general neighborhood as **Modal Location**, although he is silent as to the various relations an object might stand in to regions of space. He states, "Those substances whose essential properties are such that they must occupy space (i.e. be spatially extended) I shall call material objects. The substance that is my desk could not be a desk

On **Modal Location**, it is metaphysically impossible for material objects to exist without having a spatial location. **Modal Location** allows for immaterial entities to be spatially located, on the assumption that it is no part of their nature to be located as such.

But here those attracted to an account of the nature of human persons that involves an essential relation of some kind between body and soul— whether composite, emergent, or hylomorphic varieties of dualism—will register their discontent with **Modal Location**. On a hylomorphic conception of human persons, for example, the immaterial human soul, as the constituent that makes the organic body a *human* body in particular, is essentially such that it is integrally united to matter and spatially located *at some time or other*, even though the soul may be capable of existing disembodied in the intermediate state.[34] The same would apply to any account of human persons that takes an immaterial soul or self to be, by nature, generated in some sense from the material domain, perhaps the brain in particular. If so, then **Modal Location** will be too rigid for certain views regarding the nature and composition of human persons.

Moreover, **Modal Location** lacks the resources to accommodate the traditional theological tenet that Christ ascended with, and presently has a material human body, on the admittedly speculative assumption that Christ's resurrected body is no longer spatio-temporally located.[35] It is a consequence of **Modal Location**, together with this speculative assumption, that the resurrected body of Christ is no longer material.[36]

Yet another potential worry is that on certain historically prominent FO models of omnipresence in the Christian tradition, **Modal Location** entails that God is a material object in so far as there are no possible worlds in which God exists without being spatially located on these models.[37]

Recall from section 1 that FO models of omnipresence are those that hold that God is located at or present to each place *fundamentally*, i.e. in his

unless it occupied space . . . If there is a substance which does occupy space but need not, it does not count as a material object on my definition" (9).

[34] See Aquinas (1975) 4.79.10, "The [human] soul is, by nature, united to a body. For it belongs to its essence to be the form of a body. It is, therefore, contrary to the nature of the soul to be absent from the body."

[35] For historical reference to this theological tenet, see Crisp (2007: 133, n. 28) where he cites *The Heidelberg Catechism* in Schaff (1877: 322–35) and *The Formula of Concord*, art. 7, pp. 568–91 in Tappert (1959).

[36] But see Hudson (2005: 204), Swinburne (1994: 235–7), and Van Den Brom (1993: 309 ff.) for an interesting denial of this speculative assumption, one that tentatively appeals to Christ's body being spatially located or present in a higher-dimensional space.

[37] Thanks to R. T. Mullins for this point.

own right, and not in virtue of standing in some relation to entities that
are themselves present in the fundamental sense. Yet according to the FO
models of omnipresence espoused by the likes of Henry More, Isaac Newton,
and more recently Robert Oakes, it is metaphysically impossible that God
not be related to space in some sense or other. For More, it is part of the
nature of God to be related to space in so far as he is *identical* to space itself;
for Newton, though God is not identical to space, it is necessarily the case
that God's existence necessitates the existence of absolute space: every world
in which God exists is a world in which he is everywhere present throughout absolute space; for Oaks, it is part of the nature of God to be related to
space in so far as God is "*maximally immanent in space*—and, indeed, *necessarily* so: [since] space is an *essential aspect* of God."

Among the above FO models of omnipresence, it appears that all but
Newton's entail that God is a material object on **Modal Location**. For it
is open to the contemporary proponent of the Newtonian model of omnipresence to argue, following a move made by Fine (1994) in the area of
modal metaphysics, that essence is not reducible to modality; that something's being F, say *being spatially located*, in every possible world in
which it exists is not equivalent to saying that being F is part of its nature
or essence.

The existence of Socrates modally necessitates the existence of his single-
ton set {Socrates}, yet it is arguably not the case that *being a member of
{Socrates}* is part of the essence of Socrates. In the same way, the defender of
the neo-Newtonian account of omnipresence might argue that while God's
existing in every possible world modally necessitates the existence of absolute space in every possible world, it does not follow that God is *essentially
related to space*. Hence, adopting a more fine-grained, non-modal account
of essence can allow the defender of a neo-Newtonian account of omnipresence to endorse **Modal Location** while sidestepping the worry that God is
a material object.

For an alternative analysis of 'material object', one might consider following
the general spirit of Augustine and Anselm's above remarks: to be 'material'
is not to be essentially located in space per se, but to be essentially located in
space *in a particular kind of way*, namely, by being partly located at distinct
places via pertension.

Let's call this view **Modal Pertension** and define it as follows:

> **Modal Pertension:** x is a *material object* $=_{df}$ it is part of the nature
> of x to be located in space via pertension.

Modal Pertension rightly construes God and angelic beings as being immaterial in so far as they are, at least by the lights of most theists, in no way

essentially related to space; God and angels are essentially immaterial and contingently related to space and its occupants. The human soul also counts as immaterial on **Modal Pertension** in that while it may (on some views) be essentially located in space at some time or other, it entends rather than pertends when it is, in fact, spatially located. When the above immaterial entities are located at various places in space, they are wholly located at those places as well as wholly located at every subplace of the places in question.

Modal Pertension does, however, preclude *material* objects from entending in space. For some, this may seem much too strong for both theological and non-theological reasons alike. As pointed out by Marilyn Adams (2006), the likes of Aquinas, Scotus, and Ockham thought that in the Eucharist the physical body of Christ is literally wholly located at every place where the Eucharistic elements are located.[38] Concerning thirteenth and fourteenth century Eucharistic theology in particular, Adams notes:

> These positions shared the philosophically innovative thesis that bodies (like angels and souls) can be literally located in a place without being extended in it…Taking their cue from Augustine, scholastic philosophers reasoned that angels and intellectual souls cannot be extended in a place because they are simple and so lack parts that could be positioned at a distance from one another. But a human being's intellectual soul is located in his/her body throughout his/her *ante-mortem* career. Hence, the intellectual soul must be whole in the whole body, and whole in each part of the body (which Scotus and Ockham call being *definitively* in place). By contrast, material things do have parts, and their natural way of existing is to be extended in place, with some parts at a distance from others. Confronted with the problem of eucharistic presence…Aquinas, Scotus, and Ockham all reasoned that just because material things have parts and so can be and normally are in a place by being extended in it, it doesn't follow that it is metaphysically impossible for material things to be located in a place without being extended in it. Why would it be impossible for Divine power to make a material thing to exist in place definitively, so that the whole thing was in the whole of the place, and the whole thing was in each part of the place as well? (2006: 299–300)[39]

Someone favorable to the above view of Eucharistic presence might argue that while material objects are disposed to pertend in space, it is much too strong to say that their nature demands that they *must* be located in such a

---

[38]   For a contemporary defense see Pruss (2013).

[39]   A succinct statement of this view is given by Ockham (1991): "On the other hand, a thing is definitively in a place when (i) the whole of it is in the whole place and not outside the place and (ii) the whole of it is in each part of the place—in the way that the body of Christ is definitively in a place in the Eucharist. For the whole of his body exists together with the whole of the place of the consecrated species, and the whole of his body exists together with each part of that place" (*Quod.* I, q. 4, a. 2).

way at each moment of their existence.[40] While perhaps nothing other than divine power can make it the case that a material object be located in space via entension, one might suppose that such a state of affairs is at least metaphysically possible.

In addition to the above theological consideration, if one is a friend of the metaphysical possibility of extended *material* simples in particular, then **Modal Pertension** appears to be ruled out in so far as such objects are commonly thought to entend rather than pertend the places where they are located.[41]

It's not clear to me whether the defender of **Modal Pertension** should be moved by this worry. For one, many philosophers are inclined to think that extended material simples are metaphysically impossible, partly on the grounds that the natures or properties of extended *material* objects in particular (e.g. their being identical to spacetime regions, i.e. supersubstantivalism, or their exemplifying geometrical and topological properties) arguably preclude their being mereologically simple.[42] If one has independent grounds for thinking that extended material simples in particular are metaphysically impossible, then the worry that **Modal Pertension** precludes the possibility of such material objects loses its force. Further, one might be hesitant to lay the bulk of the argument against **Modal Pertension** on the metaphysical possibility of extended material simples. The debate over whether or not such exotic material objects are possible is a relatively recent one in contemporary metaphysics and one that even the most speculative of metaphysicians is inclined to approach rather tentatively.

Even so, the defender of **Modal Pertension** who is a friend of the possibility of extended material simples has a straightforward reply: deny that entension is the only way for such exotic material objects to be located in space. Hudson (2005: 101), for instance, has suggested that extended material simples might also *span* their respective places, where he defines the notion of spanning as follows:

> x *spans* $p =_{df} x$ is an object that is wholly and entirely located at exactly one non-point-sized place, p, and there is no proper subplace of p, p^*, such that any part of x is located at p^*.

---

[40] For a brief but helpful discussion of the various location relations employed by the medievals concerning the metaphysics of the Eucharist, see Adams (2006: 299–300). For an exhaustive treatment on these matters see Adams (2010), especially part two.

[41] For a discussion of the possibility of extended material simples see Parsons (2000), McDaniel (2007), and Simons (2004).

[42] See Hudson (2005), especially chapter 4, for a host of objections to the possibility of extended simples. Also, see Gilmore (2014) for a nice general summary of the current state of the debate.

If an extended material simple spans some non-point-sized place p, it fails to be wholly located at every subplace of p (as it would if it entended p). The relevant difference between objects that span and objects that entend in space is that the latter are wholly multi-located at every subplace where they are located, while the former are not.[43] **Modal Pertension** would, of course, need to be revised so as to include either pertension or spanning as the modes of location uniquely definitive of material objects. As long as it is open for extended material simples to span instead of entend their respective places, **Modal Pertension** so revised need not preclude the possibility of material objects of this kind.

If one is persuaded by the above theological and non-theological considerations against **Modal Pertension**, we might finally consider revising **Modal Pertension** to the following:

> **Dispositional Pertension:** x is a *material object* $=_{df}$ it is part of the nature of x to be disposed to be located in space via pertension.

As is well known, dispositions or powers can exist unmanifested; the manifestation of a power is liable to preventers, masks, finks, etc., such that an object's having the power in question does not necessitate the power's manifestation.[44] The glass may be fragile without currently manifesting its disposition to break. In the same way, one might say that material objects are disposed by nature to pertend (or span) the places where they are located, but nevertheless fail to manifest this disposition and instead entend their respective places.

As with **Modal Pertension**, **Dispositional Pertension** rightly construes God and angels as immaterial. Moreover, **Dispositional Pertension** can accommodate (if one's theological tradition dictates) the above theological account of Christ's real presence in the Eucharist: that Christ's body entends each place where the Eucharistic elements are located. The proponent of **Dispositional Pertension** who is theologically committed to real bodily presence in the Eucharist might argue that while material bodies are *disposed* by nature to either pertend or span in space, the unique presence of Christ's body in the Eucharistic elements is secured directly by divine power; perhaps the special activity of God serves to both mask or prevent the manifestation

---

[43] One potential problem with requiring extended material simples to span their respective places in the above sense is that it would seem to exclude the possibility of time-traveling scenarios involving enduring extended material simples. Such entities would be wholly multi-located at distinct places at the same time and thereby fail to span any one place in particular (though they would not entend those places in so far as they would fail to be wholly located at each of the proper subplaces of the places where they are located).

[44] See Molnar (2003).

of the powers that are part of the nature of Christ's body, as well as supply the additional power to entend each place where the elements are located.

Furthermore, **Dispositional Pertension** is also commendable on the grounds that it can accommodate a wide range of views concerning the nature and composition of human persons, particularly those that claim that the immaterial soul is, in some sense or other, essentially related to the body. While one might think that the human soul is naturally disposed to be located in space at some time or other (which perhaps explains *why* disembodiment is a radically unnatural state), the soul fails to be material on **Dispositional Pertension** precisely because it has a disposition to entend rather than to pertend or span.

Dispositional Pertension is also well-positioned to maintain the traditional theological tenet that Christ presently has a material human body, even though, as was hinted at above, Christ may fail to currently have a spatio-temporal location. Since bodies qua material objects in general (and Christ's body in particular) are by nature merely *disposed* to be located in space, their failure to manifest this disposition in no way entails that they lack this disposition and are thereby no longer material.

Finally, one might think that a theist-friendly account of the material–immaterial divide ought to be able to say something about why materiality is limiting, and thus why an unlimited or perfect being is *necessarily* immaterial.[45] Call this the *limiting constraint* for materiality.[46]

Modal Location, **Modal Pertension**, and **Dispositional Pertension** each go some way towards satisfying the limiting constraint.[47] On **Modal Location**, since it is part of the nature of material objects that they have a spatial location (if they exist), it would appear that they metaphysically depend on space for their nature and existence. Since it is part of the nature of a perfect being that it exist *a se* and thus metaphysically ungrounded, a perfect being *must* be immaterial on **Modal Location**. A similar line of reasoning can be applied to both **Modal Pertension** and **Dispositional Pertension** in so far as materiality is defined in terms of being essentially related to space *in a particular manner*.

---

[45] Thanks to Alex Pruss for this suggestion.

[46] The limiting constraint for materiality raises obvious complications for physicalist accounts of the Incarnation which maintain that God the Son was transformed into a material object, a living human body.

[47] It needs to be pointed out here that there have been a variety of different ways of satisfying the limiting constraint for materiality in the Christian tradition. Perhaps the most prominent historical grounds for thinking that materiality is limiting, and thus why an unlimited being is necessarily immaterial, turns on an Aristotelian characterization of matter in terms of potentiality. For Thomas Aquinas and medieval Aristotelians in general, it is impossible that God be material in any sense since God is pure act and matter is in potentiality.

But note that **Modal Pertension** and **Dispositional Pertension** have additional resources to ground the limiting constraint for materiality. Here I turn once again to Anselm's remarks in *Proslogion* 13 where he characterizes that which is 'absolutely limited' as that "when it is wholly in one place, cannot at the same time be somewhere else" (1998: 95). As I highlighted above, only material objects are absolutely limited in this sense for Anselm. By contrast, "That, however, is limited and unlimited at the same time which, while wholly in one place, can at the same time be wholly somewhere else but not everywhere; and this is true of created spirits" (1998: 95). Created immaterial beings, for Anselm, are 'unlimited' in that they are capable of being wholly multilocated at distinct places at one and the same time (they are 'limited' only in the sense that they are not located everywhere, as is God).

Following Anselm, then, we might say that an object's inability to be wholly multilocated is a genuine limitation, perhaps due to the fact that the scope of the object's immediate causal activity is necessarily restricted to a single place at any given time. Such a restriction is, of course, unfitting for an unlimited or perfect being. Since **Modal Pertension** and **Dispositional Pertension** construe materiality both in terms of essential dependence on space as well as location relations that are limiting in the above sense, they are doubly suited to ground the limiting constraint for materiality.

Whether the orthodox Christian theist opts for **Modal Location**, **Modal Pertension**, or **Dispositional Pertension** will, of course, depend on one's wider theological and philosophical commitments. The point remains that each furnish the theist with an account of the material–immaterial divide that allows for immaterial objects to entend the non-point-sized places where they are located, and thus be spatially located in a straightforward and strict sense.[48]

REFERENCES

Adams, Marilyn McCord. 2006. *Christ and Horrors: The Coherence of Christology*. New York: Cambridge University Press.

Adams, Marilyn McCord. 2010. *Some Later Medieval Theories of the Eucharist: Thomas Aquinas, Gilles of Rome, Duns Scotus, and William Ockham*. Oxford: Oxford University Press.

[48] I'd like to thank Jeffrey Brower, William Lane Craig, Hud Hudson, Sam Lebens, R. T. Mullins, Robert Pasnau, Alexander Pruss, Josh Rasmussen, Michael Rea, and Philip Swenson in particular for their helpful comments and discussion. I owe a debt of appreciation and gratitude to The John Templeton Foundation as this project was completed during my time as a 2013–14 Templeton Postdoctoral Fellow at the University of Notre Dame, Center for Philosophy of Religion. A warm thanks to the Fellows, directors, and staff of the Center for helping make the 2013–14 academic year productive and immensely rewarding, both personally and professionally.

Adams, Robert Merrihew. 1994. *Leibniz: Determinist, Theist, Idealist*. New York: Oxford University Press.

Anselm of Canterbury. 1998. *Saint Anselm of Canterbury: The Major Works*, edited with an introduction by Brian Davies and G. R. Evans. New York: Oxford University Press.

Anselm of Canterbury. 2007. *Anselm: Basic Writings*, ed. and trans. Thomas Williams. Indianapolis, IN: Hackett Publishing Company.

Aquinas, Thomas. 1975. *Summa Contra Gentiles*, trans. and ed. A. C. Pegis. Notre Dame, IN: University of Notre Dame Press.

Augustine. 1947. *The Immortality of the Soul*, trans. Ludwig Schopp. New York: CIMA Publishing Company.

Augustine. 1961. *Confessions*, trans. with an introduction by R. S. Pine-Coffin. Harmondsworth: Penguin Books.

Augustine. 1991. *On The Trinity*, vol. I/5, introduction, translation, and notes by Edmund Hill, O.P.; ed. John E. Rotelle, O.S.A. Hyde Park, NY: New City Press.

Augustine. 1994. *Sermons (273–305A) on the Saints*, vol. III/8, translation and notes by Edmund Hill, O.P.; ed. John E. Rotelle, O.S.A. Hyde Park, NY: New City Press.

Augustine. 2004. *Letters 156–210*, vol. II/3, translation and notes by Roland Teske, ed. Boniface Ramsey. Hyde Park, NY: New City Press.

Blount, Douglas Keith. 1997. "An Essay on Divine Presence." PhD dissertation, University of Notre Dame.

Brower, Jeffrey E. 2014. *Aquinas's Ontology of the Material World: Change, Hylomorphism, and Material Objects*. Oxford: Oxford University Press.

Carroll, John W. and Ned Markosian. 2010. *An Introduction to Metaphysics*. New York: Cambridge University Press.

Conn, Christopher H. 2011. "Anselmian Spacetime: Omnipresence and the Created Order." *Heythrop Journal*, 52: 260–70.

Craig, William Lane and J. P. Moreland. 2003. *Philosophical Foundations for a Christian Worldview*. Downers Grove, IL: InterVarsity Press.

Crisp, Oliver. 2007. *Divinity and Humanity*. New York: Cambridge University Press.

Cross, Richard. 2003. "Incarnation, Omnipresence, and Action at a Distance." *Neue Zeitschrift für Systematische Theologie und Religionsphilosophie*, 45: 293–312.

Cross, Richard. 2016. "Duns Scotus on Divine Immensity." *Faith and Philosophy*, 33: 389–413.

Descartes, René. 1985. *The Philosophical Writings of Descartes*, vol. iii, trans. John Cottingham, Robert Stoothoff, Dugald Murdoch, and Anthony Kenny. Cambridge: Cambridge University Press.

Earman, John. 1989. *World Enough and Spacetime*. Cambridge, MA: MIT Press.

Edwards, Jonathan. 1955. *The Philosophy of Jonathan Edwards From His Private Notebooks*, ed. Harvey G. Townsend. Eugene, OR: University of Oregon.

Fine, Kit. 1994. "Essence and Modality." *Philosophical Perspectives*, vol. 8: *Logic and Language*, pp. 1–16.

Gilmore, Cody. 2003. "In Defense of Spatially Related Universals." *Australasian Journal of Philosophy*, 81.3: 420–8.

Gilmore, Cody. 2014. "Location and Mereology", in Edward N. Zalta (ed.), *The Stanford Encyclopedia of Philosophy* (Spring 2014 edn). <http://plato.stanford.edu/archives/spr2014/entries/location-mereology/>.

Goetz, Stewart and Charles Taliaferro. 2011. *A Brief History of the Soul*. Malden, MA: Wiley-Blackwell.

Goris, Harm. 2009. "Divine Omnipresence in Thomas Aquinas." In Harm Goris, Herwi Rikhof, and Henk Schoot (eds), *Divine Transcendence and Immanence in the Work of Thomas Aquinas: A Collection of Studies Presented at the Third Conference of the Thomas Instituut Te Utrecht, December 15–17, 2005*. Leuven: Peeters (Publications of the Thomas Instituut te Utrecht, 13), 37–58.

Grant, Edward. 1981. *Much Ado About Nothing: Theories of Space and Vaccum from the Middle Ages to the Scientific Revolution*. Cambridge: Cambridge University Press.

Helm, Paul. 1980. "God and Spacelessness." *Philosophy*, 55: 211–21.

Hoffman, Joshua and Gary S. Rosenkrantz. 2002. *The Divine Attributes*. Malden, MA: Blackwell Publishing.

Hudson, Hud. 2005. *The Metaphysics of Hyperspace*. New York: Oxford University Press.

Hudson, Hud. 2009. "Omnipresence". In Thomas P. Flint and Michael C. Rea (eds), *The Oxford Handbook of Philosophical Theology*. Oxford: Oxford University Press, 199–216.

Hudson, Hud. 2014. *The Fall and Hypertime*. Oxford: Oxford University Press.

Leftow, Brian. 1989. "Anselm on Omnipresence." *New Scholasticism*, 63.3: 326–57.

Leibniz, Gottfried Wilhelm. 1989. *Philosophical Papers and Letters: A Selection*, translated and edited with an introduction by Leroy E. Loemker. Dordrecht: Kluwer Academic Publishers.

Locke, John. 1975. *Essay Concerning Human Understanding*, ed. and trans. Peter H. Nidditch. Oxford: Clarendon Press.

Lycan, William. 2009. "Giving Dualism its Due." *Australasian Journal of Philosophy*, 87.4: 551–63.

Malebranche, Nicolas. 1997. *Dialogues on Metaphysics and on Religion*, trans. N. Jolley and D. Scott. Cambridge: Cambridge University Press.

Markosian, Ned. 2000. "What are Physical Objects?" *Philosophy and Phenomenological Research*, 61.2: 375–95.

McDaniel, Kris. 2004. "Modal Realism with Overlap." *Australasian Journal of Philosophy*, 82.1: 137–52.

McDaniel, Kris. 2007. "Extended Simples." *Philosophical Studies*, 133: 131–41.

McDaniel, Kris. 2009. "Structure-Making." *Australasian Journal of Philosophy*, 87.2: 251–74.

Molnar, George. 2003. *Powers: A Study in Metaphysics*. New York: Oxford University Press.

More, Henry. 1995. *Manual of Metaphysics*, trans. Alexander Jacob. Hildesheim: Georg Olms.

Muller, Richard A. 2003. *Post-Reformation Reformed Dogmatics: The Divine Essence and Attributes*, vol. 3. Grand Rapids, MI: Baker Academic.

Newton, Isaac. 1934. *Mathematical Principles of Natural Philosophy*, trans. Andrew Motte and Florian Cajori. Berkeley, CA: University of California Press.

Newton, Isaac. 1962. *Unpublished Scientific Papers of Isaac Newton*. Cambridge: Cambridge University Press.

Newton, Isaac. 1999. *The Principia: Mathematical Principles of Natural Philosophy*, trans. I. Bernard Cohen and Anne Whitman. Berkeley, CA: University of California Press.

Oakes, Robert. 2006. "Divine Omnipresence and Maximal Immanence: Supernaturalism versus Pantheism." *American Philosophical Quarterly*, 43.2: 171–9.

Ockham, William of. 1991. *Quodlibetal Questions*, trans. Alfred J. Freddoso and Francis E. Kelly. New Haven, CT: Yale University Press.

O'Leary-Hawthorne, John and Jan Cover. 1998. "A World of Universals." *Philosophical Studies*, 91: 205–19.

Parsons, Josh. 2000. "Must a Four-Dimensionalist Believe in Temporal Parts?" *The Monist*, 83: 399–418.

Pasnau, Robert. 2011a. "On Existing All at Once." In Christian Tapp and Edmund Runggaldier (eds), *God, Eternity, and Time*. Burlington, VT: Ashgate, 11–29.

Pasnau, Robert. 2011b. *Metaphysical Themes 1274–1671*. Oxford: Clarendon Press.

Pruss, Alexander. 2013. "Omnipresence, Multilocation, the Real Presence and Time Travel." *Journal of Analytic Theology*, 1.1: 60–73.

Reid, Jasper William. 2008. "The Spatial Presence of Spirits among the Cartesians." *Journal of the History of Philosophy*, 46.1: 91–117.

Schaff, Philip (ed.). 1877. *Creeds of Christendom*, 4th edn. New York: Harper and Bros.

Simons, Peter. 2004. "Extended Simples: A Third Way Between Atoms and Gunk." *The Monist*, 87: 371–84.

Stump, Eleonore. 2010. *Wandering in Darkness*. New York: Oxford University Press.

Stump, Eleonore. 2013. "Omnipresence, Indwelling, and the Second Personal." *European Journal for Philosophy of Religion*, 4.4: 29–53.

Swinburne, Richard. 1993. *The Coherence of Theism*. Oxford: Oxford University Press.

Swinburne, Richard. 1994. *The Christian God*. Oxford: Clarendon Press.

Taliaferro, Charles. 1994. *Consciousness and the Mind of God*. Cambridge: Cambridge University Press.

Tappert, Theodore G. (trans. and ed.). 1959. *The Book of Concord: The Confessions of the Evangelical Lutheran Church*. Philadelphia, PA: Fortress Press.

van den Brom, Luco J. 1993. *Divine Presence in the World: A Critical Analysis of the Notion of Divine Omnipresence*. Kampen: Kok Pharos Publishing House.

van Inwagen, Peter. 1990. *Material Beings*. Ithica, NY: Cornell University Press.

Wainwright, William J. 2010. "Omnipotence, Omniscience, and Omnipresence." In Charles Taliaferro and Chad Meister (eds), *The Cambridge Companion to Christian Philosophical Theology*. Cambridge: Cambridge University Press, 46–65.

Wayne, Andrew. 2008. "A Trope-Bundle Ontology for Field Theory." In Dennis Dieks (ed.), *The Ontology of Spacetime II*. Amsterdam: Elsevier, 1–15.

Wesley, John. 1991. *John Wesley's Sermons: An Anthology*, ed. Albert C. Outler. Nashville, TN: Abingdon Press.

Wierenga, Edward. 1988. "Anselm on Omnipresence." *The New Scholasticism*, 62.1: 30–41.

Wierenga, Edward. 2010. "Omnipresence." In Charles Taliaferro, Paul Draper, and Philip L. Quinn (eds), *A Companion to Philosophy of Religion*. Malden, MA: Blackwell Publishing, 286–90.

Zagzebski, Linda. 2013. *Omnisubjectivity: A Defense of a Divine Attribute*. Milwaukee, WI: Marquette University Press.

9

'Eternity Shut in a Span': The Times of God Incarnate

Robin Le Poidevin

1. THE TEMPORAL PARADOX OF THE INCARNATION

In a sermon preached on Trinity Sunday 1621, probably at Lincoln's Inn, where he was Reader in Divinity, John Donne offered a vision of the Crucifixion that captures, in a single poignant phrase, the extraordinary paradox of the Incarnation: 'I see those hands stretched out, that stretched out the heavens.'[1] In similar vein, in one of his Holy Sonnets, he addresses the following wondering passage to the Virgin:

> Ere by the spheares, time was created, thou
> Wast in his minde, who is thy Sonne, and Brother.[2]

How is it possible that the Creator, and in particular (noting the implication in the couplet above) the *creator of time*, could become a finite, and terribly vulnerable, part of the created order? At least at first sight, a being who creates time must be time*less*. For temporal beings are dependent on time, and it makes no sense to imagine a being creating a condition of their own existence. Now, surely, if anything is an eternal and unchanging state, it is timelessness. How, then, can a timeless God take on flesh and so become part of history? For Christ is a temporal being: he is born, he begins his ministry around the age of thirty, and three years later he is arrested and put to death. There is a tension, then—indeed, to all appearances, an outright inconsistency—between the notion of God as time's creator and the notion

---

[1] Sermon 14, in Potter and Simpson (1957): 308. I am very grateful to my colleague, Chris Kenny, for drawing my attention to this phrase.
[2] 'The Annunciation', in Grierson (ed.) (1912): 319.

of God as incarnate. This is what we might describe as the 'temporal paradox of the Incarnation.'

It might seem that there is a very swift way out of this paradox in the form of the Doctrine of the Trinity. The three persons of the Trinity, it will be pointed out, have distinguishing properties. Only the Son becomes incarnate, not the Father and Creator. Still, in traditional Trinitarianism, the Son is 'of one substance' with the Father: the essential properties of divinity are exhibited by both. Among those properties, the relation to time will, surely, be fundamental. To be divine is to exhibit the maximum degree of independence from the constraints under which the created order labours, an independence which leads, by an argument we shall shortly examine, to timelessness. The timelessness of the Son seems, indeed, to be enshrined in the words of the Chalcedonian Statement on the Incarnation, according to which the Son is begotten of the Father 'before the ages'.[3]

To set out the problem explicitly:

1. God the Father is the creator of time.

So:

2. The Father is timeless.
3. The Son is of one substance with the Father.

So (from 2 and 3):

4. The Son is timeless.
5. The Son becomes incarnate.
6. To become, and so be incarnate is to be in time.

So (from 5 and 6):

7. The Son is in time.

So (from 4 and 7):

8. The Son is both timeless and in time.

This is a *reductio* of the conjunction of 1 (God as creator) and 5 (God as incarnate).

Certain components of the paradox I will not question, but pause here to comment briefly on them.

---

[3] For the complete Statement, see Stevenson (1989): 351–3. 'Before the ages' is naturally interpreted to mean simply 'before human history', but it also suggests a more radical idea: that the begetting of the Son is something that is prior—in some non-temporal sense of 'prior'—to time itself.

First, the initial premise. It may be questioned whether to be the creator of 'all things' includes or implies being creator of time. Anyone who denies this will not, of course, be exercised by the problem set out here. But they will have to have something to say in reply to the following thought: it appears to be an entirely contingent truth that time exists; and any contingent exist-ent requires the Creator for its ultimate explanation. However, there is a worry about 1, and that is that [he very notion of the creation of time is paradoxical.] For if creation is a causal process, and causes precede their effects in time, then it seems, absurdly, that the creator of time must already be in time prior to time's existence! We may, it is true, distinguish the *creative act's* being in time, as a result of what follows it, and the *creator's* being in time. The first need not imply the second. Does paradox still lurk? I will leave 1, for the time being, intact, though it clearly cries out for elab-oration, and I attempt to provide this later in the paper, returning to the paradox in section 4.

Second, the inference from 2 and 3 to 4. On Latin Trinitarianism, the inference is irresistible, since 'of one substance with the Father' is taken in a token sense, and by Leibniz's Law, if the Father is timeless, so is the Son. On Social Trinitarianism, in contrast, 'of one substance' can be given a type reading, and so there is room for a difference in the intrinsic properties of the Father and the Son.[5] Nevertheless, a radical difference in respect of their relations to time will affect their relations to each other: the Son exhibits an essential dependence not exhibited by the Father, and this might be thought theologically unacceptable. Even the Social Trinitarian, then, is unlikely to reject this particular inference.

Third, premise 5, which represents a fundamental component of trad-itional Christian doctrine. The word 'becomes' might be objected to on the grounds that this implies a change in an already temporal being, which then will immediately conflict with divine timelessness. But I suggest a more neutral reading, on which the change in question is to the world: the world is such that there are times at which it contains an incarnate God, but at earlier times it does not.

The fourth component I will not question is premise 6. As Tom Senor (1990) notes, the events of Christ's life exhibit a temporal sequence, and this is sufficient for his being in time. (Senor also argues that becoming incarnate involves a change in the Son's intrinsic properties, which in turn implies that he is in time.)

---

[4] I am grateful to an anonymous referee for pointing out this further paradox.

[5] For a defence of Latin Trinitarianism, see, e.g., Leftow (2004); for a defence of Social Trinitarianism, see, e.g., Hasker (2010).

Finally, I will not here explore the prospects for applying a reduplicative formula' to certain premises. This would involve reading 4 as 'The Son qua God is timeless', and 7 as 'The Son qua man is in time'. Although this avoids a formal contradiction, 'qua' requires interpretation. One such interpretation is a compositional account, according to which there is a composite being which has temporal and timeless elements. Whether such a being could exhibit sufficient unity to be identified as a person, or whether instead the person of Christ becomes part of an impersonal composite, is a question I simply raise, without discussing here.[6]

The part of the paradox I want to focus on is the inference from 1 to 2, from the creation of time to timelessness. To some, this may seem a small step. For others, it will require explicit argument. The key linking notion, it was suggested above, is that of *dependence*.[7] A rather short sub-argument for the inference from 1 to 2 can be provided as follows:

> 1* If x is the creator of time, then x is independent of time: there is a world in which x exists and time does not.
>
> 2* If x is temporal, then x is not independent of time: there is no world in which x exists and time does not.

Therefore:

> 3* If x is the creator of time, then x is not temporal.
>
> 3*, together with premise 1 of the original argument, then leads to 2: the Father is timeless.

This sub-argument itself may seem too quick. In particular, 2* might be contested as follows: God is independent of time in the sense that it was possible for him to exist but time not, since the creation of time was a free act. But although this entails that he is *possibly* timeless (that is, timeless in some possible world), it does not imply that he is *actually* timeless. His being actually temporal may be a necessary result of creating time. So a further assumption appears to be required, and that is the assumption that, as Brian Leftow has argued, whether an object is temporal or timeless cannot be a merely contingent matter.[8] To set out this reasoning explicitly: for x to possess a property F contingently, there must be a world in which x exists, but is not F. But for x in one world to be identical to some object y in

---

[6] For discussion, see Senor (2007), Le Poidevin (2009), and Marmodoro and Hill (2010).

[7] Thanks to Rik Peels for pressing me to explain in more detail this crucial step in the argument.

[8] What follows paraphrases Leftow (1991): 43.

another, x and y must be sufficiently similar. If x is a human, and y a beetle, they cannot be identical. So no human being could have been a beetle. If x is a table and y the number 4, they cannot be identical, and so on. Now the difference between being temporal and being timeless is too great to permit trans-world identity. Therefore, it makes no sense to suppose that God could be temporal in this world but timeless in another: the difference is too great. So God is either essentially timeless or essentially temporal. If, therefore, God is actually temporal, he is essentially so, so there is no world where he exists but time does not. He therefore would not count as independent of time, on this conception.

There is a further line of objection to the argument, and that is that God's being independent of time does not imply that there is a world in which God exists but time not. For consider the case of moral values. According to an influential theory, moral truths are dependent on God rather than *vice versa*. But as moral truths are necessary, there is no world in which God exists but those truths do not obtain. So dependence is not always appropriately spelled out in modal terms. The reply is that, although not every kind of dependence is set out in modal terms, causal dependence is. And to say that God is the *creator* of x is naturally understood as implying x's causal dependence on God.

Thus, then, the temporal paradox of the Incarnation, and the way in which its various components can be defended.

To understand the import of 1 and 2, and the validity of the inference from one to the other, requires an analysis of time and temporal existence, and that is what I shall attempt in this paper. The temporal paradox, I want to suggest, is made much worse by a certain view of (space)time, namely the substantivalist view, on which time is a container that is ontologically independent of its contents (though its geometry is perhaps causally affected by them). This bears particularly on the inference from God as creator of time to divine timelessness. In contrast, the problem is made more tractable by a radically reductionist account of time, on which time is not an object in its own right, but rather the causal structure of what we might continue to describe as time's contents: events and states of affairs. There are independent reasons in favour of that reductionist view, reasons I will allude to briefly, but my main object in this paper is simply to expound the view, show how it leads to a natural account of what it is to exist in time, and how it offers to dissolve the temporal paradox of the Incarnation. It also offers an understanding of how God can in one sense (or perhaps two senses) be independent of time as a result of being the creator of time, and yet, in the incarnate Christ, be part of it.

Here, then, are the questions I want, all-too-briefly, to address:

   (i)   What is time?
   (ii) What is it to exist in time?
   (iii) What is God's relation to time?
   (iv) Can we, in the light of our answers to those questions, resolve the temporal paradox of the incarnation?

I will take these in turn.

2. WHAT IS TIME?

One way of focusing this intimidating question is to ask what the relation is between time and the events and states of affairs that we say take place in time. Traditionally, this has been posed in the form of the question whether there can, or cannot, be time without change.[9] But there are more than two choices in this area, and the relation between time and its contents is naturally allied to a corresponding question about the relation between space and its contents. It will be convenient, then, at least initially, to talk of *spacetime*.[10] We can order the views in terms of their representation of the degree, and direction, of dependence between spacetime on the one hand and its contents on the other. At one end of the spectrum, we have:

   Supersubstantivalism, which holds that the fundamental entity is spacetime, and that concrete objects are regions of spacetime. This makes spacetime independent of its contents, and its contents not only dependent for their existence on, but also reducible to, spacetime. This is a relative newcomer to the debate.[11] More familiar is:

   Traditional *substantivalism*, which holds that there are concrete objects other than spacetime, and these are contained within a spacetime that could

---

[9] A question raised, perhaps for the first time, by Aristotle in Book IV of the *Physics* (Hussey (1983)). The classic contemporary discussion is Shoemaker (1969).

[10] 'Spacetime' here is not intended as meaning specifically relativistic spacetime. As used here, the term is neutral between different physical theories, so that we might talk of 'Newtonian spacetime', etc. I assume we would want to give the same general answer to the question 'what is the relation between time and its contents?' as the parallel question concerning space. The symmetry may however break down when we consider the connection between those contents and the direction of time, which has no obvious spatial parallel.

[11] Supersubstantivalism (under the name 'monistic substantivalism' is defended in preference to traditional substantivalism ('dualistic substantivalism') in Schaffer (2009).

exist independently of them. Those concrete objects are not, however, reducible to spacetime regions.[12]

For both supersubstantivalism and (non-super) substantivalism, spacetime relations between objects are mediated by spacetime points. (The notion of *mediation* here can be illustrated by a simple example: the relation 'being an aunt of' is a mediated relation, in that for one person to be an aunt of another there has to be a third person who is a sibling of the first person and a parent of the second. In contrast, 'being more massive than' can hold between two objects directly, without the need for any third object.) But the status of ordinary objects is perhaps somewhat anomalous on substantivalism: on the one hand, they are not *reducible* to spacetime, but on the other hand, it makes dubious sense to suppose that they could exist without it, for they would then lack extension.

Moving further along this spectrum of views, we encounter a reversal of the dependency between spacetime and its contents, in:

Modest relationism, which holds that spacetime is a construction from its 'contents.' Standardly, the spatial part of this reduction holds that space is simply the network of spatial relations between objects. This permits spatial vacua (what we would ordinarily describe as regions of space devoid of objects), which amount to no more than the holding of direct spatial relations between objects, unmediated by any other object. In contrast, the standard form of temporal relationism, familiar from the Leibniz–Clarke correspondence,[13] rules out temporal vacua (periods of time without change). But the door is open to the view that time is the network of unmediated temporal relations between events/states of affairs, permitting undifferentiated periods of time without change, while warning us not to reify these periods as objects in their own right, divisible into different parts. Further on, and now at the extreme end of the spectrum from supersubstantivalism, we have:

Reductionist relationism, which reduces not only spatial points and temporal moments, but also spatial and temporal *relations*, to something more fundamental. In the case of space, it is not immediately clear what this more fundamental relation could be.[14] But in the case of time, the obvious candidate is *causality*. Thus time, on this view, is simply the causal structure of events/states of affairs.

Finally, to be comprehensive in our survey, we should acknowledge a hybrid account, according to which spacetime is an object in its own right,

---

[12] Substantivalism is defended in Nerlich (1994), and criticized in Earman (1992).
[13] See Alexander (1956).
[14] Some speculative suggestions are made in my (2007).

ontologically independent of those contents, but whose direction is derived from the causal structure of those contents. This combines a substantivalist account of temporal separation relations (which are mediated by instants) with a reductionist account of temporal asymmetry—the asymmetry, that is, of before and after.

Although I am not here in the business of offering a decisive argument for any one of these positions, we might just pause to note an attractive feature of the radically reductionist view. My reason for doing so is that it is this position that I will later appeal to in attempting to resolve the temporal paradox of the Incarnation. It is important, then, to be clear that such an appeal is not a desperate ad hoc invocation of an otherwise unmotivated position, but to one which has merits quite independently of its role in understanding the Incarnation. One merit of reductionism is that it offers a very simple explanation of what is otherwise the puzzling fact that the arrow of causation points in the same direction as the arrow of time: causes, in other words, always precede their effects.[15] On the reductionist view, the arrow of time just *is* the arrow of causation. The reductionist view also fits very well with two characteristic features of temporal experience. Why do we not perceive the future? Because perception is a causal process: the object of a perceptual state is a cause of that state. It must therefore be earlier than that state, since temporal priority reduces to causal priority. Backwards causation is ruled out by definition. Why does the experienced order of our perceptions correspond (with, it seems, some rare but interesting exceptions[16]) to the actual order of those perceptions? Because both are determined by the causal order of those perceptions. Where a perception of, for example, a C# played on a violin is coloured by the memory of a D played a second earlier on the same instrument, what results is a perception of the C# as succeeding the D. And since causal order determines temporal order, the perception of the D was indeed prior to the perception of the C#.

An obvious objection to the reductionist view, however, is that time is much more pervasive than causation. That is, we can imagine widely separated events between which there is no causal connection nevertheless occupying a common time series. Surely it is possible for events to be temporally related without being causally related? The right response for the reductionist here,

---

[15] Is it unreasonable to rule out a priori the possibility of backwards causation? For reasons to think not, see Mellor (1998): chapter 12. For a critical discussion of the causal theory of time order, see Sklar (1977): chapters 9 and 10.

[16] See, e.g., the discussion of Benjamin Libet's 'backwards referral' experiments, which seem to show that experienced order can sometime reverse the order of perceptions, in Dennett (1991): chapter 6.

it seems to me, is to deny the implicit assumption that time is unified: that every event is temporally related to every other. Why suppose that the whole of what exists must occupy a common time series? If there are parallel causal series, series that stand in no causal relations to each other, what explanatory benefit is there in insisting that they are not also parallel time series, but one single time series? Admittedly, we do seem to have an intuition that temporal connection does not imply even indirect causal connection, but the source of this can be found in our perceptual experience: we perceive temporal order between events without necessarily also perceiving a causal order between them (though if the temporal proximity is sufficiently close, we might well seem to perceive a causal connection, especially if the events are regularly repeated). And that fact about experience is entirely compatible with the existence of unperceived causal relations between the events. Conversely, we may perceive events between which there is no direct temporal connection. Suppose that two initially independent causal series impinge at the same moment on an observer, for example light from two supernovae. The observer's perception of the supernovae as occupying a common time series does not imply that the distant events have any direct temporal relation to each other: they may instead occupy two converging time series.

On this reductionist view, then, the topological structure of time will be as complex as the network of causal connections, with their diverging and converging branches. The notion of disunified time turns out, in fact, to have theological benefits, as we shall see later.

3. WHAT IS IT TO EXIST IN TIME?

The different accounts above of what time (or spacetime) is will give rise to correspondingly different accounts of what it is to exist in time. For the supersubstantivalist, to exist in time is to be partly constituted by time, since a concrete object is just a region of spacetime—or more narrowly a region with certain properties. For the (non-super)substantivalist, to exist in time is to be contained in—without being constituted even partly by—time. What these two views have in common is the asymmetric dependence of ordinary objects on spacetime. Spacetime could exist without ordinary objects, but not vice versa. That objects depend on spacetime is a direct consequence of supersubstantivalism, since they are nothing more than modified regions of spacetime, and the directness of this consequence might seem to give the supersubstantivalist a dialectical advantage over the traditional substantivalist.[17] For the modest relationist, to exist in time is for one's life to exhibit a temporal structure: there are, in other words, temporal relations between one's instantiation of different properties. Finally, for the radical reductionist, the account is the same as the modest relationist's, except that the temporal relations in question reduce to causal relations, so that to exist in time is simply for one's life to exhibit a causal structure. It is this account that I am particularly interested in.

These accounts of time and existence in time are related in complex ways to the debate over persistence through time, specifically the debate between three-dimensionalists and four-dimensionalists.[18] If we take the supersubstantivalist view, it is hard to see how we could avoid four-dimensionalism, since regions of spacetime have parts, and if objects are just regions of spacetime then they too have parts.[19] The reductionist view, on which to exist in time is to exhibit a causal structure, raises a tricky question for three-dimensionalists, who want to reject temporal parts of objects, and hold that numerical identity can relate objects at different times. For even if we allow that continuants (as well as, or instead of, events) can be causal relata, causation, being an irreflexive relation, cannot hold between an object at one time and the numerically identical object at another time. An object by itself does not exhibit an internal causal structure: only the states of affairs of which it is part do so. In what sense, then, can a three-dimensionalist object exist at different times? The best answer the three-dimensionalist can give, it seems, is this: an object exists at different times only in a *derivative* sense, by being part of states of affairs which, in virtue of exhibiting a causal structure, exist at different times.[20] The four-dimensionalist, in contrast, will say that an object exists at different times in a *non*-derivative sense, in that what stand in causal relations to each other are different temporal parts. Their relative position in time is nothing over above their relative position in the causal series that constitutes the whole four-dimensionalist object.

Could we combine three-dimensionalism with (traditional) substantivalism? In principle, we could, but the result is an over-complex picture of what it is to exist in, and persist through time. According to this picture,

---

[17] As Schaffer (2009) argues.

[18] For an extended discussion of this debate, and a defence of the four-dimensionalist view, according to which persistence is not a matter of numerical identity over time but of being extended by virtue of having different temporal parts at different times, see Sider (2001).

[19] We might, perhaps, imagine a completely homogeneous spacetime, but part of the explanatory role of substantivalist spacetime is to ground the spatio-temporal structure of its contents. A partless spacetime could not do this.

[20] See Simons (2000).

there are two kinds of object: spacetime on the one hand and material objects on the other. Spacetime itself has perforce to be viewed in four-dimensionalist terms: it has spacetime parts, as we have already noted. It exists in spacetime in a non-derivative sense. In fact, since it constitutes a location, each spacetime point exists at itself. If we take a three-dimensionalist view of material objects, then they exist at spacetimes only in a derivative sense. Perhaps we can live with this duality, but it is, to say the least, a rather unparsimonious picture of the world.

4. WHAT IS GOD'S RELATION TO TIME?

With the theoretical background laid out, we can return to the question of God's relation to time, and how its meaning is affected by our stance on what it is to exist in time. In particular, we are concerned with the first step in the temporal paradox of the Incarnation, from creation to divine timelessness, and the sub-argument for that step. According to that argument, the creator of time must exist independently of time, so he is at least possibly timeless: there is a world in which he exists but time does not. But if he actually exists in time, then there is no world in which he exists and time does not. A being cannot be merely contingently timeless. So if God is possibly timeless, he is essentially, and so actually so.

To set it out explicitly, relabelling and rewording premises from the earlier arguments (where 'A' marks an assumption, and 'C' an intermediate or final conclusion):

A1. God[21] creates time.

A2. If God creates time, then there is a possible world in which he exists and time does not.

A3. If x exists in time in one world, and y exists in another world where time does not, then x is not identical to y.

So (from A3):

C1. If God actually exists in time, then there is no possible world in which he exists and time does not.

So (from A2 and C1):

C2. If God creates time, then he does not exist in time.

---

[21] I drop the qualification 'the Father' as not being relevant to this particular step in the temporal paradox of the Incarnation.

So (from A1 and C2):

C3. God does not actually exist in time.

That initially compelling argument depends a great deal for its plausibility on a view of time as ontologically prior to its contents, that is, on either supersubstantivalism or traditional substantivalism. For on those views, the contents of time are ontologically dependent on time: there is no world in which those objects exist but time does not. A temporal God would, as one of time's contents, be dependent on time, and therefore could not be its creator.

At this point, we should consider the strategy of treating God as an atypical occupier of time. Granted, standard occupants of time are ontologically dependent on time. But not so (it might be argued) God. We cannot conceive of what it would be for a mushroom, qua mushroom, to exist in a timeless world, for part of what makes it a mushroom is the way in which it developed. And we might take a similar view of a mountain, or planet. But perhaps God can somehow be in time without being ontologically dependent on it. If we take this line, however, we obscure the conception of being in time: are there two ways of being in time, one which implies dependence and the other not? Further (though perhaps this is simply a development of the same objection), there is the principle A3: a temporal object and a timeless object look too different to be identified.

Independently of the implications of creation, a supersubstantivalist view provides reasons to suppose God to be timeless. For on that view, if God is within spacetime, then either he is constituted by, or else he constitutes, spacetime. Either way, he is not the creator of spacetime. In addition, he must have spacetime parts, for a spacetime without structure cannot impose structure on its contents. And this in itself is an unwelcome consequence. Moreover, whether we say that God is constituted by spacetime, or constitutes it, we face difficulties. If he is constituted by spacetime, then he is a merely derivative object. And if God himself constitutes spacetime, we and every other (material) object are simply local modifications of God. We have moved rather far away from a traditional monotheistic picture and towards a pantheistic one. And this is unlikely to be embraced by any defender of a reasonably orthodox view of the Incarnation.

But once we put it in the context of relationist views, the inference from creation to divine timelessness looks much less compelling. And the part of the argument which the relationist can resist is C1 (and the general principle which motivates it, namely A3). First, for the relationist, time's occupants are not dependent on time: the dependence, rather, is the other way around. Second, when we shift from a substantivalist to a relationist view of time, the suggestion that we face a dichotomy between two starkly opposing images—a God who shares our time series versus a timeless God—becomes less plausible. There is a sense in which God is *both* outside time and within it. What we suggested in the previous section was that, for objects without temporal parts, existence in time is *derivative*: objects exist at different times only by virtue of being components of states of affairs which themselves obtain at times (in a non-derivative sense, since they exhibit a temporal structure). Considered only in itself, a continuant is not temporal—that is how it manages to be a continuant rather than a collection of temporal parts. So God too is only in time in a derivative sense: he participates in temporal states of affairs. Considered only in himself, he is not temporal. This effectively pulls the rug out from underneath A3. As long as we think of temporality as integral to an object's being (as on a supersubstantivalist or substantivalist view it is), the difference between it and a possible temporal object is too great for us to identify them. But if temporality is derivative, it is not so integral to an object, but a matter of how the states of affairs in which it participates are ordered.

This is the moment to return to a paradox noted in section 1: that if God creates time, and causality is a temporal process, then his creative act precedes time itself, which is absurd. Substantivalist views invite this paradox. For the creation of (space)time is the creation of an object in its own right, and the cause, if prior to its effect, cannot be contained within that object: so there is a time before time. The reductionist relationist account, in contrast, gives us a way of avoiding this paradox. For time on that view is just the network of causal relations between events/states. So in creating anything with a causal structure, God creates a time series. And if the creative act itself stands in a causal relation to creation, then that creative act is in time. But there is no implication that the creative act precedes time itself: it simply precedes every time it brings into existence.

(Of course, we may choose to think of the creative act as of a quite different order from the ordinary causal relations that obtain in the world, by analogy with an author and their novel.[22] In writing *Nineteen Eighty-Four*, George Orwell determined the events of the novel, and the causal relations between those events. But his so determining those events is not part of the novel, and do not stand in the same relation to those events as, say, the sinister forces of the Ministry of Truth. Anyone attracted to this picture of God's creative act will not take that act to be an event in time. Quite what the literal truth behind the analogy is, however, remains obscure. And the

---

[22] A suggestion C.S. Lewis makes in his (1952): 'Time and beyond time'.

fact that the causal relations in the novel are not real, but purely fictional, may strain the analogy to breaking point.)

It may seem that, in this account of how God is, in one sense, in time, and in another, outside it, we have removed the all-important difference between God and ordinary continuants such as ourselves. However, there still remains significant differences between our relation to time and God's.

Recall the question of unity that was raised concerning the reductionist picture. There is no a priori reason why there should not be isolated causal series. But on the radically reductionist picture, a causally disunified world would also be a temporally disunified one. Suppose, then, that part of the life of God (e.g. a phase of his mental life) forms a causal series that is isolated from the causal network in which our own lives take place. That part of God's life would not be in our time. And that means that, again in a purely derivative sense, God is not in our time either, insofar as he participates in events which are not in our time. And this is simply an illustration of God's independence from our time: he can engage in activities that do not form part of the history of our world. He can, in fact, stand in temporal relation to several distinct time series. We cannot.

There is, however, this objection to the account given of God's relation to time. We have spoken just now of individual time series, in the plural. But the inference from creation to timelessness is framed in terms of time *simpliciter*, as a single unified whole. And one might think that the existence of any time series at all is a contingent matter, given that God's creation of time is a wholly free one.[23] But if God necessarily has a mental life, and if that mental life has a causal structure, then (given the causal theory of time order) it seems that, after all, God has no choice over whether or not time exists. It is nevertheless still true—and this is surely the important part of the doctrine of the creation of time—that God is the ultimate source of any time series that does exist. So although the existence of time (that is, some time series or other) is a necessary fact, it is not independent of God.[24] Moreover, the existence of *our* time series remains contingent, and God's act in creating it entirely free.

We might further widen the gulf between ourselves and God by adopting a four-dimensionalist view of ourselves (and other ordinary objects), but not of God. We would then conceive of ourselves as time-bound in a much more radical sense. Human beings, as we might put it, are nothing more

---

[23] As Leftow (1991) insists as part of his defence of divine timelessness: see chapter 12. Thanks to Leftow for pressing this objection in correspondence.

[24] Thanks to an anonymous reviewer for pointing out a parallel here with Augustine's view of concepts as necessary existents that nevertheless depend for their being on God.

than natural processes. Consider, by analogy, a tornado. This is nothing more than a vortex of air currents, along with the debris that such currents pick up on their travels. Both of these vary from time to time. And yet the tornado gives the appearance, especially from a distance, very much of a material object that, although it may change its shape somewhat, neverthe-less manages to move from place to place while remaining something we can track over time. It is a process that behaves like an object. So, the sug-gestion might go, is each of us. There is, then, no interesting ontological (as opposed to conceptual) distinction between 'me' and 'my life': I am just an extended process that has different temporal parts at different times. God, in contrast, is a genuine continuant, not just a process, and so is more fully a substance than anything in his creation. How appealing we find the idea of such a contrast between ourselves and God, however, is likely to be affected by the stance we take on the Incarnation, to which we now, finally, turn.

5. CAN WE RESOLVE THE TEMPORAL PARADOX OF THE INCARNATION?

It will now be somewhat clearer, I hope, how we might try to make sense of the temporal aspect of God's becoming man. The 'timelessness' of God, we have suggested, can consist of two features: (i) he exists in time only in the derivative sense that his actions form a causal series; (ii) the various causal sequences that form his life may, but need not, be part of the causal sequence that involves us, and if they are not then he is not in our time ser-ies, though he is in *a* time series. This is, of course, timelessness of a much less radical kind than is represented by one tradition in Christian thought. Indeed, it allows God to be, in another sense, temporal. But it also allows God to be in our time without thereby being dependent on our time. Now this relation to time, exhibited we may suppose by the Son as well as the Father, is not at all inconsistent with a transition to a much more integrated form of life within our time. On becoming incarnate, the Son begins a life wholly contained within the causal series that constitutes our own history. And we may suppose further that, in a kenotic act of renunciation of divine powers,[25] the Son loses the ability to engage in a mental life, or any other

---

[25] On the kenotic model of the incarnation ('*kenosis*' = emptying), the Son gives up certain of the divine properties, such as omniscience and omnipotence, in becoming incarnate. He remains wholly divine in a moral sense. For discussion see, e.g., Evans (2006).

kind of life, that is causally isolated from our history. He is then wholly within time in a way in which he was not before.

Contrast this with the substantivalist picture, on which the creation of time would be a separate creative act from the creation of its contents. Thinking of Donne's vision ('I see those hands stretched out'), we may wonder how God could come to occupy a temporal structure that he had himself created. For substantival spacetime is not like a house that one might build in order subsequently to occupy it, as Pugin designed and built The Grange at Ramsgate for his own use, and in which he subsequently died. There is, unfortunately, no incarnational parallel here. Coming to occupy a house is a merely extrinsic change in the builder. In contrast, substantival spacetime does not merely contain its contents: their spatio-temporal properties are logically dependent on it. On divine supersubstantivalism, of course, spacetime does not need to be created, since God already constitutes it. But that picture will have grave difficulties accommodating an orthodox account of the Incarnation, for it seems the incarnate Son would only be part of divine spacetime, and so not the whole of the Son, unless we suppose, combining Social Trinitarianism with divine supersubstantivalism, that the Son is only part of spacetime, with the Father constituting a different part. That is not a happy result.

Earlier, we contemplated the possibility of combining a four-dimensionalist approach to our own persistence through time with an insistence that God alone is a true continuant, numerically the same God from one time to another. That would mark another sense in which we were more fully temporal beings than he. But then what exactly happens when the Son becomes incarnate? Does he remain a continuant? Then he does not truly enter into our (four-dimensionalist) condition. Does he cease to be a continuant, and become instead simply a process with different temporal parts? Then it is not truly the Son who becomes incarnate, but rather a process somehow continuous with the Son's pre-incarnate life. The Son himself goes out of existence at that point. No: incarnational doctrine does not sit happily with different approaches to divine and human persistence.

A general difficulty with kenotic accounts, on which the Son gives up at least certain of the properties of divinity, namely those that would conflict with Christ's status as truly human, is that the divine properties are not accidental, but essential to God. And nothing can lose its essential properties without ceasing to exist.[26] So is God's relation to time one of his essential

---

[26] More precisely: nothing can lose its *de re* essential properties without ceasing to exist altogether, and nothing can lose its *de dicto* essential properties—those it requires for

properties? Can we suppose that God's independence from time is something that he *could* give up? Well, one of the senses of independence we identified is something he is not required to give up. As a continuant, he is not bound by time in the way that a four-dimensionalist object is bound by time: his existence in time is derivative. This is just as true of the incarnate Son as of the pre-incarnate Son. But there is another sense of independence from time, namely God's ability to engage in a causal series that is not part of our causal series, which the Son *does* give up. And here the usual kenotic strategy for dealing with the general difficulty of not being able to give up essential properties recommends itself: the essential property is not *F* (where '*F*' can stand for omniscience, omnipotence, independence from our time, etc), but rather '*F* unless freely choosing not to be *F*'.[27]

6. CONCLUSION

At the outset, we posed four questions. We now have candidate answers to those questions, from the perspective of a reductionist relationist account of time. They are no more than sketches, but together they form what is arguably a coherent and plausible strategy for dealing with the temporal paradox of the Incarnation, the problem of how the creator of time can live a life in our time. To summarise:

(i)   *Q*: What is time? *A*: The causal structure of events and states.

(ii) *Q*: What is it to exist in time? *A*: For one's life to exhibit a causal structure. One's location at different times is just the relative position of the stages of one's life in a causal series.

(iii) *Q*: What is God's relation to time? *A*: Insofar as he is causally responsible for initiating the causal history of the cosmos, he is the creator of cosmic time. He exists in time in the derivative sense outlined in (ii). And he is capable of having a life that is not causally connected to our history.

(iv) *Q*: Can we resolve the temporal paradox of the Incarnation? *A*: Yes, given a reductionist relationist view of time. The limited notion of 'timelessness', of independence from time, outlined in (iii) is consistent with the Son's life being part of our causal

---

falling under a certain sortal—without ceasing to fall under that sortal. So the objection is that, after kenosis, God would not be God.

[27] For critical discussion of this kenotic strategy, see Morris (1986), esp. p. 97 f.

series, though he does (temporarily) give up the ability to participate in a life not in our history.

I am in partial agreement with Richard Holland, when he writes:

The important issue [in the debate over God's relation to time] does not seem to be
whether God is "in" or "outside" of time, as if the participants in the debate were
attempting to ascertain God's "temporal location." Rather it seems as if the question
at the heart of the debate is whether God experiences the coming-to-be and passing-
away of states of affairs.[28]

Although he is not explicit on the point, his remarks fit most naturally
with a relationist view of time. Holland's strategy is to make the doctrine
of the Incarnation dialectically central in the debate over God's relation
to time, and argues that our understanding of the Incarnation requires
abandonment of the traditional doctrine of the timelessness of God. What
I have argued, in effect, is that, while we may concede this argument,
there is still quite a bit that can be said concerning God's independence
from time.

The moral of our discussion is that—as both Leibniz and Clarke were
keenly aware—there are intriguing and quite complex connections between
theological issues and the relationist/substantivalist debate over the nature
of spacetime. Favouring a reductionist relationist view (for which independent reasons can be urged) over a substantivalist one goes some way towards
demystifying the mystery of time and incarnation that so beguiled the
metaphysical poets. But let the last word be theirs. Here is Richard Crashaw
(1612/13–1649), writing on the Nativity:

> Welcome to our wondring sight
> Eternity shut in a span!
> Summer in Winter! Day in Night!
> Great little one, whose glorious Birth,
> Lifts Earth to Heaven, stoops Heaven to Earth.[29,30]

---

[28] Holland (2012): 170. I say 'partial agreement' because I would want to distance
myself from the implication that time involves objective becoming. But that is another
story. I engage with this aspect of time, in connection with the incarnation, in Le
Poidevin (2016).

[29] 'Hymne of the Nativity', in Martin (1957).

[30] An earlier version of this paper was given at Queen's University, Belfast, in December
2012. I am grateful to the participants, and especially to Joseph Diekemper and Brian
Leftow, for their comments. I would also like to thank Rik Peels and an anonymous
reviewer for their comments on the penultimate version of the paper.

REFERENCES

Alexander, H. G. (1956) (ed.) *The Leibniz-Clarke Correspondence* (Manchester: Manchester University Press, 1956).

Dennett, Daniel (1991) *Consciousness Explained* (Boston, MA: Little, Brown and Company).

Earman, John (1992) *World Enough and Spacetime* (Cambridge, MA: MIT Press).

Evans, C. Stephen (2006) (ed.) *Exploring Kenotic Christology: The self-emptying of God* (Oxford: Oxford University Press).

Grierson, Herbert J. C. (1912) (ed.) *The Poems of John Donne* (Oxford: Oxford University Press).

Hasker, William (2010) 'Objections to social trinitarianism', *Religious Studies* 46: 421–39.

Holland, Richard A. Jr (2012) *God, Time and the Incarnation* (Eugene, OR: Wipf and Stock).

Hussey, Edward (1983) (ed.) *Aristotle's Physics, Books III and IV* (Oxford: Clarendon Press).

Le Poidevin, Robin (2007) 'Action at a distance', in Anthony O'Hear (ed.), *Philosophy of Science*, Royal Institute of Philosophy London Lecture Series (Cambridge: Cambridge University Press): 21–36.

Le Poidevin, Robin (2009) 'Identity and the composite Christ: An incarnational dilemma', *Religious Studies* 45: 167–86.

Le Poidevin, Robin (2016) ' "Once for All": The tense of the Atonement', *European Journal for the Philosophy of Religion* 8: 179–94.

Leftow, Brian (1991) *Time and Eternity* (Ithaca, NY: Cornell University Press).

Leftow, Brian (2004) 'A Latin Trinity', *Faith and Philosophy* 21: 304–33.

Lewis, C. S. (1952) *Mere Christianity* (London: Bles).

Marmodoro, Anna, and Hill, Jonathan (2010) 'Composition models of the incarnation: Unity and unifying relations', *Religious Studies* 46: 469–88.

Martin, L. C. (1957) (ed.) *The Poems, English, Latin and Greek of Richard Crashaw*, 2nd edn (Oxford: Oxford University Press).

Mellor, D. H. (1998) *Real Time II* (London: Routledge).

Morris, Thomas V. (1986) *The Logic of God Incarnate* (Ithaca, NY: Cornell University Press).

Nerlich, Graham (1994) *The Shape of Space*, 2nd edn (Cambridge: Cambridge University Press).

Potter, George R. and Simpson, Evelyn M. (1957) (eds) *The Sermons of John Donne*, Vol. III (Berkeley, CA: University of California Press).

Schaffer, Jonathan (2009) 'Spacetime the one substance', *Philosophical Studies* 145: 131–48.

Senor, Thomas D. (1990) 'Incarnation and timelessness', *Faith and Philosophy* 7: 149–64.

Senor, Thomas D. (2007) 'The compositional account of the Incarnation', *Faith and Philosophy* 24: 52–71.

Shoemaker, Sidney (1969) 'Time without change', *Journal of Philosophy* 66: 363–81.

Sider, Theodore (2001) *Four-Dimensionalism* (Oxford: Oxford University Press).

Simons, Peter (2000) 'How to exist at a time when you have no temporal parts', *Monist* 83: 419–36.

Sklar, Lawrence (1977) *Space, Time and Spacetime* (Berkeley, CA: University of California Press).

Stevenson, J. (1989) *Creeds, Councils and Controversies: Documents illustrating the early history of the Church 373–561* (London: SPCK).

10

The Posture of Faith

Meghan Page

While faith is often described as a cognitive state, many philosophers argue that faith includes a noncognitive factor, and is not merely a species of belief. In this paper, I develop a novel model of this affective component based on recent work in clinical psychology concerning the relationship between posture and approach motivation. I further argue that this model accurately represents many crucial features of faith: faith can motivate us to act against our desires, faith is both voluntary and passive, faith makes us vulnerable, faith is an activity, and faith can intensify belief.

1. INTRODUCTION

Perhaps faith is a species of belief. To have faith in God is to believe in God, even if you lack sufficient evidence. To have faith in your partner is to believe that your partner is faithful, even if your friend suggests otherwise. Although such cognitive portrayals of faith have an intuitive pull, it's unlikely that an exhaustive account of faith can be provided by appeals to belief alone.

For example, suppose Jennifer intends to run a marathon. Although I don't know much about her competition, I develop a confident belief that she will place first in the race. Further suppose that while I believe Jennifer will win, I despise her and desire her to lose. In such a case, I fail to exhibit faith that she will win. On the other hand, if I maintain the same belief state but change my attitude towards Jennifer, choosing to support her in her endeavor, I do display faith that Jennifer will win the race.

In each of these cases my belief state remains the same; I believe that Jennifer will win the race based on very little evidence. Nevertheless, in one case I display faith and in the other I do not. This raises a problem for merely cognitive accounts.

If faith just is a belief state, that belief state must be sufficient for having faith; our thought experiment suggests that the same belief state only produces faith on occasion.

This worry can be dissolved by means of what Mckaughan calls "belief-plus" models.

Whatever other responses (e.g. behavioral commitments, values, affections, and so forth) faith involves one cannot have faith unless one has a particular attitude, belief, towards the content in question. Call this the belief-plus conception of faith....At least among philosophers of religion who take monotheistic religions to have a stake in some truth-valued claims about reality, the belief-plus model is by far the most widely held conception of faith (Mckaughan 2013, 102–4).

According to belief-plus models of faith, although faith *necessitates* belief, belief is not sufficient for faith—a complete analysis must include something additional to belief.[1] In the marathon case, this extra component takes the form of a desire or hope that you will win the marathon. Only when this attitude is paired with the belief state is faith produced.

Other philosophers defend the stronger claim that faith is *wholly* noncognitive. On these accounts, faith is best understood as an attitude or psychological state which disposes one to certain types of assertions and interactions. For example, Clegg offers the following portrayal of faith:

Faith is inverted terror. It is strong hope or powerful trust. The declarations "My husband will get home," and "My wife is innocent" manifest a certain serenity—a serenity that we may judge to be admirable precisely because we recognize that there is much to disturb it and that in persons of weaker character, though not weaker mind, it would be missing...Genuine avowals of faith reveal states of mind. They are most accurately read as symptomatic displays that may be judged as sincere or insincere, but not as true or false (Clegg 1979, 229).

On Clegg's picture, assertions of faith are *not* expressions of belief but displays of a powerful confidence, an unwavering trust.[2]

---

[1] There are variations of the belief-plus model which deny that faith necessitates belief, replacing the cognitive element of the view with a weaker mental state. For example, Alston (1996) suggests what I will call an *acceptance-plus* account of faith. Like his belief-plus counterparts, Alston claims faith has both cognitive and noncognitive components, but the cognitive component need not be as strong as belief—acceptance will do the trick. Likewise, Howard-Snyder (2013) argues that the cognitive component of faith need not be belief but something he calls "assuming." As I don't intend to say much about the cognitive element of faith here, I won't delve too deeply into these accounts. I merely want to point out that *irrespective* of your views about the cognitive element of faith, most people at least assent to a noncognitive element in a complete account of faith.

[2] Clegg is not alone in this assessment. Audi (2011) also defends an account of faith as trust, while Pojman (2003) characterizes faith as hope.

To summarize, because of the issues like those raised in the marathon case, most philosophers agree that faith is either wholly or partially noncognitive. In this paper, I unpack this noncognitive feature.[3] In the next section, I discuss why characterizations of faith as desire, hope, or trust are inadequate and lead to various puzzles. I then provide a *model* of affective faith that resolves the worries raised by alternative accounts. For the task at hand, I ignore the question of whether a belief state is required for faith. As a result, my account does not require that any particular belief state be instantiated by faithers.

2. PROBLEMS WITH DESIRE AND HOPE

2.1. Hopeless Faith

The affective feature of faith is often equated with desire or hope.[4] Suppose that faith requires a desire or hope in its object. While this effectively captures our marathon intuition (faith that you will win the marathon requires a desire or hope that you will win the marathon), in certain paradigmatic cases of faith, it is difficult to imagine the alleged faithers *desired* or *hoped* for the object of their faith. A classic example of this dilemma occurs for the "father of faith," Abraham. Abraham had faith that God requested the sacrifice of his son, but it's hard to believe that Abraham desired or hoped God would make such a request.

Daniel Howard-Snyder claims such cases are not genuine counterexamples to the desire theory of faith, but press us to expand our conception of what sort of desire might be present in people of faith:

cognition alone cannot motivate behavior; desire is required. Like propositional fear and hope, therefore, propositional faith has desire built into it...even if one can have faith that p without desire for the truth of p, one cannot have faith that p without a desire in virtue of which one cares that p. As we've just seen, different sorts of desires might satisfy that description; so let's gather them all under the rubric of a *positive conative orientation* and say that faith that p requires a positive conative orientation towards the truth of p (Howard-Snyder 2013, 363).

According to Howard-Snyder, we might cash out this positive conative orientation through either a desire that p is true, or a desire that we desire

---

[3] If you find yourself dissatisfied by my assertion that noncognitivism is important, Jon Kvanvig argues for this position in Kvanvig (2016).

[4] For example, see Alston (1996), Howard-Snyder (2013), Clegg (1979), or Pojman (2003).

that p is true, or a desire for some consequence of p to be true. Howard-Snyder uses the example of a meth-addict who lacks the desire to stop doing meth but, acknowledging his life would likely improve were he sober, desires a desire to quit.

But even with with this liberality, it's difficult to locate *any* relevant desire within Abraham. It's doubtful that Abraham desires to desire that God requests the sacrifice of his son, or that he desires a major consequence of God's request: the death of his son. Abraham takes Isaac to the mountain because he has faith that God has commanded him to do so; nevertheless, he lacks any positive conative orientation towards this state of affairs.[5]

A parallel example can be constructed in the arena of secular faith. Suppose Jane has been informed by her commanders that the enemy is *definitely* going to attack her camp. Jane instructs the soldiers in her camp to prepare for this attack, urging them to stay awake, alert, and armed. Hours and days pass without any new word from the commanders or sign of the enemy, but Jane's disposition is unwavering. *The attack will come*, she assures her soldiers. Jane displays faith—faith that the enemy will attack her camp. But it doesn't follow that she hopes or desires the attack with either a first or second order desire.

2.2. Propositional and Attitudinal Faith

At this point, it's important to consider a common distinction in the literature on faith—the distinction between *faith that* and *faith in*. Propositional faith, or faith that, is understood as a relationship between an agent and a proposition. By contrast, attitudinal faith, or faith in, is a relationship between two agents. I don't intend to get too much into this distinction here, but I should point out that Howard-Snyder focuses on propositional faith, while I use the distinction quite loosely. While the relationship between these two sorts of faith is far from settled, one might suppose that propositional faith is ultimately grounded in attitudinal faith. On this picture, I have faith *that* my partner is faithful because I have faith *in* my partner.

---

[5] One way to get around this worry is to argue that Abraham desired to please God through obedience, and *this* was the consequence of sacrificing his son that grounds the conative element of his faith. While I am somewhat sympathetic to this line of reasoning, it seems to reflect a more *general* desire that resides in Abraham rather than one that is particularly related to his belief that God has requested him to sacrifice his son. While Abraham has faith that God has requested the sacrifice of his son, I don't think he views "pleasing God" as a necessary consequence of sacrificing his son, but a contingent consequence, given that God has requested it. Therefore, it's plausible that Abraham desires or wishes that God had never asked him to sacrifice his son in the first place.

This view allows for a possible objection to my worry about desire-hope theories. I claim, for example, that Jane has faith that the enemy will attack her camp but lacks a positive conative orientation towards this proposition. However, one might argue that Jane's faith that p is just an expression of faith *in* her commanders. While she lacks a positive orientation towards p, she enjoys a great deal of respect for her superior officers.

Although Jane's propositional faith depends on her faith in a higher authority, it does not follow that her propositional faith collapses into attitudinal faith. Jane has both propositional *and* attitudinal faith—and her propositional faith lacks the positive conative orientation characterized by Howard-Snyder.[6]

2.3. On Voluntariness

Another weakness in the desire-hope theory of faith is illuminated in the context of interpersonal relationships. We expect our partners and close friends to have faith in us. In the midst of a tenuous situation, one in which they doubt our abilities or intentions, we might exhort them to have faith in us. Such practices suppose that faith can be exercised *at will*; in this sense, faith is voluntary.[6]

But are desires voluntary? Not straightforwardly so. Unrequited love would be far less tragic were it possible to abdicate our desires in the way I can abdicate my office. Dieting would be easy as disavowing pie. But this is not our experience of desire—we are not able to control our desires *at will*. Desire is traditionally categorized as a *passion* because we experience it passively.

Is the same true for hope? I take hope to be a type of desire—a desire aimed specifically at an event or state of affairs (rather than a person or an object). If this is true, then we can control what we hope for no more than we can control what we desire.

Of course it's possible to enhance or destroy desires indirectly. For example, suppose I lack the desire to exercise. I recognize that it is good for me to exercise, and so I attempt to cultivate an appetite for fitness by reading lots

---

[6] One possible objection to this claim, raised by an anonymous referee, is that our practice of exhorting others to have faith is merely a practice of exhorting others to act "as if" they had faith. Although it's possible, this suggestion does not seem consistent with my own reflection on the practice. When I exhort my friend to have faith in me, I don't simply want her to stop acting as if she doubts me, I want her to stop doubting me. If I later discovered that she continued to doubt but "pretended" to have faith in me, I would still experience some resentment or disappointment.

of articles about the importance of exercise, hanging out with personal trainers, buying snazzy gym gear, etc. It's plausible that these actions will produce a desire within me to exercise. Nevertheless, this desire is obtained *indirectly*. I cannot produce (or destroy) a desire simply by willing to do so.[7]

 Faith, unlike desire, can be achieved by willing—or so our interpersonal practices suggest. When I am upset with you for failing to have faith in me, or when I encourage you to do so, I act as though faith is something within your control.

I want to pause for a moment and acknowledge a paradox in the nature of faith. While I argue that our interpersonal practices imply faith is voluntary, various religious traditions suggest that faith is a *gift*. Both Aquinas and Calvin take faith to be a gift from God, and passages in the Bible suggest believers ought to *request* more faith, as if it were not something they can simply acquire through willing.[8] One of the major objections to requiring faith for salvation is that faith is something we cannot always produce in ourselves just by intending to.

Though I take concerns about the absolute voluntariness of faith seriously, such worries fail to negate the objection I have raised. There is a genuine paradox: faith is voluntary in certain cases and involuntary in others. However, desire and hope are wholly involuntary, so they fail as candidates for faith. While I grant my position is mysterious, for now I can offer only a promissory note that this tension will resolve itself once my view is on the table. The model I present can account for both voluntary and non-voluntary cases of faith.

To summarize, desire and hope fail to illuminate the affective character of faith because (i) we can have faith without desire or hope and (ii) desire and hope are entirely involuntary where faith is at least partially voluntary.

3. FAITH AS TRUST

Other noncognitivists, such as Clegg, liken faith to trust. Kvanvig launches several objections to trust-based portrayals of faith in his recent paper

[7] I am following Hieronymi (2006) in suggesting that voluntary actions are those that can be done at will. Hieronymi provides a more straightforward account of voluntariness in Hieronymi (2008), where she claims that voluntariness is roughly equivalent to intentional action. Of course this account does not (and is not intended to) extend to every use of the term voluntary, but it suffices to clearly distinguish the relevant difference between faith and desire.

[8] Aquinas (2015) addresses the gift of faith in Question 6 of the *Summa Theologica*. For a discussion of Calvin's view of faith, see Shepherd (2004). For a biblical example of requesting faith, see Mark 9:23–5.

"The Idea of Faith as Trust: Lessons in NonCognitivist Approaches to Faith." Here I will draw on his work and consider several problems with analyzing faith as trust.

3.1. Reliance

On the surface, trust appears to be synonymous with faith. Abraham had faith in God insofar as Abraham trusted God. My partner doubts my faith when he questions my trust. But does equating faith with trust enhance our understanding of faith? Only if we have a clear conception of trust.

Unfortunately, the philosophical literature is filled with what Kvanvig calls a "stupefying variety of opinion" concerning the nature of trust. Nevertheless, a common thread exists among philosophers who analyze faith as trust: trust implies a kind of *reliance on the good will of another* (Kvanvig 2016). To trust God is to rely on God, to trust your students is to rely on them to do their work responsibly.

Of course, trust can't be *identical* to reliance on another's good will, for there are plenty of instances where we rely on the goodness of people we don't trust. This worry is illustrated in various sources through what Zac Cogley calls "the trickster problem" (Cogley 2012, 30). Consider a con-artist who relies on the good will of others to give him money for a company that doesn't exist. Such a trickster relies on the good will of his benefactors, but fails to *trust* them with the truth of his intentions. Cogley suggests we can resolve this worry by restricting trust to the context of a relationship that generates norms that entitle us to rely on each other. To trust is to be *entitled* to rely on the good will of others in a way that con-artists are not entitled to rely on the good will of their victims.

According to Cogley, this accounts for the other element of trust that is not captured by mere reliance: our *vulnerability to betrayal*. When our trust is breached, it is natural to feel hurt and violated. Such feelings are unwarranted for the con-artist who relies on his victims for money, but are justified for a woman whose friend broadcasts personal details about her life that she revealed in confidence.

However, Cogley's entitlement account fails to resolve all incarnations of the trickster problem. Suppose Jill is a foster child who is not fond of her foster family, but not for any serious reason. Jill knows that her social worker is required to look after her best interests and remove Jill from her foster situation should suspicious reports arise. Jill doesn't trust her social worker—she's never really trusted anyone—but she decides to tell the social worker lies about her foster family believing that the social worker will report the abuse and remove Jill from her foster home. In this case, based on the relationship between Jill and her social worker, Jill is certainly entitled to rely on her social worker's good will. *But Jill is still acting as a trickster*, and has not made herself vulnerable to betrayal by the social worker.

Although Cogley illuminates an important element of trust—its primary func tion is within the context of relationships—it fails as a complete account of the sort of reliance that is unique to trust.

Two important points can be taken from this discussion. First, equating faith with trust is not going to clarify much, given that the sort of reliance required for trust is a difficult one to crystallize. Nevertheless, whatever sort of reliance trust involves makes us vulnerable to betrayal. The vulnerability present in trust is also evident in faith, as faith can also be betrayed.

3.2. The Activity of Faith

Kvanvig raises another interesting worry about equating faith with trust:

at least when it comes to the affective faith I am focusing on here, trust-based accounts are thoroughly wrongheaded. What is distinctive about affective faith is that it is active rather than passive... time and again in Scripture, the model of commitment to the Kingdom of God is described in terms of *being a follower*. These examples of faith are not properly characterized in terms of passivity. And yet pure passivity, of the sort displayed by the successful achievement of Stoic *apatheia*, can be an expression of trust. Such an attitude toward the universe as a whole can display one's trust in the created order and in whomever or whatever is responsible for that order (Kvanvig 2016, 17–18, emphasis his).

Kvanvig appeals to the stoic notion of *apatheia*: the state in which one is at peace, undisturbed by any of the passions. He claims it's possible to *trust* in a creator just in case we free ourselves from any anxiety or worry (or positive expectation) about the future, but to have faith in a creator entails a more active approach: faith requires us to do something.

I worry about this distinction as it's presented here. The real difference between the trust of the stoic and the faith of Abraham hinges on the way God presents himself in these two different stories. Were it the case that God appeared to the stoic and commanded him to go forth into a new land, I'm not sure pure passivity on the stoic's part would count as trust. In this case, trust seems to require our stoic to act in response to God's word.

Nevertheless, Kvanvig points to a distinction of substance. Faith acts as a *motivator* in a way that trust need not. For example, you might tell me that the Pittsburgh Pirates won the World Series, and I might trust that this is correct. But if I don't know much about baseball, and don't care for the sport, this fact might never again cross my mind. This apathy does not negate my trust that the Pirates are champions, but we would be hard pressed to describe my attitude as one of faith.

I don't mean to claim that trust cannot or does not motivate our behavior, simply that we need not be motivated to act in order to trust. By contrast, faith necessitates motivation in a specific direction. This motivational component of faith underlies what Howard-Snyder attempts to capture with his "positive conative orientation." Abraham's faith that God has asked for the sacrifice of his son is fully realized in the steps he takes to fulfill this order. But, as Kvanvig points out, such motivation need not be present in order for us to trust. Therefore, faith and trust are not identical.

4. POSTURE AND ATTITUDE

I have considered several popular accounts of the non-cognitive component of faith, and discussed various problems they face. As a result, I have uncovered several fundamental features of faith: faith can occur where no desire is present, faith can be, but is not always, voluntary, faith involves a sort of reliance that makes us vulnerable, and faith motivates us towards some object or state of affairs.

In this section, rather than present a reductive metaphysical account of faith, I develop a *model* that captures these diverse elements of faith and represents them as a unified picture. In the previous sections of this paper, I have shown that current accounts of faith fail to account for *all* of the facets of faith. Hence, I suggest this model as a starting point for further work in the analysis of faith. If we are going to define faith, we must first agree on a picture of what faith is like. In addition, I aim to provide a way of thinking about faith that helps us manifest it in our own lives—to illuminate faith in a way that if our partner, friend, or God requests our faith, we have some notion of what is being asked of us and how to properly respond. While I do make claims such as "faith is a posture," the 'is' is not intended to be one of definition but of metaphor.

4.1. The model

To have faith is to maintain a posture—the posture of leaning in. To have faith in a person is to lean in to that person. To have faith that some state of affairs will come about is to lean in to that state of affairs.

Initially, this description appears opaque. What can it mean for faith to be a posture? How can a believer lean towards God, when God is hidden from their senses? Moreover, what if God is everywhere? In which direction should they lean?

Such questions follow from a traditional understanding of posture as a bodily stance. To be clear, I do not think faith is or requires any particular positioning of the body.[9] When I claim that faith is a posture, I am speaking metaphorically. However, to fully understand this metaphor, it is important to deepen our understanding of physiological postures, and the interesting relationship between posture and attitude. To do so, I will offer empirical evidence provided by research in cognitive science and clinical psychology. But before we examine these recent experimental conclusions, it's helpful to take a brief look at historical approaches to understanding the relationship between posture and attitude.

4.2. Darwin and James

The first scientist to take interest in the connection between posture and attitude was Charles Darwin. In *The Expression of Emotions in Man and Animals*, he discusses the embodiment of emotion—the instantiation of emotion in facial expressions, postures, and voice intonations.[10] Darwin observed that certain posture-emotion pairings persist throughout different cultures. One example he notes is the relationship between a sense of resignation and a shrug:

men in *all parts of the world* when they feel,—whether or not they wish to show this feeling,—that they cannot or will not do something, or will not resist something if done by another, shrug their shoulders, at the same time often bending in their elbows, showing the palms of their hands with extended fingers, often throwing their heads a little on one side, raising their eyebrows, and opening their mouths. These states of mind are either simply passive or show a determination not to act (Darwin 1998, 162, emphasis mine).

[9] One interesting feature of this account, however, is it does illuminate the use of different postures (such as kneeling, bowing, etc.) within religious practice.

[10] I'd like to thank an anonymous referee for pointing out that "emotion" is a philosophically loaded term. Some accounts of emotion, such as the one put forth by Roberts (2003) suggest that emotion itself is largely cognitive. I want to resist providing a philosophical account of emotion here, however, as I am trying to use the terms as they appear in the fields of psychology and cognitive science. I think it is an interesting question, though one outside the scope of this chapter, to consider how this work interacts with philosophical theories of emotion.

Given that the relationship of particular postures and emotional states is universal, Darwin concludes that the link between the two is biological, and not a contingent fact about culture. Attitudes extend beyond the mind and manifest in a physiological stance.

Following Darwin's observations, William James investigated the relationship between posture and emotion. He arranged a study where subjects were shown photos of a faceless mannequin instantiating various bodily postures. The study also requested the subjects to position themselves in the same postures as the mannequin and describe their resulting emotional state. James wanted to determine (i) if bodily postures actually express emotions and (ii) what effect the observance of various postures has on spectators. He concluded that postures are an effective means of expressing emotion, and further noticed that when observers mimic the postures they perceive, they tend to describe their own emotional state as conforming to the expressive content of the posture (James 1932, 435).

Both Darwin and James claim that posture is a biologically determined expresser of psychological states, while James's work further suggests that our posture can not only express but *influence* our mental or emotional state. This finding was further investigated in 1982, when Riskind and Gotay published a study concerning the *feedback* effects of posture on motivation and emotion. They found that posture strongly effects our emotional state. For example, a person placed in a slouching posture, conventionally symptomatic of depression, tends to experience emotions of helplessness more readily when later asked to complete a task. Similarly, subjects placed in crouched or threatened physical postures express greater perceptions of stress (Riskind and Gotay 1982, 296). This implies that in certain cases posture is able to cultivate, rather than merely reveal, our affective states.

4.3. Leaning in and Approach Motivation

Following the work of Riskind and Gotay, Harmon-Jones and Price experimentally investigated the relationship between leaning forward and the neural activity associated with *approach motivation*. Price and Harmon-Jones define approach motivation as *the impulse to go toward*.[11] Approach motivation is a more general concept than desire; we might go towards a thing

---

[11] They defend this definition in Harmon-Jones et al. (2013). I would like to note that this definition of approach motivation deviates from some traditional definitions which assume that approach motivation must result in a positive affective state and be motivated by external stimuli. However, I focus on the definition provided by Price and Harmon-Jones because it is the one used in the research I discuss.

without desiring it. I might, for example, approach a person out of anger rather than desire. The opposite of approach motivation is avoidance motivation. Where approach motivation acts towards the bringing about of a specific outcome, such as exercising to produce health, avoidance motivation directs us away from an outcome, such as exercising to avoid weight gain.

One study conducted by Price and Harmon-Jones involved showing participants various images while they were placed in a chair. These same pictures were shown to each participant while reclined, neutral, and leaning forward. When leaning toward the images, the participants experienced a significant increase in neural activity in the left frontal cortex—the region associated with approach motivation. The study concluded:

the results of the present experiment suggest that simply leaning forward increases a pattern of neural activation associated with approach motivation.... Practically, they suggest that leaning forward may increase desire or interest in situations (e.g. learning) or individuals (e.g. depressed) who may need such (Harmon-Jones et al. 2011, 313).

According to Harmon-Jones and Price, leaning in not only *expresses* motivation towards an object or state of affairs but intensifies or initiates motivation towards an object. A feedback loop exists between leaning forward and approach motivation. When motivated to go towards an object we lean forward, and when we lean into that object we are motivated to approach it. This, along with a large number of related studies that produced similar results,[12] has led Price and Harmon-Jones to adopt what they call a "motivational directional model" (Price and Harmon-Jones 2011, 720). Price and Harmon-Jones take psychological states to be embodied physiologically, and from this perspective motivation to approach can be understood as a leaning toward, while motivation to avoid is associated with physical withdrawal.

4.4. Extending the Model

The directional model presented by Price and Harmon-Jones to represent motivation can be used to illustrate a more nuanced conception of affective faith. According to such a model, rather than equating faith with a simple state such as desire or hope, faith involves a positioning of oneself towards

---

[12] See, for example, Price and Harmon-Jones (2011), Harmon-Jones and Peterson (2009) Peterson et al. (2008), or Harmon-Jones (2006).

the object of faith and an increased motivation towards this object as a result.

The dependency associated with faith is exemplified in this model. We can only lean forward so far without losing the ability to balance. If we lean in to another person, it not only suggests a context of intimacy but also opens us up to a unique kind of vulnerability; leaning in positions us to fall flat on our faces before the object of our faith.

But what does it mean to lean in "metaphorically"? To physically lean in is to focus and orient oneself on a specific person or goal. We can imitate this physical posture by attuning our lives, decisions and routines around the persons or states of affairs in which we place faith. In doing so, the decisions we make and attitudes we form will reflect a posture of faith.

Perhaps this metaphor is best illuminated by example. Consider a woman who, after many years of a committed romantic relationship that has grown to be lackluster, reports to her partner that she is considering separation. Her partner responds by acknowledging that the current state of their relationship is unacceptable, but implores her to have faith in him and in their future together. What is her partner requesting? In asking her to have faith in him, he requests that she continue to make herself vulnerable to him; for example, he may suggest that she approach him with her frustrations rather than letting disappointment create further distance between them. Similarly, to have faith in their future relationship is to work towards the bringing about of such a future. Seeking counseling, for example, shows a desire to approach the relationship and bring about its flourishing rather than disengage from it.

And what is the result of such engagement? Of course, it's difficult to make a generalized prediction for how, if at all, this faith will affect the future of their relationship. Still, there is a common suspicion that working on a relationship by seeking counseling or simply by prioritizing it tends to change one's attitude towards the relationship, much like posture enhances our approach motivation.

Similarly, we can consider the example of Abraham. The story of Abraham's sacrifice of Isaac appears in Genesis 22. Consider the wording of the text.

After these things God tested Abraham, and said to him, "Abraham!" And he said, "Here am I."[2] He said, "Take your son, your only son Isaac, whom you love, and go to the land of Mori′ah, and offer him there as a burnt offering upon one of the mountains of which I shall tell you."[3] So Abraham rose early in the morning, saddled his ass, and took two of his young men with him, and his son Isaac; and he cut the wood for the burnt offering, and arose and went to the place of which God had told him.[4] On the third day Abraham lifted up his eyes and saw the place afar off.[5]

Then Abraham said to his young men, "Stay here with the ass; I and the lad will go yonder and worship, and come again to you."[6] And Abraham took the wood of the burnt offering, and laid it on Isaac his son; and he took in his hand the fire and the knife. So they went both of them together.[7] And Isaac said to his father Abraham, "My father!" And he said, "Here am I, my son." He said, "Behold, the fire and the wood; but where is the lamb for a burnt offering?"[8] Abraham said, "God will provide himself the lamb for a burnt offering, my son." So they went both of them together.[9]

When they came to the place of which God had told him, Abraham built an altar there, and laid the wood in order, and bound Isaac his son, and laid him on the altar, upon the wood.[10] Then Abraham put forth his hand, and took the knife to slay his son.[11] But the angel of the Lord called to him from heaven, and said, "Abraham, Abraham!" And he said, "Here am I."[12] He said, "Do not lay your hand on the lad or do anything to him; for now I know that you fear God, seeing you have not withheld your son, your only son, from me" (Genesis 22:1–12 Revised Standard Version).

In this passage, Abraham's faith is exemplified by his response to God's instructions; he orients his behavior around the bringing about of God's will. What does Abraham do when God requests the sacrifice of Isaac? He prepares for the sacrificial journey. Abraham leans towards God by acting in a way that approaches the state of affairs God has requested. This sort of response illustrates what it means to "lean in" metaphorically.

As Kierkegaard displays in *Fear and Trembling*, scripture leaves Abraham's emotional state as the story progresses open to speculation.[13] Nevertheless, Abraham's actions display an increase in intensity as the story evolves. He begins with the simple act of embarking on a journey in the direction he was called, but the actions that follow display an increasing passion for bringing about God's will.[14] He withholds the truth of his intentions from his son, and finally removes his knife in order to slay Isaac. Abraham's actions ascend in force and severity, suggesting that, as our model predicts, Abraham's positioning of himself to carry out God's will increased his motivation to bring God's will about.

5. SORTING OUT THE PUZZLES

In sections 2 and 3, I suggested several worries for current accounts of the noncognitive aspect of faith. Now that I have presented a new model of faith, we can rely on this model to resolve them. This further reveals the virtues of using the motivational directional model to represent faith.

---

[13] See Kierkegaard (1983).

[14] Or, depending on your reading of Abraham, an intensifying mania.

5.1. The Desire Puzzle

Let's begin with the desire problem. We can't have faith that some state of affairs is going to come about if we are completely against this state of affairs; no matter how strongly I believe that you might get a certain job, if I despise you and strongly wish for your demise I can't be said to have faith in you or faith that you will get the job. On the other hand, there are certainly cases of allegedly exemplary faith, such as Abraham's willingness to sacrifice Isaac, where it's hard to imagine the faither truly desired the state of affairs towards which he strived.

Using approach motivation in place of desire resolves this tension, as approach motivation suggests we are working towards some state of affairs independently of what we desire. If I am campaigning against, or even wishing against, your acquiring a certain job I am certainly not motivated to bring about the state of affairs where you get the job. On the other hand, even though Abraham does not desire the sacrifice of his son, he is motivated towards bringing it about, and *this* is the evidence of his faith.

5.2. The Puzzle about Voluntariness

In section 2 I argue that faith is not identical to desire because desire is involuntary and faith is at least potentially voluntary. We often desire our family and friends to have faith in us. It is odd to make this request if having faith is something entirely out of their hands.

Leaning forward fulfills this requirement of voluntariness. We can choose to adopt a certain posture, and, given the relationship between this posture and approach motivation, we can choose to adopt a posture that will dispose us to a deeper connection with another person. Because of the looping effects between posture and approach motivation, the choice to manipulate one's body in a certain way *enhances* our motivation to act in a certain way. As a result, we can choose to motivate ourselves towards a relationship or state of affairs.

But some religious traditions suggest that faith is not *always* voluntary. Incidents such as Paul's conversion on the road to Damascus or the hardening of Pharaoh's heart imply that faith is a *gift*. Mark records one man's cry for faith as "I believe, help my unbelief" (Mark 9:24). The Greek word translated here as believe is *pisteuō*, the same word that much of the New Testament translates as *faith*. If faith is wholly voluntary, then the man should be able to increase his own faith rather than request the increase from Jesus.

Two points about this. First, although postures are typically acquired voluntarily, they do not have to be. I can manipulate your body into a specific posture, as was done in the experimental studies mentioned above. Certainly an almighty God could not only position our bodies as he sees fit, but also structure our lives in such a way as to bring about (or prevent) our aiming at a certain state of affairs.

Still, one might argue that it's silly for the man referenced in Mark to *ask* for more faith if faith is like leaning in. Couldn't he just lean in further? This brings me to my second point. If you've ever received physical therapy, or taken an advanced yoga class, you have experienced the *limits* of the voluntary control you have over your body. There are plenty of postures we have to *learn* and *practice*, and this process often requires the intervention of another agent. Perhaps it was precisely this sort of intervention the man desired from Jesus.

To summarize, the model of faith as the posture of leaning in is able to account for both the voluntary and non-voluntary aspects of faith.

5.3. The Trickster Puzzle

The trickster problem presents itself if we analyze faith in terms of trust. Surely one can rely on the good will of a person without *trusting* or *having faith in* them—as does the trickster. The trickster relies on the good will of others in order to exploit them for some personal gain. How can we characterize the reliance at work in faith in such a way as to avoid all versions of the trickster problem?

Thinking of faith as a posture offers a way out of this conundrum. Imagine the difference between *leaning in* to your friend or colleague and *leaning on* them. In both cases you rely on their support, but in the first you *open yourself* to them in a way you need not in the second. In fact, I can lean on someone without their explicit permission, desire, or even knowledge. While they will eventually notice the weight impinging on them, and have the ability to move in such a way that I can no longer lean on them, the posture lacks the sort of vulnerability present in leaning in. Moreover, when I lean in to a person I look *at* them; I am aware of their situation, attitude, and response to me. When I lean forward I make myself vulnerable to them, and they *see* my vulnerability.

Hence, leaning in suggests a solution to the trickster puzzle. While both the faither and the trickster exhibit reliance on the good will of another, the faither leans in while the trickster leans on.

5.4. Active Faith

Does *leaning in* capture the *active* essence of faith suggested by Jon Kvanvig? Certainly adopting a certain posture can be an activity. But what if, as I suggested in section 5.2, one is placed in a posture non-voluntarily? Is leaning enough of an activity to serve as a model of faith?

Yes, especially given the link between leaning in and motivation. Leaning in is certainly an *active* state insofar as it is a breeding ground for incentive and desire. Leaning in enhances our approach motivation and disposes us towards activities like, in Kvanvig's words, being a follower (Kvanvig 2016, 18). Therefore, leaning in is not a passive activity, and ought to pass Kvanvig's object to trust based accounts of faith.

6. CONCLUSION

I have shown that the motivational directional model of faith effectively captures many fundamental features of faith. Nevertheless, providing a model is not equivalent to providing a definition. For those who think philosophy must always aim to uncover sufficient and necessary conditions, I offer this model as a starting point: a unifying picture from which we might uncover a more robust description. For those who are skeptical that such conditions can be provided, this picture allows us to think about faith more clearly and effectively—a noble aim in itself.[15]

REFERENCES

Alston, W. P. (1996). Belief, acceptance, and religious faith. In J. Jordan and D. Howard-Snyder (eds), *Faith, Freedom, and Rationality: Philosophy of Religion Today*. Lanham, MD: Rowman & Littlefield, pp. 3–27.

Aquinas, T. (2015). *Summa Theologica*. Irvine, CA: Xist Publishing.

Audi, R. (2011). Faith, faithfulness, and virtue. *Faith and Philosophy*, 28(3): 294–309.

[15] This paper was made possible through the support of a grant from Templeton Religion Trust. The opinions expressed in this publication are those of the author and do not necessarily reflect the views of Templeton Religion Trust. Thanks to Jon Kvanvig, Daniel Howard-Snyder, and Trent Dougherty for their work orchestrating The Nature and Value of Faith Project. Many thanks to Mark Lance, Kathryn Pogin, Ryan Preston-Roedder, Lindsay Rettler, Jim Taylor, Bradley Rettler, audiences at Baylor, Georgetown, the St. Louis Conference on The Nature of Faith, and the graduate students and faculty of Baylor University for many conversations that helped shape this project.

Clegg, J. S. (1979). Faith. *American Philosophical Quarterly*, 16(3): 225–32.

Cogley, Z. (2012). Trust and the trickster problem. *Analytic Philosophy*, 53(1): 30–47.

Darwin, C. (1998). *The Expression of the Emotions in Man and Animals*. New York: Oxford University Press.

Harmon-Jones, E. (2006). Unilateral right-hand contractions cause contralateral alpha power suppression and approach motivational affective experience. *Psychophysiology*, 43(6): 598–603.

Harmon-Jones, E., Gable, P. A., and Price, T. F. (2011). Leaning embodies desire: Evidence that leaning forward increases relative left frontal cortical activation to appetitive stimuli. *Biological psychology*, 87(2): 311–13.

Harmon-Jones, E., Harmon-Jones, C., and Price, T. F. (2013). What is approach motivation? *Emotion Review*, 5(3): 291–5.

Harmon-Jones, E. and Peterson, C. K. (2009). Supine body position reduces neural response to anger evocation. *Psychological Science*, 20(10): 1209–10.

Hieronymi, P. (2006). Controlling attitudes. *Pacific Philosophical Quarterly*, 87(1): 45–74.

Hieronymi, P. (2008). Responsibility for Believing. *Synthese*, 161(3): 357–73.

Howard-Snyder, D. (2013). Propositional faith: What it is and what it is not. *American Philosophical Quarterly*, 50(4): 357–72.

James, W. T. (1932). A study of the expression of bodily posture. *The Journal of General Psychology*, 7(2): 405–37.

Kierkegaard, S. (1983). *Kierkegaard's Writings*, VI: *Fear and Trembling/Repetition*, ed. and trans. with introduction and notes by H. V. Hong and E. H. Hong. Princeton, NJ: Princeton University Press.

Kvanvig, J. L. (2016). The Idea of Faith as Trust: Lessons in Noncognitivist Approaches to Faith. In M. Bergmann and J. E. Brower (eds), *Reason and Faith: Themes from Richard Swinburne*. Oxford: Oxford University Press, pp. 4–25.

Mckaughan, D. J. (2013). Authentic faith and acknowledged risk: Dissolving the problem of faith and reason. *Religious Studies*, 49(1): 101–24.

Peterson, C. K., Shackman, A. J., and Harmon-Jones, E. (2008). The role of asymmetrical frontal cortical activity in aggression. *Psychophysiology*, 45(1): 86–92.

Pojman, L. (2003). Faith, doubt and belief, or does faith entail belief? In R. M. Gale and A. R. Pruss (eds), *The Existence of God*. Aldershot: Ashgate. pp. 1–15.

Price, T. F. and Harmon-Jones, E. (2011). Approach motivational body postures lean toward left frontal brain activity. *Psychophysiology*, 48(5): 718–22.

Riskind, J. H. and Gotay, C. C. (1982). Physical posture: Could it have regulatory or feedback effects on motivation and emotion? *Motivation and Emotion*, 6(3): 273–98.

Roberts, R. C. (2003). *Emotions: An essay in aid of moral psychology*. Cambridge: Cambridge University Press.

Shepherd, V. A. (2004). *The Nature and Function of Faith in the Theology of John Calvin* (NABPR Dissertation Series No. 2). Vancouver: Regent College Publishing.

11

Foundational Grounding and the Argument from Contingency

Kenneth L. Pearce

Unlike the *Kalam* cosmological argument for the existence of God (Craig 1979), the cosmological argument from contingency is not a request for a cause of the origination of the universe. Rather, it is a request for an explanation of the total sequence of causes and effects *in* the universe. (Call this sequence 'History'.) Many philosophers have, however, been puzzled as to how there could be such an explanation and, especially, as to how God could serve as such an explanation, as the cosmological arguer desires. This puzzlement stems from the fact that proponents of the argument from contingency are often seen as introducing God in just the same way as the proponents of the *Kalam* argument do, that is, as one more 'billiard ball' prepended to the causal sequence studied by natural science. If this is the case, then no progress has been made. We have merely added one more cause to the sequence of causes that (allegedly) needed explaining.

In response to this difficulty, I defend three theses. First, I argue that, if the argument from contingency is to succeed, the explanation of History in terms of God must *not* be a causal explanation. Second, I argue that a particular hypothesis about God's relation to History—that God is what I call the *foundational ground* of History—is intelligible and explanatory. Third and finally, I argue that the explanatory advantages of this hypothesis cannot be had within the confines of naturalism.

1. GOD IS NOT THE CAUSE OF HISTORY

Leibniz presents the argument from contingency as follows:

A sufficient reason for existence cannot be found merely in any one individual thing or even in the whole aggregate and series of things. Let us imagine the book on the

Elements of Geometry to have been eternal, one copy always being made from another; then it is clear that though we can give a reason for the present book based on the preceding book from which it was copied, we can never arrive at a complete reason, no matter how many books we may assume in the past, for one can always wonder why such books should have existed at all times; why there should be books at all, and why they should be written in this way. What is true of books is true also of the different states of the world...No matter how far we may have gone back to earlier states, therefore, we will never discover in them a full reason why there should be a world at all, and why it should be such as it is.

Even if we should imagine the world to be eternal, therefore, the reason for it would clearly have to be sought elsewhere...For even though there be no cause for eternal things, there must yet be understood to be a reason for them...These considerations show clearly that we cannot escape an ultimate extramundane reason for things, or God, even by assuming the eternity of the world (Leibniz [1697] 1969, 486–7).

In another presentation of the argument, Leibniz asserts that this 'extra-mundane reason' (God) must be "a necessary being bearing the reason for its existence within itself; otherwise we would not yet have a reason with which to stop" (Leibniz [1714] 1969, sect. 8).

Leibniz is here searching for an explanation of "the whole aggregate and series of things." From the way his argument progresses, it seems that what he has in mind is a complex *event*, which we might call the Causal History of the Universe ('History' for short). This is the event composed of all the events of the form *x causes y*. Leibniz assumes that each state of the universe can be explained by specifying its physical causes, which are to be found in earlier states of the universe, but, he says, there must be a reason why this total series is as it is and not otherwise and that reason cannot possibly be found inside the series.

I here assume that the complex event History exists and is the sort of thing that stands in need of explanation.[1] Given this assumption, the argument from contingency could function as a proof of the existence of God if we could establish that History must have an explanation (presumably by establishing a sufficiently strong Principle of Sufficient Reason) and that all possible explanations of History rely on some form of theism. Here I interpret the argument more modestly as aiming merely to show that theism has an advantage over its chief rival, naturalism, with respect to explanatory comprehensiveness. By 'naturalism' I here mean the view that any metaphysics that goes beyond natural science ought to be rejected. To show that theism has an advantage over naturalism with respect to explanatory

[1] The assumption that History exists can be dispensed with if, as Dasgupta 2014a argues, the grounding relation is irreducibly plural, for then we could argue that the causal events are plurally grounded in God's creative activity.

comprehensiveness, the cosmological arguer need only show that there exists at least one theistic explanation of History while there can be no naturalistic explanation of History.[2]

Recent presentations of the argument have often held that the way to do this is to introduce God (or God's free choice) as the cause of the origination of the universe.[3] Causal versions of the argument from contingency turn on a particular view about the causal structure of reality: they say that there is a non-physical (divine) cause that precedes all physical causes, and that this generates an explanatory advantage for the theist. This argument fails, as Graham Oppy convincingly argues, because whatever causal structure for the universe is supposed by the theist can be replicated by the naturalist (Oppy 2013). The naturalistic philosopher has wide latitude here, since there are many different live models in physical cosmology which exhibit different causal structures. To prefer one live physical hypothesis over another is not to go beyond natural science in the way the naturalist finds objectionable. Thus if the free action of God is supposed to be the indeterministic action of a necessary being, the naturalist is free to propose that the universe had an initial state which was itself necessary and indeterministically caused the organized cosmos we experience. If the theist introduces an infinite causal chain (perhaps of divine thoughts), the naturalist can introduce an infinite chain of earlier states of the universe (or parent universes). Finally, if the theist proposes an initial contingent being (rejecting divine necessity), the naturalist is free to accept an initial contingent state of the universe. Whatever advantage the theistic model is supposed to have will also be had by at least some physical models and therefore (at least as long as these models continue to be live options within physics) can be had within the confines of naturalism.

Nor does it help to point out that God is supposed to be a necessary being, and no physical entity is necessary, for God's alleged necessity must be either transparent or opaque. (That is, either we can see why God is necessary or we can't.) If the argument depends on transparent necessity, then the argument from contingency can be introduced only *after* a successful

---

[2] Analogous arguments can be made using a Big Conjunctive Contingent Fact, or the set or mereological sum of all concrete contingent beings, or any number of other (alleged) entities in place of History.

[3] See, e.g., Koons 1997; 2008, sect. 2; Pruss 2004, 170–1; 2011, 220; O'Connor 2008; 2013. Admittedly, it is unclear whether these authors intend their ascriptions of causality to God literally and univocally, but if the relation is not literally and univocally causation, then an account of the nature of that relation is owed, and none of these authors has provided such an account. I will undertake this task in the next section.

ontological argument (see Kant [1781] 1998, A606/B634–A612/B640).[4] If the argument from contingency is to stand alone, then God's necessity must be *opaque*. That is, the argument should give us reason to believe *that* a necessary being (God) exists, although we do not (yet) understand *why* the existence of this being is necessary.[5] However, if this is the theist's position, then the naturalist is free to claim that some relevant part of physical reality possesses opaque necessity.[6]

If the argument from contingency is to succeed, we must take more seriously Leibniz's statement that the argument introduces an 'extramundane reason' for History. By introducing God as one more 'billiard ball' prepended to History, causal versions of the argument make God too 'mundane' to explain anything the naturalist can't. Rather than positing a particular causal structure for the universe and giving God a privileged role in that structure, the argument from contingency must instead posit God as a non-causal explanation of *why reality has the causal structure it does*. Only in this way can theism gain an explanatory advantage over naturalism.

2. GOD IS THE FOUNDATIONAL GROUND OF HISTORY

There can be no causal explanation of History, for History is the sum of all the causal events. Accordingly, an event of the form *x's causing History* would itself be part of History and so could not, on pain of circularity, explain History. Of course, the theist is at liberty to identify another complex event, call it 'History–', which includes all of History except God's causal activity (cf. Oppy 2009, 35). This, however, would be a mistake since the naturalist is equally entitled to posit a cause of History–. If the argument from contingency is to work, we must demand an explanation of History as a whole, and this means demanding a non-causal explanation. Such an explanation can be provided by positing God as the *foundational ground* of History.

In classical philosophical theology, the term for what I am calling 'foundational grounding' is 'primary causation.'[7] I have chosen instead to use the term 'foundational grounding' because I am arguing that the (so-called)

---

[4] For discussion see Forgie 1995; Vallicella 2000; Smith 2003; Proops 2014.

[5] See Adams 1983; Forgie 1995; Gale and Pruss 1999, 462, 470; O'Connor 2008, 70–1; 2013, sect. 2.

[6] According to Joseph K. Campbell, this dilemma plays a crucial role in Hume's criticism of the argument from contingency (Campbell 1996).

[7] Latin *prima causa*. See e.g. Aquinas *Summa Theologica*, Iq19a5r2 and Iq19a6r3.

primary causation relation is *not* a causal relation (except perhaps in an analogical sense).[8]

The Greek word 'αἰτία' and its Latin translation 'causa' can refer to any answer to a 'why' question (Hocutt 1974). These terms are therefore much broader than 'cause' in contemporary English. The term 'primary causation' is misleading, since we ought not to assimilate the kind of ultimate explanation provided by God to ordinary causal explanation.

In place of the misnomer 'primary causation,' I have chosen the label 'foundational grounding.' By 'grounding' I mean the relation, or genus of relations, that obtains between more fundamental and less fundamental entities and makes metaphysical explanations of the less fundamental entities (or the facts about them) in terms of the more fundamental entities possible.[9] Thus, for instance, physicalists about the mind are to be understood as claiming that the mental is grounded in the physical.

I call God's grounding of History *foundational* because the grounding relations generate a metaphysical hierarchy, with the less fundamental things 'built on' the more fundamental things, so to speak (see, e.g., Schaffer 2009a; 2012, sect. 4.3; Fine 2012, 44–5, 51). If God grounds History as a whole, God's grounding must be somehow foundational in this hierarchy.

The aim of this section is to defend my claim that the hypothesis *God is the foundational ground of History* is intelligible and is explanatory of History.

2.1. Foundational Grounding is Intelligible

In order to show that foundational grounding is intelligible, I here construct a particular model of foundational grounding. My model is meant to be consistent with classical theistic commitments. In particular, it aims to preserve traditional divine attributes as well as the following three claims: (1) contrary to pantheism, the world is numerically distinct from God; (2) contrary to panentheism, the dependence of the world on God is

---

[8] My claim that (so-called) primary causation is not a causal relation is not an interpretive claim about Aquinas or any other classical philosophical theologian (though I do think the interpretive claim is plausible). It is, rather, a claim about how classical theists ought to understand the relation they take to obtain between God and creation.

[9] I am thus using 'grounding' more broadly than some theorists (e.g., Audi 2012, 105). In my usage, the constitution relation between statue and clay, for instance, is a type of grounding and if parts are more fundamental than wholes then so is composition. Karen Bennett refers to the members of this genus as 'building relations' (Bennett 2011).

asymmetric (God does not depend on the world); and (3) contrary to necessitarianism or emanationism, God was free to create a different world or none at all. Additionally, my model does not posit any divine causality.[10] I will not be defending the superiority of my model over other (classical or non-classical) theistic models. My aim in presenting this model is only to show that there exists at least one theistic hypothesis capable of explaining History.

My model has three stages, each involving a different grounding relation: (1) God *performs* an act of will. (2) This act of will *constitutes* History. (3) History is the *narrative ground* of particular created things like you and me. All three relations admit of non-theological examples. The first is the relation of agents to their actions. The second is the relation of a statue to its material. The third is the relation whereby fictional objects depend on fictional narratives and dream objects depend on dreams. As is to be expected, there are a number of peculiarities involved in the present application of these relations.

The performance relation is a type of grounding relation. An agent may perhaps be the (an) efficient cause of her or his action, but this is not like causing a boulder to roll down a hill, where one merely sets it going. A dance, for instance, continues to exist so long as the agent continues performing it. The agent sustains the dance in being by bearing the performance relation to the dance. This performance relation is not itself causal. In the same way, God sustains God's act in being by performing it.

Constitution is also a grounding relation: the statue exists *because* the lump exists and is so arranged. According to the model, this relation likewise obtains between God's act and History.

There are two main difficulties for this claim: first, in the paradigm cases the constitution relation is a relation between *objects*, but History and God's act are both events.[11] Second, in typical cases of 'bringing about' the state of affairs brought about is something over and above the act of bringing about, but a constituted object is nothing over and above the constituting object.

In response to the first objection, it should be noted that there are cases where it is perfectly natural to say that one event constitutes another. For instance, the discovery of the Higgs boson was constituted by the recording of certain data in certain machines. Similarly, Jones's raising her hand might constitute Jones's voting (cf. Baker 2007, 111–19). The notion that

---

[10] The model is not inconsistent with divine causality; it simply does not make use of divine causality in explaining History. It will turn out that within this model God could exercise causality (in a literal and univocal sense) only by entering into History as a character in the story. On the prospects for this kind of move, see Lebens, forthcoming.

[11] I thank Sandra Visser for this objection.

God's act could constitute an event like History is not one that we should balk at.[12]

A way of putting the second objection is to observe that God's act of creation is supposed to be an exercise of omnipotent power. Now, in typical cases of the exercise of power, the agent's act of will produces effects that are something over and above that act: if Hercules is a powerful lifter of stones, then his willing to lift a stone results in something over and above the willing itself, namely, the stone's being lifted. However, when a lump constitutes a statue we say that the statue is nothing over and above the lump. A supporter of univocal divine causality might argue that if the product of God's act is never anything over and above the act itself then God is not powerful.

This, however, gets things precisely the wrong way around. The fact that the stone's being lifted is something over and above Hercules' act is what gives rise to the possibility that Hercules' will might be thwarted. This is not the case with God.[13] As Nicolas Malebranche put it: "it suffices that [God] wills in order that a thing be, because it is a contradiction that He should will and that what He wills should not happen" (Malebranche [1674–5] 1997, 450; cf. Bonhoeffer 1997, 42–3). It is the fact that the fulfillment of God's will is nothing over and above God's willing that makes God's will perfectly efficacious.

Alexander Pruss and I have argued that perfect efficacy of will is one component of omnipotence (Pearce and Pruss 2012). (The other component is perfect freedom.) We analyze perfect efficacy of will as follows (405):

> x has perfect efficacy of will if and only if $(p)\Box((x$ wills $p)$ $\Box\!\!\rightarrow$ $(x$ intentionally brings about $p))$

In this definition, '$\Box\!\!\rightarrow$' symbolizes the subjunctive conditional and it is stipulated that all of the relevant conditionals, including those that are counterpossibles, must be non-trivially true.

A constitution relation, such as the one at issue here, can give rise to non-trivial counterpossibles of the sort required by this analysis. For comparison, consider the following counterpossible conditional:

> (Michelangelo, having artistic intentions, shapes a block of marble into a round square) $\Box\!\!\rightarrow$ (that marble constitutes a round square statue)

---

[12] On constitution relations among events/activities, see van Inwagen 1990, 82–3; Pereboom 2011, 139–41.

[13] For further examination of the difference between limited creaturely powers and the Infinite Power of God, see Pearce, forthcoming a.

This conditional is true because of certain metaphysical laws which arise from the nature of the constitution relation that obtains between a statue and its material. The law is something like, *whenever a shape is imposed on some material with artistic intentions, that material thereby comes to constitute a statue.* This law supports subjunctive conditionals, including counterpossibles.[14] In the same way, the constitution relation between History and God's act of will gives rise to a metaphysical law that supports subjunctive conditionals, including counterpossibles such as:

(1) (God wills that a certain particle be both charged and neutral) □→ (God intentionally brings it about that that particle is both charged and neutral)

and

(2) (God wills that every sentient being suffers excruciating pain during every moment of its existence) □→ (God intentionally brings it about that every sentient being suffers excruciating pain during every moment of its existence)

The antecedent of (1) is impossible due to God's essential perfect rationality; the antecedent of (2) is impossible due to God's essential moral perfection (see Pearce and Pruss 2012, 411–12). Each of these counterpossibles is, however, non-trivially true because of the constitution relation that obtains between God and History.[15] The hypothesis that God's act of will constitutes History is thus a help, rather than a hindrance, to a satisfying account of God's power.[16]

The final question to be addressed is the status of created beings like you and me. History, according to this model, is the *narrative ground* of such beings. When one dreams of Paris, one's dream is *about* Paris—the actual Paris, in the world, and not a shadowy dream Paris. This may be the case even if one dreams that Paris is in England (or Narnia) and is populated only by purple mice. However, one also sometimes dreams of persons, things, or events that do not exist outside one's dream. These items are made to exist by the dreamer's activity of dreaming. The existence of such an object is *grounded* in the dream.

---

[14] This sort of 'covering law' approach to (at least some) counterpossibles is defended in Pearce 2016.

[15] If logical and mathematical truths do not depend on History, a different account will be needed to explain the non-trivial truth of counterpossibles involving God's explicitly willing logical or mathematical propositions.

[16] In Pearce 2017 I further defend the claim that regarding God's will as grounding, rather than causing, its fulfillment is necessary for a satisfying account of omnipotence.

The case is similar for fictional objects. Sherlock Holmes, for instance, exists *because* there are stories about him. His existence is *grounded* in those stories (cf. Thomasson 1999, 35–8, et passim; Kripke 2013, 72–4).

According to the model I am proposing, this relation of narrative grounding also obtains between created objects and History. This need not imply that History is literally a narrative, but it does imply that History is similar to a narrative. This does not seem especially problematic, since a narrative— i.e. that which is narrated—is a (possibly fictitious) complex event. Whether regarding History as the narrative ground of created objects requires History to have other features typically possessed by narratives (for instance, having some meaning or significance, having certain themes, having literary structure) is not a question I will attempt to answer here, though I note that the view that History does have these features will likely be attractive to many theists.[17]

The most important objection to this proposal is that it empties created objects of their reality and causal efficacy, making God the only true reality and the only true cause. In a dream the dreamer is the one who really exists and really (though usually involuntarily) makes the things in the dream happen. The objects in the dream do not really exist (they are only dream objects) and do not really cause anything (they only dream-cause dream-events).

The classical theistic tradition has held that these results are in a sense acceptable: created objects, the tradition holds, possess diminished reality as compared to God, and the 'secondary causation' exercised by created objects is a less ultimate form of 'making it the case' than God's (so-called) primary causation. In fact, the use of the dream–dreamer and author–fiction relations to explain this contrast has precedent in the Jewish tradition (see Lebens 2015; forthcoming; Citron 2015). The comparison has also been employed by Thomists such as James Ross (1969, 255–8). However, considerable care must be exercised in interpreting the diminished reality thesis if one is to maintain classical theism. To hold that nothing but God strictly speaking exists would be to collapse into pantheism, and to deny causal efficacy to creatures would surely make God the author of sin. We must therefore carve out some space for the existence and causal efficacy of creatures.[18]

In plain language, we say that *there is* a fictional detective named 'Holmes', and *there are* several species of *Star Trek* aliens, and so forth. These are

---

[17] I thank Sandra Visser for emphasizing this point.
[18] A similar collection of difficulties for the dream model is discussed by Lebens 2015, 185–94.

perfectly ordinary and perfectly literal uses of the existential 'is'.[19] At the same time, however, we say that Sherlock Holmes is not a *real* detective, but rather a fictional character, and that we do not know whether there is *really* life on other planets. A satisfactory metaphysical picture should not only preserve the truth of these claims, but give some metaphysical weight to them. The objection that my model has the consequence that ordinary created objects are not real is best understood as claiming that the model undermines the metaphysical significance of the plain language distinction between real objects, on the one hand, and dream objects and fictional objects on the other.

This distinction is indeed elided when one attempts to accommodate the existence of fictional objects within the framework of a Quinean meta-ontology (as in van Inwagen 1977), for on such a view 'really' can only mean something like 'literally' or 'strictly speaking'. Accordingly, on this kind of view, fictional objects really exist, since quantification over fictional objects is ineliminable.[20] One could escape this objection by adopting an ontology with two modes of existence, real and unreal, where unreal existence would be accorded not only to fictional objects, but also to dream objects, imaginary objects, posits of false scientific theories, and so forth. My model, however, suggests that we are related to God in something like the way fictional objects are related to us. It might be thought that we therefore fall on the unreal side of the distinction.

In fact, the grounding approach to ontology which is here presupposed provides a neat solution to these problems. The metaphysical significance of 'real' stems from its association with 'fundamental': the real objects are the fundamental objects. But fundamentality comes in degrees, with grounded entities being less fundamental than the entities that ground them. Accordingly, since dreams are grounded in dreamers, the dreamers are more fundamental than the dreams. It is in this sense that dreamers and the objects in their waking environs are real but dream objects are not. My model does not undermine the dependence of dreams on dreamers; it merely posits that the dreamers, in turn, depend on God. Accordingly, the ordinary distinction between real objects and dream objects is in no way

---

[19] This claim is, admittedly, somewhat controversial, and there is not space to defend it here. For such defenses, see van Inwagen 1977; Thomasson 1999; Schnieder and Solodkoff 2009; Kripke 2013, 69–83. For an opposing view, see Everett 2005; 2007. For an overview of the debate about sentences that apparently quantify over fictional objects, see Friend 2007.

[20] This is closely connected to the objection of Everett 2007 that such views cannot accommodate the truth of sentences such as 'Sherlock Holmes does not (really) exist,' which plain language takes to be true in many contexts.

undermined, for the real objects are more fundamental than the dream objects, and this is what we mean in calling them 'real'.[21]

So much for the existence of created objects. What of their causal efficacy? According to the model, the causal relations within History are the *only* genuine causal relations; there is not some more basic level of causation underlying History. There are, of course, dream causes and fictional causes and so forth, but the causal relations that make up History are the most real (i.e. most fundamental) causal relations there are. Foundational grounding is not (literally, univocally) causal, and so does not pre-empt creaturely causation.

Nevertheless, one might worry that, on this view, causation is not a genuine 'making it the case' relation: God's ultimate 'making it the case' pre-empts any creaturely activity. There are really three distinct objections in the neighborhood here. First, one might worry that the model leads to divine omnidetermination, and this kind of omnidetermination is inconsistent with genuine activity on the part of creatures, and especially human freedom. Second, one might worry that, on this view, creatures do not genuinely depend on their causes, since it was not the created cause but rather the will of God that made the creatures exist. Third, one might worry that on this view created causes can no longer serve as explanations, their explanatory force having been pre-empted by God.

To the first objection I respond that I have no particular commitment to avoiding omnidetermination since I find it far from obvious that omnidetermination is inconsistent with human freedom. Nevertheless, for those philosophers who do find omnidetermination problematic, there is a way of endorsing my model while avoiding omnidetermination. The objection assumes that, when two objects are related by constitution, the features of the constituted object are fully determined by the features of the constituting object. However, this assumption would be denied by various sorts of anti-reductionists. For instance one might suppose that a human organism constitutes a human person while holding that the human person has and exercises causal powers in a way that is not determined by the human

---

[21] In my view, fundamentality is actually only one of several criteria included in the plain language notion of reality, but it is the criterion that is relevant to the present objection. The relative weight of the several criteria and the location of the 'cut-off' employed in drawing the binary real/unreal distinction vary contextually. For further development and defense of this approach to reality, see Pearce, forthcoming b, sect. 1.3.

The model does, of course, make created objects less fundamental than God and there is therefore a sense in which the model holds that, from God's perspective, created objects are not real (cf. Lebens, forthcoming). However, it is more accurate to say that ordinary created objects are more real than dream objects but less real than God. Reality and fundamentality come in degrees.

organism.[22] This approach to constitution would open up the possibility
that History might be constituted by God's act of will without being determined by God in every respect. If more than one possible history could
have been constituted by the very same divine creative act (or if History
could have differed in certain ways without any difference in God's creative
act), then standard theistic options for avoiding omnidetermination (simple
foreknowledge, open theism, Molinism) are available.[23]

In response to the second objection, which claims that the model prevents created objects from depending on their created causes, note that, on
my model, objects exhibit robust counterfactual dependence on their
causes. Were it not for the causal chain leading up to the encounter of a
certain sperm with a certain egg, I would not exist. Why not? Because my
very being depends on (more specifically: is narratively grounded in) that
causal sequence. It is, of course, a disputed matter exactly how much of an
object's causal history is essential to it, but if created objects are narratively
grounded in History—which, recall, is the complete *causal* story of the
world—then clearly they *do* depend counterfactually, and indeed ontologically, on their causes.

In response to the third objection, that created causes do not, on this
model, explain their effects, note that even in dreams and fictions there are
causes, and these causes do explain their effects. Thus it is *because* Tybalt is
stabbed by Romeo that Tybalt dies. Of course, it is also *because* Shakespeare
wrote the play that way that Tybalt dies. The second explanation is more
fundamental than the first, but it does not pre-empt the explanation in
terms of fictional causes. Similarly, the constitution of History by God's act
of will provides a more fundamental explanation than the causal explanation of a particular event, but it does not pre-empt the causal explanation.

2.2. Foundational Grounding is Explanatory

Having completed the exposition of my model of foundational grounding
and defended its intelligibility, I now proceed to argue that the model is
explanatory of History. I assume that there is such a thing as objective
explanation and that it is a relation that obtains between true propositions

---

[22] For anti-reductionist views similar (but not identical) to the one contemplated here,
see Baker 2000; 2007, chs 3–5; Merricks 2003.

[23] An anonymous referee worries that if this route is taken then God will no longer
provide a complete explanation of History. However, many libertarians hold that an
agent's action may have a complete explanation even though the agent could have done
otherwise. See Pruss 2006, ch. 7.

or obtaining states of affairs (see Pruss 2006). Explanatoriness is a relation that obtains between a hypothesis and some data just in case *if the hypothesis were true it would explain the data*. Accordingly, my aim in this subsection is to argue that if the hypothesis *God is the foundational ground of History* were true it would explain the fact that History exists and is as it is.

I presuppose that grounding is intelligible. While some philosophers dispute this (e.g., Hofweber 2009, sect. 2; Daly 2012), it is now widely held. Most defenses of the intelligibility of grounding proceed by pointing to our ordinary explanatory practices and, in particular, to plain language uses of 'because'. Thus Fabrice Correia gives the following examples of explanatory claims (Correia 2008, 1022):[24]

- The ham sandwich exists because the slice of ham is between the two pieces of bread;
- Sam is experiencing pain because his brain is in a physical state which is [here an appropriate description];[25]
- The event that was Sam's walking yesterday exists because Sam was walking yesterday;
- The redness of this apple exists because the apple is red;
- The set {Socrates} exists because Socrates does.

In the same way, on the model I have proposed, History exists and is as it is because God's act of will exists and is as it is, and God's act of will exists because God performs it.

Objections to the explanatoriness of my hypothesis, unless they are objections to the very notion of grounding, should therefore not be objections to its basic structure: if the notion of grounding has a place in philosophy at all, then grounding relations are explanatory. There are, however, three more serious objections. First, it may be thought that the model is too vague and schematic to be an explanation. Second, it may be thought that the explanation is objectionably ad hoc. Third, it may be thought that this model does not give us the "reason with which to stop" that Leibniz sought, and therefore does not make explanatory progress.

To the first objection I reply that in general vague and schematic explanations are explanations. It is true that we ought (*ceteris paribus*) to prefer explanations that are more precise and detailed. This, however, is not because vague explanations are not explanatory. It is because precision and detail are good-making features of explanations. So, for instance, the question

---

[24] Correia's term is 'ontological dependence,' but all of these examples can plausibly be regarded as instances of what I call 'grounding'.

[25] Brackets original.

'why did Smith die?' can be answered, 'he died because of illness' or 'he died because he was murdered (by someone somehow for some reason)'. Both of these answers are vague and schematic. If we are engaged in an inference to the best explanation, then a more specific and detailed explanation is *ceteris paribus* preferable. Furthermore, it is difficult to determine which of two vague and schematic explanations is best without having recourse to more specific variants of them. So, for instance, if the hypothesis that Smith died due to illness is superior to the hypothesis that he was murdered, this will typically be because some specific illness hypothesis does a better job of explaining the data than any murder hypothesis does. This is not a difficulty about whether the hypotheses are explanatory; it is a difficulty about whether the hypothesis is the *best* explanation. However, even opponents of the Principle of Sufficient Reason generally admit that any 'non-disastrous' explanation is better than none (see Kleinschmidt 2013, 77). Thus, although a detailed and specific hypothesis is better than a vague and schematic one, and although it is difficult to compare vague and schematic hypotheses, it is nevertheless true that the vague and schematic hypothesis that God is the foundational ground of History may be accepted as the best explanation of History if no other explanation is available, or if it is all-things-considered superior to competing hypotheses (cf. O'Connor 2013, sect. 4).

My reply to the second objection is the same as my reply to the first: ad hoc hypotheses are explanatory, but an ad hoc explanation is rarely the best explanation. Consider the ad hoc hypothesis that traffic lights change as they do because tiny gnomes run around in the mechanism flipping switches. If there really were such gnomes, then this would be a correct explanation. The problem with the gnome hypothesis is not that it is un-explanatory, but simply that there are other explanations available that explain just as much of the data and better accord with our overall picture of the world.

Whether (and to what degree) my model (or classical theism in general) should be regarded as ad hoc will therefore depend on how independently plausible one finds classical theism (and the other elements of the model), whether it turns out to be able to do other explanatory work elsewhere, whether there are other independent lines of evidence in its favor, and so forth. These issues cannot be addressed here, but they are relevant only to comparing competing explanations. Since (as I will soon argue) naturalism leaves the explanandum completely unexplained, these factors are not relevant to the present project.

Perhaps some will think that my model is ad hoc in a more specific way that prevents it from making explanatory progress. According to this third objection, because the posits of my model themselves stand in need of explanation, the inference to the best explanation is here unjustified.

This is a sensible thing to say about the gnome traffic light hypothesis: that there should be such gnomes is far more puzzling than that traffic lights should change. Hence if explanation is meant to involve the removal of puzzlement or mystery (Pruss 2006, 18, *et passim*), it would seem that the gnome hypothesis must be regarded as a failed explanation unless and until the gnomes are explained. Some might regard the existence of God as similarly puzzling or mysterious, so that overall puzzlement is not reduced by my model.

In response, consider three structures explanation might have. First, there may be an infinite chain of explanations, which never terminates at all. Second, the chain of explanations may terminate in brute facts. Brute facts are facts that stand in need of explanation, but nevertheless do not have explanations. Third, the chain of explanations may terminate in what Shamik Dasgupta calls 'autonomous facts'—facts for which it makes no sense to ask why (Dasgupta 2014b, 575–80; 2016, 383–7).

Consider the first case first. My model is consistent with the existence of an infinite chain of causal explanations, but claims that this infinite chain nevertheless *itself* has an explanation. The objection claims that the entity involved in that explanation (God) stands in need of further explanation. But if we are comfortable with infinite chains of explanation, this ought not to bother us. Instead, it ought to send us searching for the next link in the chain.

Now consider the second case. Intuitively, some brute facts are worse than others. Many physicalists think that taking as brute the initial configuration of the physical universe, together with the laws of nature, is more satisfying than taking as brute the existence of God and God's creative act (e.g., Oppy 2013, 55–6). Other philosophers regard the existence of God as a better candidate for a brute fact (e.g., Swinburne 1979, ch. 5; 1996, ch. 3). Although considerations of simplicity, systematicity, and so forth can be (and have been) brought to bear here, it seems likely that this debate will ultimately come to an unresolvable clash of intuitions.

The third scenario would clearly be the most intellectually satisfying, if it could be made to work without unacceptable consequences. I will focus on this case, since it has been widely held within the tradition that classical theism does allow for the truth of the Principle of Sufficient Reason—understood here as the claim that everything that stands in need of explanation is in fact explained—without unacceptable consequences. I will argue that this traditional view is correct.

What sorts of facts might be autonomous? The most obvious candidates are the various sorts of definitions. Thus although the fact that the English word 'bachelor' means an unmarried male admits of a historical/etymological explanation, the fact that bachelors are unmarried males needs no explanation. If there are such things as Aristotelian 'real definitions'— definitions not of words but of things—then these are likewise good candidates for autonomous facts. Real definitions would be statements of essences, and they would not require further explanation (cf. Dasgupta 2014b, 577–80; 2016, 385–90).

On the model under discussion, the answer to the question, 'why is History occurring the way it is?' is 'because God so willed.' Although this may sound like a causal explanation, it is not, since God's act of willing does not cause, but rather constitutes, History. The next question we can ask is, 'why did God so will?' Here, of course, we fall upon the thorny problem of the explanation of free actions, but we may assume that God's free act of willing is explained in whatever way free acts are generally explained.[26] We may then go on to ask, why is it that God existed and was free so to will? Merely asserting that this is true necessarily does not give us a 'reason with which to stop', for necessary truths can and often do have explanations. A more subtle strategy is needed.

According to Thomas Aquinas, "the proposition, 'God exists,' of itself is self-evident... [but] because we do not know the essence of God, the proposition is not self-evident to us" (Aquinas *Summa Theologica*, Iq2a1). The idea here is that the real definition of God is unknown to us, but a being who knew it would be in a position to demonstrate God's existence a priori (see Forgie 1995). If this were true of God, then the fact that God exists and is free would either itself be autonomous (as part of the real definition of God), or would be explained by the autonomous fact that God's essence is as it is.

If this strategy is correct, then there is a sound modal ontological argument. To construct this argument, we stipulate that the word 'God' shall stand for the (unknown) real definition of God. We then assert that God's existence is possible, and that God exists necessarily if at all. God is therefore necessary, and therefore actual. On the view described, the premises of this argument would follow directly from the divine essence, and the fact that the divine essence is as it is would be autonomous.

This strategy does not, however, make the argument from contingency depend on the ontological argument. On the contrary, the ontological

---

[26] In my view, any version of libertarianism that holds that free actions cannot be explained succumbs to the randomness objection (the event is not an action of yours unless you appear in the right sort of way in an explanation of its occurrence), but there is not space here to defend that claim. For a discussion of various ways in which libertarians might allow that free actions *can* be explained, see Pruss 2006, ch. 7.

argument depends on the argument from contingency: *after* we have posited God in order to explain History, we see that our explanation can bottom out in autonomous facts, and therefore give us a maximally satisfying explanatory structure, only if the real definition of God has certain features. This gives us reason to hypothesize that the real definition of God *does* have these features—that is, that there is a sound ontological argument. Because we do not have independent grounds for believing the premises of this ontological argument, we cannot use it to *establish* the existence of God. This does not, however, prevent us from using it to *explain* God's existence and, indeed, God's necessary existence.

Having explained why God exists and is free, we can go on to explain God's free act in (something like) the usual way in which free acts are explained (whatever that is). This act in turn explains History—not by causing it, but by constituting it. In this way, explanation bottoms out in the definition of God.

This additional stage of explanation—the explanation of why God exists and is free—is vague and schematic like the earlier stage, insofar as we don't actually know the real definition of God which is employed in our modal ontological argument. Nevertheless, the schema is a satisfying one which, unlike naturalism, posits no brute facts.

3. NATURALISM LEAVES HISTORY UNEXPLAINED

Naturalism, as I use the term here, is the view that any metaphysics that goes beyond natural science ought to be rejected. In this section, I argue that History cannot be explained within the boundaries of this view.

Although most naturalist philosophers simply accept that their view requires them to posit brute facts, and would no doubt include the occurrence of History among these facts (see, e.g., Grünbaum 2004; Fahrbach 2005), some have attempted to accommodate ultimate explanation within naturalistic boundaries. The reason these attempts fail is simple. As long as we stay within the bounds of (current) natural science, the only available variety of non-necessitating explanation is indeterministic causation. However, on pain of circularity, no causal explanation of History can be given. Therefore, naturalistic explanations of History will be necessitating explanations. But to give a necessitating explanation of History is to restrict the scope of possibility in a way that is at odds with current science and hence cannot be accepted by the naturalist.

To see how this problem arises, we will consider two recent attempts at ultimate naturalistic explanation. The first, due to Shamik Dasgupta, argues that essentialist explanation is a scientifically accredited variety of explanation, and that there is some entity (or there are some entities) known to science whose existence can be given essentialist (rather than causal) explanations. The second, due to Marc Lange, argues that the laws of nature non-causally explain certain facts, and that among these may be some existence facts.[27]

Dasgupta defends a Principle of Sufficient Reason according to which every fact that stands in need of an explanation has one. He concedes (at least for the sake of argument) that existence facts, if they are to be explained at all, must be explained in terms of other existence facts. These two claims, together with the rejection of explanatory circles and regresses, entail that not all existence facts stand in need of explanation (Dasgupta 2016, 397). Given Dasgupta's view, discussed above, that the autonomous facts are essentialist facts (real definitions), this implies the existence of one or more beings whose essence includes existence, as was traditionally said of God.

Despite this consequence, Dasgupta denies that his theory is anti-naturalistic.[28] He suggests that our best scientific theories might in fact be committed to entities whose essence includes existence. If there is just one such entity, then Dasgupta's model will look quite similar to mine, simply substituting some entity known to science into the place of God. If, however, there is a plurality of such entities, then the structure will be somewhat different.

Dasgupta suggests spacetime as a candidate for a unique essentially existing entity. On this view,

at rock bottom there is some kind of physical "space" (in the broad sense of the term) in whose nature it is to exist and instantiate some kind of structure...The view will then be that all other (substantive) facts—about my armchair, my mental states, my duties and obligations—are grounded in the existence and structure of that underlying physical space (398).

Let us grant the plausible, but not uncontroversial, assumption that space-time in modern physics should be given a substantivalist interpretation, so that spacetime is a naturalistically respectable entity.[29] Granting this assumption, the first problem with Dasgupta's approach is that, according to

---

[27] If, as some philosophers suppose (e.g., Bird 2005; Yates 2013), laws of nature are grounded in essences, these proposals may be equivalent.

[28] Dasgupta considers the claim that his theory has anti-naturalistic consequences as an objection that may be raised against his theory but does not explicitly endorse naturalism himself.

[29] For a carefully nuanced discussion of the extent to which modern physics supports substantivalism, see Maudlin 1993. Dasgupta 2011 attacks standard substantivalist interpretations of General Relativity and proposes a non-standard version of substantivalism.

straightforward interpretations of General Relativity, the geometric structure of our spacetime is physically contingent. There are many global solutions to Einstein's Field Equations, and it is part of the practice of physics to distinguish among those solutions that are and are not 'physical' (or, as philosophers would say, physically possible).[30] Many different solutions are regarded as 'physical,' and these correspond to different possibilities for the global structure of spacetime. However, if it is in the essence of spacetime to exist and have the structure it does, then no alternative structures are possible. Consistency with actual physics requires either that our spacetime exist only contingently (so that a different spacetime with an alternative structure might have existed) or that our spacetime has its geometric structure only contingently.

Let us suppose, then, that spacetime exists essentially, but has its geometric structure accidentally (and so, in some sense, contingently).[31] If this is to explain History, presumably it will do so by grounding the existence of the entities (or states) within History, including the causal powers of these entities, which will then give rise to the sequence of causes and effects.[32]

Although this approach may, in a certain sense, provide an explanation of History, by holding that History is constituted by certain features of spacetime, it cannot provide the kind of explanation Leibniz demanded, an explanation of "why the thing is as it is and not otherwise" (Leibniz [1714] 1969, sect. 7). This is because, as has been observed, the global structure of spacetime is physically—and hence metaphysically—contingent. Thus the global structure of spacetime cannot follow from the essence of spacetime. Yet this global structure will, on this view, be (directly or indirectly) responsible for History having the structure it does. Furthermore, on this sort of view, the global structure of spacetime cannot, on pain of circularity, be directly or indirectly explained in terms of any of the events in History— which is to say, it cannot be explained causally. This is again inconsistent with straightforward interpretations of General Relativity, since that theory is usually understood to say that the shape of spacetime can be explained (perhaps causally) in terms of the distribution of mass-energy.[33]

I argued above that an explanation should not be regarded as a failure simply because the explanans requires further explanation. In this case,

---

[30] For accounts of some historical disputes about which solutions are physical, see Earman 1995, ch. 1; Singh 2004, 151–5.

[31] Dasgupta allows for contingency only in a relatively weak sense, but admits that the essentialist facts are not contingent in any sense.

[32] A theory of this sort is developed in detail by Schaffer 2009b.

[33] "Matter and energy, like the sun, *cause* space (and spacetime) to warp and curve" (Greene 2005, 69, emphasis added).

however, naturalism renders the explanans (the global structure of space-time) in principle inexplicable, since the proposal under consideration rules out both essentialist explanations and causal explanations, and no other scientifically accredited sorts of explanation have been identified. Accordingly, even if this is to be regarded as a successful explanation of History, we could just run the argument from contingency again by demanding an explanation of the global structure of spacetime. This contrasts with the theistic model I have proposed, where contingency is introduced in a non-causal, but intelligible, way by God's choice.

On Marc Lange's alternative proposal, the laws of nature provide non-causal explanations of certain facts. The laws, Lange says, may entail certain propositions without saying that anything causes them. Lange makes no concrete proposals about what such a proposition might be in modern physics, but he suggests that Newton may have been correct in holding that his physics entailed the existence of space and time (Lange 2013, 244).

The idea of interest for our purposes is that the laws of physics may somehow entail, and thereby explain, the global structure of History. This proposal, however, runs into the same difficulty as Dasgupta's: the global causal structure is not physically necessary. Both proposals turn out to be revisionary with respect to physics.

The general problem is this: current physics knows only one way of selecting between multiple, genuinely possible outcomes, and this is by indeterministic *causation*. But History cannot be explained causally. Other naturalistically respectable patterns of explanation render the explanandum (at least) physically necessary. But the global structure of History is *not* physically necessary.[34] Accordingly, no naturalistic explanation of History is possible.

4. CONCLUSION

The cosmological argument from contingency can be understood as a demand for an explanation of History, the total sequence of causes and effects in the universe. Such an event, however, cannot, on pain of circularity, have a causal explanation. A non-causal explanation of History is possible given classical theism but impossible given naturalism. Accordingly, the argument from contingency succeeds in providing excellent reason for

---

[34] In sect. 1, I said that the naturalist was free to accept a necessary initial state of the universe. This open possibility is significantly weaker than the claim here rejected, that the global structure of History and/or spacetime might be necessary.

favoring theism over naturalism. Of course, this reason will be *decisive* only if a sufficiently strong Principle of Sufficient Reason is endorsed and I have given no argument in favor of such a principle. If the Principle of Sufficient Reason is rejected, a more holistic comparison of theories will be necessary. Additionally, naturalism and classical theism are not the only perspectives to be considered and there are many possible classical theistic models besides the one here proposed. Thus considerable work remains to be done if it is to be shown that my classical theistic model is in fact the *best* explanation of History. Nevertheless, the fact that such a model exists shows that theism has a substantial explanatory advantage over naturalism, and this result is quite significant enough.[35]

REFERENCES

Adams, Robert Merrihew. 1983. "Divine Necessity." *Journal of Philosophy* 80 (11): 741–52.

Aquinas, St. Thomas. 1920. *The Summa Theologica of St. Thomas Aquinas*, 2nd edn, trans. Fathers of the English Dominican Province. London: Burns Oates & Washbourne.

Audi, Paul. 2012. "A Clarification and Defense of the Notion of Grounding." In Fabrice Correia and Benjamin Schnieder, eds, *Metaphysical Grounding: Understanding the Structure of Reality*. Cambridge: Cambridge University Press, 101–21.

Baker, Lynne Rudder. 2000. *Persons and Bodies: A Constitution View*. Cambridge Studies in Philosophy. Cambridge: Cambridge University Press.

Baker, Lynne Rudder. 2007. *The Metaphysics of Everyday Life*. Cambridge: Cambridge University Press.

Bennett, Karen. 2011. "Construction Area (No Hard Hat Required)." *Philosophical Studies* 154 (1): 79–104.

Bird, Alexander. 2005. "Laws and Essences." *Ratio* 18 (4): 437–61.

Bonhoeffer, Dietrich. 1997. *Creation and Fall*. Edited by John W. de Gruchy. Translated by Douglas Stephen Bax. Dietrich Bonhoeffer Works, vol. 3. Minneapolis, MN: Fortress Press.

Campbell, Joseph K. 1996. "Hume's Refutation of the Cosmological Argument." *International Journal for Philosophy of Religion* 40 (3): 159–73.

[35] This paper benefited from the comments of two anonymous referees and from discussions with Sandra Visser, Kenneth Silver, Joshua Rasmussen, Alexander Pruss, Samuel Lebens, and the participants at the 2015 St. Thomas Summer Seminar in Philosophy of Religion and Philosophical Theology, especially Bob Hartman, Blake McAllister, Michael Rota, and Dean Zimmerman.

Citron, Gabriel. 2015. "Dreams, Nightmares, and a Defense Against Arguments From Evil." *Faith and Philosophy* 32 (3): 247–70.

Correia, Fabrice. 2008. "Ontological Dependence." *Philosophy Compass* 3 (5): 1013–32.

Craig, William Lane. 1979. *The Kalam Cosmological Argument*. New York: Barnes & Noble Books.

Daly, Chris. 2012. "Scepticism about Grounding." In Fabrice Correia and Benjamin Schnieder, eds, *Metaphysical Grounding: Understanding the Structure of Reality*. Cambridge: Cambridge University Press, 81–100.

Dasgupta, Shamik. 2011. "The Bare Necessities." *Philosophical Perspectives* 25 (1): 115–60.

Dasgupta, Shamik. 2014a. "On the Plurality of Grounds." *Philosophers' Imprint* 14 (20): 1–28.

Dasgupta, Shamik. 2014b. "The Possibility of Physicalism." *Journal of Philosophy* 111 (9/10): 557–92.

Dasgupta, Shamik. 2016. "Metaphysical Rationalism." *Noûs* 50 (2): 379–418.

Earman, John. 1995. *Bangs, Crunches, Whimpers, and Shrieks: Singularities and Acausalities in Relativistic Spacetimes*. New York: Oxford University Press.

Everett, Anthony. 2005. "Against Fictional Realism." *Journal of Philosophy* 102 (12): 624–49.

Everett, Anthony. 2007. "Pretense, Existence, and Fictional Objects." *Philosophy and Phenomenological Research* 74 (1): 56–80.

Fahrbach, Ludwig. 2005. "Understanding Brute Facts." *Synthese* 145 (3): 449–66.

Fine, Kit. 2012. "Guide to Ground." In Fabrice Correia and Benjamin Schnieder, eds, *Metaphysical Grounding: Understanding the Structure of Reality*. Cambridge: Cambridge University Press, 37–80.

Forgie, J. William. 1995. "The Cosmological and Ontological Arguments: How Saint Thomas Solved the Kantian Problem." *Religious Studies* 31 (1): 89–100.

Friend, Stacie. 2007. "Fictional Characters." *Philosophy Compass* 2 (2): 141–56.

Gale, Richard M., and Alexander R. Pruss. 1999. "A New Cosmological Argument." *Religious Studies* 35 (4): 461–76.

Greene, Brian. 2005. *The Fabric of the Cosmos: Space, Time, and the Texture of Reality*. New York: Vintage Books.

Grünbaum, Adolf. 2004. "The Poverty of Theistic Cosmology." *British Journal for the Philosophy of Science* 55 (4): 561–614.

Hocutt, Max. 1974. "Aristotle's Four Becauses." *Philosophy* 49: 385–99.

Hofweber, Thomas. 2009. "Ambitious, Yet Modest, Metaphysics." In David J. Chalmers, David Manley, and Ryan Wasserman, eds, *Metametaphysics: New Essays on the Foundations of Ontology*. Oxford: Clarendon Press, 260–89.

Kant, Immanuel. [1781] 1998. *Critique of Pure Reason*, ed. and trans. Paul Guyer and Allen W. Wood. The Cambridge Edition of the Works of Immanuel Kant. Cambridge: Cambridge University Press.

Kleinschmidt, Shieva. 2013. "Reasoning Without the Principle of Sufficient Reason." In Tyron Goldschmidt, ed., *The Puzzle of Existence: Why Is there Something Rather Than Nothing?* New York: Routledge, 64–79.

Koons, Robert C. 1997. "A New Look at the Cosmological Argument." *American Philosophical Quarterly* 34 (2): 193–211.

Koons, Robert C. 2008. "Epistemological Foundations for the Cosmological Argument." *Oxford Studies in Philosophy of Religion* 1:105–33.

Kripke, Saul A. 2013. *Reference and Existence: The John Locke Lectures.* New York: Oxford University Press.

Lange, Marc. 2013. "Are Some Things Naturally Necessary?" In Tyron Goldschmidt, ed., *The Puzzle of Existence: Why Is there Something Rather Than Nothing?* New York: Routledge, 235–51.

Lebens, Samuel. 2015. "God and His Imaginary Friends: A Hassidic Metaphysics." *Religious Studies* 51 (2): 183–204.

Lebens, Samuel. Forthcoming. "Hassidic Idealism: Kurt Vonnegut and the Creator of the Universe." In Tyron Goldschmidt and Kenneth L. Pearce, eds, *Idealism: New Essays in Metaphysics.* Oxford: Oxford University Press.

Leibniz, Gottfried Wilhelm. [1697] 1969. "On the Radical Origination of Things." In *Philosophical Papers and Letters*, 2nd edn, ed. and trans. Leroy E. Loemker. Dordrecht: Kluwer Academic Publishers, 486–91.

Leibniz, Gottfried Wilhelm. [1714] 1969. "The Principles of Nature and Grace, Based on Reason." In *Philosophical Papers and Letters*, 2nd edn, ed. and trans. Leroy E. Loemker. Dordrecht: Kluwer Academic Publishers, 636–42.

Malebranche, Nicolas. [1674–5] 1997. *The Search after Truth*, ed. and trans. Thomas M. Lennon and Paul J. Olscamp. Cambridge Texts in the History of Philosophy. Cambridge: Cambridge University Press.

Maudlin, Tim. 1993. "Buckets of Water and Waves of Space: Why Spacetime is Probably a Substance." *Philosophy of Science* 60 (2): 183–203.

Merricks, Trenton. 2003. *Objects and Persons.* Oxford: Clarendon Press.

O'Connor, Timothy. 2008. *Theism and Ultimate Explanation: The Necessary Shape of Contingency.* Malden, MA: Blackwell.

O'Connor, Timothy. 2013. "Could There Be a Complete Explanation of Everything?" In Tyron Goldschmidt, ed., *The Puzzle of Existence: Why Is there Something Rather Than Nothing?* New York: Routledge, 22–45.

Oppy, Graham. 2009. "Cosmological Arguments." *Noûs* 43 (1): 31–48.

Oppy, Graham. 2013. "Ultimate Naturalistic Causal Explanations." In Tyron Goldschmidt, ed., *The Puzzle of Existence: Why Is there Something Rather Than Nothing?* New York: Routledge, 46–63.

Pearce, Kenneth L. 2016. "Counteressential Conditionals." *Thought: A Journal of Philosophy* 5 (1): 73–81.

Pearce, Kenneth L. 2017. "Counterpossible Dependence and the Efficacy of the Divine Will." *Faith and Philosophy* 34 (1): 3–16.

Pearce, Kenneth L. Forthcoming a. "Infinite Power and Finite Powers." In Benedikt Paul Göcke and Christian Tapp, eds, *The Infinity of God: Scientific, Theological, and Philosophical Perspectives*. Notre Dame, IN: Notre Dame University Press.

Pearce, Kenneth L. Forthcoming b. "Mereological Idealism." In Tyron Goldschmidt and Kenneth L. Pearce, eds, *Idealism: New Essays in Metaphysics*. Oxford: Oxford University Press.

Pearce, Kenneth L., and Alexander R. Pruss. 2012. "Understanding Omnipotence." *Religious Studies* 48 (3): 403–14.

Pereboom, Derk. 2011. *Consciousness and the Prospects for Physicalism*. New York: Oxford University Press.

Proops, Ian. 2014. "Kant on the Cosmological Argument." *Philosophers' Imprint* 14 (12): 1–21.

Pruss, Alexander R. 2004. "A Restricted Principle of Sufficient Reason and the Cosmological Argument." *Religious Studies* 40 (2): 165–79.

Pruss, Alexander R. 2006. *The Principle of Sufficient Reason: A Reassessment*. Cambridge Studies in Philosophy. Cambridge: Cambridge University Press.

Pruss, Alexander R. 2011. *Actuality, Possibility, and Worlds*. Continuum Studies in Philosophy of Religion. New York: Continuum.

Ross, James F. 1969. *Philosophical Theology*. Indianapolis, IN: Bobbs-Merrill.

Schaffer, Jonathan. 2009a. "On What Grounds What." In David J. Chalmers, David Manley, and Ryan Wasserman, eds, *Metametaphysics: New Essays on the Foundations of Ontology*. Oxford: Clarendon Press, 347–83.

Schaffer, Jonathan. 2009b. "Spacetime the One Substance." *Philosophical Studies* 145 (1): 131–48.

Schaffer, Jonathan. 2012. "Grounding, Transitivity, and Contrastivity." In Fabrice Correia and Benjamin Schnieder, eds, *Metaphysical Grounding: Understanding the Structure of Reality*. Cambridge: Cambridge University Press, 122–38.

Schnieder, Benjamin, and Tatjana von Solodkoff. 2009. "In Defence of Fictional Realism." *Philosophical Quarterly* 59 (234): 138–49.

Singh, Simon. 2004. *Big Bang: The Origin of the Universe*. London: Fourth Estate.

Smith, Donald P. 2003. "Kant on the Dependency of the Cosmological Argument on the Ontological Argument." *European Journal of Philosophy* 11 (2): 206–18.

Swinburne, Richard. 1979. *The Existence of God*. Oxford: Clarendon Press.

Swinburne, Richard. 1996. *Is There a God?* New York: Oxford University Press.

Thomasson, Amie L. 1999. *Fiction and Metaphysics*. Cambridge Studies in Philosophy. Cambridge: Cambridge University Press.

Vallicella, William F. 2000. "Does the Cosmological Argument Depend on the Ontological?" *Faith and Philosophy* 17 (4): 441–58.

van Inwagen, Peter. 1977. "Creatures of Fiction." *American Philosophical Quarterly* 14 (4): 299–308.

van Inwagen, Peter. 1990. *Material Beings*. Ithaca, NY: Cornell University Press.

Yates, David. 2013. "The Essence of Dispositional Essentialism." *Philosophy and Phenomenological Research* 87 (1): 93–128.

12

Religious Assertion

Michael Scott

According to a widely adopted interpretation of talk of God the affirmation of an indicative sentence about God, such as

1. God created the universe,

is an assertion with the propositional content *that God created the universe* that conventionally expresses the speaker's belief in that content. This account has the advantage of treating such utterances at *face value*, in the same way as non-religious assertions, and appears to offer a promising basis for the interpretation of other religious utterances.[1] However, there is a long-standing position in the philosophy of religion and in theology that regards this face value theory as seriously mistaken or incomplete. Opponents to face-value interpretations have often proposed radical alternatives: that indicative religious utterances are not assertions but express a different speech act, or that religious utterances do not communicate religious beliefs. Examples of the radical theory include interpretations of seemingly literal assertoric utterances like (1) as metaphors (Kenny 2004, McFague 1983), principles of conduct (Hare 1992, Arnold 1873), the expression of plans or intentions (Braithwaite 1955), or practical recommendations (Santayana 1905).[2] Wittgenstein proposes that religious utterances express 'a passionate commitment to a system or reference' (1994: 64) and says of belief in predestination that 'it is less a theory than a sigh or a cry' (1994: 30). This departure from the face-value interpretation is usually motivated by characteristics of religious discourse that purportedly distinguish it from

---

[1] I take an utterance to be the production of a sentence in speech or writing or by some other means of communication. By 'religious utterance' I mean an utterance that represents a religious entity (such as God) or property (such as holiness); I will be concerned with (indicative) utterances about God but the interpretation can be extended to a much wider range of religious utterances.

[2] See also Don Cupitt (1984), D. Z. Phillips (1976) and Gordon Kaufman (1993).

observational, historical, scientific, and other representational fields of discourse. Some of the proposed differences are the standards employed in justifying religious claims, the distinct kinds of commitment expressed by religious claims, and the relationship between religious propositions and evidence.

Proponents of the face-value approach are fully aware that there is a rich variety of religious expression in the form not only of religious utterances that are non-literal or non-assertoric—such as metaphors, questions, fictional stories, expressions of hope, awe, or devotion—but also of non-linguistic religious activities.[3] However, they reject the attempt to assimilate religious assertions with other kinds of speech act. The numerous objections include: the unwarrantedly revisionary nature of the alternative proposals (Swinburne 1993, ch. 6), the positions implausibly depart from the face-value account without being sufficiently supported by arguments, the theories involve intellectually questionable reinterpretation of religious discourse (Plantinga 2000: ch. 2, particularly in reference to Kaufman), they are promoted with an atheistic agenda, or they are an historical aberration of (mainly) the early twentieth century (van Inwagen 2006: 156).

The complaints that radical opposition to the face-value approach has a recent vintage or that it is tied to atheism are misplaced. Maimonides (*c.*1135–1204) treats much of what we say about God as non-literal (1963: ch. 52), while Gregory Palamas, writing a couple of centuries later, doubts that either our thoughts or language should be taken as accurately representing God (1983: 32). The early Christian theologian Dionysius (1987) and the unknown medieval author of *The Cloud of Unknowing* (2001), while they appear to regard assertions about God's nature as a relatively harmless mistake, think that a closer relationship with God is achieved through the recognition that no utterance represents the way that God is. George Berkeley (1950) argues that affirmations of certain Christian doctrines do not express beliefs in them; Kant (in his more radical moments) suggests that religious judgements are action-guiding principles rather than beliefs (1999: A671, A686). However, the more substantive objections made by face-value theorists look more compelling. It is hard to square the radical position that religious utterances are metaphors or plans, or express intentions or feelings, with speakers' use of religious language. Speakers may say, for example, that (1) is true, which we would not expect if it merely

---

[3] Non-assertoric expression is, of course, commonplace in non-religious discourse. On metaphor in religious and scientific discourse see Soskice (1985). Additionally, indicative religious sentences may be uttered without asserting them, consistently with their conventionally being asserted; (1), for instance, could be used ironically.

expressed a feeling. (1) can be employed in valid arguments and the negation of (1) is both meaningful and inconsistent with its affirmation. This is difficult to explain if speakers do not take what they say to represent the way the world is.

There is, however, theoretical space between the face-value theory and its radical opposition that I will defend in this paper. There could be systematic differences between assertion and the speech act of affirming an indicative religious sentence without it following that religious utterances are non-literal or that they are not used to communicate religious beliefs. According to this moderate position, the prevailing speech act for expressing indicative religious sentences is governed by norms that are different to those that govern assertion. The moderate theory therefore sides with the radical opposition by endorsing significant and pervasive differences between religious discourse and other representational fields of discourse. However, moderate theory sides with the face-value account by preserving the connection between religious affirmations and the speaker's belief in the truth of what is said. If successful, the moderate theory can do justice to the evidence for the distinctiveness of religious discourse that motivates the more radical theories, while retaining the appeal of a face-value approach.

In section 1, I will set out a theory of the constitutive norms of assertion and argue, in section 2, that religious affirmations are normatively different. In section 3 I will develop a positive account of religious affirmation and address some objections. Although the focus in the paper is on religious language and its use, there are related epistemological questions that interestingly parallel this issue. In section 4 I will show how the moderate theory fits with some recent accounts of religious epistemology.

1. THE NORMS OF ASSERTION

Since we will be considering whether a given indicative utterance is an assertion I will use the expression *affirmation* to refer to an indicative utterance or putative assertion. The idea of a speech act is in part due to J. L. Austin's (1975: 94–5) famous distinction between locutionary and illocutionary acts (or speech acts). A locutionary act is the act of saying something, or articulating a meaningful utterance. Illocutionary acts are classes of locutionary acts that include asking questions, making wishes, making requests, giving orders, and so on. So, using Austin's terminology, in this section we will consider some of the norms and individuating conditions for the speech act of assertion; in the next section we will consider whether religious affirmations satisfy those conditions or belong to a different illocutionary class.

A useful way into the debate about assertion is to consider Robert Stalnaker's influential account (1999). He points out that assertions are usually made in conversational contexts where the participants have shared assumptions that determine what possibilities they rule out and what they take to be actual. At a given point in the conversation, there is a 'common ground' of propositions presupposed by the speakers and hearers. In the course of the conversation, new propositions that are asserted and accepted are added to this collection of assumptions. Making an assertion modifies the conversation by affecting the attitudes of the participants: the speaker proposes to add the asserted proposition to the common ground. Notably, Stalnaker's theory characterizes assertion by its 'essential effects', specifically the effects on the development of a conversation, rather than by its causes or relationship with the speaker's mental states. So assertion is not, on this theory, essentially the expression of the speaker's belief. Moreover, Stalnaker's theory allows for the possibility, in certain conversational contexts, that both speaker and hearers know that an asserted proposition is untrue but play along with it. A case of this sort occurs when the participants in a conversation maintain a polite untruth about somebody in order to preserve that person's sensibilities. In such contexts, a speaker may make an openly insincere assertion on the basis of false presuppositions where neither the speaker nor hearers believe the asserted claim. However, we can see why an assertion would usually express what the speaker believes: since the participants in a conversation are usually aiming to avoid error and to get closer to the truth, speakers typically contribute by putting forward propositions that they also believe to be true.

Despite the attractions of Stalnaker's theory that assertion puts forward a proposition for inclusion in the common ground, it is not clear that assertion requires the background of a conversational context and shared presuppositions. For example, one could assert something without an audience. As Linda Zagzebski points out: 'If I overhear you reciting your creed, I hear you making assertions that express your beliefs' (2012: 120). Perhaps such cases could be understood, consistently with Stalnaker's account of assertion, as speakers having conversations with themselves. However, one could also make assertions in a context where one does not share enough assumptions with the hearers to have any prospect of contributing to a common ground. John MacFarlane (2011) also highlights the issue of retracting an assertion. We are able to take back or render 'null and void' an assertion after having made it; retracting an assertion also appears to be a speech act that is the corollary of assertion and there are similar corollaries for questioning, commanding, and apologizing. Stalnaker's theory does not provide a straightforward way of understanding retraction. If an assertion is a proposal to contribute information into the shared presuppositions of a conversation, (it could be withdrawn before it has reached the point of being accepted) However, after it has been accepted and the conversational context changed and various additional assertions are introduced, it is unclear how the proposal is undone. Finally, as Stalnaker notes, his theory has difficulty in distinguishing assertions from other speech acts that change the shared presuppositions in a conversation. For example, suppose that a proposition is put forward for the purposes of a debate without supposing that it is true. The utterance meets the proposed conditions for an assertion but it does not seem to have been asserted. Notwithstanding these difficulties, there are two particularly interesting features of Stalnaker's theory that I will use to develop an account of assertion. First, assertions can be distinguished from other speech acts by their normative characteristics, second, assertions have certain essential effects.

An idea implicit in Stalnaker's treatment of assertion is that a speech act can be understood as a practice with distinctive norms. A normative practice is an activity with rules that provide standards of proper conduct when pursuing the activity. Sports and games with defined rules are familiar examples. There are standard rules of tennis and should I break them by, say, cheating, then I am playing the game improperly. We can also think of speech acts as linguistic practices governed by rules for their correct employment with different speech acts—assertion, questions, testimony, apologies, promises, expressions of intentions, and so on—each having characteristic norms. This has become a widely adopted approach to understanding assertion and distinguishing it from other kinds of speech act. If someone has violated a norm of assertion, according to Williamson, it is 'much as if he had broken a rule of a game: he has cheated. On this view, the speech act, like a game and unlike the act of jumping, is constituted by rules.' (2000: 238) I will call the *constitutive norms* of a practice those that must be followed to engage correctly in the practice. While I will follow the widely adopted approach of characterizing assertion by its constitutive norms, I will address some alternatives in section 2.

Before turning to the other aspect of Stalnaker's account, here are two further points of clarification about constitutive norms. First, there are requirements that must be met to qualify as engaging in a given activity that are not constitutive norms. Take the activity of jumping. It seems plausible that in order to jump one must take off from the ground. Jumping, however, is not an activity governed by norms. So what distinguishes this requirement from a constitutive norm? While taking off from the ground seems to be a condition that must be met to jump, it does not provide a standard for correct or incorrect jumping: if one failed to meet it, one would not thereby have incorrectly jumped but not have jumped at all. A norm, in contrast, sets an evaluative standard; a constitutive norm sets a standard that must be met to engage in the practice correctly. We can similarly distinguish between requirements for the participation in a speech act from the constitutive norms that characterize it. For example, it is plausible that one of the requirements for S to make a promise to H to do *p* is that S tell H that he will do *p*.[4] In contrast, John Rawls suggests a constitutive norm of promising that 'reads roughly as follows: if one says the words "I promise to do X" in the appropriate circumstances, one is to do X, unless certain excusing conditions obtain' (1971: 345). The former is a requirement that must be met to make a promise, the latter is a standard against which we can judge whether a promise is defective or infelicitous. Second, there are many standards relevant to the evaluation of what one does in the course of participating in a practice that are not constitutive norms of that practice. This arises from the fact that one can engage at the same time in a number of different practices—social, moral, epistemic, linguistic, and so on—with different constitutive norms. Jumping up and down during a funeral, for example, might be a significant failure of etiquette and good taste; cheating in a game of who can jump highest might be considered bad form. In both cases, evaluative standards are brought to bear on the activity of jumping. They are not, however, constitutive norms of jumping because they do not establish that the jumper has defectively or infelicitously jumped; rather, it is the norms of etiquette or of fair play that have been breached. Similarly, assertion and other speech acts are subject to various norms that are not constitutive norms of the speech act. A question may be impertinent, or repeated in an offensively insistent matter, without being linguistically defective.

The other aspect of Stalnaker's theory is that assertion has distinctive and essential effects. Charles Peirce, who anticipated this view, proposed that 'to assert a proposition is to make oneself responsible for its truth' (1934: 384) and this idea that the speaker makes commitments in asserting something has been developed by various philosophers including MacFarlane (2005), Robert Brandom (1994: ch. 3), Michael Rescorla (2009) and Gary Watson (2004). Various norms have been proposed and debated. For example, Brandom characterizes the assertion of *p* as a commitment to vindicating one's entitlement to *p* when one is challenged. In asserting something, on Brandom's view, one is obliged to offer some justification of what one has asserted if it is disputed. A closely related commitment is that one should

---

[4] This example is simplified for the purposes of illustrating the distinction. For example, I am excluding cases where a promise is implied by what S says rather than explicitly stated. For a detailed treatment see Searle (1969).

withdraw the assertion if it is shown to be untrue.[5] Two commitments stand out as plausible constitutive norms of assertion:

The justification norm (JN): the onus is on the speaker to justify what is asserted when faced with a legitimate challenge to its truth.[6]

The retraction norm (RN): the speaker should retract and not continue to assert something that has been shown to be untrue.

I will call the theory that assertion is governed by these two norms the *normative commitment theory*.

For example, suppose S and H are walking through a forest and S asserts

2. That tree is a white willow

and H questions (2) because the tree looks too tall to be a willow. According to the normative commitment theory (and specifically JN), the onus is now on S to offer a reason in support of what he has said. The justification need not be elaborate (JN does not require that speakers be particularly articulate to make felicitous assertions). For example, S might say: 'It looks like the picture I saw of a white willow.' Also, H might not find S's justification persuasive. The point is that if JN is a norm of assertion then there is a reasonable expectation on S to have something to say that supports (2) where it is legitimately challenged. Accordingly, the failure to provide justification for (2) is reason for thinking that S's assertion is defective. For instance, if H raises legitimate doubts about whether the tree is a white willow rather than a weeping willow and S has no response, then it seems that S should retract (2) or else revise or weaken it. Perhaps S should have weakened the assertion to 'That tree looks like a white willow' or 'In my opinion that tree is a white willow' (which are both assertions but much easier to justify), or used a different speech act, for example, 'I wonder if that tree is a white willow?' Although S could continue to insist on (2) without thereby ceasing to have made an assertion, by acting in this way S would have 'broken a rule of a game' by failing to carry out the normative commitments of assertion: the assertion is defective.[7] Both the justification norm

---

[5] Brandom adds a second commitment that in asserting something a speaker licenses hearers to rely on the asserted proposition. However, as Max Kölbel (2011: 67–9) argues, the licence to rely on someone else's assertion can be understood as following from the asserter's obligation to justify the asserted proposition.

[6] I will focus on legitimate challenges that, to be satisfactorily addressed, require a reason in favour of what has been asserted. However, a challenge could also be met by showing that it is unpersuasive.

[7] On the distinction between intuitions about the defectiveness of assertions that are due to the fault of the speaker or where the assertion itself is defective see Alston (2000: 57) and Rescorla (2009).

and the retraction norm, therefore, seem to characterize linguistic practice in the use of utterances of indicative sentences about (at least) observable occurrences.

The normative commitment theory does not require that assertions occur in the conversational contexts posited by Stalnaker. It also has a more plausible account of retracting an assertion. To retract an assertion is to back out of the commitment to stand by the truth of the asserted proposition. More importantly, JN and RN do look like plausible constitutive norms of assertion. They explicate the way in which speakers are committed to the truth of the stated proposition that distinguishes the speech act from, for example, suppositions or expressions of hope or intentions. Moreover, if S asserts *p* and fails to satisfy JN or RN that seems a basis for legitimate criticism of what the speaker says: the speaker should not have asserted *p* but instead asserted a weaker proposition, employed a different speech act, or retracted *p* entirely.

The normative commitment theory allows for non-defective assertion where the speaker does not believe what is said: one can 'make oneself responsible' for an assertion, and satisfy RN and JN, without believing it.[8] However, since we generally take an assertion to express the speaker's belief, should the theory be supplemented with a belief norm?

The belief norm (BN): in asserting *p* the speaker should believe *that p*.

The argument against making BN a norm of assertion is that there seem to be cases of linguistically respectable assertions that the speaker does not believe. There is the example given earlier, of a polite untruth.[9] There also cases of speakers asserting *p* without believing *p* that appear commendable. Jennifer Lackey (2007) gives the following example. A respected paediatrician who has researched childhood vaccines recognizes that the evidence shows that there is no causal connection between vaccines and autism. However, shortly after his 18-month-old daughter receives one of her vaccines she develops autism. While he is aware that signs of autism typically emerge at around this age, he abandons his earlier belief that vaccines do not cause autism. When one of his patients asks him of the rumours surrounding

---

[8] The differences between believing a proposition and arguing for and defending that proposition are clearly set out by Alston (1989) and Audi (1993).

[9] That this is not a conclusive counterexample to a belief norm. Defenders of BN can argue that such cases only show that in certain circumstances the belief norm may be overridden by other non-linguistic norms—in this case the norm of polite behaviour—that are not specific to assertion (Williamson 2000: 256). Note that rejecting BN as a constitutive norm of assertion, we are also rejecting an even stronger knowledge norm, as defended by Williamson (2000).

vaccines and autism, he appreciates that his current doubts were likely due to the traumatic experiences of dealing with his daughter's condition and he asserts:

3. There is no connection between vaccines and autism.

Although he recognizes that there is good evidence for his assertion, he does not believe (3) at the time of uttering it. Far from being grounds to regard the assertion as defective, it seems praiseworthy that the speaker has recognized his emotional distress may have distorted his beliefs and has asserted something that he does not believe. Although BN therefore seems inappropriate as a constitutive norm of assertion, it would be an advantage if our account of assertion explained the fact that we do generally expect that an assertion expresses a speaker's belief. Fortunately, the normative commitment theory has the resources to do so: one does not normally undertake commitments to defend a proposition, or to retract it if one cannot defend the proposition, unless one also believes that it is true.

The theory that assertion involves normative commitments JN and RN therefore has a number of advantages. It preserves the intuitive connection between assertion and belief, accounts for cases where assertions are made without belief, as well as avoiding some of the counterintuitive consequences of Stalnaker's theory. I do not propose that JN and RN *completely* exhaust the norms of assertion; it may be that additional norms are needed to fully specify the speech act. JN and RN are, however, the key norms of assertion identified by the normative commitment theory.[10] It is possible to make an assertion, albeit a defective one, if an utterance fails to satisfy JN or RN. But the utterance of an indicative sentence will not be an assertion if it is not governed by these normative commitments.

2. ASSERTION AND RELIGIOUS AFFIRMATION

Armed with an account of (at least some of) the normative standards of assertion, let us return to the issue raised earlier: is there a systematic difference between religious affirmations and assertions?

How should we establish that JN and RN characterize religious discourse? We are concerned with whether they are *constitutive* norms of religious affirmations, i.e. whether such affirmations must satisfy them to be linguistically appropriate. Showing that linguistic practice accords with a principle

---

[10] See Alston (2000) for a theory of assertion that combines commitments with other norms.

is not sufficient to establish that the principle is a constitutive norm. By comparison, imagine a community in which individuals say things like 'I promise to do *p*' (where *p* is some future action that they can perform) and invariably go on to do *p*, but if someone were not to do *p* their action would not thereby be deemed inappropriate nor their earlier utterance defective. While their behaviour is in accordance with Rawls's norm, it is not a constitutive norm of their practice because not acting on *p* is not a failing. However, we can show that a constitutive norm is not in play for a given practice if there are examples of actions that form part of that practice and fail to obey the norm without thereby being defective. So do religious affirmations include non-defective examples that fail to exhibit JN or RN?

Suppose a speaker affirms the following:

4. God is almighty.

If challenged on the truth of (4) on the grounds that God does not exist or that an omnipotent being is impossible (because, say, of the paradox of the stone), the speaker might attempt to supply a justification that addresses the challenge. But it would not be surprising if the speaker responded that no evidence or argument is needed or refused to engage in debate, or said it is a matter of faith, reiterated the proposition (perhaps in different terms or with a different tone).[11] More generally, these are legitimate conversational responses to challenges to religious affirmations. Taking this stance will not of course satisfy the sceptic and it may be seen as an epistemic failing. However, it is not a *linguistic* failing on the part of religious believers that they cannot or do not address doubts about the truth of their religious affirmations. So it appears that, by virtue of affirming (4), there does not seem to be an obligation on the part of the speaker to either attempt to address doubts about its truth or retract the affirmation. It follows that JN and RN are not constitutive norms of religious affirmation.[12]

Saying that JN and RN are not constitutive norms of religious affirmation does not imply that religious affirmations are not justifiable or that evidence and argument is not relevant either to the belief in or affirmation

---

[11] Justification, insofar as it is required by JN, need not be in the form of arguments *from other beliefs* that the speaker has. In affirming (4), a speaker might be expressing a basic belief and the justification of (4) might include the report of experiences of God. See Plantinga (2000) for a defence of the reasonableness of this position.

[12] Are weaker versions of JN or RN applicable to religious affirmation? Watson (2004: 68–9) proposes a weaker version of JN, whereby a speaker is committed to the *defensibility* of what is said rather than the actual defence of it. However, I do not believe that the weaker version of JN is a constitutive norm of affirmation; that is, a speaker may make a religious affirmation without the confidence that the affirmed proposition could be successfully argued.

of religious propositions. Arguments and evidence are frequently presented in favour of religious beliefs and a great deal of philosophy of religion and theology is focused on the construction and evaluation of such arguments and evidence. Moreover, there may be non-linguistic norms that make the provision of a justification for (4) appropriate when it is challenged. For example, according to evidentialists (such as William Clifford 1999) a belief is only reasonable if it is held on the basis of sufficient evidence. If this is right, there is an epistemic obligation on a speaker expressing their religious belief to be in possession of a sufficiently strong justification for the truth of what is affirmed. It may also be desirable for religious believers to be able to respond to challenges both from atheists and other believers with a view to defeating sceptics and persuading others. But these are epistemic and social norms; only *linguistic* norms are relevant to our assessment of the constitutive norms of religious affirmation. The epistemological obligation to supply or have a justification for a religious affirmation is one thing; the linguistic requirement on speakers to provide support for a religious affirmation when challenged on its truth is another. This is not to say that epistemological considerations are not part of the constitutive norms of assertion. For example, according to Williamson it is a norm of the assertion of p that the speaker knows that p. However, the epistemological and linguistic appropriateness of an assertion are distinct issues. Even if assertion imposes certain epistemological demands on the speaker, whether the satisfaction of these demands is sufficient for epistemological respectability is a separate question.

Take the utterance

5. Jesus is the only-begotten son of God and is of one substance with the Father.

Suppose it is argued that an incorporeal being cannot have children, or that a being cannot be both the son of God and of one substance with God. As with (4), the speaker might respond by claiming that it is a matter of faith or that it is not appropriate to question Scripture. Or the speaker might say that the issue cannot be assessed by evidence. These responses ignore the demands of RN and JN, that is, that reasons to reject the truth of what is said commit the speaker to defend it or withdraw the claim. Is this a linguistic failing—a deliberate or unintentional misunderstanding of what it is to assert something? Suppose someone affirms

6. 2018 is a leap year

and this is challenged because, say, 2018 is not evenly divisible by 4. If the speaker responds that (6) is a matter of faith or otherwise resists justifying

(6) we would suppose that the speaker was either confused about what they had said or was being mischievous. In religious cases, in contrast, responses that deflect JN or RN are not only routine but we do not take them to be indicative of a linguistic blunder. Religious sentences are affirmed without the speaker needing to satisfy these norms. As mentioned above, failing to satisfy these norms may be—according to some—socially, epistemologically, or morally ill-advised and inappropriate. Many religious believers aim to meet them for these reasons. But this is a distinct matter to whether these obligations are imposed by the speech act of affirmation. Neither RN nor JN, therefore, are constitutive norms of affirmation: religious affirmation is a speech act that is distinct from assertion.

3. THE NORMS OF RELIGIOUS AFFIRMATION

Notwithstanding the normative differences I have set out between religious affirmations and assertions, there are some important points of similarity between these speech acts. First, in making a religious affirmation *that p* the speaker presents the proposition *p* as suitable to be added—to put it in Stalnaker's terms—to the common ground of judgements adopted by hearers. That is, in affirming *p*, one upholds *p* and rules out other possibilities that are inconsistent with it. In affirming 'God only does what is good', for example, one rules out God doing bad things. In this respect, religious affirmations are conversationally like assertions. Second, assertions and affirmations are similarly related to belief. I argued earlier that BN is not a constitutive norm of assertion because there are legitimate assertions where the speaker does not believe what is said. For similar reasons it is not a constitutive norm of affirmation. However, just as assertion is the principal linguistic method of expressing belief, affirmation is the principal linguistic method of expressing religious belief. Third, Peirce's proposal that speakers take on the responsibility for the truth of what they say seems right for affirmations as well as assertions. For example, there is something amiss with a speaker affirming (5) and promptly disowning the proposition they have affirmed, or entirely ignoring it in their subsequent thought and action. In contrast, this wouldn't be grounds for criticism if the speaker had *pretended* to assert (5), or had conjectured (5) as a possibility, rather than affirmed it.

Consistently with these points, the instances in which religious affirmation seems misplaced are where the speaker fails to employ the stated proposition in theoretical reasoning or in practical evaluations. For example, if a speaker affirms that God created the world but makes no use of the proposition in thinking about the universe and the judgement exerts no influence on the speaker's attitudes or motivations, this would be grounds for criticizing the affirmation. Or suppose that a speaker affirms:

7. By the grace of God we are saved by faith in Jesus Christ.

If the proposition has no practical consequences in decisions or actions of the speaker, then it seems that the proposition should not have been affirmed. This suggests the following norm of affirmation:

The practical/theoretical norm (PN): in affirming *p*, the speaker should uphold *p* in theoretical reasoning and practical judgements, where they apply.

PN is a defeasible norm. It may be overruled, in some contexts, by other norms: a creationist who is by profession a biochemist might not use in their academic research religious propositions that they would otherwise affirm, in order to follow the prevailing norms of biological science. An affirmation may not have a practical effect for compelling reasons: a speaker who affirms (7) and because of their belief in (7) goes to church, might cease to do so in a context in which the lives of churchgoers are under threat. This is consistent with PN being a commitment a speaker takes on in religious affirmation.

An advantage of PN is that it preserves the relationship between religious affirmation and belief without relying on either RN or JN: in affirming a proposition that one uses in reasoning and making decisions, one also usually believes it to be true. It also accounts for the appropriateness of criticisms of affirmations highlighted above. If S comes to regard *p* as a mistake, that is a reason for S to retract *p*; if S ignores *p* in thinking and decisions that is a reason to think S should not have affirmed it. PN additionally draws support from the widely canvassed feature of religious belief, noted both by radicals and face-value theorists, which is its influence on a person's life.[13] The adoption of a new religious belief normally goes along with a variety of changes in the behaviour, dispositions, and attitudes of the believer; the changes in a person's life that usually follow from a religious conversion are the most easily observable examples of the changes in a person's motivations that accompany religious belief. Since religious affirmations typically express beliefs, it is unsurprising that this motivational aspect of religious belief

---

[13] The normative connection between religious affirmations and motivations is an important respect in which they differ from religious assertions. For a more detailed treatment of the relationship between religious judgements and motivations see Scott (2013: ch. 5).

should extend to religious affirmations. PN makes it a norm of religious affirmation in general.

I will say more about the practical commitment of religious affirmation in the following section. In the remainder of this section, I will consider some alternative proposals for the norms of religious affirmation and then consider some objections to the way in which I have differentiated religious affirmation from assertion. To avoid confusion, I will call an affirmation governed by PN (and not JN or RN) an *avowal.* So my position is that religious affirmations are conventionally avowals rather than assertions.

Rather than taking PN as the norm of religious affirmation, do religious affirmations instead fall under another familiar type of speech act? This is an objection that might come from supporters of the radical interpretations of religious discourse described in the introduction. If religious affirmations are really expressions of intentions, recommendations, or expressions of feeling, then we can see why they would not satisfy the justification or retraction norms. Since, on any of these options, speakers are not taking on any commitment to uphold the truth of what is said, reasons for thinking that the propositional content of a given religious utterance is false are not reasons for withdrawing it or providing a justification for it. However, by assimilating religious affirmations with such apparently different speech acts, these theories sever the relationship between what the believer says and the speaker's belief in what is said, which seems to undermine the point of making an affirmation. Radical theories also run into difficulties in explaining the details of the proposed interpretations of religious affirmations. For instance, if

    1. God created the universe

is a recommendation or the expression of an intention, what is being recommended or what intention is being expressed? Even if a suitable recommendation or intention could be found, these theories will have to explain the interaction between religious and non-religious discourse. For example, (1) can be combined with

    8. If God created the universe then scientists will not be able to explain the origins of the universe

to conclude

    9. Scientists will not be able to explain the origins of the universe.

But how could this argument be logically valid if (1) is the expression of a recommendation or intention?

Perhaps a speech act that is more closely related to assertion can provide a more promising model for religious affirmation. To the extent that religious affirmations are not governed by JN and RN they are normatively comparable to suppositions. Notably, Andrei Buckareff (2005) proposes that faith could be an action-guiding assumption rather than a belief.[14] On this basis, religious affirmations, to the extent that they express faith, might be taken to express assumptions. Could religious affirmations therefore be akin to suppositions? In stating a supposition, a speaker puts forward a proposition, usually for some practical reason, without a commitment to justify its truth. However, the normative similarity between religious affirmations and suppositions is superficial. Here are two differences.

A supposition is put forward conditionally on the practical considerations that make it useful. For example, a supposition can be made on a whim—let's suppose that Archduke Franz Ferdinand had not been assassinated in 1914 and imagine what would have happened, purely for the interest in entertaining it rather than due to any consideration of its truth or grounds for believing it. A supposition may also be made out of some practical or moral requirement: for example, if one is in a situation of having to rely on somebody one does not know, one might act on the supposition that that person is trustworthy even though one lacks good evidence to suppose that it is true. Suppositions are accordingly often temporary and changeable depending on the interests and needs of those adopting the supposition. The affirmation of a religious proposition, in contrast, is not normally put forward to further some other interest. A religious affirmation rules out alternatives rather than sets them aside in a potentially only temporary way for whatever purposes the affirmation was made. Second, religious affirmations appear to exhibit different linguistic behaviour to suppositions. For instance, if someone affirms (1) we take them to disagree with an agnostic who refuses to affirm (1). However, someone who merely supposes (1) does not seem thereby to be in disagreement with someone who does not make that supposition. Also, if someone affirms (1) and another affirms that (1) is false, it seems that one of these two speakers must have made a mistake. However, this does not seem to be the case if affirmations are suppositions since it need not be a mistake to suppose something that is false.

---

[14] See also Howard-Snyder (2013) and Swinburne's (2005) discussion of 'pragmatist' accounts of faith; Swinburne, however, differs from Buckareff in seeing the faithful as also committed to various religious beliefs (2005: 148). For an overview and critique of non-doxastic theories of faith see Malcolm and Scott (forthcoming).

In general, these problems—how to provide a plausible analysis of the content of religious affirmations, to explain the linguistic behaviour of religious utterances and their interaction with non-religious utterances—present prima facie obstacles to radical accounts that have not as yet been met.[15] Religious affirmation should not, therefore, be assimilated with the other speech acts suggested by the radical opposition to face-value theory. This is not to say, however, that feelings, hopes, plans and other states emphasized by many radical theories are not communicated by religious affirmations. Indeed, commitments other than belief may play a role in the explanation for the expressive value of discourses that employ affirmation rather than assertion.[16] That is, affirmation can give voice to beliefs that a speaker may be unable to justify (or be uninterested in justifying) but to which the speaker is also committed for reasons other than its truth.

A different objection to my account is that assertions are an insufficiently distinct and cohesive group of utterances to be assessed for distinctive normative characteristics. For example, Janet Levin (2008) argues that assertions are governed by *context-sensitive* norms. Rather than assertion being constituted by norms that are applicable for all assertions, the norms vary according to the circumstances in which the assertion is made. For example,

3. There is no connection between vaccines and autism

seems to be an example of a non-defective assertion that the speaker does not believe; but on the context-sensitive theory of norms, this does not provide a conclusive counterexample to the belief norm BN. Rather, BN could be a norm of assertion in some contexts but not others (such as cases in which the speaker has ground for thinking their beliefs are misguided). A more radical 'no assertion' position is proposed by Herman Capellen (2011). He argues that 'assertion' is a philosophical term of art that does not pick out a unified collection of speech acts: there is no speech act of assertion with distinct constitutive norms or even variable norms. Instead, locutionary acts that express indicative sentences are governed by a variety of different norms, no subset of which characterizes assertions.

These alternatives to the constitutive norm account of speech acts are not widely agreed on. However, the argument of this paper can be expressed in a way that is not dependent on the constitutive norm model. The contrast

---

[15] Problems akin to these are discussed in detail in metaethics (Schroeder 2008). For an overview of research in the philosophy of religion see Scott (2013).

[16] For a theory that takes religious affirmations to express both beliefs and non-cognitive attitudes see Scott (2013: chs 5–6).

I draw between religious affirmations and assertions, and the distinction between religious discourse and other areas of discourse that it illustrates, can be made in other terms. If Levin is right, it may not be correct to conclude that religious affirmations are not assertions; rather, avowals *are* assertions but exhibit certain normative characteristics that differentiate them from other classes of assertion. On the no-assertion view, my argument does not establish anything about assertions in general, however, it does point up characteristic differences between religious indicative utterances and utterances of other indicative sentences that face-value theorists contend behave in the same way. These ways of expressing the argument still capture the central point that there are differences between religious affirmations and other apparently descriptive indicative utterances that they appear, at face value, to resemble. To this extent, the changes that would be imposed on the argument of this paper by positions that are critical of the constitutive norm model of assertion are more terminological than substantial.

If we accept the prevailing view that assertion is a normatively distinct speech act, a related worry about my argument is whether religious affirmations should be considered as a distinct and unified type of speech act. I have treated religious affirmations as a class by virtue of their subject matter. But this could be challenged in two ways: on the grounds that the selection of religious affirmations is artificially narrow and should include non-religious utterances, or that it is too broad and that while PN may be the norm of some religious affirmations, other religious affirmations may be assertions.

The first challenge is entirely reasonable: speech acts are acts that we perform in uttering various meaningful sentences and it would be odd if a speech act were restricted to sentences with a specific subject matter. However, it is also unproblematic to the case that I am making. I have picked out religious affirmations (in particular affirmations about God) because they are central to the traditional focus of philosophical interest in religious discourse and the question of whether it differs in a systematic way from other areas of discourse (and specifically historical, observational, and scientific areas of discourse).[17] I have argued that there are such differences. Now suppose that, say, ethical affirmations also exhibited the same normative characteristics as religious affirmation (something I believe not to be the case). This would show that PN governs a much larger class of affirmations

---

[17] These examples of other discourse may not themselves have uniform norms governing their affirmations. For instance, Bas van Fraassen (1980: 57) argues that affirmations of scientific theories do not assert those theories but instead claim certain virtues for them, in particular, that they have 'empirical adequacy' by their usefulness in organizing and deriving results about observables.

than originally anticipated: both ethical and religious affirmations are avowals. But it would not undermine the argument against the face value theory that religious discourse employs speech acts (avowals) that distinguishes it from discourses that employ assertion.

The second challenge is that religious affirmations are not a unified class of speech acts. For example, while some religious affirmations may be avowals, perhaps others might exhibit one or both of JN or RN. As I set out in section 2, the most straightforward way of showing that the justification and retraction commitments are not constitutive norms for religious affirmations is to find examples of religious affirmations that fail to observe these norms without thereby being defective. To show that there is no subclass of religious affirmations governed by JN or RN is trickier to establish: I have no a priori argument for this, nor space for a more comprehensive survey of examples. However, I think that the examples that *look* as if they are governed by RN or JN usually fall into one of the following three categories. (A) There are many examples of speakers providing justifications for their religious affirmations, or being in a position to do so if challenged. Many religious affirmations express beliefs that the speaker has because they have been persuaded of them by supporting evidence. But as we have seen, this does not establish that the speaker's affirmation is subject to the *constitutive* norm of justification. For JN and RN to be constitutive, there would need to be grounds for criticizing the affirmation as defective or unsuitable if the speaker did not make the relevant commitments. However, there does not seem to be anything linguistically wrong with a speaker's affirmation of (1) without being able or willing to defend it and being unwilling to retract what is said if unable to answer reasonable objections. (B) There are cases where there *is* an obligation on a speaker to justify a religious affirmation or retract it if the proposition cannot be given a respectable defence. For instance, in the context of debate in a philosophy seminar. However, the obligations imposed on speakers in these contexts are due to the norms relating to debating standards in academic seminars rather than the constitutive norms of religious affirmation. (C) Speakers may, in uttering a religious sentence, make the justification and retraction commitments. In so doing, they would have met the standards for assertion. However, while this shows that religious propositions can be asserted it does not show that religious affirmations should in general be interpreted as assertions. Religious propositions can be used in a variety of speech acts, including metaphors, fictions, and the expression of intentions and hopes, as well as assertions; these are not counterexamples to a theory about the prevailing constitutive norms for religious indicative utterances.

4. LANGUAGE AND EPISTEMOLOGY

I have argued that the constitutive norms of religious affirmation impose fewer epistemological demands on speakers than assertion, at least with respect to the provision of a justification in support of what is said. Religious affirmation also involves other theoretical and practical commitments that account for its similarities with assertion and in particular the relationship between what is said and what the speaker believes. But this may seem a hollow victory against the face-value theory if justification is an epistemic requirement for a religious belief to be reasonable. There seems little advantage in employing a speech act that lifts the normative demands for justification, if similar epistemic demands are still in place on the beliefs expressed by that speech act. This would be like playing a variant of basketball only to find that the changes to the rules are considered against the spirit of the game. A critic could argue: 'If RN and JN are not linguistic norms of religious affirmation, that just goes to show that the reasonableness of religious beliefs is not built in to the epistemologically permissive norms that govern this speech act. But we should not expect that we can read off what is epistemologically appropriate from what is linguistically appropriate.' However, the linguistic and epistemic issues cannot be detached. Avowing, like assertion, is the principal and most direct and simple way of communicating what one believes. So why should speakers avow rather than assert religious propositions? In this section I will consider two accounts of the epistemology of religious belief that explain the epistemic value of religious avowals. The first is due to John Bishop (2007), the second to Linda Zagzebski (2012).[18]

Bishop distinguishes between two different aspects of belief: *holding true* a proposition and *taking a proposition to be true in reasoning.* The former is an attitude toward a proposition that it is true; the latter is the action of taking a proposition to be true in one's theoretical and practical reasoning. For example, suppose that Mary believes her pet tortoise is liable to roam, so when she shows it off to guests she keeps an eye on the tortoise to avoid it getting lost. Mary holds true the proposition that her tortoise is liable to roam. Moreover, in a context in which the tortoise is liable to escape and she intends not to lose it, '[t]hrough an effortless piece of practical reasoning in which, *inter alia*, she *takes* this proposition about the tortoise to be true there results Mary's action in keeping a close eye on it'. (p. 34) Often, these two aspects of belief go together because holding true a proposition (i.e. having the attitude of belief towards the proposition) disposes the believer

---

[18] This is far from a comprehensive survey. See also Audi (2008) and Alston (1996).

towards taking that proposition true in reasoning. However, Bishop argues holding-true and taking-true aspects of belief are distinct. This is shown by the fact that they can come apart: one can choose not to act on what one takes to be true. He gives the example of a racist suspecting his beliefs may emerge from prejudice and then not acting on them, even though he has not shaken free of the beliefs.

Using this distinction, Bishop introduces the idea of a *doxastic venture.* In doxastic venture one takes a proposition as true while recognizing that its truth is not supported by the available evidence. A religious doxastic venture is therefore 'an active venture in practical commitment to the truth of faith-propositions that the believer correctly recognizes not to be adequately supported by his or her evidence.' (106) Religious doxastic venture provides an account of faith that Bishop takes to be closely aligned to William James: 'a defence of our right to adopt a believing attitude in religious matters in spite of the fact that our merely logical intellect may not have been coerced.' (1956: 1–2)[19] Bishop also takes faith to involve holding-true what one believes. However, since in a doxastic venture one lacks evidence for belief and one cannot simply choose to believe in God, Bishop proposes that this aspect of belief has other non-evidential, *passional* causes. For example, in encounter with a religious tradition, one can find oneself with the attitude towards *p* that it is true even without finding it to be supported by evidence.[20]

Suppose that a speaker takes a doxastic venture on

6. By the grace of God, we are saved by faith in Jesus Christ

and accordingly affirms (6). In doing so, the speaker would not make the commitment required by JN (because of lack of justification for the proposition) nor RN (because persuaded that it is true despite being evidentially undecidable). However, on Bishop's account, 'faith has an element of active commitment to it' (107) and the speaker makes theoretical and practical commitments to uphold (6). For example, 'To be a person of Christian faith, one has to *do* something in virtue of one's faith-beliefs, namely *commit* oneself to God—and that involves entrusting oneself to God and seeking to do God's will.' (106) These commitments accord with the practical and theoretical commitments proposed by PN. So it appears that Bishop's theory

---

[19] See also Kierkegaard: 'an objective uncertainty held fast in an appropriation process of the most passionate inwardness' (1968: 180).

[20] Bishop introduces a number of constraints on when a doxastic venture is epistemically respectable. For example, it must be in a situation where the proposition believed is evidentially undecidable (which Bishop takes to be true for a number of religious propositions) and where the choice to make a practical commitment is pressing.

offers an epistemological basis for the reasonable exercise of religious avowal
and explains why the linguistic legitimacy of such linguistic expression
is valuable: it provides for the communication of religious convictions
and practical commitments that, while lacking justification, are reasonable
to hold.

Central to Linda Zagzebski's account of religious epistemology is a distinction between theoretical and practical reasons. Theoretical reasons for *p*
are facts that lend support to a logical or probabilistic case for the truth of
p. She takes theoretical reasons to be 'third personal' in that they can be
shared with others and are relevant to the truth of *p* from any person's
perspective: they provide a reasonable person who comes to believe them
reasons to believe *p*. A deliberative reason, in contrast, provides only first
personal reason for an agent to regard *p* as true. It has 'an essential connection to *me and only to me* in my deliberations about whether *p*'. (64) For
example, if I have a powerful moral intuition that a certain act is wrong,
that intuition provides me with a deliberative reason to believe that it is
wrong. I can also use intuition as a theoretical reason, for example, I can cite
my intuition in moral argument with you on whether that act is wrong. But
deliberative reasons lend support to our having beliefs without providing a
justification for them. Experiences and emotions, Zagzebski argues, can
provide deliberative reasons to change our beliefs and adopt new beliefs
independently from any evidence or arguments in favour of the truth or
falsity of those beliefs. The passional causes and experiences that Bishop
proposes can lead to religious belief would be among the deliberative
reasons for belief.

Zagzebski contends that a crucial deliberative reason for religious belief is
provided by an offer of trust made by the speaker that she takes to be made
in the act of giving religious testimony.[21] Rather than construing testimony
as providing evidence for the truth of what is said, she proposes that it can
be understood as presenting the hearer that is being addressed with an invitation to believe what the speaker is saying; this is a deliberative reason for
the addressee to accept the testimony. Moreover, it is (in line with the distinction between theoretical and practical reasons) a deliberative reason
only for the hearer, rather than evidence that could be appreciated by anybody. 'The speaker asks the hearer to give her trust and she may grant it or
she may not. Her reason for granting it depends upon her relationship with

---

[21] Zagzabski defends the rationality of trust more generally on the basis that it is
rational to place trust in one's own epistemic faculties and, therefore, in others that we
take to be as sincere in what they say and in turn it is rational to trust those in whom
those I trust place their trust.

the speaker.' (130) The deliberative reason may be persuasive to this hearer because her deliberative verdict is that accepting the invitation will yield the acquisition of knowledge, or an understanding of how to do good, or the means to better live her life or have a more integrated self than she could achieve on her own. Trust may be grounded in other deliberative reasons, such as a religious experience or admiration for a religious tradition or Scripture.

Zagzebski argues that religious testimony need not be made by an individual but could come from a religious institution or through Scripture. Moreover, testimony may communicate an invitation to trust in an agent other than the speaker: the audience of testimony 'can be groups of people distant from the teller in time or space, and the teller need not be an individual. It can be a religious or scientific or political community.' (122) This is what she thinks can happen in the case of religious testimony. Proposing various models of revelation—such as a chain of testimonies from people with direct contact with the divine transmitted to the present, or an ongoing possibility of relationships with God through Scripture or the actions of the Holy Spirit—Zagzebski proposes that religious testimony can be understood as an invitation to trust that is ultimately made by God. Although an individual or institution may mediate the invitation via testimony, the hearer places their trust in God.

If God tells me that *p*, God takes responsibility for the truth of *p* for me and for all other intended recipients of his revelation. God intends that I believe him, and he acknowledges that we who are the recipients place epistemic trust in him by believing him.... My position is that the ground of faith is trust in God, which gives me a deliberative, first-person reason to believe what God tells me. (190)

Zagzebski's account of religious faith as a commitment to trust in God prompted by deliberative reason rather than theoretical considerations presents another way in which religious avowals are of value. A speaker given first personal deliberative reasons to believe the teachings of a religion and who decides to trust in God can voice those beliefs in avowals, without making justification or retraction commitments with respect to those avowals.

In staking out a middle path between the face-value interpretation of religious utterances and its radical opposition, I recognize that *both* sides of this debate will likely disagree with a moderate compromise. But the theory that religious affirmations are avowals has two key attractions. It provides space to the practical aspects of religious affirmations that tend to get forgotten in face-value interpretations of religious discourse, without succumbing to radical reinterpretations of what religious believers say or undermining either the representational content or belief-reporting role of indicative religious utterances. It also shows how it is possible to do justice to the distinctiveness of religious discourse, while staying in line with the evidence of how speakers use religious language and treating what they say at face value.[22]

REFERENCES

Alston, William P. 1989. *Epistemic Justification: Essays in the Theory of Knowledge.* Ithaca, NY: Cornell University Press.

Alston, William P. 1996. 'Belief, Acceptance and Religious Faith', in Jeff Jordan and Daniel Howard-Snyder (eds), *Faith, Freedom and Rationality: Philosophy of Religion Today.* Lanham, MD: Rowman and Littlefield.

Alston, William P. 2000. *Illocutionary Acts and Sentence Meaning.* Ithaca, NY: Cornell University Press.

Anonymous. 2001. *The Cloud of Unknowing*, trans. A. C. Spearing. Harmondsworth: Penguin Books.

Arnold, Matthew. 1873. *Literature and Dogma.* London: Smith, Elder.

Audi, Robert. 1993. *The Structure of Justification.* Cambridge: Cambridge University Press.

Audi, Robert. 2008. 'Belief, Faith, and Acceptance'. *International Journal for Philosophy of Religion* 63: 87–102.

Austin, J. L. 1975. *How to Do Things with Words.* 2nd edn, ed. J. O. Urmson and M. Sbisa. Oxford: Oxford University Press.

Berkeley, George. 1950. *Alciphron or the Minute Philosopher*, in *The Works of George Berkeley*, vol. 3, ed. A. A. Luce and T. E. Jessop. London: T. Nelson.

Bishop, John. 2007. *Believing by Faith: An Essay in the Epistemology and Ethics of Religious Belief.* Oxford: Clarendon Press.

Braithwaite, R. B. 1955. *An Empiricist's View of the Nature of Religious Belief.* Cambridge: Cambridge University Press.

Brandom. Robert B. 1994. *Making it Explicit: Reasoning, Representing, and Discursive Commitment.* Cambridge, MA: Harvard University Press.

Buckareff, Andrei. 2005. 'Can faith be a doxastic venture?' *Religious Studies* 41: 435–45.

Capellen, Herman. 2011. 'Against Assertion', in Jessica Brown and Herman Capellen (eds), *Assertion: New Philosophical Essays.* Oxford: Oxford University Press, pp. 21–48.

Clifford, W. K. 1999 [1877]. 'The ethics of belief', in *The Ethics of Belief and Other Essays*, ed. Timothy J. Madigan. Amherst, MA: Prometheus, pp. 70–96.

Cupitt, Don. 1984. *The Sea of Faith.* London: BBC Books.

---

[22] Thanks to Gabriel Citron for his comments on an earlier draft of this paper.

Dionysius. 1987. *Pseudo-Dionysius: The Complete Works*, trans. Paul Rorem. New York: Paulist Press.

Hare, R. M. 1992. *Essays on Religion and Education*. Oxford: Oxford University Press.

Howard-Snyder, Daniel. 2013. 'Propositional Faith: What It Is and What It Is Not'. *American Philosophical Quarterly* 50 (4): 357–72.

James, William. 1956. *The Will to Believe and Other Essays in Popular Psychology, and Human Immortality*. New York: Dover.

Kant, Immanuel. 1999. *Critique of Pure Reason*, ed and trans. Paul Guyer, Allan W. Wood. Cambridge: Cambridge University Press.

Kaufman, Gordon. 1993. *In Face of Mystery*. Cambridge, MA: Harvard University Press.

Kenny, Anthony. 2004. *The Unknown God: Agnostic Essays*. London: Continuum.

Kierkegaard, Søren. 1968. *Concluding Unscientific Postscript*, trans. David F. Swenson and Walter Lowrie. Princeton, NJ: Princeton University Press.

Kölbel, Max. 2011. 'Conversational Score, Assertion, and Testimony', in Jessica Brown and Herman Cappelen (eds), *Assertion: New Philosophical Essays*. Oxford: Oxford University Press, pp. 49–78.

Lackey, Jennifer. 2007. 'Norms of Assertion'. *Noûs* 41: 594–626.

Levin, Janet. 2008. 'Assertion, Practical Reason, and Pragmatic Theories of Knowledge'. *Philosophy and Phenomenological Research* 76: 359–84.

MacFarlane, John. 2005. 'Making Sense of Relative Truth'. *Proceedings of the Aristotelian Society* 105: 321–39.

MacFarlane, John. 2011. 'What is Assertion?', in Jessica Brown and Herman Capellen (eds), *Assertion: New Philosophical Essays*. Oxford: Oxford University Press, pp. 79–96.

Maimonides, Moses. 1963. *The Guide of the Perplexed*, vol 1, trans. Shlomo Pines. Chicago: University of Chicago Press.

Malcolm, Finlay and Michael Scott. Forthcoming. 'Faith, Belief and Fictionalism'. *Pacific Philosophical Quarterly*.

McFague, Sallie. 1983. *Metaphorical Theology: Models of God in Religious Language*. London: SCM Press.

Palamas, Gregory. 1983. *The Triads*, ed. John Meyendorff, trans. Nicholas Gendle. New Jersey: Paulist Press.

Peirce, C. S. 1934. 'Belief and Judgment'. In C. Hartshorne and P. Weiss (eds), *Collected Papers*, volume V. Cambridge, MA: Harvard University Press.

Phillips, D. Z. 1976. *Religion without Explanation*. Oxford: Blackwell.

Plantinga, Alvin. 2000. *Warranted Christian Belief*. New York: Oxford University Press.

Rawls, John. 1971. *A Theory of Justice*. Cambridge, MA: Harvard University Press.

Rescorla, Michael. 2009. 'Assertion and its Constitutive Norms'. *Philosophy and Phenomenological Research* 79: 98–130.

Santayana, George. 1905. *The Life of Reason*, vol III: *Reason in Religion*. New York: Scribner.

Schroeder, Mark. 2008. *Being For: Evaluating the Semantic Program of Expressivism*. Oxford: Clarendon Press.

Scott, Michael. 2013. *Religious Language*. Basingstoke: Palgrave Macmillan.

Searle, J. 1969. *Speech Acts: An Essay in the Philosophy of Language*. Cambridge: Cambridge University Press.

Soskice, Janet Martin. 1985. *Metaphor and Religious Language*. Oxford: Clarendon Press.

Stalnaker, Robert C. 1999. *Context and Content: Essays on Intentionailty in Speech and Thought*. Oxford: Oxford University Press.

Swinburne, Richard. 1993. *The Coherence of Theism*. Oxford: Oxford University Press.

Swinburne, Richard. 2005. *Faith and Reason*. Oxford: Oxford University Press.

Van Fraassen, Bas C. 1980. *The Scientific Image*, Oxford: Oxford University Press.

Van Inwagen, Peter. 2006. *The Problem of Evil: The Gifford Lectures Delivered in the University of St Andrews in 2003*. Oxford: Oxford University Press.

Watson, Gary. 2004. 'Asserting and Promising'. *Philosophical Studies* 117: 57–77.

Williamson, Timothy. 2000. *Knowledge and Its Limits*. Oxford: Oxford University Press.

Wittgenstein, Ludwig. 1994. *Culture and Value*, rev. edn, ed. G. H. von Wright, trans. P. Winch. Oxford: Blackwell.

Zagzebski, Linda Trinkaus. 2012. *Epistemic Authority: A Theory of Trust, Authority, and Autonomy in Belief*. New York: Oxford University Press.

13

There is no Free-Will Defense

James P. Sterba

My thesis is that there is no Free-Will Defense for the degree and amount of moral evil in our world. I am not denying the Free-Will Defense made famous by Alvin Plantinga which maintains that it is logically possible that any world that God would create with free creatures in it would have some moral evil in it as well, or at least, I am not denying this defense given my own interpretation of it. Rather, I am denying that God's creating our world with the degree and amount of moral evil that exists, or has existed, in it could be defended in terms of the freedom that it provides, or has provided, to its members. However, I am not denying that God's creating our world with all its evil could be justified on other grounds. Accordingly, it may be argued that the securing of some other good, or goods in an afterlife is the justification for the degree and amount of moral evil in our world. I am not contesting that possibility. My thesis here is simply that the freedom that exists, or has existed, in our world could not constitute a justification for the moral evil that exists, or has existed, in it.

I

My argument begins by noting that political states, particularly those aiming at securing a significant degree of justice for their members, are structured to secure a range of important freedoms for all their members even when doing so requires interfering with the freedoms of some of their members.[1]

---

[1] Alvin Plantinga understands important or significant freedom in a broader way than I am here. For Plantinga, to be significantly free is to be free with respect to an action that is morally significant, which is an action it would be wrong for an agent to perform but right to refrain from performing or vice versa. For me, significant freedoms are those freedoms a just political state would want to protect. Accordingly, evils that interfere with

For example, consider the laws against assault. Such laws are designed to help protect people against assault, where assault is understood characteristically as intentionally acting to cause serious physical injury to another person. These laws are thus designed to help secure freedom from assault by attempting to prevent assaults whenever possible, and when assaults do occur, they assist by having additional provisions for apprehending their perpetrators and restricting their freedom in appropriate ways. Such laws are clearly not structured so as never to interfere with the freedom of any of their members.

Thus, suppose that Nat, a law-enforcement officer, is responding to an emergency call in a state whose laws purport to secure a significant degree of justice, and she comes upon Matt who is about to assault Pat, his domestic partner. Here there is no question that Nat would take steps to stop Matt from carrying out his assault on Pat. She would not be concerned to allow Matt the freedom to carry out the harmful consequences of his act. Rather, she would be concerned to secure Pat's freedom from Matt's assault. The freedom of Matt to carry out his assault would have virtually no weight at all against Pat's freedom not to be assaulted by Matt.

Moreover, whenever such assaults occur, they result in a morally unacceptable distribution of freedom. What happens is that the freedom of the assaulters, a freedom no one ideally should have, is exercised at the expense of the freedom of their victims not to be assaulted, an important freedom that everyone ideally should have.[2]

Of course, even in just states, people can still fantasize about assaulting others. Think about Jackie Gleason's character, Ralph Kramden in *The Honeymooners* fantasizing about what he would do to his wife, Alice, played by Audrey Meadows.[3] People can even intend to carry out assaults, and take very general, multiple-use preparatory steps to do so. Yet it is only when they take clear steps toward committing an assault that normally they are interfered with in societies that purport to be just.

such liberties are, for me, significant evils. God, of course, could secure for us significant freedom in my sense and significant freedom in Plantinga's sense, but there is more justification for God, like the just political state, to focus, at least first, on securing significant freedom in my sense. My significant freedoms are like the freedom from assault, while Plantinga's significant freedoms include those freedoms and much more. See Alvin Plantinga, *God, Freedom and Evil* (New York: Harper Torchbacks, 1974) p. 30.

[2] I qualify my claim with "ideally" because under certain circumstances a reactive (or pre-emptive) assault against an actual (or would-be) assaulter can be justified used in order to put an end to (or prevent) an actual assault.

[3] Part of the humor in *The Honeymooners* was that both characters "knew," Alice from her wiser perspective, that Ralph would never do, or even intend to do, what he was fantasizing about doing.

Of course, not infrequently, even political states intent upon securing justice for their citizens are unsuccessful at constraining the freedom of would-be assaulters and protecting the freedom of their would-be victims. And there are many political states that are far less concerned about securing justice for their citizens where law enforcement officers just allow assaults to be committed, or even participate in carrying them out themselves. Still, the practice of constraining the freedom of would-be assaulters in favor of the freedom of their would-be victims is characteristic of societies that aim to be just.

II

Now in the law, assaults are acts that cause serious injury and thus impose significant evils on their victims. But are these evils horrendous evils? Marilyn Adams defines horrendous evils as evils "the participation in which (that is, the doing or suffering of which) constitutes prima facie reason to doubt whether the participant's life could (given their inclusion in it) be a great good to him/her on the whole."[4] Now while some assaults impose horrendous evils, as Adams defines them, some do not. Nor are horrendous evils, so defined, just a subclass of assaults. One reason for this is that some horrendous evils are the result of natural disasters, and so are not the result of assaults at all. Moreover, given that my focus is on the Free-Will Defense of moral evil, I am not concerned with outcomes, even horrendously evil ones, which are simply the result of natural forces. Rather, I am concerned with significant moral evil that results from human freedom or the lack thereof.[5]

Now it might be objected here that I cannot separate off natural evils in the way I propose because God, unlike humans, could be held to be morally responsible for natural evils. But while this objection has merit, I propose to set it aside, and simply focus on the question of whether a Free-Will Defense can exonerate God from responsibility for the moral evil in the world. So my attention is directed only at those significant moral evils that have their origin in human freedom and the lack thereof.

---

[4] Marilyn Adams, *Horrendous Evils and the Goodness of God* (Ithaca, NY: Cornell University Press, 1999), p. 26.
[5] I understand "significant moral evils that have their origin in the lack of freedom" to themselves have resulted, in turn, from morally wrong actions because otherwise they would not be lacks of freedom but lacks of something else.

III

This means that the evils I am concerned with represent a broader class of evils than those that simply result from assaults. In assaults, a freedom no one ideally should have is obtained by sacrificing the freedom of their victims to be without such assaults, which is an important freedom that everyone ideally should have.[6] This results in a morally unacceptable distribution of freedom in society. But obviously morally unacceptable distributions of freedom can come about by means other than assaults. So we need to consider not just the significant moral evils that result from assaults but the broader class of significant moral evils that have their origin in human freedom and the lack thereof.

Now to better appreciate this broader range of evils, consider conflicts between the rich and the poor. In these conflict situations, the rich, of course, have more than enough resources to satisfy their basic needs. In contrast, imagine that the poor lack the resources to meet their basic needs to secure a decent life for themselves even though they have tried all the means available to them that libertarians, who value freedom above all, regard as legitimate for acquiring such resources.[7]

Now the lack of resources to meet their basic needs clearly constitutes a significant evil for the poor. However, whether it is a moral evil or not depends on whether the poor are morally entitled to such resources.[8] So it is relevant that under circumstances like these, libertarians maintain that the rich should have the freedom to use their resources to satisfy their luxury needs if they so wish. Libertarians recognize that this freedom might well be enjoyed with the consequence that the satisfaction of the basic needs of the poor will not be met; they just think that freedom always has priority over other political ideals, and since they assume that the freedom of the poor is not at stake in such conflict situations, it is easy for them to conclude that the rich should not be required to sacrifice their freedom so that the basic

---

[6] With respect to the qualification "ideally," see n. 2.

[7] By "libertarians" here I mean "political libertarians" who, as I say in the text, value freedom above all. Accordingly, they also endorse the ideal that each person should have the greatest amount of freedom morally commensurate with the greatest amount of freedom for everyone else. The political libertarian is thus different from the metaphysical libertarian who endorses contra-causal freedom. However, in section VII, I show how the two are closely related.

[8] I think this is right. Assume that others should help you out in some regard, but only in a supererogatory sense. This would mean that you are not entitled to that help and others are not obligated to provide it. It does not seem then that the failure of others to provide that help would be a moral evil. It would be morally good for them to help you out, but their not doing so is not morally bad, and hence it is not a moral evil.

needs of the poor may be met. According to libertarians, therefore, the poor's lack of resources is not a moral evil imposed on them by the rich.

Of course, libertarians allow that it would be nice of the rich to share their surplus resources with the poor. Nevertheless, according to libertarians, such acts of charity are not required because the freedom of the poor is not thought to be at stake in such conflict situations. So, at least initially, libertarians do not see the poor as suffering from a moral evil at the hands of the rich because they do not see the freedom of the poor at stake in their conflict with the rich. As libertarians see it, the conflict is simply one between the freedom of the rich and the needs of the poor.

Now it turns out that libertarians are wrong about the conflict between the rich and the poor. They are right to see it as a conflict between the freedom of the rich and the needs of the poor. What they fail to see is that it is also a conflict between the freedom of the rich and the freedom of the poor. The freedom of the poor is truly at stake in such conflict situations with the rich. What is at stake is the freedom of the poor not to be interfered with in taking from the surplus possessions of the rich what is necessary to satisfy their basic needs.

Needless to say, libertarians want to deny that the poor have this freedom. But how can they justify such a denial? As this freedom of the poor has been specified, it is not a positive freedom to receive something but a negative freedom of non-interference. Clearly, what libertarians must do is recognize the existence of such a freedom and then claim that it unjustifiably conflicts with other freedoms of the rich. But when libertarians see that this is the case, they are often genuinely surprised for they had not previously seen the conflict between the rich and the poor as a conflict of freedoms.[9]

Now when the conflict between the rich and the poor is viewed as a conflict of freedoms, we can either say that the rich should have the freedom not to be interfered with in using their surplus resources for luxury purposes, or we can say that the poor should have the freedom not to be interfered with in taking from the rich what they require to meet their basic needs. If we choose one freedom, we must reject the other. What needs to be determined, therefore, is which freedom is morally enforceable: the freedom of the rich or the freedom of the poor.

Elsewhere, I have argued that the freedom of the poor, which is the freedom not to be interfered with in taking from the surplus resources of others what is required to meet one's basic needs, is morally enforceable over the

[9] Tibor Machan, *Libertarianism Defended* (Burlington, VT: Ashgate, 2006), ch. 20; Eric Mack, "Libertarianism Untamed," *Journal of Social Philosophy* (1991), pp. 64–72; Jan Narveson, *Libertarian Idea* (Peterborough, CA: Broadview Press, 2001) p. 35.

freedom of the rich, which is the freedom not to be interfered with in using one's surplus resources for luxury purposes.[10] This means that within the bundle of freedoms allotted to each person by the basic principle of libertarianism, there must be the freedom not to be interfered with (when one is poor) in taking from the surplus possessions of the rich what is necessary to satisfy one's basic needs. I argue that this must be part of the bundle that constitutes the greatest amount of freedom for each person because this freedom is morally superior to the freedom with which it directly conflicts, that is, the freedom not to be interfered with (when one is rich) in using one's surplus possessions to satisfy one's luxury needs.

So my argument is that a libertarian ideal of freedom, by favoring the freedom of the poor over the freedom of the rich, can be seen to support a right to welfare. Assuming further that we can meaningfully speak of distant peoples and future generations as having rights against us and we corresponding obligations to them, there is no reason not to extend my argument for a right to welfare to distant peoples and future generations. This is because for libertarians, fundamental rights are universal rights, that is, rights possessed by all people, not just those who live in certain places or at certain times.

Of course, to claim that rights are universal does not mean that they are universally recognized. Rather, to claim that rights are universal, despite their spotty recognition, implies only that they ought to be recognized because people at all times and places have or could have had good reasons to recognize these rights, not that they actually did or do so.

Nor need universal rights be unconditional. This is particularly true in the case of the right to welfare, which is conditional upon people doing all that they reasonably can be expected to do to provide for themselves. In addition, this right is conditional upon there being sufficient resources available so that everyone's welfare needs can be met. So where people do not do all that they can reasonably be expected to do to provide for themselves, or where there are not sufficient resources available, people do not normally have a right to welfare.

Given the universal and conditional character of this libertarian right to welfare, I argue that this right should be extended to distant peoples, and I agree with Peter Singer that this can be done at minimal costs to the rich. But, unlike Singer, I don't stop with distant peoples. I further argue that this right should be extended to future generations. The upshot is that until we have a technological fix, recognizing a universal right to welfare applicable

---

[10] Most recently, in *From Rationality to Equality* (Oxford: Oxford University Press, 2015).

both to existing and future people requires us to use up no more resources than are necessary for meeting our own basic needs, thus securing for ourselves a decent life but no more. For us to use up more resources than this, without a technological fix, we would be guilty of depriving at least some future generations of the resources they would require to meet their own basic needs, thereby violating their libertarian-based right to welfare. Obviously, this would impose a significant sacrifice on existing generations, particularly those in the developed world, clearly a far greater sacrifice than Singer maintains is required for meeting the basic needs of existing generations. Nevertheless, these demands do follow from a libertarian-based right to welfare. In effect, then, recognizing a right to welfare, applicable to all existing and future people, leads to an equal utilization of resources over place and time.

Now my argument is that the libertarian ideal of freedom leads to a right to welfare which, of course, welfare liberals endorse, and that this right to welfare extended to distant peoples and future generations leads to the equality that socialists endorse. Assuming that my argument is correct, it shows how far we are from a morally defensible distribution of significant freedom in most societies across the world, and that this has been true throughout most of human history.[11]

Yet even if one did not accept my argument, it would still be hard to reject its conclusion that we have not yet achieved a morally acceptable distribution of significant freedom in most societies around the world and that this has been true throughout most of human history. As we noted earlier, even in political states that aim at securing justice for their members, their laws against assault still operate imperfectly, and thus result in a distribution of freedom that is unjust to some degree. The problem is more severe when we consider the effect that significant evils other than assaults have on the distribution of freedom in society. Here I would maintain, particularly in the economic arena, that the rate of failure even in political states that aim to be just is much more pronounced, because, unlike cases of assault, the maldistribution of significant freedom is less easy to see. Of course, problems are much more severe in political states that are far less, or not at all, concerned about justice for their members. Accordingly, we humans have almost always lived in societies that are marred, or even characterized, by unjust distributions of freedom. We either have brought about the injustice

---

[11] Although prehistoric humans did not aggress against their natural environments as much as we do today, they did unnecessarily drive many species into extinction and thereby threaten the basic needs of future generations, and they also failed to secure a morally acceptable distribution of freedom in their existing in-group and between group relations.

ourselves, simply benefited from it, or even when not benefiting from it have not done what we can to correct it. Alternatively, we ourselves may be the victims who are suffering under injustice. In any case, that there is an unjust distribution of freedom in virtually all societies around the world, and that this has been true for most of human history seems difficult to challenge.

The clear upshot is that we humans are at least partially responsible for the unjust distribution of freedom that has characterized human history. The world would be far more just if many of us acted differently, if we did more to bring about a just society. There is no escaping the blame that many of us bear. We could do better, but we don't, and people in the past could have done better as well.

IV

Suppose, however, there were among us persons with superhuman powers for making our societies more just than they are. Suppose comic book and cinematic persons like Superman, Wonder Woman, Spider-Man, and Xena really did exist. What would we expect of them? Would we not expect them to do what they can to make our societies more just than they are, and thereby bring about a better distribution of significant freedom?

Now it is true that these fictional superheroes are often pitted against supervillains who rival them in power. However, from time to time, these superheroes come up against ordinary villains, and it just takes a minimal exercise of their superhuman powers for them to prevent significant evils from occurring, thereby, securing significant freedoms for those who would otherwise suffer those evils. And when that happens, no one really protests, except possibly the villains themselves. In fact, inaction by the superheroes in such contexts is broadly condemned by virtually everyone, again, save the villains themselves.

Spider-Man/Peter Parker, for example, is exercised by the motto: With great power, there must also come great responsibility. It is in fact pressed upon him by his Uncle Ben who raised him just before his uncle dies in a tragic set of circumstances that result, in part, from Spider-Man's initial failure to live by that motto. After the death of his uncle, Spider-Man does strive to live by the motto, and his main problem becomes how to do so while still maintaining some kind of a personal life. Similar commitments are also made by other superheroes, although they too have comparable difficulties figuring out how to live by those commitments while maintaining a personal life.

Nevertheless, among superheroes, the idea that they should limit the freedom of would-be villains to protect would-be victims is just taken for granted. Of course, superheroes are more frequently shown protecting people from serious assault. They are less frequently portrayed as protecting people from the significant evils of an unjust economic system, thereby securing people's freedom in that area of their lives. This may be because showing just transfers of income from the rich to the poor do not tend to make great theater. One place where this has been effectively dramatized, however, is in the semi-fictional account of the adventures of Robin Hood, where a dispossessed nobleman, Robin of Loxley, fights against the attempt by the Sheriff of Nottingham to deprive people—especially poor people— of their rightful property. So inspiring is this moral tale that the hero's name has come to be applied to virtually anyone who uses extra-legal, but justi- fied, means to transfer economic resources from the rich to the poor. Thus, at least in the world of comic book and cinematic superheroes, much is done to bring about a more just distribution of significant freedoms in soci- ety, and we, who also imaginatively live in that world, generally think this is the way it should be.[12]

V

Why then in the actual world couldn't God, like the superheroes in our fictional world, be more involved in preventing evils that result in the loss of significant freedom for their victims?

Consider the case of Matthew Shepard who was befriended by two men in a bar in Laramie, Wyoming in 1998. The two men, who were reportedly anti-gay, offered to give Shepard a lift and then drove him to a remote loca- tion where they robbed, severely beat, and tortured him, and then left him to die hanging on a fence, where he lapsed into unconsciousness and was discovered the next day by a passing cyclist who thought he was a scarecrow. Shepard died two days later in a Laramie hospital never having regained consciousness.[13]

---

[12] For more on the role superheroes have in our moral imagination, see *The Gospel According to Superheroes*, ed. B.J. Oropeza (New York: Peter Lang, 2008) and *Superheroes and Philosophy: Truth, Justice and the Socratic Way*, ed. Tom Morris and Matt Morris (Peru, IL: Open Court, 2005).

[13] For more on the Matthew Shepard story, see Judy Shepard, *The Meaning of Matthew: My Son's Murder in Laramie and a World Transformed* (New York: Hudson Street Press, 2009). There is now conflicting evidence surrounding exactly why Matthew Shepard was killed. At the trial, there was testimony that the two men "just wanted to beat [Shepard]

Now surely God could have intervened in this case, maybe just by causing the car Shepard was in to have a flat tire as it was being driven out of the bar's parking lot. Then Shepard could have gotten a ride with someone else or walked to his lodging near the University of Wyoming campus where he was a first-year student. Now if God had done this, Shepard's two assailants would still have been able to freely imagine, intend, and even take initial steps toward carrying out their presumably anti-gay motivated robbery, torture, and murder of Shepard. They would just have been prevented from carrying out the final step of their action with its horrible consequences for their victim. Their freedom not to be interfered with in taking action to bring about the anti-gay motived robbery, torture, and murder of Matthew Shepard would surely have been restricted by God's causing them to have a flat tire. But clearly that was not an important freedom for them to have. Even the legal authorities in Laramie had taken steps to prevent their residents from exercising such freedom. Their laws were just not that effective. The authorities surely did not think that would-be assailants should have the freedom to assault their intended victims.

Consider as well the very significant freedom Matthew Shepard would have enjoyed if the freedom of his would-be assailants had been restricted in this regard. He would have enjoyed the freedom not to be assaulted, tortured, and murdered which would have presumably led to his enjoying other freedoms such as the freedom to complete his education and the freedom to find meaningful work.[14] Surely, these and other freedoms that Shepard would have enjoyed if his assault had been prevented are a lot more important than the freedom his assailants exercised. This is clearly why virtually no one would protest the action of a superhero who would prevent the harmful consequences of the actions of Shepard's would-be assailants in order to secure such important freedoms for Shepard. There seems to be no question about what a more morally justified distribution of freedom would look like in this case.

---

up bad enough to teach him a lesson not to come on to straight people," but now there is other evidence brought to light by Stephen Jimenez in his *The Book of Matt: Hidden Truths about the Murder of Matthew Shepard* (Hanover, NH: Steerforth Press, 2013) that drugs may have figured importantly in the killing. However, the exact motives of Shepard's killers is not relevant to determining the net loss of significant freedoms resulting from his death, which is what I am concerned about in this paper.

[14] These last two freedoms should be more fully expressed as the freedom not to be interfered with in completing an education and the freedom not to be interfered with in finding meaningful work.

VI

Yet what if God, a superhero, or someone else had intervened and prevented Shepard's murder so that he was able to continue on with his life. Suppose that Shepard later chose to be a pro-gay vigilante who sought out people with anti-gay sentiments and did to them what his unsuccessful assailants had intended to do to him. Would this then show that failing to prevent Shepard's assault would have been justified because it would have resulted in preventing the far more horrendous evils that Shepard would have gone on to commit himself?

Surely this does raise a problem with regard to the justification for preventing the assault on Shepard. However, the appropriate solution would not be for God or someone with superhuman powers to permit the assault against Shepard, but rather for the intervener to go on to prevent any further significant assaults by Shepard that he would attempt in the future. In each such case, the intervention would restrict a not very important freedom of the would-be assailant in order to secure significant freedoms for those who would otherwise be victims. Surely, that would be the best way to bring about a morally defensible distribution of freedom in this regard.

Now consider a different scenario. Consider the possibility that allowing the loss of significant freedoms in the present could lead either to either a gain in significant freedoms in the future or to the prevention of the loss of significant freedoms in the future. So in the case of Matthew Shepard, imagine that the loss of significant freedom for Shepard could lead to the gain of significant freedom in the future. Actually, as things turned out, this was, in fact, the case. Shepherd's death did result in the freedom for Shepard's mother to respond to his death by building support for a federal law that better protected gays and lesbians from discrimination as well as the freedom for Shepard's assailants to respond to his death by repenting their actions and reforming themselves. Although it does not appear that Shepard's assailants took advantage of these freedoms, they were still available to them. However, these freedoms, even taken together, are in no way as significant as the freedoms that Shepard lost, and so they alone could not justify that loss. In fact, something like these same freedoms would still have been available to Shepard's mother and to his assailants even if Shepard had not suffered his horrible loss. Thus, Shepard's mother would still have had the freedom, maybe this time in cooperation with her son, to take on the task of building support for a federal law that better protected gays and lesbians from discrimination. Likewise, Shepard's assailants would still have had the freedom to repent their discriminatory ways and reform themselves, even if they had not murdered Shepard. The only way that allowing

Shepard's loss of significant freedom could ever possibly be justified in terms of freedom is if that loss had been logically necessary to secure a greater gain in comparable freedoms or to prevent a greater loss of comparable freedoms in the future.

Thus, suppose you are in circumstances where if you intervened to stop a deadly assault on someone you end up exposing a large group of people to the same kind of deadly assault. Surely, in such circumstances, given your lack of power to affect a better resolution, you would be justified in allowing the deadly assault on the one person. But this is nothing like Matthew Shepard's case. The particular freedoms of Shepard's mother and his assailants that are logically connected to his murder are clearly not as important as the freedoms that Shepard would lose in order for them to obtain those freedoms. Moreover, as we noted, there are comparable freedoms that Shepard's mother and his assailants would have even without the loss of his life. Even if there were a causal chain extending from Shepard's murder through the action of his mother in building support for a federal law that better protected gays and lesbians to an actual reduction of deadly assaults on gays and lesbians, there is nothing logically necessary in such a train of events. Surely, an Omni-God, or even humans operating under circumstances where Shepard's murder had been prevented, could have achieved those same good results. So clearly for God, and even for us, there was no way that failing to prevent Matthew Shepard's murder could have been justified in terms of a gain in significant freedom or the prevention of a loss of significant freedom in the future when compared to the loss of significant freedom that resulted from his murder.

So clearly with respect to the board range of actual cases in the world, God has not chosen to secure the significant freedoms of those who are morally entitled to those freedoms by restricting others from exercising freedoms that they are not morally entitled to exercise. As a consequence, significant moral evil has resulted that could otherwise have been prevented. So if God is justified in permitting such moral evils, it has to be on grounds other than freedom because an assessment of the freedoms that are at stake would require God to act preventively to secure a morally defensible distribution of freedom, which, of course, God has not done. So if God is to be justified with respect to cases like Matthew Shepard's, it must be because there is a justification for God's inaction in terms other than freedom. It would have to be a justification for permitting moral evil on the grounds that it secures some other good, or goods in this life, or other goods in an afterlife. Now I am not contesting the possibility of that sort of a justification for the moral evil in our world here. What I am claiming here is simply that the freedom that exists, or has existed, or even will exist, in our world could not constitute the justification for the moral evil that exists, or has existed, in it. My claim is simply that there is no Free-Will Defense of the moral evil that exists in this world now or in the past.

VII

Yet how does my argument against the Free-Will Defense relate to Plantinga's attempt to advance that defense beyond his solution to the so-called logical problem of evil?[15] Plantinga's solution to the so-called logical problem of evil depends on the claim that it may not be within God's power to bring about a world containing moral good but no moral evil. Plantinga argued that this is because to bring about a world containing moral good, God would have to permit humans to act freely, and it may well be that in every possible world where God actually permits humans to act freely, every human being would suffer from a malady that Plantinga labeled Transworld Depravity (TD), and so every human being would act wrongly at least to some degree. However, recently Richard Otte has shown that given Plantinga's original definition of TD, it is necessarily false that all human essences would suffer from TD.[16] Otte went on to helpfully offer a different definition of TD that is free of this logical difficulty.[17] Yet other philosophers have questioned whether TD, however formulated, is any more plausible than Transworld Sanctity (TS), an opposing view that holds that necessarily at least one human essence in any world God actualized would never act wrongly.[18] Faced with such dissension, Plantinga has entertained another suggestion from Otte that all he really needs to counter the argument from

[15] I refer here to "the so-called logical problem of evil" because, as I explain below, the proposed solution I favor depends on a moral principle that applies to both God and ourselves, and to the logical relations of that principle to the circumstances in which we find ourselves. Now it may turn out that a defensible solution to the problem of evil that takes into account the degree and amount of evil in the world also depends on the logical relations between certain moral principles and the circumstances in which we find ourselves. If so, we would not have any good reason to call one problem of evil a logical problem, but not the other.

[16] Richard Otte, "Transworld Depravity and Unobtainable Worlds," *Philosophy and Phenomenological Research* (2009) pp. 165–77.

[17] Otte, "Transworld Depravity," pp. 168–73.

[18] See Daniel Howard-Snyder, "The Logical Problem of Evil," in *The Blackwell Companion to The Problem of Evil*, ed. Justin McBrayer and Daniel Howard-Synder (Malden, MA: John Wiley and Sons, 2013), pp. 19–33) and Daniel Howard-Synder and John O'Leary-Hawthorne, "Transworld Sanctity and Plantinga's Free Will Defense," *International Journal for Philosophy of Religion* (1998) pp. 1–21. See also Alexander Pruss, "A Counterexample to Plantinga's Free Will Defense," *Faith and Philosophy* (2012),

evil posed by John Mackie is simply to espouse the One Wrong Thesis (OW), which just claims that if God tried to actualize a morally perfect world, at least one human being would act wrongly.[19] Thus, OW makes no assumption, as TD does, about how all human beings would act.

No doubt, OW is far more plausible than TD, and thus more useful for a solution to the so-called logical problem of evil. Nevertheless, I think there is a better way to approach the problem of evil posed by Mackie. The general approach favored by Plantinga and others has been to come up with possible, even plausible, constraints on God's power that would serve to account for evil in the world. But what about seeing evil in the world as required by God's goodness rather than simply by constraints on God's power?[20] Surely, we have no difficulty seeing at least some of the natural evil in the world in this light. Think, for example, of the pain most of us experience when we get too close to fire. Clearly, a good God would want us to experience pain in such contexts. Now consider a doctor who pushes and shoves her way through a crowded subway in order to come to the aid of someone who is having a heart attack. Or, *pace* Kant, consider your not being fully honest with a temporarily depressed friend to keep him from committing suicide.[21] Arguably, a good God would have no difficulty permitting (hence, not interfering with) such minor moral wrongs, given the greater good that would thereby result. Fortunately, that admission is all that is needed to solve the problem of evil posed by Mackie. It is a solution based on an appeal to God's goodness rather than simply to any constraint on God's power.[22] So the idea is to appeal to God's goodness to explain why

pp. 400–15. Michael Bergmann, "Might-Counterfactuals, Transworld Untrustworthiness and Plantinga's Free Will Defense," *Faith and Philosophy* (1999), pp. 336–51.

[19] Otte, "Transworld Depravity," p.173ff.

[20] There is also an important advantage to my approach. On Plantinga's view, the explanation of at least some moral evil in the world is the constraints on God's power, and these constraints come from the truth of counterfactuals of freedom. But there doesn't seem to be any further explanation for why these counterfactuals are true. (See Robert Adams, "Plantinga and the Problem of Evil," in *Alvin Plantinga*, ed. James Tomberlin and Peter van Inwagen (Dordrecht: Reidel, 1985), pp. 225–33.) On my account, the explanation for some moral evil in the world is God's goodness, and we are helped in understanding how a good God would permit some moral evil by analogy with how good human beings would permit moral evil in comparable circumstances. In this way, I think we can have a more satisfying explanation of the compatibility of the existence of God with some moral evil.

[21] Imagine you are certain that your friend will come back to you later after he gets over his temporary depression and profusely thank you for not being fully honest with him in these circumstances.

[22] Notice that while the human agents act as they do in these cases partly because of limitations of power, God's permissive acts are to achieve some good.

God's power has not been exercised in a certain regard rather than appeal to (a limitation of) God's power to explain why God has not done some particular good.

Notice that underlying this alternative approach to solving the problem of evil posed by Mackie is a commitment to the following moral principle:

Every moral agent has reason not to interfere with the free actions of other moral agents when the slightly harmful consequences of their actions would lead to a significant good.   (NI)

NI holds of ourselves, but it also holds of God, and, on that account, it permits a solution to the problem of evil posed by Mackie. And, this seems right. The morality that is operative here is appropriately a morality that applies to all moral agents, ourselves as well as God. Clearly, what we now need to do is turn to the task of determining what moral principles holding of God and ourselves apply to the degree and amount of moral evil in the world.

Yet I don't think this new task should be seen as moving from a logical problem of evil to something else—an evidential problem of evil. In dealing with the so-called logical problem of evil posed by Mackie, I argued that it could be solved by appealing to the moral principle NI, which we should take to hold of God and ourselves. Thus, given NI, any world that God would create with human beings in it would have some moral evil in it as well. Thus, given NI, the existence of God and (some) moral evil are logically compatible.

Accordingly, in attempting to determine the compatibility of God and the degree and amount of moral evil in our world, I see no reason to think that we are dealing with a really different kind of problem of evil from the one posed by Mackie. To me, it looks like just another logical problem of evil where the question at issue is whether there are moral principles that hold of ourselves, and should hold of God as well, which are consistent or inconsistent with the existence of God.

Now it may be that we will not be able to come up with any moral principles that can conclusively be shown to hold of God and ourselves in this regard. Maybe there will turn out to be just good reasons favoring moral principles compatible with the existence of God, and comparably good reasons favoring alternative moral principles that are incompatible with the existence of God. If that happens, then, we may end up with an "evidential" problem of evil after all. Still, at first blush, we appear to be facing just another logical problem of evil involving an appeal to moral principles, no different in kind from the one to which we appealed to deal with the problem of evil originally posed by Mackie.

Now Plantinga also wanted to extend his Free-Will Defense and show that the existence of God is logically compatible with a world that has at least as much moral evil in it as does our world. So he imagined God creating us and placing us in a situation where we are free and where, Plantinga claimed, the amount of moral evil that exists in the world is simply the result of how we exercise that freedom. Here Plantinga assumed that God cannot act otherwise without reducing the freedom in the world and thereby also reducing the moral good that comes from exercising that freedom.

Yet Plantinga's extended Free-Will solution to the problem of the degree and amount of moral evil in the world fails to take into account that there are two ways that God can promote freedom in the world. It recognizes that God can promote freedom by not interfering with our free actions. However, it fails to recognize that God can also promote freedom, in fact, promote far greater significant freedom, by actually interfering with the freedom of some of us at certain times. God's relevant activity for Plantinga appears to be limited to simply creating us and making us free. For Plantinga, what happens after that, particularly the evil consequences that result from our actions, is our responsibility, not God's. But it is far more plausible to see God as also interacting with us continually over time, always having the option of either interfering or not interfering with our actions, and especially with the consequences of our actions.[23]

Of course, the same holds true for ourselves. We frequently have the option of interfering or not interfering with the freedom of others, and we have to decide what we should do. Because Plantinga failed to see that God, in particular, can promote more significant freedom over time by sometimes interfering with our free actions, he failed to see that the problem of the compatibility of God and the degree and amount of moral evil that actually exists in the world is not settled by just noting God's act of creation and placing us in an initial situation where we are free. We have to further take into account the extent to which God has promoted freedom by restricting the far less significant freedom of some of us in order to secure the far more significant freedom of others.

Nor would it do to claim that the freedom relied on by the Free-Will Defense is contra-causal freedom, not the freedom as non-interference cherished by political libertarians. This is because contra-causal freedom presupposes freedom as non-interference: you cannot be contra-causally

[23] It seems clear that the idea that God would, or should, be continually intervening in human affairs to secure the more important freedoms of would-be victims at the expense of the less significant freedoms of would-be wrongdoers is not part of his Free-Will Defense.

free to do X if you are interfered with such that you are kept from doing X. To have contra-causal freedom, you must have freedom as non-interference as well. Moreover, if you lack the contra-causal freedom to do X, according to the defenders of this analysis of freedom, this is frequently because you also lack the freedom of non-interference with respect to doing X. Nevertheless, for defenders of this analysis of freedom, there can be other explanations for the lack of contra-causal freedom, such as inner compulsions or crippling fears. Still, the connection between contra-causal freedom and freedom as non-interference is understood to be quite close, and supporters of the Free-Will Defense must acknowledge that this is the case.[24] The loss of the one sort of freedom is tantamount to a loss of the other; a gain in the one is tantamount to a gain in the other.[25]

Nor does my critique of the Free-Will Defense depend on there being counterfactuals of freedom to which God would have access. In fact the whole Molinist debate in philosophy of religion turns out to be irrelevant to my critique. For my critique to work, God doesn't need to be able to determine our internal free acts, something that if indeterminism is true even God may not be able to do, according to Molinism. Rather, for my critique to work, God simply needs to be able to prevent the external consequences of our significant or horrendous immoral acts, something that superheroes or even well-placed third parties should be able to do.

Even on a contra-causal account of free action, there is a point where the significantly evil consequences of free acts have a purely causal history (their contra-causal origins coming before this purely causal history begins). At that point, an omniscient and all-powerful God would surely be aware of these causal processes as they get going to divert them or put a stop to them.[26] In so doing, God would be interfering with the less significant freedom of would-be wrongdoers for the sake of securing the more significant freedom of their would-be victims.

---

[24] The same connections with freedom as non-interference obtains if one rejects contra-freedom in favor of compatibilist freedom.

[25] Nor would it do to claim that the freedom that is at issue here is an inner freedom of the will that could not be effected at all by external intervention. This is because if that were the only freedom that was at issue here, God could have prevented all the evil in the world without interfering with this freedom at all. Thus, freedom in this sense provides no grounds at all for why God does not intervene. For this conception of freedom, see Rene Descartes, *Passions of the Soul* I Article XLI and Rogers Albritton, "Freedom of Will and Freedom of Action," *Proceedings and Addresses of the American Philosophical Association* (1985), pp. 239–51.

[26] I want to thank Tom Flint and Linda Zagzebski for helping me work through this point.

VIII

Now we have seen that political states, especially those that aim to achieve a certain degree of justice, are committed to restricting the far less significant freedoms of would-be aggressors in order to secure the far more significant freedoms of their would-be victims. We have also seen that political states can restrict freedoms in other areas, particularly the economic sphere, with the same justification for promoting more significant freedoms. And something similar holds true for us as individuals. We too have options to promote greater and more significant freedoms by restricting some people's lesser freedoms.

In our imaginations, we have also taken on the task of promoting significant freedoms by conceiving of superheroes restricting the freedoms of ordinary villains to prevent them from restricting the more significant freedoms of their would-be victims. Given that there is much that political states and individuals still have not done to promote significant freedom in the world, superheroes manage to play an important role in our imaginations bringing about a more just distribution of significant freedom than exists in the world as we find it. For many of us, the role that superheroes play in our imaginations closely parallels the role we ourselves think we should play in the actual world if we only had the superhuman powers to do so.

Accordingly, the actual world we live in is such that there is much more that God could have done to promote significant freedom in it. The problem is not with God's creating us and giving us free will. Rather, the real problem comes later in time when God fails to restrict the lesser freedoms of wrongdoers to secure the more significant freedoms of their victims. Hence, the world we live in cannot be justified by the distribution and amount of significant freedom that is in it. There are too many ways that political states and human individuals could have increased the amount of significant freedom by restricting lesser freedoms of would-be wrongdoers. Likewise, there is much that God could have done to promote freedom by restricting freedom that simply has not been done.

So we cannot say that God's justification for permitting the moral evil in the world is the freedom that is in it because God could have reduced the moral evil in the world by increasing the freedom in the world, and that has not been done. Hence, there is no Free-Will Defense of the degree and amount of moral evil in the world. If the moral evil in the world is justified it cannot be because of the freedom in the world, because God could have decreased the moral evil in the world by justifiably restricting the freedoms of some to promote significant freedoms for others. Accordingly, if there is a justification for the moral evil in the world that renders it compatible with the existence of God, it has to be in terms of something other than the distribution and amount of freedom in our world. The justification would have to be provided in terms of securing of some other good, or goods, or securing the freedom that exists, or will exist, in an afterlife. Once then it is settled that there is no Free-Will Defense of the moral evil in this world, we need to take up the question of whether the moral principles that govern the production and distribution of other goods can serve to justify God's permission of the degree and amount of moral evil in the world as we know it. If we are successful in finding such a justification we will have a defense of the degree and amount of moral evil in the world. But it will not be a Free-Will Defense.

Still, a critic might respond that while I have shown that the degree and amount of moral evil that exists in the world cannot be justified by the distribution and amount of freedom in the world, I have not, by my own admission, shown that the evil could not be justified by the amount and distribution of moral good that is in the world. This is true. But if this is all that the Free-Will Defense wants to hold then the view is surely mischaracterized as a "Free-Will Defense," and should really be called a Greater Moral Good Defense, since it concedes that our world has considerably less significant freedom and as a result considerably more moral evil in it than God could have otherwise effected.[27] Moreover, this Greater Moral Good Defense itself requires a defense. As I suggested earlier, there is a need to show that moral principles binding on ourselves and on God would permit the trade-off of our significant freedoms in our world in order to secure more moral good. Accordingly, even allowing that I have shown that there that really is no Free-Will Defense, it remains to be seen whether there a Greater Moral Good Defense for the lack of significant freedom and the consequent greater moral evil that exists in our world.[28]

[27] The idea here is that God by not preventing significant evils in our world thereby increases the amount of evil that comes into our world and thereby also decreases that amount of significant freedom in our world that the evils themselves eliminate.

[28] For their helpful comments on earlier versions of this paper, I wish to thank Robert Audi, Justin Christy, Samuel Lebens, Nevin Climenhaga, Evan Fales, Thomas Flint, Samuel Newlands, Alvin Plantinga, Meghan Schmitt, Meghan Sullivan, and Stephen Wykstra, as well as thank the John Templeton Foundation for their financial support.

14

How to Think of Religious Commitment as a Ground for Moral Commitment: A Thomistic Perspective on the Moral Philosophies of John Cottingham and Raimond Gaita

Mark R. Wynn

1. INTRODUCTION

John Cottingham has argued that certain traits that are widely considered ideals of character will only count as virtues granted the truth of a religious worldview or 'background of significance', so giving those with the relevant moral commitments a reason for subscribing to theism. Writing from an atheistic or perhaps agnostic perspective, Raimond Gaita has proposed that the language of religion provides a useful aid for the moral imagination, by allowing us to occupy a possibly fictional vantage point from which certain truths about our fellow human beings, and the claims they make upon us, become newly salient. In this paper, I aim to show how Thomas Aquinas's category of infused moral virtue can be used to extend and integrate the work of these influential authors, so as to produce a further, broadly based account of the relationship of religious and moral commitment.

Since they set out their respective positions relatively briefly, I shall begin by expounding and at points sympathetically elaborating upon the views of Cottingham and Gaita, in order to present each approach in its strongest form. I shall then consider how each can be further developed by appeal to Thomas Aquinas's account of the goods that are the object of the infused moral virtues. I begin with Cottingham's case.

2. INTERPRETING COTTINGHAM'S CASE

In his book *Why Believe?* John Cottingham has argued that various widely acknowledged ideals of character—notably those of hope, humility, gratitude, and wonder or awe—fit very readily within a theistic conception of human beings and their metaphysical context, but can be subsumed only with some difficulty, if at all, within rival metaphysical schemes.[1] It is an implication of Cottingham's account that many of our contemporaries subscribe to a conception of the virtues that derives from the predominantly theistic culture of former centuries, from which 'our' culture (the culture of early twenty-first century, urban, western people) has arisen. And our culture, on this view, exhibits a kind of incoherence, for while many of us no longer count ourselves as theists, we have retained our allegiance to various ideals of character whose natural home conceptually is within a theistic worldview; and collectively we have failed to notice that in these respects our moral commitments have come adrift from our worldview.[2]

I am going to take as one example of this line of argument Cottingham's proposal that hope as an ideal of character makes good sense given a theistic worldview and not otherwise. Once again, it is worth recalling that his discussion of this point forms part of a larger case that extends to other virtues, such as humility and gratitude. Here is an excerpt from his account of hope:

'O Israel, *trust* in the Lord,' says the Psalmist, 'for in him there is mercy, and in him is plenteous redemption.' Or again, 'I *hope* for the Lord; my soul doth *wait* for him; in his word is my *trust*.' [Ps. 129[130]:5–7] , , , [T]here is no proper placeholder for these traits in classical virtue theory. On the contrary, one of the characteristic features of ancient Greek thought, both in Aristotle and in the tradition he inherited, was a distinctly sober, not to say gloomy, awareness of how often hopes can be disappointed, of how easily human life can be overturned, even for the most virtuous and prosperous, by the swings of fortune. 'Call no man happy until he is dead', ran the proverb, etched deep into the mindset of most of the philosophers and poets of classical antiquity. But the cry of Job, 'Though he slay me, yet will I trust in him'

---

[1] See *Why Believe?* (London: Continuum, 2009). Cottingham has also argued that the categorical form of some moral norms fits best within the context of a theistic worldview. See, for example, his essay 'The Source of Goodness', in H. Harris, ed., *God, Goodness and Philosophy* (Aldershot: Ashgate, 2011), ch. 2. But for present purposes, I am going to concentrate on his claim that certain familiar ideals of life are best understood in theistic terms.

[2] Of course, this general thesis is familiar from other contexts. See for example Alasdair MacIntyre, *After Virtue* (London: Duckworth, 2nd edn 1985), and Friedrich Nietzsche, 'Twilight of the Idols, or How to Philosophise with a Hammer', in Friedrich Nietzsche, *The Anti-Christ, Ecce Homo, Twilight of the Idols*, tr. J. Norman, ed. A. Ridley and J. Norman (Cambridge: Cambridge University Press, 2005), pp. 153–230.

[Job 1:4] or St Paul's 'neither height nor depth nor...things present nor things to come...shall be able to separate us from the love of God' [Rom. 8:38], express something quite outside the range of this classical fatalism: an indomitable determination to trust and to keep hope alive, to 'hope against hope', as Paul put it in his letter to the Romans [Rom. 4:18].[3]

Although the hope that interests Cottingham here is clearly God-directed, he is not making the superficial point that hope in the biblical or theistic God is not evident in classical traditions. He is referring to a certain demeanour in life, a certain confidence in how things will turn out, or at least a certain confidence in how we can receive events, however they turn out; and if classical culture does not exhibit this sort of confidence this is not trivially because Aristotle and others did not have the concept of, let alone believe in, the biblical God, but because their worldview does not invite this sort of confidence in the way things will turn out, or in how events can be received however they turn out. In the remainder of this essay, I shall read the notion of 'hope' in this way.[4]

So Cottingham's case turns in part on a cultural observation: look at non-theistic cultures, and you will find that they simply do not think about, or at least do not recognize as an ideal, the kind of trust that is considered normative for human beings in biblical traditions. Of course, making this case in full would be a challenging task: it would require reviewing not only the cultures of the Greco-Roman world but any number of other cultures as well, to show that the confidence in question is found in, and only in, theistic societies—along with societies such as our own, which derive from a theistic culture, even if they are not themselves uniformly theistic. Even if this sort of cross-cultural generalization were possible, we would still want some account of what it is in the worldview of theistic cultures that enables such hope, and what it is in the worldview of non-theistic cultures that prevents its emergence, to assure ourselves that we are dealing here with a relevant causal or conceptual connection. So as presented here, Cottingham's case is not meant to be conclusive: it is intended simply to shake us into a recognition that the traits that many of us count as virtues have not been considered as virtues in other cultures. And on this basis, he is inviting his

---

[3] *Why Believe?*, pp. 154–5.

[4] Of course, some strands of classical culture, notably Stoicism, include the idea of a divine, providential ordering of events. To the extent that these traditions reproduce relevant elements of the biblical worldview then Cottingham would, I take it, allow that there is nothing to prevent them regarding hope in his extended sense as a virtue. Aristotle himself believed that there was a God, but this is not a God with knowledge of the world, let alone one who exercises providential care of the world. So for present purposes, I shall not count Aristotle as a 'monotheist'.

reader to ask: mustn't there be something distinctive about our culture (or the earlier cultures from which our culture's values derive) that will explain why this conception of the virtues should have flourished here but not elsewhere?

Alongside this case from cultural observation, Cottingham has a further line of argument, which aims to establish that this cultural correlation does indeed rest on a conceptual connection. In the recent philosophical literature, there have been various attempts to construct secular counterparts for traditional theistic virtues such as hope. Cottingham finds these accounts unpersuasive, and takes their failure as further evidence of the integral connection between theistic assumptions and the kind of hope that is exemplified in the biblical narratives. Here, for example, is his summary of Erik Wielenberg's search for a secular counterpart to the theistic ideal of hope in his book *Value and Virtue in a Godless Universe*:

> The central theological virtue of hope, maintained in the face of radical vulnerability and the ever-present human tendency to buckle under external misfortune or internal weakness, becomes for Wielenberg a confidence in the power of science to ameliorate our lot (including by pharmacological means), pointing us towards 'the upper limits of justice and happiness' that 'remain to be discovered'.[5]

From Cottingham's point of view, the difficulty for a Wielenbergian conception of the human condition is not, of course, that it cannot ground any kind of trust or hope. It is possible after all to have a well-grounded hope in the capacity of the sciences to effect fundamental change in human lives in various respects. For Cottingham, the difficulty is, rather, that this hope is very far from the encompassing, life-sustaining kind of confidence that is depicted in the biblical texts that we noted just now. It is worth recalling that there are many secular commentators who would side with Cottingham on this issue and grant that, from a naturalistic point of view, our attitude to the human condition should be, at root, one of deep pessimism and even despair. Bertrand Russell and William James (who, if not a secular commentator, is not writing as an orthodox monotheist anyway) would be obvious examples.[6] So in these ways, drawing both on cultural history, and on recent

---

[5] *Why Believe?*, p. 157. The quotation is taken from Erik Wielenberg, *Value and Virtue in a Godless Universe* (Cambridge: Cambridge University Press, 2005), p. 139.

[6] See for example Bertrand Russell in his essay 'A Free Man's Worship' (1903) reproduced in L. Pojman, ed., *Ethical Theory* (Belmont, CA: Wadsworth, 4th edn 2001), pp. 606–10. Russell sets out his naturalistic assessment of our circumstances at the very beginning of his essay, noting for example how 'Man is the product of causes which had no prevision of the end they were achieving'. He continues: 'Only within the scaffolding of these truths [such as the lack of any providential ordering of events], only on the firm foundation of unyielding despair, can the soul's habitation henceforth be safely built.' James's position

ventures in avowedly secular ethics, Cottingham aims to show that in surrendering a theistic worldview, we are also relinquishing, if only we see matters clearly enough, various humanly important attitudinal possibilities.

Cottingham's case on these matters is to be read at least in part, I take it, in metaphysical terms: it is because they lack the requisite metaphysical commitments that Wielenberg and others find themselves unable to produce secular counterparts for traditional theistic virtues such as hope. This construal of Cottingham's general position is perhaps more easily justified for his remarks on humility rather than hope. In the case of humility, he says for example that: 'Religious language offers a ready expression for this complex framework of affective and cognitive responses [those involved in being a humble person].' And he adds by way of explanation: 'Man is not self-creating.'[7] So it is the believer's conception of God as the source of being, among other things, that provides the ideal of humility with a secure conceptual home, and ensures that the trait constitutes a fitting response to the nature of things. While I shall not rehearse his case, Cottingham is struck here, once again, by the contrast between Christian and Aristotelian perspectives, and the distinction between, for instance, the person of Christian humility and Aristotle's 'great-souled man'.[8]

At other points, Cottingham's case seems to be focused more on particular theistic practices, such as the practice of grace before meals, rather than, directly, the metaphysical commitments that are distinctive of theism, as in this passage:

> in the absence of morning prayer, one will simply get up in the morning and start the day; in the absence of a habit of saying Grace, one will simply pick up the knife and fork and start eating. These, and many other differences in habitual patterns of behaviour and affective response, often give us a more significant indicator of the differences between atheism and theism than if we focus on abstract metaphysical claims.[9]

In this text, the accent is upon habits of feeling and action, understood somewhat in distinction from metaphysical commitments. But I take it that Cottingham's thought is that these habits embody or in some way derive from distinctively theistic metaphysical claims, so that the habits remain dependent on a theistic metaphysic, even if that metaphysic is not asserted

---

on this question is evident from his treatment of the regenerative power of religious conversion: see *The Varieties of Religious Experience: A Study in Human Nature* (London: Longmans, Green, and Co, 1910 [1902]), Lectures IX and X.

[7] *Why Believe?*, p. 153.
[8] For Aristotle's account of the great-souled man, see *Nichomachean Ethics*, Book IV.
[9] *Why Believe?*, p. 164.

in the 'abstract'. Even if I am mistaken on the exegetical question of whether Cottingham is to be read in these terms, the case that I am sketching is of independent interest, not least because, as I have noted, something like it has been endorsed by various secular philosophers. The case can, then, be discussed simply on this basis. But for the remainder of the paper, I will attribute it to Cottingham, allowing that there is a degree of exegetical uncertainty on this point.

So far, Cottingham has proposed that there is an integral connection between, for instance, commitment to hope as an ideal of character and theism. He is also of the view that his secular interlocutor will, most likely, agree that hope, humility, and other such traits are genuine virtues. And he feels able, therefore, to put to his interlocutor this choice: you can keep your value commitments by continuing to regard hope and humility, for example, as virtues, but in that case you have good reason to be a theist; or you can keep your naturalism, but in that case, you have good reason to give up your value commitments. Here is one representative passage in which he develops this challenge:

the naturalist faces a dilemma here. On the one hand, it is hard to deny that there is something admirable about this ethic of hope and trust. And the value is something we seem to recognize not just on a prudential level.... Over and above such utilitarian considerations, most of us have a strong intuitive sense of something splendid, something moving, about the human being weighed down with misfortunes and difficulties, who nevertheless manages to keep alive the radiance of hope, as is done in the straining yet resonant self-exhortation at the end of Psalm 43: 'Why are thou cast down, O my soul, and why are thou disquieted within me? Hope in God for I shall yet praise him who is the health of my countenance, and my God.' [Ps. 42[43]:11] The position so far reached, then, is that these so-called theological virtues are ones which many or most of us, almost irrespective of religious persuasion or its absence, can intuitively recognize as admirable and valuable. And hence, short of biting the bullet and suppressing such intuitions, the naturalist has to construct some secular analogue for these virtues, which will allow them to be preserved as ethically desirable traits of character. But I have suggested that this will not be easy, without a suitable framework in which to locate them.[10]

So Cottingham is presenting the naturalist with this dilemma: you recognize hope (in the relevant, broadly defined sense that Cottingham has delineated) to be an ideal of life; and yet there is no naturalist framework that will allow us to display why hope is rightly regarded as an ideal of life, or that will underwrite the practices that are required for the nurturing of hope in

---

[10] *Why Believe?*, pp. 155–6.

human communities; so you face a choice between giving up your naturalism and giving up your commitment to hope as an ideal of life.

Cottingham presents the case I have been discussing relatively briefly, and does not attempt to defend it at any length from objections. So there remains a question about how his argument might be developed, and perhaps strengthened, in the face of objections. I turn to this question next.

3. ELABORATING ON COTTINGHAM'S ARGUMENT

In this section, I shall introduce two objections to Cottingham's position, and consider how his case might be extended, or on certain points re-affirmed, so as to meet these objections.

It might be said that Cottingham's argument depends on an equivocation in its reading of the key claim that 'hope is a virtue'. As Cottingham says here: 'most of us have a strong intuitive sense [that there is] something splendid' in the ideal of hope. And in keeping with this observation, we could take the claim 'hope is a virtue' in a purely descriptive sense: on this reading, what is being asserted is simply that many of us take hope to be a virtue. But Cottingham's argument surely depends, the objector may continue, on a normative reading of the claim 'hope is a virtue', according to which hope is rightly taken as an ideal of character. We can after all explain the fact that people believe that hope is a virtue by noting that they believe that there is a God, or stand within a culture whose values derive from a predecessor culture in which people believed that there is a God. It is only if hope is rightly believed to be a virtue that Cottingham has given us reason to conclude that there is a God, and not simply that people believe, or once believed, that there is a God.

In brief, God's reality is required not to secure the sociocultural truth that many people believe hope to be a virtue, but only to secure the normative truth that hope is indeed a virtue. So doesn't Cottingham's case appeal to the plausible claim that many people take hope to be a virtue, while it actually requires the different and not properly substantiated claim that hope is rightly thought to be a virtue? To put the matter otherwise, doesn't Cottingham commit something like the error that many commentators have associated with J. S. Mill's argument in Chapter IV of *Utilitarianism* when he slides, so it is alleged, from a descriptive to a normative reading of the claim that 'happiness is desirable'?[11]

[11] See Mill's comment: 'the sole evidence it is possible to produce that anything is desirable, is that people do actually desire it.... No reason can be given why the general

This objection invites us to think about the role of sociocultural generalizations in Cottingham's argument. These generalizations can be assigned two roles in the discussion. Cottingham is inviting the naturalist to endorse each of these claims:

> [1] Hope (of the relevant kind) is a genuine virtue (rather than simply a trait that is taken by many to be a virtue).

And

> [2] Hope can only be a genuine virtue if the biblical worldview or something relevantly like it is true.

Sociocultural generalization is relevant to both these claims. Cottingham reasons: if we find that hope is taken to be a virtue in theistic cultures, and in cultures which have grown out of theistic cultures, and not otherwise, doesn't this give us an initial reason for thinking that there is a deep-seated connection between commitment to theism and commitment to hope as a virtue? Here sociocultural generalization is used to support [2]. I don't find any illicit slide from the descriptive to the normative case here. The thought is just that if people in theistic cultures (and cultures that derive from theistic cultures) take hope to be a virtue, and people in other cultures do not, then this provides an initial reason for supposing that a theistic worldview is in some way presupposed in the idea that hope is a genuine virtue. So this association gives us prima facie reason to endorse [2].

Sociocultural generalization can also be introduced to support [1]. But here it functions as an appeal to the reader, who is being asked to locate themselves within the relevant generalization. In other words, the reader is being invited to recognize that, like many others in 'our' culture, they too believe that hope is a genuine virtue. So here again there is, I think, no slide from the descriptive to the normative case: the reader is being called upon to recognize that they are already committed to the idea that hope is a genuine virtue; they are not being drawn into a transition from the thought that many people take it to be a virtue to the thought that it is a genuine virtue. So Cottingham is not really arguing for [1] at all, but appealing to an already established consensus on this question, and inviting his reader to locate themselves within that consensus.

happiness is desirable, except that each person, so far as he believes it to be attainable, desires his own happiness': John Stuart Mill, *Utilitarianism*, ed. George Sher (Indianapolis, IN: Hackett Publishing Company, 2001), ch. IV. Mill moves here from the claim that happiness is in fact desired to the claim that it is 'desirable', where the latter claim may be read either descriptively ('happiness is capable of being desired') or normatively ('happiness ought to be desired').

Let's suppose that Cottingham is right to think that he has presented a prima facie case for [2]: hope can only be a genuine virtue if the biblical worldview or something relevantly like it is true. And let's also suppose that his addressee stands within the relevant sociocultural generalization, so has an 'intuitive sense' (to use Cottingham's form of words) that hope is a genuine virtue. If the addressee is also a naturalist, what should she say at this point?

The naturalist might respond by saying: having rehearsed Cottingham's argument, I have come to see that, while I remain a naturalist, I cannot retain my belief that hope, of the relevant kind, is a virtue. They might then conclude that their 'intuitive sense' that hope is a genuine virtue is nothing more than a cultural artefact, which derives from their upbringing within a theistic culture or a culture with roots in earlier theistic traditions. Naturalists who are persuaded by Cottingham's dilemma will have good reason to respond in this way if they takes themselves to have powerful reasons for favouring naturalism. But we might wonder: hasn't Cottingham given naturalists a reason of some sort, even if not a very powerful reason, for supposing that theism is true, given their initial 'intuitive sense' that hope is indeed a virtue?[12] Elaborating on this question will allow us to put a second objection to Cottingham's case.

In support of the idea that Cottingham's case has supplied such grounds, it might be said: in general, our initial attitude towards our 'intuitive sense' of how things stand should be one of trust or 'credulity'; in such cases, the burden of proof surely rests on the person who doubts what we find ourselves intuitively inclined to believe.[13] If that is so, then the naturalist's intuitive sense that hope is a virtue ought to be given some initial weight. And while other considerations may in the end prove overriding, this intuitive sense does give the naturalist who accepts the terms of Cottingham's dilemma a reason for thinking that theism is true.

---

[12] This is to ask whether Cottingham's case has any epistemic force. So far as I can see, this is not a question that Cottingham puts directly to himself, and for present purposes, I bracket the question of whether he intends his case to be read in these terms. It is clear that Cottingham does intend to present the secularist with a forced choice between certain moral commitments and their naturalism. But this train of thought does not of itself commit him to a view about whether naturalists should treat their moral commitments as providing support for the truth of theism. Whatever the correct exegesis here, I hope the ensuing discussion will establish that these issues are of some interest in their own right.

[13] This principle, or others rather like it, has been defended by many philosophers. See for example Richard Swinburne, *The Existence of God* (Oxford: Oxford University Press, 2nd edn 2004), ch. 13.

In response to this proposal, it might be objected that, on Cottingham's account, there is nothing in the experience of hope, or in features of the world that are accessible to the senses, to mark out hope as a virtue. For whether or not hope is a virtue depends, on his account, upon our metaphysical context: the confidence that is a mark of biblical hope would not be appropriate, in his judgement, if naturalism were true; indeed, in such circumstances hope would presumably count as a vice, since it would then be an ideal of life that is incongruous with its metaphysical context. This suggests that if we are to have a reliable 'intuitive sense' of whether or not hope is a virtue, then our cognitive faculties will need to be attuned in some relevant way to the truth or otherwise of theism; since it is the truth or otherwise of theism that fixes whether or not hope is a virtue. But we might ask: why suppose that we are capable of any such attunement?

If theism is true, then perhaps we have some reason to attribute to human beings such a capacity. Perhaps God wants our intuitive judgements concerning which traits are virtues to track the truth, because God wants us to lead good lives, and for this reason confers upon us the requisite cognitive powers? This is not to say that we need to be explicitly aware of the connection between the existence of God and hope's status as a virtue; it may be, for example, that God gives us simply a disposition to grasp unreflectively that hope is a virtue. Such a disposition, conferred on this basis, will of course be truth-directed. But if, on the other hand, we take naturalism to be true, then why would we suppose that we have an 'intuitive sense' of which traits are virtues that is responsive to our metaphysical context, so that its verdicts track the truth or otherwise of naturalism? Again, such a sense need not involve any explicit awareness of the connection between naturalism and the moral status of a given trait, nor need it involve any explicit awareness of whether naturalism is true. But if its verdicts on these matters are to be trustworthy, then those verdicts will need to track the truth or otherwise of naturalism, if it is the truth or otherwise of naturalism that fixes whether or not a given trait is a virtue. In fact, the objector may continue, if naturalism is true, and if our cognitive capacities are to be explained in evolutionary terms, then we surely have good reason to deny that we have any such intuitive sense of which traits count as virtues. After all, evolutionary theory has nothing to say about any such sense; and this is as it should be, because what connection could there be between an appreciation of which traits count as virtues, where this appreciation at least indirectly tracks the truth or otherwise of a large scale metaphysical hypothesis (that is, naturalism), and 'fitness' understood in evolutionary terms?[14] Here we have a second objection to Cottingham's case, when it is read in epistemic terms.

This objection does not imply that in general we cannot argue from an 'intuitive sense' that P to some conclusion Q, on the grounds that Q is a condition of the truth of P. The proposal is just that if such an argument is to be persuasive, then it cannot be the case that the falsity of Q would imply the unreliability of the 'intuitive sense' that P. For if the case were to have that character, then in taking our intuitive sense of these matters to be reliable, at the outset, we will have begged the question in favour of Q: for this sense will only be reliable if Q. To take the case in hand, if naturalism is true then we should not be disposed to trust the findings of any 'intuitive sense' we may have concerning whether hope, in Cottingham's sense, is a virtue. And in that case, we can't very well construct an argument for theism that assumes the reliability of our intuitive sense that hope is a virtue. So here is a reason for doubting whether the considerations adduced by Cottingham give the naturalist a reason, not even a weak reason, for supposing that theism is true.

In response to this objection, we might say that Cottingham's claim that hope is a virtue should be read rather differently. Compare the case where I say that it is better to be sitting restfully than running flat out in a state of terror. Of course, this ranking will vary once we start to build in context. If a hungry tiger is approaching me, then it may well be better for me to be running flat out in a state of terror than to be sitting restfully. But the preference in question is to be read as the claim that, considered in themselves, the state of sitting restfully is to be preferred to the state of running flat out in a state of terror. There is I take it some sense in such judgements. And similarly we might take 'hope is a virtue' to affirm that in itself, and bracketing context, hope is to be preferred to rival demeanours in life, such as those favoured in the Greco-Roman world. Perhaps it is in this sense that hope is superior to contrary traits, so that it is, as Cottingham urges, 'admirable'?

---

[14] Alvin Plantinga has raised the question of whether evolutionary naturalists have an account of the development of our cognitive faculties that is consistent with their claim to know that evolutionary naturalism is true. Here, we are concerned with a related debate, but our particular focus is the question of whether naturalism is consistent with our capacity to know certain moral truths, when the ground of those truths is understood along the lines that Cottingham proposes. A solution to the difficulty that Plantinga has posed need not amount to a solution to the difficulty that we are considering. See Alvin Plantinga, *Warranted Christian Belief* (Oxford: Oxford University Press, 2000), pp. 227–40.

This response does engage with the objection that our intuitive sense of whether or not hope is a virtue is not to be trusted if naturalism is true. After all, the evolutionary origin of our cognitive apparatus is entirely compatible, I take it, with our being able to judge reliably that sitting restfully is to be preferred, other things being equal, to running flat out in a state of terror; and why should we not suppose that the evolutionary origin of our cognitive powers is similarly compatible with our being able to judge reliably that hope in Cottingham's sense is to be preferred, on the same context-free kind of basis, to the gloominess of the Greeks? However, while this manoeuvre saves Cottingham's argument from the objection, it also means that the claim 'hope is a virtue' no longer supports the claim that theism is true. Why? Because the claim 'hope is a virtue' is now being read context-independently, so that its truth is no longer tied to the truth of theism. And accordingly, our reasons for thinking that hope is a virtue, when the claim is interpreted in this way, are no longer reasons for thinking that theism is true.

We could develop another response to the objection by building in context. For example, we could compare these four scenarios: (a) being a hopeful person when theism is true; (b) being a hopeful person when theism is false; (c) being a gloomy person (or exhibiting some other trait contrary to hope) when theism is true; and (d) being a gloomy person when theism is false. We might then take the claim that hope is a virtue to amount to the claim that scenario (a) (being a hopeful person when theism is true) is in itself a better scenario than any of (b) to (d) in themselves, bracketing out any other information about the character of these scenarios. Here we have a context-laden reading of the claim that hope is to be ranked above contrary traits. And again, we might suppose that there is nothing in an evolutionary account of the development of our cognitive faculties that would prevent us from being able to make such a judgement reliably.

However, this reading of the claim that hope is a virtue is also incapable of providing the basis of an inference to theism. For on this reading, to say that hope is a virtue is to make a claim about which of various possible scenarios is optimal; it is not to be committed to a view about whether this optimal scenario in fact obtains. So (a) may indeed be the best of these scenarios; and this truth may allow us to give some content to the claim that hope is superior to contrary traits, and therefore a virtue. But the fact that (a) is a theistic scenario gives us no reason to think that theism is in fact true; it tells us only that if the optimal scenario were to obtain, then theism would be true.

In sum, it is not clear that Cottingham's discussion provides the naturalist with a reason for thinking that theism is true. If the claim that hope is a virtue is taken to mean that hope is a virtue relative to our actual meta-physical context, then the naturalist should refuse to grant that we have a reliable 'intuitive sense' that this is so. Alternatively, we could read the claim that hope is a virtue in context-independent terms (abstracting from context, hope is to be preferred to contrary traits) or in context-laden terms of the kind we have considered (hope granted the truth of theism is to be preferred to all the alternative pairings of traits and worldviews). The naturalist can grant that we can make these discriminations reliably; but allowing that hope is a virtue in these senses does not determine whether hope is properly an ideal of character in our metaphysical context, and so does not provide the basis of an argument for theism.

So this second objection to Cottingham's case, when that case is read epistemically, has, I think, some force. Nonetheless, our willingness to judge that hope is a virtue in the context-laden sense may still be of some interest, if our intention is to develop a pragmatic, rather than epistemic, case for theism. I shall come to that question shortly, but first of all, let us turn to another account of the relationship between religious and moral thought.

As we have seen, on Cottingham's view, certain moral commitments—notably, to take our focal example, commitment to hope as an ideal of character in our world—call for a religious 'framework of reference' if they are to be coherent. To put the point in traditional terms, I need to subscribe to the truth of some story about God's providence if my commitment to hope as an ideal of life, in our universe, is to be coherent. Raimond Gaita's work points to another, rather different way of formulating the idea that religious narratives and moral commitments are mutually implicating. In the next section, I set out the main elements of Gaita's approach, and consider its relationship to Cottingham's discussion. I shall then argue that both accounts can be constructively extended, and integrated, by reference to Thomas Aquinas's category of infused moral virtue.

4. INTERPRETING GAITA'S ACCOUNT OF THE RELATIONSHIP BETWEEN MORAL AND RELIGIOUS THOUGHT

Gaita's discussion of the relationship between moral and religious commitment is marked by his profound scepticism of the capacity of moral theory to serve as a source of moral insight. For Gaita, rather than theory, the sources of deep moral understanding are the enacted witness of moral exemplars, and a vocabulary for talking about human beings that is fundamentally religious in content. Let's see how he develops these themes.

In his book *A Common Humanity*, Gaita describes an episode from his youth, when he was working as an assistant on a psychiatric ward. One day, a nun came to the ward, and in seeing her demeanour in the presence of the patients—'the way she spoke to them, her facial expressions, the inflexions of her body'—he takes himself to have acquired a deepened understanding of the sense in which the patients are, in moral terms, his equals.[15] Before witnessing the nun's conduct, Gaita would have said, in all sincerity, that the patients were his equals. But her enacted, bodily example, rather than anything she says, shows him that until now, he did not believe this 'in his heart'. Her example 'reveals', he says, the full equality of the patients with himself and all other human beings, so disclosing our 'common humanity'.[16]

Gaita evidently thinks that it is possible to arrive at this insight into the full humanity of another human being, even an afflicted human being such as the patients on the ward, without first of all committing oneself to a religious worldview. And he is clear that his own recognition of the equality of the patients depended simply on the nun's enacted example: it did not require any prior, explicit commitment to a religious or any other worldview. (Indeed, although Gaita does not say so, I take it that his religious stance at that time, as in later life, was agnostic or atheistic.) In this respect, Gaita's position resembles Cottingham's: for Cottingham too, it seems, it is possible to grasp the appropriateness of certain ideals of life—such as the appropriateness of hope as an ideal of life, in our world—without first of all adopting, explicitly, a theistic perspective. It is for this reason that it is possible, on his account, to start with the recognition that hope is an ideal of life, and to move from there to a commitment to theism. However, by contrast with Cottingham, Gaita does not think that reflective endorsement of the value judgement with which he is concerned (the judgement that these patients are fully his equals) calls for the introduction of a theistic 'framework of significance'. In fact, he maintains that the truth about human beings that is revealed in the nun's behaviour is incapable of being supported by any framework whatsoever. He remarks:

Whatever religious people might say, as someone who was witness to the nun's love and is claimed in fidelity to it, I have no understanding of what it revealed

---

[15] Raimond Gaita, *A Common Humanity. Thinking About Love and Truth and Justice* (Melbourne: Text Publishing, 1999), p. 18.

[16] The example is developed in *A Common Humanity*, pp. 18–19. Gaita relates the example of the nun to other themes in his moral philosophy, and confirms its central place in his thinking, in the second edition of his book *Good and Evil: An Absolute Conception* (Abingdon: Routledge, 2004). See especially the Preface, pp. xii–xxi. Gaita's sensitivity to the role of examples in informing a moral perspective is also evident in his autobiographical work *Romulus, My Father* (Melbourne: Text Publishing, 1998).

independently of the quality of her love. If I am asked what I mean when I say that even such people as were patients on that ward are fully our equals, I can only say that the quality of her love proved that they are rightly the objects of our non-condescending treatment, that we should do all in our power to respond in that way. But if someone were now to ask me what informs my senses that they are *rightly* the objects of such treatment, I can appeal only to the purity of her love. . . . I allow for no independent justification of her attitude.[17]

So for Gaita, the example of the nun, and of others like her, reveals a moral truth to which we have no independent access, and their conduct therefore plays an indispensable role in our moral thought.[18]

However, while Gaita differs from Cottingham in supposing that there is no need to ground, nor even is there any possibility of grounding, moral truths in religious or metaphysical terms, his position turns out to be strikingly similar to Cottingham's in a further respect, because like Cottingham he thinks that the language of religion is vital for the articulation of the most basic of our value commitments. Consider for example these remarks:

For us in the West, the claim that all human beings are sacred is the one that bears most directly on the question of how to characterise the nun's behaviour. Only someone who is religious can speak seriously of the sacred, but such talk informs the thoughts of most of us whether or not we are religious, for it shapes our thoughts about the way in which human beings limit our will as does nothing else in nature. If we are not religious, we will often search for one of the inadequate expressions which are available to us to say what we hope will be a secular equivalent of it. We may say that all human beings are inestimably precious, that they are ends in themselves, that they are owed unconditional respect, that they possess inalienable rights, and, of course, that they possess inalienable dignity. In my judgment these are ways of trying to say what we feel a need to say when we are estranged from the conceptual resources we need to say it. Be that as it may: each of them is problematic and contentious. Not one of them has the simple power of the religious ways of speaking.[19]

Despite their difference on the question of whether some of our fundamental value commitments require, or even permit, the underpinning of a theistic

---

[17] *A Common Humanity*, pp. 21–2. Gaita's position on this point is clearly related to the thought of his doctoral supervisor, R. F. Holland. See especially Holland's essay 'Is Goodness a Mystery?', *Against Empiricism: On Education, Epistemology and Value* (Oxford: Basil Blackwell, 1980), pp. 126–42.

[18] Gaita does defend, and not just assert, the idea that there is 'no independent justification of the nun's attitude', but his argument on this point is not directly relevant to our concerns. For discussion of his case here, see Mark Wynn, 'The Moral Philosophy of Raimond Gaita and Some Questions of Method in the Philosophy of Religion', *New Blackfriars*, Vol. 90 (2009), pp. 639–51.

[19] *A Common Humanity*, p. 23.

metaphysics, in this text Gaita sounds very like Cottingham. Just as Cottingham maintains that there is no secular way of talking that will serve as a substitute for religious ways of talking if we want to articulate with any authority the idea that hope is a genuine virtue (see again his critique of Wielenberg), so Gaita suggests that there is no secular way of talking (employing notions such as dignity, rights, respect, and preciousness) that we can substitute for the language of religion if we want to articulate with any depth the thought that, whether we be psychiatric patients or philosophers, we all of us share a common humanity.

Gaita's stance on this point becomes clearer if we recall that on his view, we are sensitized to the moral importance of other human beings above all in so far as we see them in the light of someone's love. In this spirit, Gaita notes that: 'One of the quickest ways to make prisoners morally invisible to their guards is to deny them visits from their loved ones, thereby ensuring that the guards never see them through the eyes of those who love them.'[20] It is for this reason that the love of parents is so important for Gaita, since parental love is defined by the ideal of unconditionality, and can therefore light up the moral reality of human beings who might otherwise seem un-lovable. But even parental love sometimes fails, and it is in the nature of the case restricted in its scope. And it is more fundamentally, therefore, Gaita explains, the example of figures such as the nun that sustains our commitment to the common humanity of all human beings, or to the idea that all of us, regardless of our particular traits or attributes, are intelligibly the objects of someone's love.[21] But the love of figures such as the nun—the love of people Gaita calls saints—is not simply a natural endowment of certain individuals, he insists. It is instead a cultural achievement, made possible by particular ways of speaking, and associated disciplines of thought and feeling.

It is at this juncture that Gaita appeals to the language of religion, and in particular the language that represents God's love as a special kind of parental love: one that does not fail, but extends reliably and impartially and unconditionally to all human beings. The nun's capacity to act as she does is a product, for Gaita, of her participation in a relevant cultural tradition and it depends in particular on her formation in the discipline of seeing other human beings as the objects of God's unfailing parental love. As Gaita says of the nun's saintly love and of parental love:

Both forms of love are unconditional but they are not unconditioned. Their existence depends upon certain practices and customs as much as it informs them, and

---

[20] *A Common Humanity*, p. 26.   [21] *A Common Humanity*, p. 24.

also upon certain facts of the human condition. Neither is universally an ideal amongst the peoples of the earth, and even in cultures such as ours where they are (or have been) celebrated, people's hold on them is often fragile. They are, I believe, dependent upon one another. I doubt that the love expressed in the nun's demeanour would have been possible for her were it not for the place which the language of parental love had in her prayers.[22]

Here again, Gaita's stance sounds very much like Cottingham's, albeit that Gaita is concerned with love and Cottingham with hope and other virtues distinct from love. In the language of religion, Gaita is saying, we have a way of representing all human beings as the objects of an unwavering parental love, and therefore as fully our equals; and we do not have a secular discourse that might serve as a satisfactory substitute for the presentation of this same insight. And the example of figures such as the nun, he seems to claim here, depends in the end upon the enabling power of religious thoughts, and especially the thought of God's universal parental love.

Allowing for these similarities, Gaita's formulation of the idea that our moral thought depends upon the language of religion has a rather different cast from Cottingham's rendering of this idea. Gaita is not supposing, it seems to me, that anyone who grasps, in any depth, the common humanity of human beings must be familiar with the language of divine parental love. And he is certainly not suggesting, as Cottingham seems to be, that the fully reflective person who subscribes to the ideal of saintly love, or some other relevant ideal of life, is required to use the language of religion devotionally. Gaita is clear, for example, that there can be secular saints, and he does not think of this position as in any way unstable, or as inviting completion in the form of religious commitment.[23] Nonetheless, Gaita does seem to be affirming that it is because our culture has emerged from theistic cultures that we have the idea of a common humanity; and he seems to be saying that it is only in so far as at least some of us continue to use the language of divine parental love prayerfully that this ideal will continue to be presented to us authoritatively in the lives of 'the saints'. So it seems to be an implication of his position that if theistic forms of thought and spiritual discipline were

---

[22] *A Common Humanity*, p. 22.

[23] On this point, Gaita's position is reminiscent of Pierre Hadot's account of the philosophical schools of the ancient world, such as Stoicism and Epicureanism. According to Hadot, these schools introduced various ways of representing the universe (think for instance of Epicurean atomism) not fundamentally because they took themselves to have evidence for the truth of these worldviews, but because they believed that the worldview would provide a spiritually helpful focus of thought. See Pierre Hadot, *Philosophy as A Way of Life: Spiritual Exercises from Socrates to Foucault*, tr. M Chase (Oxford: Blackwell, 1995), ch. 11.

to disappear from our culture altogether, then we would with time lose our grip upon the idea that we all of us share a common humanity.

It is noteworthy that for Gaita, it is not theological discourse that is important in sustaining the practice of figures such as the nun. It is, rather, religious stories and anthropomorphic representations of the divine life that play this role. In this sense, it is the religious imagination, and not fundamentally abstractly discursive forms of religious thought, that is integral to the enduring vitality of our moral understanding. He puts the point thus:

Philosophers and theologians are, for reasons that go deep in their disciplines, inclined to say that the language of prayer, anthropocentric and often poetic, merely makes moving and therefore psychologically accessible to less than perfectly rational beings, things whose intellectual content is more clearly revealed in the abstract deliverances of theological and philosophical theories. I suspect that the contrary is closer to the truth—that the unashamedly untheoretical, anthropocentric language of worship has greater power to reveal the structure of the concepts which make the nun's behaviour and what it revealed intelligible to us.[24]

Given his account of the example of the nun, we should expect Gaita to take this view. He has proposed that the nun differs from the psychiatrists who work on the ward, and from Gaita himself in his 'pre-conversion' state, not fundamentally in what she says (it's not apparent, in fact, that Gaita hears anything of what she says on her visit to the ward), but in her bodily demeanour towards the patients. It is, then, enacted example that is the source of deep-seated moral understanding. And if there is to be a divine counterpart for the nun's enacted example, then it will presumably be found in closely observed narratives of what God or the gods have done in their relations with human beings, and not in abstract, doctrinal claims about God's relation to the world.

5. REVIEWING GAITA'S CASE

What should we make of Gaita's discussion? His case depends in part on what is, surely, a plausible claim about the moral formation of human beings: for many of us, growth in moral understanding depends upon our exposure to the enacted witness of exemplary individuals. More controversially, Gaita is advancing a complex counterfactual sociocultural claim: but for the presence in 'our' culture of the language of divine parental love, the very idea of a common humanity, in the sense that he intends, would never

---

[24] *A Common Humanity*, p. 23.

have emerged. That may be doubted. It has been urged, for example, that the stories of non-theistic religious traditions can secure our sense of the moral importance of our fellow human beings on the same sort of basis, and with the same sort of authority, as the idea of divine parental love.[25] But for our purposes, perhaps the most interesting of Gaita's proposals is the thought that we human beings are incapable of fashioning a purely secular, or purely theoretical, language that will serve as an adequate substitute, in our moral discourse, for image-laden, anthropomorphic religious ways of talking.

It is hard to assess the plausibility of this claim. It is, Gaita seems to be saying, a deep truth of human nature that religious ways of talking have this capacity to structure our moral thought: there is no abstractly conceptual necessity that moral thought should be so structured, but given the sort of creatures we are (given that we culture-bound, image-bound, and story-bound kinds of creature) religious forms of thought are essential, he seems to be saying, for the enduring vitality of *our* moral thought. It may be that he thinks of this truth as relative not only to human nature, but also to the particular set of cultural traditions that has in fact evolved in human history. Perhaps Gaita would allow that, for all we know, there might in principle have been secular cultural traditions that could have played the role that is played in our cultural history by the language of divine love. But in the world as it is constituted, he seems to be saying, none of the secular cultural traditions that has in fact evolved is capable of playing this role.

And although he does not say so, perhaps Gaita also thinks that if a body of stories and images is to play this sort of role, then it cannot be constructed here and now, but has to be elaborated, and refined, along with associated literary, visual and musical traditions, across generations, if it is to exercise the deep imaginative pull of established religious forms of thought. So perhaps Gaita would allow that it may be just a contingent truth of cultural history that we find ourselves dependent on religious forms of thought in the way that he has suggested. But whatever he thinks on this point, it appears to be an implication of his position that this dependence runs deep: on Gaita's view, it would be futile, as well as, very likely, morally impoverishing, to seek some secular counterpart to religious traditions that

[25] For instance, Michael McGhee has argued that taking on a moral perspective requires an external vantage point upon the human condition. And while agreeing with Gaita that the language of divine parental love provides one way of assuming such a vantage point, he argues that the stories of, for example, Boddhisattva figures are just as capable of playing this role, and of sustaining thereby a concern for human beings as such. See Michael McGhee, 'Is Nothing Sacred? A Secular Philosophy of Incarnation', *Philosophical Investigations* 34 (2011), pp. 169–88.

could be substituted for them with no loss of moral efficacy. Here again, his position has obvious affinities with Cottingham's.

So Cottingham and Gaita agree that religious categories have an important role to play in nourishing our moral thought. But on Cottingham's view, hope can only count as an ideal granted a theistic metaphysics, whereas for Gaita, whatever the metaphysical facts may be, a life that acknowledges a common humanity is to be preferred to a life informed by any contrary value. Religion is relevant on Gaita's scheme not because saintly love will only count as an ideal granted a theistic metaphysic, but because we are culture-bound, image-bound, exemplar-dependent creatures, and accordingly our capacity to apprehend the humanity of other human beings depends on our acquaintance with religious stories, and especially stories that speak of human beings as the objects of a universal, unconditional love. To this extent, the dependence of moral thought on religion is, for Gaita, more a matter of the imagination than of metaphysics.

6. COTTINGHAM, GAITA AND THOMAS AQUINAS'S CONCEPTION OF INFUSED MORAL VIRTUE

Neither Cottingham nor Gaita intends to give a fully developed account of the relationship between moral and religious commitments. So part of my concern here has been to argue for a particular reading of their comments, and at points to expand on those comments in the light of potential objections. In concluding, I am going to consider how these accounts, read as I have read them, may be further extended, and at the same time integrated, so as to present a single overarching account of the relationship between moral and religious commitment. For this purpose, I am going to read these accounts through the lens provided by Thomas Aquinas's notion of infused moral virtue. So I begin by briefly introducing this notion.[26]

Aquinas inherited from Aristotle the idea that there are acquired moral virtues, and from his theological forebears the idea that there are infused theological virtues.[27] Combining these approaches, he proposes that along with the acquired moral and infused theological virtues, there are also

---

[26] I give a fuller account of the notion in my paper 'Between Heaven and Earth: Sensory Experience and the Goods of the Spiritual Life', in David McPherson, ed., *Spirituality and the Good Life* (Cambridge: Cambridge University Press), forthcoming, 2017.

[27] See Aristotle, *The Ethics of Aristotle: The Nichomachean Ethics*, tr. J. A. K. Thomson, rev. H. Tredennick (Harmondsworth: Penguin, 1976), Book II. The theological virtues of faith, hope and love are distinguished famously in 1 Cor. 13.

infused moral virtues.[28] The infused moral virtues aim not simply at this-worldly goods (such as the good of bodily health, which is the goal of acquired temperance), nor simply at other-worldly goods (such as the good of relationship to God, which is the immediate goal of the theological virtues), but at what we may think of as a hybrid kind of good, namely, our flourishing in relation to creatures, where the measure of that flourishing is provided by relationship to God. Hence infused temperance, for example, involves 'abstinence' from food, that is, a pattern of consumption of food that is consistent with health of the body, but where the measure of right consumption is fixed by reference to relationship to God. Aquinas explains the relationship between the theological and infused moral virtues in these terms:

> The theological virtues are enough to shape us to our supernatural end as a start, that is, to God himself immediately and to none other. Yet the soul needs also to be equipped by infused virtues in regard to created things, though as subordinate to God.[29]

So, in brief, the infused moral virtues are concerned with our relations to 'created things' (so they share their subject matter with the acquired moral virtues), but 'as subordinate to God', so that the standard of success in these relations is provided not simply by reference to human nature but in terms of relationship to God (so the infused moral virtues share their teleology with the theological virtues). Hence Aquinas takes neighbour love, for example, to be appropriate for us, because this way of relating to other human beings is fitting relative to the truth that we will one day share with them in the beatific vision.[30] So the good that is realized in the practice of neighbour love concerns, of course, our relations to creatures, but is

---

[28] The key text here is *Summa Theologiae* 1a.63.4, where Aquinas asks 'whether any moral virtues are in us by infusion'. See the Benziger Bros. edition, translated by the Fathers of the English Dominican Province, 1947, available here: <http://dhspriory.org/thomas/summa/index.html>. The example of consumption of food that I go on to give is developed here. A helpful account of Thomas's development of earlier traditions of thought can be found in John Inglis, 'Aquinas's Replication of the Acquired Moral Virtues', *Journal of Religious Ethics* 27 (1999), pp. 3–27.

[29] *Summa Theologiae*, ed. T. Gilby (London: Eyre & Spottiswoode, 1964–74), vol. 23, 1a2ae. 63. 3.

[30] See for instance this remark: 'As stated above (Q 23, Art. 1), the friendship of charity is founded upon the fellowship of everlasting happiness, in which men share in common with the angels. For it is written (Mt. 22:30) that "in the resurrection...men shall be as the angels of God in heaven." It is therefore evident that the friendship of charity extends also to the angels' (*Summa Theologiae* 2a2ae. 25. 10, ellipsis in the original, tr. Fathers of the English Dominican Province). Here Thomas grounds the appropriateness of love of the angels in a truth concerning our theological context, namely, our shared eschatological future; and he takes the same considerations to ground the appropriateness of neighbour love that is extended to human beings.

grounded in our theological context, since it consists in the fittingness of those relations relative to theological truths, in this case, the truth that we will share with other human beings in the vision of God. In this sense, this is a hybrid good, one that consists in our relations to creatures being properly ordered to our relation to God.

Granted this account of the goods that are the object of the infused moral virtues, let us return first of all to Cottingham's discussion. Drawing on Aquinas's notion of infused moral virtue, we can think of Cottingham's case as an invitation to lead a life of hope, so as to realize a significant hybrid good, namely, the good of leading such a life in a theistic universe. The good that will then be realized can be considered as a Thomistic hybrid good for the reasons that Cottingham gives: if we do not inhabit a theistic universe, then it may be doubted whether hope will count as an ideal of life; but within a theistic universe, hope will constitute a fitting response to our theological context, and will thereby realize the good that consists in living congruently with that context. So as with other hybrid goods, this is a good that concerns not simply our relationship to the material order, nor simply our relationship to God, but our relationship to created things in so far as that relationship is fitting relative to our relationship to God.

It is worth recalling here that Cottingham is concerned with a kind of hope that is not directed simply at God, even if it depends for its appropriateness on the existence of God. After all, his secular interlocutor is supposed to be committed to a life of hope, in the sense that is relevant to Cottingham's case, yet their hope cannot be directed, at least not explicitly, at God. Instead, hope, in this sense, involves, once again, our attitudes towards this-worldly events. Understood in these terms, hope realizes a good of the same structure as the good that is realized, according to Aquinas, by abstinence: in each case, our thoughts, feeling and actions in our dealings with the material world turn out to be congruent with our theological context, and realize thereby a significant good.

We can elaborate on this case by returning to our earlier reading of the claim that hope is a virtue. Suppose we read this claim as the claim that of the following four scenarios, the first is the best, other things being equal: (a) being a hopeful person when theism is true; (b) being a hopeful person when theism is false; (c) being a gloomy person (or exhibiting some other trait contrary to hope) when theism is true; and (d) being a gloomy person when theism is false. This ranking reflects Cottingham's judgement that hope will only count as a virtue granted the truth of the theism: it is for this reason that (a) is to be preferred to (b). And as we have seen, the secular person can trust their intuitive judgement that this ranking is appropriate, without thereby begging the question against secularism. Granted the ranking, we could represent Cottingham's case as an appeal to lead a life of hope, so as to realise scenario (a), on the grounds that this is the best of the available scenarios. On this reading, his case provides a pragmatic justification for theistic commitment: we are to order our lives to realize goods that will obtain only if theism is true.

Of course, if we can't be sure that theism is true, then we can't be sure that in leading a life of hope we will realise (a) rather than (b). But in this respect, it may be urged, this practical choice is no different from the many others we make when acting under conditions of uncertainty. What matters in these cases is having some prospect of realizing a significant good; for when that good is indeed significant, then we can have good reason to aim at it, even if we cannot be certain of success. And similarly, if scenario (a) involves a sufficiently great good, then will we not have a good reason to aim at that good, by leading a life of hope, even if we are uncertain of success?[31]

Let's think further about this case by reflecting on the ranking of scenarios (a) to (d). It may be said: even if the first scenario (of a life of hope in a theistic universe) is objectively the best—best, as it were, from the perspective of the universe—might it, even so, not be the best scenario for me?[32] Might I not realize a better outcome for me by leading a life of gloom (or a life involving some other trait that is contrary to hope)? It is hard to see how the claim that my being gloomy is better for me than my being hopeful could be maintained in the abstract. But an objector may urge that there is something in the character of our particular universe, or in my character, or in my location in our universe, even if this is a theistic universe, which

---

[31] The practical reasonableness of such a choice could be understood in the terms provided by William James in his classic treatment of the practical rationality of religious belief, 'The Will to Believe'. In James's terms, the realization of (a) involves a 'momentous' good. The choice here is also 'forced', in the sense that only a life of hope will give the person the possibility of realizing (a). We are also assuming, of course, that the choice is 'living': if a person is psychologically incapable of leading, say, a life of hope, then the choice of such a life will not be open to them. And lastly, the case also presupposes that epistemic considerations are not decisive, and following James we may wish to cast this idea in terms of the thought that the truth of theism 'cannot by its nature be settled on intellectual grounds' (Section IV). See William James, 'The Will to Believe' in James, *Essays in Pragmatism* (New York: Hafner Press, 1948), pp. 88–109. Aquinas's account of the rationality of faith has, I would say, a similar structure, at least implicitly. See for instance his insistence that faith is voluntary, rather than being the product of evidence or signs. Hence he writes: 'the act of faith is belief, an act of mind fixed on one alternative by reason of the will's command' (Gilby, ed., *Summa Theologiae* 2a2ae. 4. 1). For the point that genuine, or 'formed' faith, is not produced by signs, see Aquinas's discussion of the faith of the devils in *Summa Theologiae* 2a2ae 5. 5. ad. 3.

[32] Compare Guy Kahane's discussion of the question of whether the truth of theism would be good for human beings in his essay 'Should We Want God To Exist?', *Philosophy and Phenomenological Research* 82: 3 2011, Section VII.

means that my leading a life in which my attitude is fundamentally one of gloom rather than of hope is better for me. Or perhaps the objector will say that I should exhibit neither hope nor gloom as a fundamental life attitude, since it is best for me simply to respond to some situations with gloom and to others with hope, without either attitude becoming a generalized stance in life of the kind that Cottingham describes.

As we have seen, Cottingham claims that in theistic traditions, there is broad agreement that a life of hope, rather than gloom, is fitting for a person regardless of their personal circumstances, and even in the face of considerable personal affliction. This claim is relevant to our objection, for, if this consensus view is right, then when I lead a life of hope in a theistic universe my thoughts and actions and desires, so far as they are relevant to my hope, will be aligned with what is most fundamentally of value, whatever may be true of the details of my circumstances. And if that is so, then when I lead a life of hope within a theistic universe a very significant good will accrue to me, and not just to the universe. And while it may be true that other goods would accrue to me were I to give up my hope, how might those goods outweigh the good of a life that is congruent, in these respects, with the incommensurable good of the divine life?[33]

Alternatively, it may be objected that even if the first scenario is the best of the four, whether objectively or for me, the other scenario in which hope features may be much the worst outcome of the four for me—and if that is so, then should I not prioritize avoiding this outcome, and therefore choose gloom rather than hope? If we are concerned with a ranking that reflects simply the 'perspective of the universe', then arguably one of the non-theistic scenarios should be ranked lowest, since God's existence is, after all, on standard accounts, an unrivalled good. And from the point of view of the universe, perhaps my leading a life of hope in a non-theistic universe is a worse state of affairs, other things being equal, than is my leading a life of gloom in such a universe—since in the first case, and not in the second, my life fails to be aligned with my context (if Cottingham is right about these matters).

But even if this is the correct objective ranking, there is reason to concentrate not upon the overall good that is exhibited in these scenarios, but upon the good that is sensitive to my choices, since that is the only good over which I have control, and therefore the only good that is at stake in my

---

[33] Thinking of the relevant good in terms of alignment with context, rather than simply, say, pleasant feelings, helps to show that the ranking reflects hope's contribution as an ideal of character, rather than on account of its securing benefits of another kind. My thanks to a reviewer for this point.

choosing. And what is this good that is sensitive to my choice? On the approach we have been taking, this is the good of a life that is properly aligned with my context; and the corresponding bad will be a life that is misaligned with my context. So if we ask 'which choice should I be most concerned *not* to make?', we should answer: the choice which risks bringing about the worst misalignment of my life with its context. In (a) to (d) there are two scenarios where my life is misaligned with my context: (b) when I lead a life of hope in a non-theistic universe, and (c) when I lead a life of gloom in a theistic universe. Which of these failures of alignment is the worse, and therefore more to be avoided? Arguably, it is (c). Why? Because here my life fails to be aligned not simply with the finite good of a non-theistic universe, but with the boundless good of the divine life. And this second kind of misalignment looks like a more radical falling short, because it involves a failure to properly acknowledge not simply a finite good, but the divine good. If that is right, and if my priority is avoiding bad outcomes rather than bringing about good outcomes, then it seems that I should choose a life of hope. Why? Because only so can I be sure of avoiding the bad of a life that fails to be aligned with its divine context.

So here in outline is a way of applying Cottingham's discussion to the question of whether theistic commitment is rationally motivated, in practical terms. This approach turns on the idea that the goods realized by the traits of character that Cottingham discusses are like the goods that are realized by the infused moral virtues, understood as Aquinas understands them; that is, in each case, whether through the practice of a Thomistic virtue such as infused temperance or through lived commitment to an ideal of character such as hope and humility, understood in Cottingham's terms, it is possible to realize a significant hybrid good, if we inhabit a theistic universe. Granted this parallel, then we can adopt a Thomistic reading of the connection between commitment to hope as an ideal of life and commitment to theism: we have good reason to commit ourselves to a life of hope, and therefore good reason to think of such a life as an ideal, because we have thereby the prospect of realizing a particularly profound hybrid good, namely, the good of a life that is aligned with a divine context. In this way, we can avoid the objections to the epistemic reading of Cottingham's case that we considered earlier, while building on his core insight that hope will count as an ideal of life only if theism is true. In brief, what this Thomistic reading of the case allows us to do is to take that insight as the basis for a practical project, namely, the project of realizing the relevant hybrid good.

Let us consider now how the notion of infused moral virtue may be relevant to Gaita's discussion. As we have seen, Gaita thinks that religious stories, and especially the idea of God's universal and unconditional parental love, have played an important part in producing our conception of a 'common humanity'. However, Gaita also thinks that to appreciate the revelatory power of these stories, it is enough to hold the requisite thoughts in mind: there is no need to take them to be true. The notion of infused moral virtue allows us to expand on this typology, by identifying a further possibility, one which involves neither the thought that theistic stories are evidently true nor the thought that they are to be treated simply as instructive fictions. Let us consider this possibility a little further. I shall begin by arguing that the notion of infused moral virtue enables us to read the example of the nun with new insight.

As we have seen, Gaita writes that he doubts 'that the love expressed in the nun's demeanour would have been possible for her were it not for the place which the language of parental love had in her prayers'. He glosses this idea by supposing that the nun has been formed in the discipline of addressing God as parent in her prayers, and has, accordingly, become habituated to thinking of other human beings as the objects of divine love, so that she is able to see the patients in the light of that love. Here, then, is one way of grounding moral motivation in religious thought. The notion of infused moral virtue points to another way of making this connection.

If we follow Aquinas's account of the rationale for neighbour love, then we should say that such love realizes an important hybrid good, because it is appropriate relative to our theological context. We could put this point simply by recalling that, as Aquinas puts it, 'if we loved a certain man very much, we would love his children though they were unfriendly towards us'.[34] From this vantage point, what motivates the nun is not simply her character-grounded appreciation of the patients on the ward as loved by God, but also her understanding that in loving them, her actions will be congruent with her theological context, and specifically with her friendship for God. Gaita's examples of the nun and of the prisoners obscure this connection, because in these cases there is not evidently a question about Gaita's relationship to the nun, or about the guards' relationship to those who visit the prisoners: for instance, Gaita's new appreciation of the patients is informed by the nun's regard for them, but not by any thought of the relation in which he stands to her. But the parent–child relationship, which is central to Gaita's case, does standardly have this additional feature.

When I see my brothers and sisters in the light of my parents' love, I am moved to love them not only because I now see them in the light of someone's love, but also because I see them in the light of the love of someone to

---

[34] *Summa Theologiae* 2a2ae. 25. 8, Benziger Bros edn.

whom I bear a special relation. My love for my siblings is especially fitting given that it is my parents who love them. Why? Because if I love my parents, then it is appropriate for me to love what they love, as an expression of my love for them. In the same way, to revert to Aquinas's example, my love for a friend's children is a natural overflow of my love for the friend, because appropriate relative to the love that I bear the friend.

So Aquinas's discussion of neighbour love suggests an extension of Gaita's treatment of the nun's love. Both accounts involve the idea that in recognizing God's love for our fellow human beings, we will thereby be motivated to love them ourselves. But Gaita's account turns simply on our seeing others in the light of God's love, whereas Aquinas offers a thicker description of the object of love: the other human being is to be seen not simply as the object of love, but as the object of the love of someone to whom I am bound in a special sort of relationship, since I am, in the theological sense, their child or friend.

So a Thomistic reading of the nun's conduct suggests a further connection between religious thought and moral motivation, by allowing us to see her behaviour as motivated by the prospect of realizing a significant hybrid good. Once again, a person can be so motivated even if they do not think it overall likely that there is a God who stands to us in the relationship of parent or of friend, providing that they consider the relevant good a weighty enough good. This account allows us, therefore, to distinguish a further possibility, in addition to the two that figure directly in Gaita's discussion: a person may take the stories of divine parental love as simply a morally instructive fiction, or they may suppose that such stories are likely to be true, or if they take this further approach, they may commit themselves in practical terms to the truth of such stories, without taking them to be evidently true, by seeking to realise various hybrid goods that would be realized were the stories to be true.

This Thomistic reading of the nun's story also captures a further feature of Gaita's account. We have seen that Gaita is resistant to the idea that the authority of the nun's example depends on the support of any metaphysical hypothesis. As he says, 'Whatever religious people might say, as someone who was witness to the nun's love and is claimed in fidelity to it, I have no understanding of what it revealed independently of the quality of her love'. The rationale for his position here is in part the thought that if the appropriateness of the nun's behaviour were to depend on the evident truth of a metaphysical claim (for instance, the claim that God loves all human beings), then her example could be no more persuasive than the case in support of that claim, which is to say that our commitment to the appropriateness of her conduct would have to be, at best, rather tentative, and to fluctuate in accordance with fluctuations in the evidence for the relevant metaphysical hypothesis.

The account we have been developing provides another way of preserving this element of Gaita's account. For if the nun is motivated by the prospect of realizing a hybrid good of the kind we have been discussing, then her conduct can be seen to be appropriate independently of any commitment to the thought that it is likely that there is a God who loves all human beings. In this case, what grounds the thought that her behaviour is appropriate is not fundamentally an epistemic judgement—the judgement that it is probable that there is a God—but a value judgement—the judgement that if there is a God, then her behaviour will realise a hybrid good of great worth. We might add that the judgement that this good is indeed of great worth is presumably most readily sustained not in the language of creeds, but in the vivid celebrations of divine-human friendship that are to be found in religious poetry and story and song. So in these various respects, a Thomistic reading of Gaita's example of the nun can extend his position, while adhering to some of the fundamental insights that provide the basis for that position.

CONCLUSION

As we have seen, John Cottingham and Raimond Gaita both foreground the practical importance of religious thoughts. Hence Cottingham focuses upon religious practices, such as grace before meals, rather than doctrinal claims considered in the abstract, and Gaita sets aside creedal language in favour of morally motivating, anthropomorphic stories of God's relationship to human beings. The case we have been exploring allows us to combine these approaches, by understanding the connection between religious thought and practice that each seeks to draw in terms of the idea of hybrid goods, that is, goods of the kind that Aquinas introduces when explaining the teleology of the infused moral virtues. Cottingham's account of hope as an ideal of life, and Gaita's account of the nun, and of the authority of her example, can both be read with new insight in the light of the idea of hybrid goods. And accordingly, these accounts can be folded into the view that we have been developing here, according to which religious thoughts motivate moral practices by extending the prospect of hybrid goods, which will be realized should those thoughts be true. In these ways, I have tried to draw out, and then to bring together, two important strands in the recent moral philosophical literature. And in the process, I hope to have shown the enduring interest of the medieval concept of infused moral virtue, and to have produced an account of the relationship of religious and moral commitment that will speak to the concerns of diverse philosophical traditions.[35]

[35] I am grateful for comments on drafts of this paper that I received at the Centre for Ethics and Metaethics, University of Leeds, and the Philosophy Department, The Open University. I would also like to thank two referees from the Press for their most helpful remarks.

Index